Democracy

DEMOCRACY

1,000 Years in Pursuit
of British Liberty

PETER KELLNER

MAINSTREAM
PUBLISHING

EDINBURGH AND LONDON

First published in Great Britain in 2009 by
MAINSTREAM PUBLISHING COMPANY
(EDINBURGH) LTD
7 Albany Street
Edinburgh EH1 3UG

ISBN 9781845965068

A catalogue record for this book is available
from the British Library

Typeset in Caslon and Requiem

Printed in Great Britain by
CPI Mackays of Chatham Ltd, Chatham, ME5 8TD

Dedicated to the memory of my father, Michael Kellner.
This book contains some of the reasons why he chose to become British.

Acknowledgements

I am grateful to the following for allowing me to publish copyright material:

Tony Benn for the speech he wrote but never delivered in 1961.

Christopher Booker and Sir David Frost for *That Was the Week That Was* (London: W.H. Allen, 1963).

Paul Dacre for his speech to the Society of Editors, 2008.

Antony Jay and Jonathan Lynn for *Yes, Prime Minister* (London: BBC, 1986).

Anthony King for *The British Constitution* (Oxford: OUP, 2007). Reproduced with the permission of Oxford University Press.

Neil Kinnock for his 1987 speech to the Welsh Labour Party Conference.

The Times for William Rees-Mogg's 1967 editorial 'Who breaks a butterfly on a wheel?'

The estate of the late Sonia Brownell Orwell and Secker & Warburg Ltd for *Coming Up for Air* (London: Victor Gollancz, 1939).

The estate of the late Lord Hailsham and the BBC for the extract from Lord Hailsham's Dimbleby Lecture.

Parliamentary material is reproduced with the permission of the Controller of HMSO on behalf of Parliament.

All royalties are being donated to charity: the money is being divided between the Kitchen Table Charities Trust and the Gareth Butler History Trust.

Contents

FOREWORD 21

PREFACE 24

c.930   'IF IT BE WATER, LET IT BE HEATED TILL IT REACHES BOILING POINT'
         The Dooms of King Athelstan 34

c.1000   'IT'S HARD WORK, SIR, BECAUSE I AM NOT FREE'
         Aelfric's account of the lack of freedom in daily life 37

1070   'LET HIS EYES BE PUT OUT AND LET HIM BE CASTRATED'
         The laws of William the Conqueror 40

1166   'UPON OATH THAT THEY WILL SPEAK THE TRUTH'
         The Assize of Clarendon 42

1215–7   'TO NO ONE WILL WE SELL, TO NO ONE DENY OR DELAY RIGHT OR JUSTICE'
         Magna Carta 45

1258–95 'TO DEAL WITH THE BUSINESS OF THE REALM AND OF THE KING'
         The Provisions of Oxford 49
         Summons to de Montfort's Parliament 50
         Summons to the Model Parliament 51

1305–20 'IT IS NOT FOR GLORY, NOR RICHES, NOR HONOURS THAT WE ARE
         FIGHTING, BUT FOR FREEDOM'
         William Wallace's speech denying treason 53
         The court's sentence against William Wallace 54
         The Declaration of Arbroath 55

1351   'THE STRAIGHTS OF THE MASTERS AND THE SCARCITY OF SERVANTS'
         The Statute of Labourers 58

1376–7   'THE AMENDMENT OF SEVERAL ERRORS IN THE GOVERNMENT, AND THE
         PRESERVATION OF THE REALM'
         Sir Peter de la Mare's speech to the Good Parliament 61

1381   'ARE WE NOT ALL DESCENDED FROM THE SAME PARENTS, ADAM AND EVE?'
         William Langland: Piers Plowman 63
         John Ball's speech at Blackheath 64
         The Anonimalle Chronicle's account of the Peasants' Revolt 65

1401   'THE SAID LORD BENEDICT SHALL BRAND AS HERETICS AND CAUSE
         TO BE TORTURED IN THE USUAL MANNER, HENRY OF LANCASTER AND
         HIS ADHERENTS'
         Owain Glyn Dŵr's letter to the king of Scotland 68
         Glyn Dŵr's letter to a lord in Ireland 69

Glyn Dŵr's Pennal Letter 70

1471   'BLESSED BE GOD, THIS LAND IS RULED UNDER A BETTER LAW'
Sir John Fortescue: *The Difference Between an Absolute and Limited Monarchy* 72

1516–23   'A CONSPIRACY OF RICH MEN PROCURING THEIR OWN COMMODITIES UNDER THE NAME OF THE COMMONWEALTH'
Sir Thomas More: *Utopia* 74
Sir Thomas More's speech to the king on the rights of MPs 76

1563   'NO PERSON RETAINED SHALL DEPART FROM HIS MASTER, MISTRESS, OR DAME UNLESS IT BE FOR SOME REASONABLE AND SUFFICIENT CAUSE'
The Statute of Artificers 78

1576   'THERE IS NOTHING SO NECESSARY FOR THE PRESERVATION OF THE PRINCE AND STATE AS FREE SPEECH'
Sir Peter Wentworth's speech to the House of Commons on freedom of speech 81

1602   'O, WHEN DEGREE IS SHAKED, / WHICH IS THE LADDER TO ALL HIGH DESIGNS, / THEN ENTERPRISE IS SICK!'
William Shakespeare: *Troilus and Cressida* 84

1606   'HAVE HIS PRIVY PARTS CUT OFF AND BURNT BEFORE HIS FACE'
The trial of the Gunpowder Plot conspirators 86

1607–10   'THE KING OUGHT NOT TO BE UNDER ANY MAN, BUT UNDER GOD AND THE LAW'
Sir Edward Coke's notes on his ruling on the divine right of kings 89
King James's speech to Parliament defending the divine right of kings 92

1628   'RIGHTS AND LIBERTIES, ACCORDING TO THE LAWS AND STATUTES OF THIS REALM'
The Petition of Right 94

1641–2   'A MALIGNANT AND PERNICIOUS DESIGN OF SUBVERTING THE FUNDAMENTAL LAWS AND PRINCIPLES OF GOVERNMENT'
The Grand Remonstrance 97
Charles I's letter to Parliament 99
Charles I's exchange with Speaker Lenthall 100
Report of the Commons committee considering the safety of the kingdom 101

1644   'WHO KILLS A MAN KILLS A REASONABLE CREATURE; BUT HE WHO DESTROYS A GOOD BOOK, KILLS REASON ITSELF'
John Milton: *Areopagitica* 104

1646   'HAVE YOU SHOOK THIS NATION LIKE AN EARTHQUAKE TO PRODUCE NO MORE THAN THIS?'

The Levellers: *A remonstrance of many thousand citizens and other freeborn people of England to their own House of Commons* 107

1647   'EVERY MAN HAS A VOICE BY RIGHT OF NATURE'

The Putney Debates 111

1649   'A TYRANT, TRAITOR, MURDERER AND PUBLIC ENEMY'

The charges against Charles I 117

Charles I's defence 118

Bradshaw's ruling against Charles 120

Charles I's speech from the scaffold 121

1649   'THE OFFICE OF KING IS UNNECESSARY, BURDENSOME, AND DANGEROUS TO LIBERTY'

The declaration of Cromwell's Rump Parliament abolishing the monarchy 123

1649   'OUR LIBERTIES AND FREEDOMS, THE TRUE DIFFERENCE AND DISTINCTION BETWEEN MEN AND BEASTS'

John Lilburne: 'England's New Chains' 126

Lilburne defends himself in Parliament 127

Cromwell tells the Council of State to act against Lilburne and his allies 128

1651   'THE PASSIONS OF MEN ARE COMMONLY MORE POTENT THAN THEIR REASON'

Thomas Hobbes: *Leviathan* 130

1652   'EVERY PERSON OF THE POPISH RELIGION SHALL FORFEIT ONE THIRD PART OF THEIR ESTATES'

Act for the Settlement of Ireland 1652 135

1653   'GO! GET OUT! MAKE HASTE, YE VENAL SLAVES, BEGONE!'

Cromwell's speech dissolving the Rump Parliament 138

1653   'OLIVER CROMWELL IS HEREBY DECLARED TO BE LORD PROTECTOR FOR LIFE'

The Instrument of Government 140

1660   'THE CIVIL RIGHTS AND ADVANCEMENTS OF EVERY PERSON ACCORDING TO HIS MERIT'

John Milton: *The Ready and Easy Way to Establish a Free Commonwealth, and the Excellence Thereof, Compared with the Inconveniencies and Dangers of Readmitting Kingship in this Nation* 145

1660   'LET ALL OUR SUBJECTS RELY UPON THE WORD OF A KING'

The Declaration of Breda 148

1679   'FOR THE SPEEDY RELIEF OF ALL PERSONS IMPRISONED'

Habeas Corpus Act 1679 151

1689   'THE BEST MEANS FOR VINDICATING AND ASSERTING THEIR ANCIENT RIGHTS AND LIBERTIES'

The Bill of Rights: An Act Declaring the Rights and Liberties of the Subject and Settling the Succession of the Crown 155

1690 'MAN HATH BY NATURE A POWER TO PRESERVE HIS LIFE, LIBERTY AND ESTATE'

John Locke: *The Second Treatise of Civil Government* 160

1695 'A VOTE WHICH HAS DONE MORE FOR LIBERTY AND FOR CIVILISATION THAN THE MAGNA CARTA OR THE BILL OF RIGHTS'

The House of Commons' resolutions on the Licensing Bill 164

1701 'A TRUE-BORN ENGLISHMAN'S A CONTRADICTION, / IN SPEECH AN IRONY, IN FACT A FICTION'

Daniel Defoe: *The True-Born Englishman* 168

Daniel Defoe: *The Shortest Way with Dissenters* 171

1701 'WHOSOEVER SHALL COME TO THE POSSESSION OF THIS CROWN, SHALL JOIN IN COMMUNION WITH THE CHURCH OF ENGLAND'

Act of Settlement 1701 172

1707 'ONE KINGDOM BY THE NAME OF GREAT BRITAIN'

Act of Union 1707 176

1726 'THE HIGHEST TAX WAS UPON MEN WHO ARE THE GREATEST FAVOURITES OF THE OTHER SEX'

Jonathan Swift: *Gulliver's Travels* 179

1738 'NO MAN CAN BE SO GUARDED IN HIS EXPRESSIONS, AS TO WISH TO SEE EVERYTHING HE SAYS IN THIS HOUSE IN PRINT'

The House of Commons debate on the legality of reporting parliamentary speeches 183

1741 'HE HAS MONOPOLIZED ALL THE FAVOURS OF THE CROWN. THIS IS A MOST HEINOUS OFFENCE AGAINST OUR CONSTITUTION'

The House of Commons debate on the removal of Sir Robert Walpole 188

1741 'RIGHT IS OF TWO KINDS, RIGHT TO POWER AND RIGHT TO PROPERTY'

David Hume: 'Of the First Principles of Government' 192

David Hume: 'Of National Characters' 194

1759 'THEY ARE LED BY AN INVISIBLE HAND'

Adam Smith: *The Theory of Moral Sentiments* 196

Adam Smith: *The Wealth of Nations* 199

1763–75 'THE MOST ABANDONED INSTANCE OF MINISTERIAL EFFRONTERY EVER ATTEMPTED TO BE IMPOSED ON MANKIND'

John Wilkes: *The North Briton* 201

William Pitt's speech calling for Wilkes to be readmitted to the House of Commons 203

John Wilkes's speech calling for his expulsion to be expunged from the record 205

1768   'THE GOOD AND HAPPINESS OF THE MAJORITY IS THE GREAT STANDARD'
          Joseph Priestley: *Essay on the First Principles of Government* 208

1770–4   'YOUR REPRESENTATIVE OWES YOU HIS JUDGEMENT; AND HE BETRAYS
          YOU IF HE SACRIFICES IT TO YOUR OPINION'
          Edmund Burke: *Thoughts on the Cause of the Present Discontents* 211
          Edmund Burke: Speech to the electors of Bristol 212

1772   'SLAVERY IS SO ODIOUS THAT NOTHING CAN BE SUFFERED TO SUPPORT
          IT BUT POSITIVE LAW. THEREFORE THE BLACK MUST BE DISCHARGED'
          Lord Mansfield's ruling on Sommersett's case 216

1789   'A TRADE FOUNDED IN INIQUITY, AND CARRIED ON AS THIS WAS, MUST
          BE ABOLISHED'
          William Wilberforce's speech advocating the abolition of the slave
          trade 218

1790–1   'THOSE WHO ATTEMPT TO LEVEL, NEVER EQUALIZE'
          Edmund Burke: *Reflections on the Revolution in France* 221
          Thomas Paine: *Rights of Man* 224

1792   'IT IS VAIN TO EXPECT VIRTUE FROM WOMEN TILL THEY ARE, IN SOME
          DEGREE, INDEPENDENT OF MEN'
          Mary Wollstonecraft: *A Vindication of the Rights of Woman* 227

1792   'LET REASON BE OPPOSED TO REASON, AND ARGUMENT TO ARGUMENT,
          AND EVERY GOOD GOVERNMENT WILL BE SAFE'
          Thomas Erskine's speech to the jury in the trial of Thomas Paine 230

1795   'NATURAL RIGHTS IS SIMPLE NONSENSE, RHETORICAL NONSENSE
          – NONSENSE UPON STILTS'
          Jeremy Bentham: *Anarchical Fallacies*, 'Critique of the Doctrine of
          Inalienable, Natural Rights' 235

1795   'THAT MAN TO MAN, THE WORLD O'ER, / SHALL BROTHERS BE FOR
          A' THAT'
          Robert Burns: 'A Man's a Man For A' That' 239

1800   'ONE KINGDOM, BY THE NAME OF "THE UNITED KINGDOM OF GREAT
          BRITAIN AND IRELAND"'
          Act of Union 1800 241

1809   'FURTHER PROVISION FOR PREVENTING CORRUPT PRACTICES IN THE
          PROCURING OF ELECTIONS'
          Curwen's Act 243

1817   'IT IS NOT ANARCHY YE ARE AFRAID OF: WHAT YE ARE AFRAID OF IS
          GOOD GOVERNMENT'
          Jeremy Bentham: *Plan of Parliamentary Reform, in the Form of
          a Catechism* 245

1818   'HE TOSSED AWAY THE RULE AND THE SCALE ALTOGETHER, AND
       WITHOUT RESTRICTION LET IN ALL: YOUNG OR OLD, MEN OR WOMEN,
       SANE OR INSANE, ALL MUST VOTE'
       The House of Commons debate on the franchise and the conduct
       of elections 248

1819   'FROM THIS MOMENT THE YEOMANRY LOST ALL COMMAND OF TEMPER'
       The Annual Register: The Peterloo Massacre 252

1819   'LET A GREAT ASSEMBLY BE / OF THE FEARLESS AND THE FREE'
       Percy Bysshe Shelley: 'The Mask of Anarchy' 255

1820   'DEMOCRATIC REPRESENTATION CANNOT EXIST AS PART OF A MIXED
       GOVERNMENT'
       George Canning's speech to his constituents in Liverpool opposing
       widening the franchise 262

1828–9 'I AM READY TO GO TO PRISON TO PROMOTE THE CAUSE OF THE
       CATHOLICS, AND OF UNIVERSAL LIBERTY'
       Daniel O'Connell's address to the electors of Clare on Catholic
       Emancipation 265
       The Duke of Wellington's speech supporting Catholic Emancipation 268

1830   'IF REFORM WERE NOT ATTENDED TO IN TIME, THE PEOPLE WOULD
       LOSE ALL CONFIDENCE IN PARLIAMENT'
       The House of Lords debate on the Reform Bill 271

1830   'IT IS NO TEMPORARY CAUSE THAT IS AT WORK; IT IS A DEEP SENSE OF
       GRIEVOUS WRONGS'
       William Cobbett: 'Rural Wars' 274

1831–2 'THE PRINCIPLE IS TO ADMIT THE MIDDLE CLASS TO A DIRECT SHARE
       IN THE REPRESENTATION, WITHOUT ANY VIOLENT SHOCK TO THE
       INSTITUTIONS OF OUR COUNTRY'
       The House of Commons debate on the Reform Bill 277

1834   'THE WHOLE PROCEEDINGS WERE CHARACTERISED BY A SHAMEFUL
       DISREGARD OF JUSTICE AND DECENCY'
       George Loveless: Victims of Whiggery 285

1834   'THE FIRM MAINTENANCE OF ESTABLISHED RIGHTS, THE CORRECTION
       OF PROVED ABUSES AND THE REDRESS OF REAL GRIEVANCES'
       Sir Robert Peel: The Tamworth Manifesto 289

1837   'WE HAVE OPENED ALL THE PUBLIC-HOUSES, AND LEFT OUR
       ADVERSARY NOTHING BUT THE BEER-SHOPS – MASTERLY STROKE OF
       POLICY THAT, MY DEAR SIR, EH?'
       Charles Dickens: The Pickwick Papers 292

1839   'WE PERFORM THE DUTIES OF FREEMEN; WE MUST HAVE THE
       PRIVILEGES OF FREEMEN'

The People's Charter 296

Benjamin Disraeli's speech to the House of Commons 297

The Chartists' proposed bill 299

1842–6 'TO HAVE A USEFUL AND A PROSPEROUS PEOPLE, WE MUST TAKE CARE
THAT THEY ARE WELL FED'

Richard Cobden's speech attacking the Corn Laws 302

Lord Stanley defends the Corn Laws 305

Sir Robert Peel's resignation speech 307

1843 'I AM HERE THE REPRESENTATIVE OF THE IRISH NATION, AND IN
THE NAME OF THAT MORAL, TEMPERATE, VIRTUOUS AND RELIGIOUS
PEOPLE, I PROCLAIM THE UNION A NULLITY'

Daniel O'Connell calls for Irish independence 309

1845 'TWO NATIONS; BETWEEN WHOM THERE IS NO INTERCOURSE AND NO
SYMPATHY'

Benjamin Disraeli: *Sybil, or, The Two Nations* 311

1851–69 'THE DIVISION OF MANKIND INTO TWO CASTES, ONE BORN TO RULE
OVER THE OTHER, IS AN UNQUALIFIED MISCHIEF'

Harriet Taylor Mill: 'The Enfranchisement of Women' 315

Sir James Easte Willes's ruling that women should not have the right
to vote 318

1854 'THE CIVIL SERVICE IS FOR THE UNAMBITIOUS, AND THE INDOLENT OR
INCAPABLE'

The 'Northcote–Trevelyan Report': the Report on the Organisation of the
Permanent Civil Service 319

1856 'IF YOU ADMIT EVEN ONE LIFE PEERAGE, YOU INTIMATE YOUR
READINESS TO ASSENT TO ANYTHING THE HOUSE OF COMMONS MAY
DICTATE'

The Earl of Derby's speech opposing the creation of life peers 324

1859–61 'THE ONLY PURPOSE FOR WHICH POWER CAN BE RIGHTFULLY
EXERCISED OVER ANY MEMBER OF A CIVILIZED COMMUNITY IS TO
PREVENT HARM TO OTHERS'

John Stuart Mill: *On Liberty* 326

John Stuart Mill: *Considerations on Representative Government* 329

1864 'HOW CAN WE BEST ADMIT THE WORKING CLASSES TO SOME POWER
WITHOUT GIVING THEM THE WHOLE POWER?'

Walter Bagehot: 'A Simple Plan of Reform' 332

1865 'ENGLAND IS THE MOTHER OF PARLIAMENTS. WHY SHOULD YOU BE
THUS TREATED IN YOUR OWN LAND?'

John Bright's speech on reforming the franchise 336

John Bright opposes women having the vote 339

1867   'A POLITICAL BETRAYAL WHICH HAS NO PARALLEL IN OUR
PARLIAMENTARY ANNALS'

Lord Cranborne and Benjamin Disraeli debate the Reform Bill 340

1869–86 'WHEN THE HOUSE OF COMMONS IS AT ONE WITH THE NATION, THE
VOCATION OF THIS HOUSE HAS PASSED AWAY'

Lord Salisbury's speech on the role of the House of Lords 345

Lord Salisbury's letter to Lord Carnarvon 346

Lord Salisbury's speech on the second reading of the Parliamentary
and Municipal Elections Bill 346

Gladstone's speech at Greenwich advocating reform 347

Queen Victoria's letter to Gladstone, 7 March 1886 350

1886   'CAN ANYTHING STOP A NATION'S DEMAND, EXCEPT ITS BEING PROVED
TO BE IMMODERATE AND UNSAFE?'

Gladstone's speech to Parliament on Irish Home Rule 351

1901   'THE TRUE TEST OF PROGRESS IS NOT THE ACCUMULATION OF WEALTH
IN THE HANDS OF A FEW, BUT THE ELEVATION OF A PEOPLE AS A WHOLE'

Keir Hardie's motion promoting socialism 355

Keir Hardie's speech 356

1908   'IT FOLLOWS THAT NOTHING SHOULD EVER BE DONE FOR THE FIRST TIME'

F.M. Cornford: *Microcosmographia Academica* 359

1909–11 'THEY SAY: "YOU THIEVES!" I SAY THEIR DAY OF RECKONING IS AT HAND'

Lloyd George's speech defending the People's Budget 361

Parliament Act 1911 364

1913–8 'EITHER WOMEN ARE TO BE KILLED OR WOMEN ARE TO HAVE THE VOTE'

Emmeline Pankhurst's speech to the Connecticut Women's Suffrage
Association, 13 November 1913 367

Herbert Asquith's speech to Parliament, 14 August 1916 370

Herbert Asquith's speech to Parliament, 28 March 1917 371

1921   'IRELAND SHALL BE STYLED AND KNOWN AS THE IRISH FREE STATE'

Anglo-Irish Treaty 374

1931   'FREEDOM FOR THE PIKE IS DEATH FOR THE MINNOWS'

R.H. Tawney: *Equality* 378

1939   'HATE, HATE, HATE. LET'S ALL GET TOGETHER AND HAVE A GOOD HATE'

George Orwell: *Coming Up for Air* 381

1940   'I HAVE NOTHING TO OFFER BUT BLOOD, TOIL, TEARS AND SWEAT'

Winston Churchill's speech to Parliament 384

1941   'THAT SOCIETY IS BEST WHICH CAN MAKE THE MOST PROGRESS WITH
THE LEAST RESTRAINT'

Herbert Morrison's speech defending his ban of the *Daily Worker* and *The Week* 387

Aneurin Bevan's speech to Parliament opposing the ban 389

1941–2   'A REVOLUTIONARY MOMENT IN THE WORLD'S HISTORY IS A TIME FOR REVOLUTIONS, NOT FOR PATCHING'

Anthony Eden's speech at the Mansion House on Britain's war aims 392

The 'Beveridge Report': the Report of the Inter-Departmental Committee on Social Insurance and Allied Services 395

1945   'NO SOCIALIST GOVERNMENT COULD AFFORD TO ALLOW FREE EXPRESSIONS OF PUBLIC DISCONTENT. THEY WOULD HAVE TO FALL BACK ON SOME FORM OF GESTAPO'

Winston Churchill's election broadcast 399

Clement Attlee's election broadcast 401

1946   'THE NINETEENTH-CENTURY LIBERAL EXPONENTS OF OUR CONSTITUTIONAL SYSTEM GRIEVOUSLY MISLED THE OUTSIDE WORLD'

Leo Amery's Chichele Lecture: 'The Essential Nature of the Constitution' 405

1948   'DESPITE OUR FINANCIAL ANXIETIES, WE ARE STILL ABLE TO DO THE MOST CIVILISED THING IN THE WORLD'

Aneurin Bevan's speech to the House of Commons on the National Health Service 408

1948   'NOW IS THE TIME TO RESTORE THE SENSE OF THE ULTIMATE VALUE OF EVERY HUMAN BEING'

Sydney Silverman's speech to Parliament proposing an end to the death penalty 413

1948–50   'IN THE CENTRE OF OUR MOVEMENT STANDS THE IDEA OF A CHARTER OF HUMAN RIGHTS, GUARDED BY FREEDOM AND SUSTAINED BY LAW'

Winston Churchill's speech to the Congress of Europe, The Hague 417

The European Convention on Human Rights 419

1957   'A MAN'S JUDGMENT IS GENERALLY MORE LOGICAL AND LESS TEMPESTUOUS THAN THAT OF A WOMAN'

Earl Ferrers's speech on the Life Peerages Bill 423

1957   'THERE MUST REMAIN A REALM OF PRIVATE MORALITY AND IMMORALITY WHICH IS NOT THE LAW'S BUSINESS'

The 'Wolfenden Report': the Report of the Departmental Committee on Homosexual Offences and Prostitution 426

James Dance's speech opposing the legalisation of homosexuality 429

1959   'WE CANNOT, WE DARE NOT, IN AFRICA OF ALL PLACES, FALL BELOW OUR OWN HIGHEST STANDARDS'

Enoch Powell's speech in the Hola Camp debate 431

1961   'In Parliament tradition has always served as a valued link, reminding us of our history, never as a chain binding us to the past'

Tony Benn's case for being allowed to remain an MP 434

1963   'This Is Your Life, Henry Brooke – and was theirs'

Christopher Booker and David Frost: *That Was the Week That Was* 438

1966–8   'Like the Roman, I seem to see "the River Tiber foaming with much blood"'

Roy Jenkins's speech on racial integration 442

Enoch Powell's 'Rivers of Blood' speech 445

1967   'Who breaks a butterfly on a wheel?'

Times editorial on Mick Jagger's arrest for possessing drugs 449

1969   'Think of it! A second Chamber selected by the Whips. A seraglio of eunuchs'

Michael Foot's speech to Parliament opposing plans to reform the House of Lords 453

1970   'We intend to make equal pay for equal work a reality, and to take women workers out of the sweated labour class'

Barbara Castle's speech on the Equal Pay Bill 457

1975   'Gone is the principle of accountability to Parliament. The new doctrine is to pass the buck to the people'

Margaret Thatcher's speech to Parliament in the referendum debate 460

1975   'Let our children grow tall and some taller than others'

Margaret Thatcher's speech to the Institute of Socio-Economic Studies 464

1976   'We live in an elective dictatorship'

Lord Hailsham's Dimbleby Lecture 468

1979   'The interference with the applicants' freedom of expression was not justified'

The ruling of the European Court of Human Rights on the *Sunday Times* article on thalidomide 472

1986   'You see, Bernard, you're the perfect balanced sample'

Antony Jay and Jonathan Lynn: *Yes, Prime Minister* 475

1987   'If we accept the motion, we would be placing the House of Commons for-ever under the effective control of the Government'

Tony Benn's speech on the Zircon Affair 477

1987   'They live in a free country, but they do not feel free'

Neil Kinnock's speech to the Welsh Labour Party Conference 481

1988   'WE HAVE NOT SUCCESSFULLY ROLLED BACK THE FRONTIERS OF THE
        STATE IN BRITAIN, ONLY TO SEE THEM REIMPOSED AT A EUROPEAN LEVEL'
        Margaret Thatcher: the 'Bruges Speech' 484

1993   'WE SHOULD TRUST THE PEOPLE'
        The Maastricht debate 488

1995   'THE PEOPLE OF SCOTLAND WANT AND DESERVE DEMOCRACY'
        Report of the Scottish Constitutional Convention 494

1997   'THE TIME HAS COME TO ENABLE PEOPLE TO ENFORCE THEIR RIGHTS
        AGAINST THE STATE IN THE BRITISH COURTS'
        White Paper: 'Rights Brought Home' 498

1998   'OUR TOTAL AND ABSOLUTE COMMITMENT TO EXCLUSIVELY DEMOCRATIC
        AND PEACEFUL MEANS OF RESOLVING DIFFERENCES ON POLITICAL ISSUES'
        The Good Friday Agreement 502

1998   'TWO RAINY DAYS OUT OF FIFTEEN WOULD CERTAINLY BE AN
        ACCEPTABLE RISK FOR PLANNING A PICNIC'
        The 'Jenkins Report': the Report of the Independent Commission on
        the Voting System 506

1999   'NO-ONE SHALL BE A MEMBER OF THE HOUSE OF LORDS BY VIRTUE OF
        A HEREDITARY PEERAGE'
        House of Lords Act 1999 509

2005   'IF WE USE UNDEMOCRATIC MEANS SUCH AS THESE, WE MAY
        UNINTENTIONALLY WILL NEW AND AWFUL ENDS'
        Barbara Follett's speech to the House of Commons 512

2007   'LIBERTY IS NOT THE ONLY VALUE WE PRIZE AND NOT THE ONLY
        PRIORITY FOR GOVERNMENT'
        Gordon Brown's speech on liberty 516

2007   'WHAT, THEN, IS TO BE DONE? THE SHORT ANSWER IS: NOTHING'
        Anthony King: The British Constitution 519

2008   'THE FREEDOM OF THE PRESS IS FAR TOO IMPORTANT TO BE LEFT TO
        THE SOMEWHAT DESICCATED VALUES OF A SINGLE JUDGE'
        Paul Dacre's speech to the Society of Editors 522

BIBLIOGRAPHY 526
INDEX 529

FOREWORD

It is mildly unsettling to open the newspaper and discover that you are responsible for the collapse of civilisation as we know it. This singular honour was awarded jointly to me and my esteemed colleague Jeremy Paxman. Our specific crime, according to the star columnist of *The Guardian* and liberal conscience of the intelligent left, Polly Toynbee, was that the way we interview politicians has so lowered them in the esteem of the electorate that people could no longer be bothered to cast their ballots. Why vote for a bunch of people whom we regularly portrayed as a bunch of blackguards?

Ms Toynbee was not the first to indict aggressive interviewers – a relatively recent phenomenon in our island history – on this charge, and I daresay she will not be the last. Where she was demonstrably accurate was in her observation that voter turnout at general elections has fallen steeply over the decades. It was below 60 per cent in 2001. Half a century earlier, it had been well above 80 per cent. As Peter Kellner shows so convincingly in this book, the British contribution to democracy around the globe has been second to none, but it has been a long struggle: a thousand years to achieve the freedoms we now take for granted. That liberty rests on two pillars: the power to elect those who govern us and the power to throw them out when we deem they have failed us. The universal franchise, where it exists, is the ultimate expression of democracy. So, things must have come to a pretty pass if even we British can no longer be bothered to vote. The charge, therefore, is a grave one: every time Paxman raises a disbelieving eyebrow or I interrupt a cabinet minister in full flow, another few thousand voters decide to have nothing more to do with these dodgy characters and democracy takes another hit.

But I suspect there may be another explanation for voter apathy. When turnout was at its highest, life in Britain was hard. We were barely five years out of the bloodiest war in history, and millions struggled to put enough food on the table and raise their children in decent homes. Crucially, the choice in the polling booth was clear: socialism or Conservatism.

Fifty years later, we were enjoying what may turn out to have been the most benign and prosperous period in our history. And the choice for the voter? Suffice to say, it had become increasingly difficult to slide a voting slip, let alone a cigarette paper, between the politics of New Labour and those of the compassionate Conservative. Farewell divisive ideology; welcome big tent. If everyone was reasonably content with their lot and the choice was so fuzzy, why bother leaving home and hearth to queue up at the polling station?

That, at least, will be my defence when Prosecutor General Toynbee assumes her rightful position in the High Court of Democracy and I face the charges against me. Assuming a merciful Toynbee has not had my tongue removed, I might plead that the existence of robust interviewing (oddly, I prefer that adjective to 'hectoring' or even 'aggressive') may actually serve the great cause of democracy. I have yet to meet a competent and confident politician with a decent case to argue who has failed to see off the most persistent of interviewers. And if we do overstep the mark (yes, Polly, I admit it has been known), the audience is very quick to spot it and the politician benefits.

My other objection to the charge is that democracy is a more resilient institution than it is sometimes given credit for. It will take more than a little apathy, whatever its cause, to see it off. If we have had another election by the time you read these words, I will offer a small wager that turnout has increased. I write at a time of recession with both main parties offering different rescue plans, so the problems are evident and the choice is clear. In those circumstances, I'm willing to bet that many more people will want to make their views known through the ballot box.

Whether one approves of a particular style of political interviewing or not, the thing that matters is what its existence says about free speech. Either we have it or we don't, and there can be no democracy without it. So far, I reckon the British media has done pretty well in its most solemn responsibility: speaking truth to power. Journalists may quibble about the way our libel laws or privacy laws are enforced, but the defence of libel still lies in the truth and the defence of invasion of privacy lies in proving public interest. That seems fair enough to me. Others may argue that the forces of so-called political correctness are limiting our ability to call a spade a bleedin' shovel. If that also means we must stop using vile, degrading and inflammatory language to describe people with a different colour skin from us, I'm pretty happy with that too. Freedom of speech has never meant being able to shout fire in a crowded theatre.

Does all this sound pretty complacent? Quite possibly, but it is beyond doubt that we have become a more tolerant society in the last few decades. We could have used our vote to throw out politicians who wanted to end discrimination against homosexuals, for instance, but we chose not to. Those who marched against the invasion of Iraq may feel their voices were not heard, but they could have voted for another party in the next election and they did not – or at least, not in enough numbers to make a difference to the outcome. Which is not to say that many important questions remain. Would our democracy be more secure with:

- a written constitution?
- a clearer separation of power between law-makers, judiciary and executive?
- the establishment of a republic so that we become citizens rather than subjects?
- a system of proportional representation?

Again, the answer is quite possibly, but if we want any or all of these changes, we have the power to argue for them and, indeed, march in protest if we are not happy with what Westminster decides. And if our politicians refuse to do our bidding, we can throw the rascals out.

Should we not be on constant guard against those who seek, from time to time, to subvert our basic freedoms? Certainly. As I write, there are various campaigns being waged against a perceived threat to habeas corpus, the growth of vast government databases and the introduction of identity cards. The objectors have already enjoyed some successes against the government. In the end, as it always must be in an effective democracy, it is down to us to decide where we want to go.

Abraham Lincoln got one thing wrong in his address at Gettysburg. It was the sentence that began: 'The world will little note, nor long remember what we say here . . .' The truth is that a century and a half has passed and time has not even begun to dim our memory of the closing sentence of that speech, which remains the finest evocation of democracy that has ever been delivered: 'that government of the people, by the people, for the people, shall not perish from the earth'.

We can argue over whether – in our parliamentary democracy – we have government *by* the people. Ours is a representative system. We choose our representatives and tell them to get on with it. Binding referendums are rare. But so long as we are able to make that choice, we are in with a pretty fair chance of making it work – even if some of us do choose to stay at home on voting day. That's our choice, too.

John Humphrys
January 2009

PREFACE

L iberty is Britain's gift to the world. From Magna Carta to the
European Convention on Human Rights, from trial by jury to the
Enlightenment, from habeas corpus to America's ban on 'cruel and unusual
punishment', from freedom of speech to the notion that rich and poor should
be equal before the law – Britain has led the way. We provided the world with
its first written constitution, its first Bill of Rights and its first proposal of a
'social contract' between the state and the individual.

This book sets out to tell the story of Britain's journey towards liberty and
democracy – two different but closely related virtues. It does so through the
words of the people and documents that determined that journey's speed and
route. Some are well known, others less so. As well as mapping the road to
democracy, the pages that follow also include examples of resistance to reform,
because argument has been at the heart of the process and this process cannot
be understood without glimpsing both sides. It also contains the contributions
of rebels, poets, satirists and novelists. Here are Shakespeare and Milton, Swift
and Defoe, Wilkes and Pankhurst, Burns and Shelley, Dickens and Orwell, *Yes,
Prime Minister* and *That Was the Week That Was*. All have often helped to inform
and shape the debate about liberty more than many politicians would wish or,
in some cases, acknowledge.

In making the claim that Britain has blazed the trail for liberty, I should
make clear what I am not saying. I do not contend that all democratic ideals
first emerged from these islands: that would be nonsensical given the histories of
ancient Athens and pre-Imperial Rome. Nor do I make the elementary mistake
of supposing that Westminster is the 'mother of parliaments': Iceland's Althing
first met three centuries before Simon de Montfort summoned the barons and
bishops to Westminster.

Nor do I argue that Britain was always ahead of other countries. Elements
of liberty were promoted in Continental Europe during the Reformation.
France and the United States leapfrogged Britain with their revolutions and

their republican determination that people should be citizens and not subjects. And in the past two centuries, the British have often lagged behind others: in giving women the vote, for example, or in ridding ourselves of the hereditary principle in selecting our legislators. Indeed, the phrase 'mother of parliaments' comes from a speech that, far from complacently congratulating ourselves on our historic role in the evolution of democracy, actually complained that we had lost the lead by denying the franchise to the great majority of men. What John Bright the Liberal MP said to his constituents in 1865 was: 'England is the mother of parliaments. I ask you men of Birmingham . . . why [should you] be thus treated in your own land?'

Moreover, while liberty was being extended within Britain, it was being denied in other lands that we controlled. At best, the British Empire was an intermittent advertisement for the practical benefits of ruling by some form of consent – the consent, that is, of local satraps and other functionaries. And the evolution of the abolition debate is instructive, for while slavery was banned in England in 1772, it took a full six decades for it to be outlawed across the Empire.

Finally, it is clear that our story contains few unsullied heroes. Most reforms were advanced by those promoting their own interests, rather than either the principle of liberty or the well-being of people as a whole. Trial by jury was a beneficial outcome of Henry II's turf war with the Church over who controlled England's legal system. The rights of 'free men' guaranteed by Magna Carta were designed to bolster the powers of the barons and their friends, not to give succour to the vast majority of un-free men and women. Sir Thomas More wanted MPs to have the right to speak their minds – but not for ordinary men and women to read the Bible in English, lest they made up their own minds about Christ's teachings. Sir Edward Coke alternated between a fawning and an independent stance towards the monarchy, depending on which would profit him more; his groundbreaking ruling that the law stood higher than the king occurred during one of his more independent phases. David Hume was arguably Britain's finest philosopher of liberty, but his views on 'naturally inferior' black Africans would have assured him a warm welcome in apartheid-era South Africa. John Wilkes was unquestionably brave in defending free speech, yet even his closest friends knew not to leave either their wallet or their daughter unattended in his company. And some of the most important contributions to the nineteenth-century debate about widening the franchise came from people such as Thomas Macaulay and Walter Bagehot, who wanted the middle classes to have the vote not as a stepping stone on the way to votes for all, but to prevent the kind of insurgency that could give political power to working-class men. (Votes for women were way off their radar.)

Yet, for all these qualifications, I contend that the essential proposition holds good: most of today's tenets of liberty and democracy (and, for much of the world, common law) can be traced back, directly or indirectly, to arguments, ideas and/or reforms within these islands. One modest example was provided, perhaps unwittingly, by President Obama in his inauguration speech. Towards the end, he quoted words that George Washington had ordered to be read to his troops during the American nation's painful birth: 'Let it be told to the future world that in the depth of winter, when nothing but hope and virtue could survive, that the city and the country, alarmed at one common danger, came forth to meet it.' Those words were, in fact, written by Thomas Paine, one of the great English Radicals of his age. Nor is this an isolated example of British influence on America's founding fathers. Their constitution and early amendments drew heavily on our struggles for liberty, from the principle of habeas corpus to their ban on 'cruel and unusual punishments' – a phrase lifted directly from our Bill of Rights almost a century earlier.

Sometimes the launch pad for our progressive leaps forward was Britain-wide, sometimes more narrowly English, and, from time to time, Scottish, Welsh or Irish. In fact, the fluctuating relationships between the nations of the British Isles provide a crucial part of our story – as, more recently, do Britain's relations with the rest of Europe.

Other themes have dominated at different times: the monarchy versus the Church, barons and Parliament; the plight, rights and struggles of the poor; the independence of the judiciary; freedom of speech; religious tolerance and intolerance; the nature of equality, the rights of women and the extension of the franchise; the division of power between the two houses of Parliament; the relationship between economic power and political liberty; and the power of the state to coerce the individual. As the scope of the issues connected with liberty and democracy has widened, so has the potential for conflict between them. Once upon a time, the struggle for fairness and the struggle for freedom were much the same thing. For centuries, both were concerned with the right to speak out, to ensure justice for all, and to prise power and wealth from the hands of a tiny minority. Things are no longer so clear. Freedom and fairness are often at odds with each other. We face conundrums that different democrats, all with the best of intentions, will answer in different ways. For example, how far should economic freedom be curtailed in order to ensure basic welfare and opportunities for all? Where press freedom and personal privacy collide, what principles should determine which should prevail? Have we struck the right balance between the independent sovereignty of Parliament and our pooled-sovereignty commitments to the European Union, United Nations and other international organisations? When should we be free, and when should the law curb our freedom, to proclaim and act upon our dislike of certain of our fellow Britons? Today, the cause of liberty is as much about arbitrating between freedom and fairness as about battling against oppression.

One of the characteristics of our story is that as certain debates subside – such as those over the power of the monarchy, the scandal of slavery or the right to vote – others arise to take their place. In recent decades, equality has broadened from concerns about income and gender to embrace race and sexuality. We have also acquired a constitution that gives rise to a new set of controversies, for in recent years it has become one of the most complex in the world. We employ at least six different electoral systems to choose people for public office. England, Wales, Scotland and Northern Ireland are all run according to different rules. Referendums, once unheard of in the United Kingdom, now play a spasmodic role in deciding major issues without the government having made any real attempt to establish coherent principles for drawing the line between direct and representative democracy. And today's bizarrely constituted, theoretically indefensible, but somehow workable House of Lords demonstrates that, in society as in biology, evolution has the power to trump intelligent design. The result of all this is aesthetically offensive, but whether the UK 'works' less well as a result is a separate question. For what it's worth, my own view – like that of Professor Anthony King in *The British Constitution*, of which an extract appears in this book – is that the system manages to work surprisingly well despite, or perhaps because of, its variety and untidiness.

Indeed, the reason that Britain's increasingly messy constitution somehow manages to work may help us to answer an even larger question: why has Britain played such a central role in the development of liberty and democracy around the world? The individual components of this book tell us about the what, when, who and how of the journey. What is less clear is whether it was just happenstance that Britain led the way or whether there was (and still is?) something specific, distinct and fundamental that explains our extraordinary role.

I confess immediately that I have not spent my adult life pondering this question. It crept up on me while I was compiling this book. The more progress I made, the more it nagged, and eventually I arrived at a tentative answer. It is, however, no less tentative than those of the politicians, political scientists and historians I have asked to help me think this through. None of them has provided a confident, emphatic response. Maybe, in time, a clearer view will emerge. If it does, I have little doubt that what follows here will appear feeble and wrong-headed. Still, if only to help get the debate going, here is the view that I hold for the time being.

Let's start with the mess that is Britain's constitution. It is messy, and it works, because it has evolved organically. In no other major democracy has the evolution of liberty and democracy taken place so continuously over so long a period. Even when that story has been interrupted – most strikingly between 1649 and 1660, when we had no monarch – normal service has subsequently always been resumed. This continuity allowed the principles of liberty to become more entrenched – even if not always perfectly observed – in Britain than in countries whose history is marked by more frequent disruptions. The evolution of liberty in Britain has been appallingly slow (something we tend to forget when we criticise some other countries for failing to democratise ten times faster than we did ourselves), but once basic principles have been established, they have tended to stay established.

One result is that we have inherited a set of traditions that are so enduring that we are apt to regard them as fundamental to being 'British'. This can have its nasty, arrogant side, such as when claims are made of our supposed superiority over other peoples. But these traditions have also provided us with export-ready toolkits of liberty that others, lacking an equivalent history of organic reform, have been able to adopt. One example is the way in which America's founding fathers drew upon our Bill of Rights when designing their Constitution. More recently, when Churchill proposed a set of common standards of human rights across Europe after the Second World War, it was probably only a British leader who could carry conviction and only a British lawyer/politician (David Maxwell Fyfe) who could draw on his country's own lasting principles in taking charge of the drafting process.

If continuity and organic development play a big part in the history of liberty in Britain, this prompts a further question: why has that process been more continuous and more organic than those of other countries? One obvious explanation is that the Channel separates the British Isles from the rest of Europe. We are hard to invade. Nobody has managed to do so successfully for almost 1,000 years (unless you count the arrival in 1688 of the Orange troops loyal to William and Mary, which was as much an invasion-by-invitation as a seriously contested assault). It is unlikely to be an accident that Iceland, the only country with an even older parliament, also has the sea to protect it against invasion. On the other hand, unlike Iceland, Britain is only a short distance from mainland Europe. Goods, people and ideas have always been able to travel easily to and fro. Throughout our history, we have been close enough to encourage trade, but far enough to deter aggression.

Island status confers another benefit: it settles disputes about external borders. Give or take the Channel Islands, there is no argument about where England ends and France begins. Land borders are more conducive not only to raids and invasions but also to violent disputes about where the border itself should be. Such disputes ultimately raise the question of whether the nations on either side can survive.

Yet that is, at best, only a partial explanation of Britain's distinct history. The sea offers some defence, but is a less than total guarantee of independence – as the Irish know only too well. And we also need to explain why conflicts within the main island of Britain – between England and Scotland, between England and Wales, and between rivals inside England, as in the Wars of the Roses – have not disrupted our history as much as violent conflicts have disrupted the history of the European mainland. For although England's relations with the rest of the British Isles have been subjects of perpetual controversy and sometimes war, there has been little argument over the past thousand years about the integrity of England itself. Its internal wars – such as the Wars of the Roses and the Civil War – have been about control of the whole country, not whether England should be broken up or kept together.

I believe (and here I admit that the ice on which this theory skates is becoming dangerously thin) that Sir John Fortescue got it right in his 1471 analysis of the differences between France and England. He observed that French kings raised taxes by decree, while taxes in England were determined by negotiation between Parliament and the monarch. As a result, both poverty and public alienation were greater in France. The English, he argued, were less likely to rise up against the Crown. Fifteenth-century England had, in today's parlance, a massive democratic deficit, but there was just about enough consent from enough people most of the time to keep the show on the road.

That consent was made possible by the absence, most of the time, of a single ruler wielding absolute power. With rare exceptions, control of the British state has been dispersed since at least the middle of the twelfth century. In practice, if not in theory, some sort of separation of powers has been the norm for almost 900 years. As Alan Macfarlane pointed out in *The Origins of English Individualism*, this was reflected in, and possibly caused by, more widely dispersed property rights – and, to some extent, tenants' rights – in England than in most of Europe in the early centuries of the second millennium. Such property rights gave enough people (though, admittedly, very far from a majority) the kind of stake that not only encouraged the kind of negotiation that Fortescue observed; they also required a legal system that recognised such rights. Over time, the tussles over property rights and the quality of the legal system expanded into battles over how England, and later Britain, should be run and for whose benefit. Without the early establishment of property rights, the evolution of liberty and democracy would surely have been far slower.

At one level, then, our story is that of an endless series of tugs-of-war – between the monarchy and the Church, the monarchy and the barons, the monarchy and Parliament, landowners and merchants, the Lords and the Commons, and so on. These contests have often been bitter and sometimes violent, but, without exception, each side has wanted to win the argument as well as the war – and the arguments usually shaped the negotiations that brought most contests to their conclusion and restored some element of consent. Even when negotiation and consent broke down completely, as in the Peasants' Revolt or the Civil War, argument thrived. Guns and swords may have settled immediate battles, but of greater lasting influence were John Ball's speech at Blackheath in 1381 and the Putney Debates between the Levellers and the Cromwellians in 1647.

Negotiation, debate and consent: these provide the thread to our story, linking each century to the next. Today's liberties have been shaped more by words than by weapons.

It would be absurd to say that words have mattered only in Britain. However, I would contend that words have mattered more, and in a particular way, in these islands. We have tended to ground our arguments less in abstract principles than in pragmatism, empiricism and the need to find practical solutions to immediate problems. Morality has mattered, but, on the whole, ideology has not. When Harold Wilson said that British socialism owed more to Methodism than to Marxism, he was expressing a truth that has a wider application and older roots than the Left in the twentieth century.

Moreover, our history fertilised the soil in which the idea of the Enlightenment could grow. Its shoots appeared first in Scotland, then in the rest of Britain. Initially, the idea that reason should be the fount of legitimacy – whether in philosophy, science or politics – was hard for most people to accept. For some, it still is today. But its impact on Western culture and, more widely, today's world is hard to overstate. Looking back, we can see that there is a good reason why the principles of the Enlightenment were first established in these islands. Not only did our empirical habits steer us away from abstract ideologies, but we also demonstrated the enduring truth that new thinking can never flourish in an atmosphere of tyranny and oppression. One of the great lessons of the Enlightenment is profound, but simply stated: liberty is the air in which reason can breathe. Hence Britain's record of producing far more than its share of great empirical thinkers and problem-solvers: people such as Isaac Newton and Charles Darwin, James Watt and Isambard Kingdom Brunel, Adam Smith and John Maynard Keynes, John Harrison and Alan Turing, Joseph Lister and Alexander Fleming, Charles Babbage and Tim Berners-Lee.

To return to the question: why did Britain lead the way? Why are we able to tell such a unique story of argument and negotiation, protest and consent, empiricism and free thought? I suspect (and now I can hear the ice creaking beneath my feet) that our geography and climate play a part. It is not just that Britain is a group of islands; our weather and the seas around our shores are variable and can be volatile. The Gulf Stream combines with our latitude to prevent our summers becoming too hot or our winters too cold. (Other parts of the world, the same distance from the equator, tend to be hotter in the summer and colder in the winter.) By a process of social evolution, we have discovered that temperate behaviour is the best way to deal with a temperate climate, that the often unpredictable problems we face require practical skills rather than distant theories, that to survive changeable conditions we need to rub along together, that the best way to tackle the shared challenges posed by an erratic environment is to pool our ideas and our experience, and that tolerance is not just morally superior to tyranny but is also a more effective ally of safety and security. After all, Charles Darwin showed how geography and climate shaped the way life on earth evolved; why should they not help to shape how societies evolve? Had the British Isles and its people been removed a millennium ago from the edge of the Atlantic to, say, the eastern Mediterranean or the Gulf of Arabia, our social evolution would have surely taken a very different course.

That is one set of explanations for the nature of the story. There are others – including, perhaps, the idea that there is no single overarching explanation: that Britain has been shaped by a series of separate events that occurred by chance and that might have worked out differently and set our history on an utterly different course. Perhaps our liberties grew like a snowball rolling down a winter hill, starting with a random stone and gathering mass as it zigzagged down the bumpy slope: a process that might have occurred anywhere, but happened to take place in Britain. Or maybe the explanation is a mixture of the two: a Darwin's snowball, in which geography and climate have created a distinctive terrain in which accidental events and exceptional individuals were able to achieve extraordinary things.

The aim of this book is not to settle the matter. The only certainty on which it insists is that words have been supremely important in the way the story has unfolded. Some of the most important of those words are in these pages. They remind us of not only the intensity and passion of the struggles for our liberty and democracy, but also the richness of our language. Naturally I hope readers will share my interest in the content of the unfolding arguments; I also hope they – you – will share some of my pleasure in the way many of those arguments were expressed.

My selection is inevitably subjective. This book could easily have been far longer – with more, and fuller, extracts. To those who complain that I have skimmed only the surface, I say: this book is probably not for you. Others will be more to your taste, such as Cambridge University Press's excellent four-volume series, published in the 1960s, of constitutional documents from the Tudor era to the nineteenth century, or the even weightier series, English Historical Documents, that Oxford University Press and other publishers have provided in recent decades.

This book is intended for a wider audience. That is why the longer documents have been edited down to, typically, extracts of around 1,000 words. This is the length of a newspaper's normal 'op-ed' commentary. It is today's most familiar unit of political discourse: long enough to provide an insight into the author's line of reasoning, but short enough not to pall. I have also tidied up some of the English in the older documents. On balance, I felt that it was more important to achieve clarity than to avoid offending purists. (I haven't touched Shakespeare's language, though: there are limits.)

Anyone who needs or desires the full-length version of any document in its original English (or, for that matter, Latin) can go elsewhere – and probably has done already, or knows where to look. For those who don't want to go that far, but who wish to explore any of the episodes depicted in this book a little further, I list at the end a number of books and, perhaps more importantly, websites that I have found useful. And there is always Google.

Three of the documents cannot be traced through any of these routes, so I wish to offer special thanks to those who provided them. These are: the National Library of Wales, for supplying an English translation of Owain Glyn Dŵr's 'Pennal Letter'; David Butler, for lending me his copy of *Select British Eloquence*, published in 1859, which contains George Canning's uncompromising denunciation of progressive reform; and Tony Benn, for making available one of his finest speeches, but one that he was never allowed to deliver, setting out his case for remaining a Member of the House of Commons rather than being forced to go to the House of Lords following the death of his father, Lord Stansgate, in 1960.

There are others who made this book possible either through their general advice and encouragement or by pointing me towards documents that, though publicly available, I might not have found but for their friendly and unstinting help. In alphabetical order these were: Don Berry, Vernon Bogdanor, Bill Campbell (who doubles as my publisher), Shami Chakrabarti, Barbara Follett, Sabina Frediani, Helene Hayman, Simon Jenkins, Tony Judt, Anthony King, Anthony Lester, Richard Preston, Greg Rosen, Simon Schama, Jean Seaton, Liz Symonds, Stewart Wood and Tony Wright.

Jonathan Pearse deserves particular gratitude. His knowledge of, and ability to find his way around, some of the less readily available source materials was extraordinary, as was his dedication to the task of finding them. Finally, I am certain I would have given up long ago without the love and support of Cathy, my wife, whose own work provides a constant reminder that our history is not some remote, dead land, to be glimpsed and dissected from afar, but a living entity, whose consequences affect the daily lives of us all. The story told in this book is about our past, but it is also about our present – and our future.

Peter Kellner
St Albans, January 2009

c.930

'IF IT BE WATER, LET IT BE HEATED TILL IT REACHES BOILING POINT'

Athelstan the Glorious, the grandson of Alfred the Great, ruled England from 924 to 939 – and, indeed, the whole of Britain after his victory at the Battle of Brunanburh (most likely the modern-day Wirral) in 937. His 'dooms', or statutes, provide one of the earliest surviving sets of laws and systems of tithes, fines and punishments intended to apply to the country as a whole. Whether the dooms were implemented fully throughout the country is open to debate, but the concept of national rules and payments can be traced back to before the Norman Conquest. In the centuries that followed, there would be arguments, battles and confrontations over the content of the rules and who should decide and enforce them – and whether they should apply outside England – but the idea of having a nationwide legal system was never reversed.

THE DOOMS OF KING ATHELSTAN

I, Athelstan king, with the counsel of Wulfhelm, archbishop, and of my other bishops, make known to the reeves [local officials] of each borough, and beseech you, in God's name, and by all his saints, and also by my friendship, that you first of my own goods render the tithes both of livestock and of the year's earthly fruits, so that they may most rightly be either meted, or told, or weighed out; and let the bishops then do the like from their own goods, and my aldermen and my reeves the same.

You may not unjustly anywhere acquire anything for me; but I will grant to you your own justly, on this condition, that you yield to me mine; and shield both yourselves, and those whom you ought to exhort, against God's anger and against my orders.

First: that no thief be spared above twelve years, and above eight pence. And if any one so do, let him pay for the thief according to his worth. But if he will defend himself, or flees away, then let him not be spared. If a thief be brought into prison: that he be forty days in prison, and let him be released with 120 shillings, and let him pledge that he evermore desist. And if after that he steal, let them pay for him according to his worth, or bring him again therein: and if any one stand up for him, let him pay for him according to his worth, as well to the king as to him to whom it lawfully belongs: and let every man of those there who stand by him pay to the king 120 shillings.

And we have ordained respecting witch-craft and murder: if any one should be thereby killed, and he could not deny it, that he be liable in his life. But if he will deny it, and at threefold ordeal shall be guilty; that he be 120 days in prison: and after that let kindred take him out, and give to the king 120 shillings, and pledge that he evermore desist from the like.

And let no man exchange any property without the witness of the reeve, or of the mass-priest, or of the landlord, or of the steward, or of other upstanding man. If any one do so, let him give thirty shillings, and let the landlord take possession of the exchange.

But if it be found that any of these have given wrongful witness, that his witness never again be believed, and that he also pay a fine of thirty shillings.

If any one, when summoned fail to attend the court three times; let him pay the king for his disobedience. But if he will not do right, nor pay the fine, then let all the chief men belonging to the borough ride to him, and take all that he has. But if any one will not ride with his fellows, let him pay the king's fine.

If any one chooses trial by ordeal, then let him come three days before to the mass-priest who is to hallow it; and let him feed himself with bread and with water, and salt, and herbs, before he shall go to it; and let him attend mass each of the three days, and go to the house on the day that he shall go to the ordeal: and then swear the oath that he is innocent, before he goes to the ordeal. And if it be water, that he dive an armlength and a half by the rope; if it be iron ordeal, let it be three days before the hand be undone. And let every man begin his charge with an oath, and be each of those fasting on either hand, who may be there together, by God's command and the archbishop's: and let there be on either side not more than twelve. If the accused man be with a larger company than some twelve, then be the ordeal void, unless they will go from him.

And he who buys property with witnesses, and if after obliged to vouch it to warranty, then let him receive it from whom he before had bought it. And let no marketing be on Sundays; but if any one do so, let him forfeit the goods, and pay a fine of thirty shillings.

And he who shall swear a false oath, and it be made clear against him; that he never after be oath-worthy, nor let him lie within a hallowed burial-place, though he die, unless he have the testimony of the bishop in whose shrift-shire he may be, that he has made such remedy as his confessor prescribed to him.

And concerning the ordeal we enjoin by command of God, and of the archbishop, and of all the bishops: that no man come within the church after the fire is borne in with which the ordeal shall be heated, except the mass-priest. If it be water, let it be heated till it reaches boiling point. And be the kettle of iron or of brass, of lead or of clay. And if it be a single accusation, let the hand dive after the stone up to the wrist, and if it be threefold, up to the elbow. And when the ordeal is ready, then let two men go in of either side; and be they agreed that it is so hot as we before have said.

c.1000

'IT's HARD WORK, SIR, BECAUSE I AM NOT FREE'

T he story of British liberty and democracy is not only a story of laws
and constitutions but also a story of morality, philosophy, religion and
economics, and of tyrants, rebels and daily life. Around the end of the first
millennium, Aelfric, a Wessex monk, devised translation exercises for his pupils.
These included the following dialogues, which describe the daily tribulations of
British people before the Norman Conquest. They offer an early example of a
strand of progressive thinking: that people with no economic power cannot be
truly free.

AELFRIC'S ACCOUNT OF THE LACK OF FREEDOM IN DAILY LIFE

MASTER: What do you say ploughman? How do you carry out your
work?

PLOUGHMAN: Oh, I work very hard, dear lord. I go out at daybreak driving
the oxen to the field, and yoke them to the plough; for fear of my lord,
there is no winter so severe that I dare hide at home; but the oxen having
been yoked and the share and coulter fastened to the plough, I must plough
a full acre or more every day.

MASTER: Have you any companion?

PLOUGHMAN: I have a lad driving the oxen with a goad, who is now also
hoarse because of the cold and shouting.

MASTER: What else do you do in the day?

PLOUGHMAN: I do more than that, certainly. I have to fill the oxen's bins
with hay, and water them, and carry their muck outside.

MASTER: Oh, oh! It's hard work.

PLOUGHMAN: It's hard work, sir, because I am not free.

MASTER: What do you say shepherd? Do you have any work?

SHEPHERD: I have indeed, sir. In the early morning I drive my sheep to their pasture, and in the heat and in cold, stand over them with dogs, lest wolves devour them; and I lead them back to their folds and milk them twice a day, and move their folds; and in addition I make cheese and butter; and I am loyal to my lord.

MASTER: You, shoemaker, what do you work at for our use?

SHOEMAKER: My trade is certainly very useful and necessary to you.

MASTER: How so?

SHOEMAKER: I buy hides and skins. And by my craft prepare them and make them into various kinds of footwear, slippers and shoes, leggings and leather bottles, reins and trappings, flasks and leather vessels, spur-straps and halters, bags and purses. And not one of you would want to pass the winter without my craft.

MASTER: Salter, what good is your craft to us?

SALTER: My craft is very useful to all of you. Not one of you enjoys satisfaction in a meal or food, unless he entertain my craft.

MASTER: How so?

SALTER: What man enjoys pleasant foods to the full without the flavour of salt? Who fills his pantry or storeroom without my craft? Indeed you will lose all butter and cheese-curd unless I am present with you as a preservative; you couldn't even use your herbs without me.

MASTER: What do you say baker? What is the use of your trade; or can we survive without you?

BAKER: You might live without my trade for a while, but neither for long nor very well. Truly, without my craft every table would seem empty; and without bread all food would turn distasteful. I make people's hearts strong; I am the stamina of men, and even the little ones are unwilling to pass me by.

MASTER: Oh, oxherd, what do you work at?

OXHERD: Oh, I work hard, my lord. I go out at daybreak driving the oxen to the field, and yoke them to the plough; for fear of my lord, there is no winter so severe that I dare hide at home; but the oxen having been yoked and the share and coulter fastened to the plough, I must plough a full acre or more every day. I have a lad driving the oxen with a goad, who is now also hoarse because of the cold and shouting. I have to fill the oxen's bins with hay, and water them, and carry their muck outside. It's hard work, sir, because I am not free.

1070

'LET HIS EYES BE PUT OUT AND LET HIM BE CASTRATED'

Four years after the Battle of Hastings, William the Conqueror set out the main laws by which he would govern England. They were, in effect, the rules of occupation: his troops were still in the process of subduing the north of England by torching homes, crops and livestock, and spreading salt on the land to reduce its fertility. Note that, whether the accuser or the accused, any Englishman caught up in a criminal case involving a Frenchman risked 'the ordeal of hot iron or by wager of battle', yet no such ordeal was to be inflicted upon a Frenchman.

William's laws refer to 'scot and lot'. This was the name given to local taxation. It derives from the French of the period: *escot*, meaning payment, and *lot*, meaning share. It provides the origin of the phrase 'scot-free' – a term originally applied to people who managed to get away without paying taxes.

THE LAWS OF WILLIAM THE CONQUEROR

The new law of the land as set down by William the Conqueror and his magnates:

First that above all things he wishes one God to be revered throughout his whole realm, one faith in Christ to be kept ever inviolate, and peace and security to be preserved between English and Normans.

We decree also that every freeman shall affirm by oath and compact that he will be loyal to king William both within and without England, that he will preserve with him his lands and honour with all fidelity and defend him against his enemies.

I will, moreover, that all the men I have brought with me, or who have come after me, shall be protected by my peace and shall dwell in quiet. And if any one of them shall be slain, let the lord of his murderer scize him within five days, if he can; but if he cannot, let him pay me 46 marks of silver so long as his substance avails. And when his substance is exhausted, let the whole hundred in which the murder took place pay what remains in common.

And let every Frenchman who, in the time of king Edward, my kinsman, was a sharer in the customs of the English, pay what they call 'scot and lot', according to the laws of the English. This decree was ordained in the city of Gloucester.

We forbid also that any live cattle shall be bought or sold for money except within cities, and this shall be done before three faithful witnesses; nor even anything old without surety and warrant. But if anyone shall do otherwise, let him pay once, and afterwards a second time for a fine.

It was decreed there that if a Frenchman shall charge an Englishman with perjury or murder or theft or homicide or 'ran', as the English call open rapine which cannot be denied, the Englishman may defend himself, as he shall prefer, either by the ordeal of hot iron or by wager of battle. But if the Englishman be infirm, let him find another who will take his place. If one of them shall be vanquished, he shall pay a fine of 40 shillings to the king. If an Englishman shall charge a Frenchman and be unwilling to prove his accusation either by ordeal or by wager of battle, I will, nevertheless, that the Frenchman shall acquit himself by a valid oath.

This also I command and will, that all shall have and hold the law of the king Edward in respect of their lands and all their possessions, with the addition of those decrees I have ordained for the welfare of the English people.

Every man who wishes to be considered a freeman shall be in pledge so that his surety shall hold him and hand him over to justice if he shall offend in any way. And if any such shall escape, let his sureties see to it that they pay forthwith what is charge against him, and let them clear themselves of any complicity in his escape. Let recourse be had to the hundred and shire courts as our predecessors decreed. And those who ought of right to come and are unwilling to appear, shall be summoned once; and if for the second time they refuse to come, one ox shall be taken from them, and they shall be summoned a third time. And if they do not come the third time, a second ox shall be taken from them. But if they do not come the fourth summons, the man who is unwilling to come shall forfeit from his goods the amount of the charge against him, 'ceapgeld' as it is called, and in addition to this a fine to the king.

I prohibit the sale of any man by another outside the country on pain of a fine to be paid in full to me.

I also forbid that anyone shall be slain or hanged for any fault, but let his eyes be put out and let him be castrated. And this command shall not be violated under pain of a fine in full to me.

1166

'UPON OATH THAT THEY WILL SPEAK THE TRUTH'

The Assize of Clarendon is one of the most important documents in the evolution of the rule of law in Britain – and, indeed, around the world. It introduced such concepts as evidence given under oath, trial by jury, the impartial administration of justice and the beginning of the idea of habeas corpus. Most of the basic tenets of common law (i.e. laws common to the whole of England and developed through court judgements) can be traced back to the Assize.

Yet the man who dreamed all this up is better remembered for provoking the death of Thomas à Becket, the Archbishop of Canterbury. Henry II ruled England from 1154 until 1189. The murder of Becket took place in 1170. What Henry should be remembered for was the document he issued four years earlier at a convocation of lords at the royal hunting lodge of Clarendon in Wiltshire. It, too, flowed from the running conflict between the Crown and the Church. Both sought to dominate the legal system. In 1164, the king had issued the Constitutions of Clarendon, which ended the clergy's right to be tried by ecclesiastical courts alone, even when accused of criminal offences.

Now Henry went further. He wanted not only to marginalise the Church but also to stop each baron running his own separate legal system in his own area. In the Assize of Clarendon, the king set out the principles of justice that were to apply uniformly throughout the land. In short, the Assize of Clarendon was Henry's ambitious bid to nationalise the law and address the eternal controversies of crime and miscarriages of justice. As with so much of the story of how British democracy evolved, the long-term significance of the event is more impressive than the mixed motives that gave rise to it.

THE ASSIZE OF CLARENDON

> In the first place the aforesaid king Henry, by the counsel of all his barons, for the preservation of peace and the observing of justice, has decreed that an

inquest shall be made throughout the separate counties, and throughout the separate hundreds, through twelve of the more lawful men of the hundred, and through four of the more lawful men of each township, upon oath that they will speak the truth: whether in their hundred or in their township there be any man who, since the lord king has been king, has been charged or published as being a robber or murderer or thief; or any one who is a harbourer of robbers or murderers or thieves. And the Justices shall make this inquest by themselves, and the sheriffs by themselves.

And he who shall be found through the oath of the aforesaid persons to have been charged or published as being a robber, or murderer, or thief, or a receiver of them, since the lord king has been king, shall be taken and shall go to the ordeal of water, and shall swear that he was not a robber or murderer or thief or receiver of them since the lord king has been king.

And if the lord of him who has been taken, or his steward or his vassals, shall, as his sureties, demand him back within three days after he has been taken, he himself, and his chattels, shall be remanded under surety until he shall have done his law.

And when a robber or murderer or thief, or harbourers of them, shall be taken on the aforesaid oath, if the Justices shall not be about to come quickly enough into that county where they have been taken, the sheriffs shall send word to the nearest Justice through some intelligent man, that they have taken such men; and the Justices shall send back word to the sheriffs where they wish those men to be brought before them: and the sheriffs shall bring them before the Justices. And with them they shall bring, from the hundred or township where they were taken, two lawful men to bear record on the part of the county and hundred as to why they were taken; and there, before the Justice, they shall do their law.

And the sheriffs who take them shall lead them before the Justice without other summons than they have from him. And when the robbers or murderers or thieves, or receivers of them, who shall be taken through the oath or otherwise, are given over to the sheriffs, they also shall receive them straightway without delay.

And, in the different counties where there are no jails, such shall be made in the burgh or in some castle of the king from the money of the king and from his woods if they be near, or from some other neighbouring woods, by view of the servants of the king; to this end, that the sheriffs may keep in them those who shall be taken by the servitors who are accustomed to do this, and through their servants.

The lord king wills also that all shall come to the county courts to take this oath; so that no one shall remain away, on account of any privilege that he has, from coming to take this oath.

And if any one shall be taken who shall be possessed of robbed or stolen goods, if he be notorious and have evil testimony from the public, and have no warrant, he shall not have law. And if he be not notorious, on account of the goods in his possession, he shall go to the water.

And if any one shall confess before lawful men, or in the hundred court, concerning robbery, murder, or theft, or the harbouring of those committing them, and afterwards wish to deny it, he shall not have law.

The lord king wishes also that those who shall be tried and shall be absolved by the law, if they be of very bad testimony and are publicly and disgracefully defamed by the testimony of many and public men, shall forswear the lands of the king, so that within eight days they shall cross the sea unless the wind detains them; and, with the first wind which they shall have afterwards, they shall cross the sea; and they shall not return any more to England unless by the mercy of the lord king: and there, and if they return, they shall be outlawed; and if they return they shall be taken as outlaws.

And if any sheriff shall send word to another sheriff that men have fled from his county into another county on account of robbery or murder or theft, or the harbouring of them, or for outlawry, or for a charge with regard to the forest of the king, he (the sheriff who is informed) shall capture them: and even if he learn it of himself or through others that such men have fled into his county, he shall take them and keep them in custody until he have safe pledges from them.

And all sheriffs shall cause a register to be kept of all fugitives who shall flee from their counties; and this they shalt do before the county assemblies; and they shall write down and carry their names to the Justices when first they shall come to them, so that they may be sought for throughout all England, and their chattels may be taken for the service of the king.

The lord king forbids that monks or canons or any religious house receive any one of the petty people as monk or canon or brother, until they know of what testimony he is, unless he shall be sick unto death.

And the lord king wills that this assize shall be kept in his kingdom as long as it shall please him.

1215–7

'TO NO ONE WILL WE SELL, TO NO ONE DENY OR DELAY RIGHT OR JUSTICE'

From Athelstan to Henry II, the story of Britain's political and legal evolution is one of kings exerting their authority. Magna Carta marks the start of the struggle, over seven centuries, to wrest power from the monarchy and, later, nobles and landowners, and give it to the people.

King John came to the throne in 1199, and within ten years he was in trouble. He had lost Normandy. He had raised taxes sharply to pay for the Third Crusade. He had been at loggerheads with Pope Innocent III. Unless he could strike a deal with nobles and clerics, his authority risked erosion. He might even be overthrown. In 1213, Stephen Langton, the Archbishop of Canterbury, proposed such a deal: the Church and the nobility would continue to support the king if he granted them greater freedom. Two years later, King John acceded to Langton's plan in a ceremony at Runnymede, an island in the River Thames.

Most of Magna Carta was devoted to the interests of the Church, landowners and merchants. It contains a whiff of anti-Semitism. But it did assert that no 'free man shall be seized or imprisoned, or stripped of his rights or possession, or outlawed or exiled, or deprived of his standing in any other way . . . except by the lawful judgement of his equals by the law of the land'. Although at the time they constituted only a tiny proportion of the population, the concept of 'free' men (and women) broadened over subsequent centuries, and this doctrine became a cornerstone of civil liberties and the rule of law in Britain and many other countries.

MAGNA CARTA

> JOHN, by the grace of God King of England, Lord of Ireland, Duke of Normandy and Aquitaine, and Count of Anjou, to his archbishops, bishops, abbots, earls, barons, justices, foresters, sheriffs, servants, and to all his officials and loyal subjects, Greeting.

KNOW THAT BEFORE GOD, for the health of our soul and those of our ancestors and heirs, to the honour of God, the exaltation of the holy Church, and the better ordering of our kingdom:

FIRST THAT WE HAVE GRANTED TO GOD, and by this present charter have confirmed for us and our heirs in perpetuity, that the English Church shall be free, and shall have its rights undiminished, and its liberties unimpaired. This freedom we shall observe ourselves, and desire to be observed in good faith by our heirs in perpetuity.

TO ALL FREE MEN OF OUR KINGDOM we have also granted, for us and our heirs for ever, all the liberties written out below, to have and to keep for them and their heirs, of us and our heirs:

Neither we nor our officials will seize any land or rent in payment of a debt, so long as the debtor has movable goods sufficient to discharge the debt.

If anyone who has borrowed a sum of money from Jews dies before the debt has been repaid, his heir shall pay no interest on the debt for so long as he remains under age, irrespective of whom he holds his lands. If such a debt falls into the hands of the Crown, it will take nothing except the principal sum specified in the bond.

The city of London shall enjoy all its ancient liberties and free customs, both by land and by water. We also will and grant that all other cities, boroughs, towns, and ports shall enjoy all their liberties and free customs.

Ordinary lawsuits shall not follow the royal court around, but shall be held in a fixed place.

We ourselves, or in our absence abroad our chief justice, will send two justices to each county four times a year, and these justices, with four knights of the county elected by the county itself, shall hold the assizes in the county court, on the day and in the place where the court meets.

For a trivial offence, a free man shall be fined only in proportion to the degree of his offence, and for a serious offence correspondingly, but not so heavily as to deprive him of his livelihood. In the same way, a merchant shall be spared his merchandise, and a husbandman the implements of his husbandry, if they fall upon the mercy of a royal court. None of these fines shall be imposed except by the assessment on oath of reputable men of the neighbourhood.

Earls and barons shall be fined only by their equals, and in proportion to the gravity of their offence.

A fine imposed upon the lay property of a clerk in holy orders shall be assessed upon the same principles, without reference to the value of his ecclesiastical benefice.

No town or person shall be forced to build bridges over rivers except those with an ancient obligation to do so.

No constable or other royal official shall take corn or other movable goods from any man without immediate payment, unless the seller voluntarily offers postponement of this.

No sheriff, royal official, or other person shall take horses or carts for transport from any free man, without his consent.

Neither we nor any royal official will take wood for our castle, or for any other purpose, without the consent of the owner.

In future no official shall place a man on trial upon his own unsupported statement, without producing credible witnesses to the truth of it.

No free man shall be seized or imprisoned, or stripped of his rights or possessions, or outlawed or exiled, or deprived of his standing in any other way, nor will we proceed with force against him, or send others to do so, except by the lawful judgement of his equals or by the law of the land.

To no one will we sell, to no one deny or delay right or justice.

To any man whom we have deprived or dispossessed of lands, castles, liberties, or rights, without the lawful judgement of his equals, we will at once restore these. In cases of dispute the matter shall be resolved by the judgement of the twenty-five barons referred to below in the clause for securing the peace.

No one shall be arrested or imprisoned on the appeal of a woman for the death of any person except her husband.

If we have deprived or dispossessed any Welshmen of lands, liberties, or anything else in England or in Wales, without the lawful judgement of their equals, these are at once to be returned to them. A dispute on this point shall be determined in the Marches by the judgement of equals. English law shall apply to holdings of land in England, Welsh law to those in Wales, and the law of the Marches to those in the Marches. The Welsh shall treat us and ours in the same way.

SINCE WE HAVE GRANTED ALL THESE THINGS for God, for the better ordering of our kingdom, and to allay the discord that has arisen between us and our barons, and since we desire that they shall be enjoyed in their entirety, with lasting strength, for ever, we give and grant to the barons the following security:

The barons shall elect twenty-five of their number to keep, and cause to be observed with all their might, the peace and liberties granted and confirmed to them by this charter.

If we, our chief justice, our officials, or any of our servants offend in any respect against any man, or transgress any of the articles of the peace or of this security, and the offence is made known to four of the said twenty-five barons, they shall come to us – or in our absence from the kingdom to the chief justice – to declare it and claim immediate redress.

In the event of disagreement among the twenty-five barons on any matter referred to them for decision, the verdict of the majority present shall have the same validity as a unanimous verdict of the whole twenty-five, whether these were all present or some of those summoned were unwilling or unable to appear.

We will not seek to procure from anyone, either by our own efforts or those of a third party, anything by which any part of these concessions or liberties might be revoked or diminished. Should such a thing be procured, it shall be null and void and we will at no time make use of it, either ourselves or through a third party.

Given by our hand in the meadow that is called Runnymede, between Windsor and Staines, on the fifteenth day of June in the seventeenth year of our reign.

Almost immediately, and with the Pope's support, King John repudiated Magna Carta, saying he had signed under duress. A group of barons enlisted the help of Prince Louis of France to overthrow John. The following year, John lost his life, succumbing to dysentery (though there were rumours that he was poisoned).

John's nine-year-old son, Henry, succeeded to the throne. The rebel barons were defeated, but a deal was done to keep Magna Carta. Moreover, in 1217, it was supplemented with the 'Charter of the Forest', which scrapped the death penalty for stealing venison and allowed free men access to forests to collect firewood and provide pasture for their pigs.

1258–95

'To deal with the business of the realm and of the king'

In 1258, following the failure of a harvest the previous year that caused something close to famine in large parts of England, Henry III and his allies met at Oxford with a group of (relatively) reformist barons led by Simon de Montfort. Short of cash, Henry needed the barons' support. They agreed to back him – but, under the 'Provisions of Oxford', Henry had to cede much of his power to a 15-man 'King's Council', whose decisions would be monitored by Parliament. The king was allowed to nominate only three members. This effectively took over from a larger, 24-man council, of whom 12 had been appointed by the king. Local power was to be devolved to each shire, where four knights would gather grievances and forward them to a national 'justiciar' – an early version of today's Ombudsman.

Had an official copy of the Provisions of Oxford survived, it would rank alongside Magna Carta as a seminal document charting the road to democracy as, for the first time, it curbed the day-to-day power of the king. What has survived is a second-hand account written by monks at the Benedictine Abbey of Burton-on-Trent.

The Provisions of Oxford

It was provided that from each county there are to be chosen four discreet and law-worthy knights who, on every day when the county is held, are to meet to hear all complaints of any trespass and injuries whatsoever inflicted upon any persons whatsoever by sheriffs, bailiffs, or whatsoever others, and to make the attachments arising out of the said complaints pending the first coming of the chief justiciar to those parts.

Be it noted that the twenty-four have decreed that there shall be three parliaments every year. To these three parliaments shall come the elected councillors of the king, even if they are not summoned, to review the state of the realm and to deal with the common business of the realm and of the king together; and at other times by the king's summons when need shall be.

Be it also noted that the community should choose twelve sound men who shall come to the parliaments, and at other times when need shall be, when the king and council shall summon them to deal with the business of the king and of the realm: and the community will accept as settled whatever these twelve shall do. And this shall be done to spare the cost to the community.

The fifteen who are to be of the king's council shall be confirmed by the twenty-four or by a majority of them. And they shall have the power to advise the king in good faith on the government of the kingdom and on all things touching the king and kingdom; and to amend and redress everything that they shall consider to need redress and amendment; and over the chief justiciar and all other persons.

In 1261, Henry, emboldened both by a recovery in his fortunes and by divisions among the barons, renounced the Provisions. Three years later, de Montfort struck back, raising an army that defeated King Henry III at the Battle of Lewes. De Montfort became England's de facto ruler. In December 1264, acting on de Montfort's instructions, the king summoned bishops, earls and barons and elected representatives of each county and borough to a new Parliament. This was the first British parliament to contain commoners, and the first to involve a rudimentary form of election. The franchise was severely restricted: only better-off landowners and property owners had the vote. But the principle of elected commoners was established. This is one of the surviving summonses – the one sent to the Bishop of Durham.

SUMMONS TO DE MONTFORT'S PARLIAMENT

Henry, by the grace of God king of England, lord of Ireland, and duke of Aquitane, to the venerable father in Christ, Robert by the same grace bishop of Durham, greeting. Since after the grave occurrences of disturbance which have long prevailed in our kingdom, our dearest first-born son Edward has been given as a hostage for securing and confirming peace in our realm, and as the said disturbance, blessed be God, is abated, for providing deliverance in a salutary manner for the same and confirming and thoroughly completing full security of tranquillity and peace to the honour of God and the profit of our whole kingdom, as well as concerning divers other matters which we are unwilling to decide without your counsel and that of the other prelates and magnates of our realm, it is needful that we have speech with them.

We command you, desiring you by the faith and love by which you are bound to us, that putting aside all excuse and other business, you will be with us in London on the octave of St Hilary next, to treat and to give your advice on the said matters, with the prelates and barons whom we shall summon thither. And this, as you love us and our honour, and your own and the common tranquillity of the kingdom, in no wise omit.

Witness the king,
at Worcester, the 14th of December

De Montfort did not savour his triumph for long. Henry's son Edward (later Edward I) escaped imprisonment, raised an army and fought de Montfort, killing him at the Battle of Evesham in August 1265. However, de Montfort's concept of Parliament survived. Thirty years later, in 1295, Edward I summoned what became known as the 'Model Parliament'. This, too, contained elected commoners as well as bishops, earls and barons.

By this time, Parliament had acquired the right to levy taxes. Edward needed money to fight the Scots and the French. Whereas de Montfort's Parliament was asked merely to provide 'advice', Edward asked the 1295 Parliament 'to consider, ordain and provide' the means to help the king achieve his aims. This was the summons sent to the Archbishop of Canterbury.

SUMMONS TO THE MODEL PARLIAMENT

The King to the venerable father in Christ Robert, by the same grace archbishop of Canterbury, primate of all England, greeting. As a most just law, established by the careful providence of sacred princes, exhorts and decrees that what affects all, by all should be approved, so also, very evidently should common danger be met by means provided in common. You know sufficiently well, and it is now, as we believe, divulged through all regions of the world, how the king of France fraudulently and craftily deprives us of our land of Gascony, by withholding it unjustly from us.

Now, however, not satisfied with the before-mentioned fraud and injustice, having gathered together for the conquest of our kingdom a very great fleet, and an abounding multitude of warriors, with which he has made a hostile attack on our kingdom and the inhabitants of the same kingdom, he now proposes to destroy the English language altogether from the earth, if his power should correspond to the detestable proposition of the contemplated injustice, which God forbid.

Because, therefore, darts seen beforehand do less injury, and your interest especially, as that of the rest of the citizens of the same realm, is concerned in this affair, we command you, strictly enjoining you in the fidelity and love in which you are bound to us, that on the Lord's day next after the feast of St. Martin, in the approaching winter, you be present in person at Westminster; citing beforehand the dean and chapter of your church, the archdeacons and all the clergy of your diocese, causing the same dean and archdeacons in their own persons, and the said chapter by one suitable proctor, and the said clergy by two, to be present along with you, having full and sufficient power from the same chapter and clergy, to consider, ordain and provide, along with us and with the rest of the prelates and principal men and other inhabitants of our kingdom, how the dangers and threatened evils of this kind are to be met.

Witness the king,
at Wangham, the thirtieth day of September

The king did not quite raise all the money he hoped for – and even that involved a bargain. The elected commoners did not see why they should stump up the cash Edward wanted unless they had the chance to air their grievances against poor administration. As well as marking an advance in the powers of Parliament, 1295 also marked the beginning of a tilt towards power for England's growing urban population. Of 292 commoners elected to the parliament, 219 represented towns and only 73 the shires.

In 1309, Parliament formalised its increased powers by withholding some money from the new king, Edward II, until he redressed a list of 21 grievances. Some of them concerned high-handed actions taken in the king's name; others were less to do with the hardships faced by ordinary people than with the Church's desire to maximise its power and retain its autonomy. The grievances included demands to remove secular pressures from the appointment of clerics and to deprive lay judges of hearing cases of bigamy. But, as is so often the case, a battle fought to secure the narrow interests of a few set a precedent with far-reaching long-term consequences for British democracy and the power of the monarchy.

Up to this point, England had had a unicameral parliament – bishops, peers and commoners all sat together. This soon changed. In the 1330s, Lords and Commons made separate grants to the king. This marks the point at which Parliament divided into an upper and a lower chamber, becoming a bicameral institution.

1305–20

'IT IS NOT FOR GLORY, NOR RICHES, NOR HONOURS THAT WE ARE FIGHTING, BUT FOR FREEDOM'

William Wallace was one of Scotland's most prominent military leaders during the Wars of Scottish Independence. Although heavily outnumbered, his troops defeated the Earl of Surrey's English forces at the Battle of Stirling Bridge in 1297. The following year, however, Wallace was defeated at the Battle of Falkirk, and he ceded control of his forces to Robert the Bruce. Wallace then travelled to France to seek King Philip IV's help in fighting the English. While he was away, Robert the Bruce settled his differences with Edward I. When Wallace returned from France, he was a wanted man. In August 1305, he was captured and put on trial for treason. As an outlaw, he was not allowed to engage a lawyer or even to speak in his own defence. But he shouted out these words from the dock when Sir Peter Mallorie formally accused him of treason.

WILLIAM WALLACE'S SPEECH DENYING TREASON

I cannot be a traitor, for I owe him [Edward] no allegiance. He is not my Sovereign; he never received my homage; and whilst life is in this persecuted body, he never shall receive it. To the other points whereof I am accused, I freely confess them all. As Governor of my country I have been an enemy to its enemies; I have slain the English; I have mortally opposed the English King; I have stormed and taken the towns and castles which he unjustly claimed as his own. If I or my soldiers have plundered or done injury to the houses or ministers of religion, I repent me of my sin; but it is not of Edward of England I shall ask pardon.

Not only was Wallace, inevitably, found guilty, but the court also handed down a sentence that was savage even by the standard of the times.

THE COURT'S SENTENCE AGAINST WILLIAM WALLACE

That the said William, for the manifest sedition that he practised against the Lord King himself, by feloniously contriving and acting with a view to his death and to the abasement and subversion of his crown and royal dignity, by opposing his liege lord in war to the death, be drawn from the Palace of Westminster to the Tower of London, and from the Tower to Aldgate, and so through the midst of the City, to the Elms;

And that for the robberies, homicides, and felonies he committed in the realm of England and in the land of Scotland, he be there hanged, and afterwards taken down from the gallows.

And that, inasmuch as he was an outlaw, and was not afterwards restored to the peace of the Lord King, he be decollated and decapitated; and that the heart, the liver and lungs as well as all the other intestines of the said William, from which such perverted thoughts proceeded, be cast into the fire and burnt;

And further that the body of the said William be cut up and divided into 4 parts, and that the head, so cut off, be set up on London Bridge, in the sight of such as pass by, whether by land or by water; and that one quarter be hung on a gibbet at Newcastle-upon-Tyne, another quarter at Berwick, a third quarter at Stirling, and the 4th at St. Johnston [Perth], as a warning and a deterrent to all that pass by and behold them.

The following March, Robert the Bruce was crowned king of Scotland. However, it was not until the Battle of Bannockburn in 1314 that he established full control over the whole of Scotland. Under his rule, Scotland's parliament passed a number of laws. According to one of the few surviving documents from the time, the Ayr Manuscript, these included the following early statement of the principle of equality before the law: 'The lord king wishes and orders that common law and common justice be done as well to poor people as to rich people according to the old laws and liberties justly used before these times.'

Robert's rule was popular, but not secure. English raids into Scotland continued, and the Pope did not recognise Scottish independence. In 1320, an appeal was sent to the Pope to change his mind. Its author was probably Bernard, Abbot of Arbroath and Chancellor of Scotland. It served not just as a request to help the Scots against the English but also as an assertion of the case that monarchs owe their place to the consent of their subjects and therefore that allegiance would always be conditional rather than blind. The declaration says that 'we are bound [to the king] both by law and by his merits'. Thus, were Robert or some future king to defy the law and/or cease to display 'merit', he would have to go. Specifically, the declaration says that should their 'Prince, King and Lord', Robert I, attempt to 'make us or our kingdom subject to the King of England' then 'we should drive him out as our enemy . . . and make some other man . . . our king'.

The declaration's sentiments trump its suspect historical analysis to make it arguably the most important document in Scotland's history.

THE DECLARATION OF ARBROATH

Most Holy Father and Lord, we know and from the chronicles and books of the ancients we find that among other famous nations our own, the Scots, has been graced with widespread renown. They journeyed from Greater Scythia by way of the Tyrrhenian Sea and the Pillars of Hercules, and dwelt for a long course of time in Spain among the most savage tribes, but nowhere could they be subdued by any race, however barbarous. Thence they came, twelve hundred years after the people of Israel crossed the Red Sea, to their home in the west where they still live today. The Britons they first drove out, the Picts they utterly destroyed, and, even though very often assailed by the Norwegians, the Danes and the English, they took possession of that home with many victories and untold efforts; and, as the historians of old time bear witness, they have held it free of all bondage ever since. In their kingdom there have reigned one hundred and thirteen kings of their own royal stock, the line unbroken by a single foreigner.

Thus our nation did indeed live in freedom and peace up to the time when that mighty prince the King of the English, Edward, the father of the one who reigns today, came in the guise of a friend and ally to harass us as an enemy. The deeds of cruelty, massacre, violence, pillage, arson, imprisoning prelates, burning down monasteries, robbing and killing monks and nuns, and yet other outrages without number which he committed against our people, sparing neither age nor sex, religion nor rank, no one could describe nor fully imagine unless he had seen them with his own eyes.

But from these countless evils we have been set free, by the help of Him Who though He afflicts yet heals and restores, by our most tireless Prince, King and Lord, the Lord Robert. He met toil and fatigue, hunger and peril, like another Macabaeus or Joshua and bore them cheerfully. Him, too, divine providence, his right of succession according to our laws and customs which we shall maintain to the death, and the due consent and assent of us all have made our Prince and King. To him, as to the man by whom salvation has been wrought unto our people, we are bound both by law and by his merits that our freedom may be still maintained, and by him, come what may, we mean to stand.

Yet if he should give up what he has begun, and agree to make us or our kingdom subject to the King of England or the English, we should exert ourselves at once to drive him out as our enemy and a subverter of his own rights and ours, and make some other man who was well able to defend us our King; for, as long as but a hundred of us remain alive, never will we on any conditions be brought under English rule. It is in truth not for glory, nor riches, nor honours that we are fighting, but for freedom — for that alone, which no honest man gives up but with life itself.

Therefore it is, Reverend Father and Lord, that we beseech your Holiness with our most earnest prayers and suppliant hearts, inasmuch as you will in your sincerity and goodness consider all this, that you will look with the eyes of a father on the troubles and privation brought by the English upon us and upon the Church of God. May it please you to admonish and exhort the King of the English, who ought to be satisfied with what belongs to him since England used once to be enough for seven kings or more, to leave us Scots in peace, who live in this poor little Scotland, beyond which there is no dwelling-place at all, and covet nothing but our own.

We are sincerely willing to do anything for him, having regard to our condition, that we can, to win peace for ourselves. This truly concerns you, Holy Father, since you see the savagery of the heathen raging against the Christians, as the sins of Christians have indeed deserved, and the frontiers of Christendom being pressed inward every day; and how much it will tarnish your Holiness's memory if (which God forbid) the Church suffers eclipse or scandal in any branch of it during your time, you must perceive. Then rouse the Christian princes who for false reasons pretend that they cannot go to help of the Holy Land because of wars they have on hand with their neighbours. The real reason that prevents them is that in making war on their smaller neighbours they find quicker profit and weaker resistance.

But how cheerfully our Lord the King and we too would go there if the King of the English would leave us in peace, He from Whom nothing is hidden well knows; and we profess and declare it to you as the Vicar of Christ and to all Christendom. But if your Holiness puts too much faith in the tales the English tell and will not give sincere belief to all this, nor refrain from favouring them to our prejudice, then the slaughter of bodies, the perdition of souls, and all the other misfortunes that will follow, inflicted by them on us and by us on them, will, we believe, be surely laid by the Most High to your charge.

To conclude, we are and shall ever be, as far as duty calls us, ready to do your will in all things, as obedient sons to you as His Vicar; and to Him as the Supreme King and Judge we commit the maintenance of our cause, casting our cares upon Him and firmly trusting that He will inspire us with courage and bring our enemies to nought. May the Most High preserve you to his Holy Church in holiness and health and grant you length of days.

Given at the monastery of Arbroath in Scotland on the sixth day of the month of April in the year of grace thirteen hundred and twenty and the fifteenth year of the reign of our King aforesaid.

Pope John XXII responded by recognising Robert as the king of an independent Scotland. In 1327, England's king, Edward II, was deposed by his wife and her lover in favour of Edward's son. The new king, Edward III, had a quick go at dominating Scotland, failed, and in 1328 signed a peace treaty with Robert, renouncing England's right to rule the Scots in return for a payment of £20,000 to England's treasury. This sum was raised by a special 'peace levy' throughout Scotland.

1351

'THE STRAIGHTS OF THE MASTERS AND THE SCARCITY OF SERVANTS'

The Black Death arrived in England in June 1348. By the time it was finally over, two years later, England's population had fallen by around one third, to an estimated 2.5 million. One immediate effect was a labour shortage. Workers could, in best free-market manner, bid up their wages. In 1349, King Edward III sought to stop this by decree, and two years later Parliament backed him with a detailed law, the Statute of Labourers, which sought to freeze wages, and the prices of food and drink, at the levels of 'the twentieth year' of Edward's reign – that is, 1346–7.

Not only did the law foreshadow prices and incomes laws in the twentieth century, it also paved the way for laws on poverty relief, by drawing a distinction between the 'able bodied' who could work and those who could not.

THE STATUTE OF LABOURERS

> Because a great part of the people, and especially of the workmen and servants, has now died in that pestilence, some, seeing the straights of the masters and the scarcity of servants, are not willing to serve unless they receive excessive wages, and others, rather than through labour to gain their living, prefer to beg in idleness: We, considering the grave inconveniences which might come from the lack especially of ploughmen and such labourers, have held deliberation and treaty concerning this with the prelates and nobles and other learned men sitting by us; by whose consentient counsel we have seen fit to ordain: that every man and woman of our kingdom of England, of whatever condition, whether bond or free, who is able bodied and below the age of sixty years, not living from trade nor carrying on a fixed craft, nor having of his own the means of living, or land of his own with regard to the cultivation of which he might occupy himself, and not serving another, if he, considering his station, be sought after to serve in a

suitable service, he shall be bound to serve him who has seen fit so to seek after him; and he shall take only the wages, liveries, gift or salary which, in the places where he sought to serve, were accustomed to be paid in the twentieth year of our reign of England, or the five or six common years next preceding. Provided, that in thus retaining their service, the lords are preferred before others of their bondsmen or their land tenants: so, nevertheless that such lords thus retain as many as shall be necessary and not more; and if any man or woman, being thus sought after in service, will not do this, the fact being proven by two faithful men before the sheriffs or the bailiffs of our lord the king, or the constables of the town where this happens to be done, straightway through them, or some one of them, he shall be taken and sent to the next jail, and there he shall remain in strict custody until he shall find surety for serving in the aforesaid form.

And if a reaper or mower, or other workman or servant, of whatever standing or condition he be, who is retained in the service of any one, do depart from the said service before the end of the term agreed, without permission or reasonable cause, he shall undergo the penalty of imprisonment, and let no one, under the same penalty, presume to receive or retain such a one in his service. Let no one, moreover, pay or permit to be paid to any one more wages, livery, gift or salary than was customary as has been said; nor let any one in any other manner exact or receive them, under penalty of paying to him who feels himself aggrieved from this, double the sum that has thus been paid or promised, exacted or received and if such person be not willing to prosecute, then it (the sum) is to be given to any one of the people who shall prosecute in this matter; and such prosecution shall take place in the court of the lord of the place where such case shall happen.

And if the lords of the towns or manors presume of themselves or through their servants in any way to act contrary to this our present ordinance, then in the Counties, Ridings and Districts, suit shall be brought against them in the aforesaid form for the triple penalty (of the sum) thus promised or paid by them or the servants; and if perchance, prior to the present ordinance any one shall have covenanted with any one thus to serve for more wages, he shall not be bound by reason of the said covenant to pay more than at another time was wont to be paid to such person; nay, under the aforesaid penalty he shall not presume to pay more.

Likewise saddlers, skinners, leather-workers, shoemakers, tailors, smiths, carpenters, masons, tilers, shipwrights, carters and all other artisans and labourers shall not take for their labour and handiwork more than what, in the places where they happen to labour, was customarily paid to such persons in the said twentieth year and in the other common years preceding, as has been said; and if any man take more, he shall be committed to the nearest jail in the manner aforesaid.

Likewise let butchers, fishmongers, stablemen, brewers, bakers, pullers and all other vendors of any victuals, be bound to sell such victuals for a reasonable price, having regard for the price at which such victuals are sold in the adjoining places: so that such vendors may have moderate gains, not excessive, according as the distance of the places from which such victuals are carried may seem reasonably to require; and if any one sell such victuals in another manner, and be convicted of it in the aforesaid way, he shall pay the double of that which he received to the party injured, or in default of him, to another who shall be willing to prosecute in this behalf; and the mayor and bailiffs of the cities and Burroughs, merchant towns and others, and of the maritime ports and places shall have power to enquire concerning each and every one who shall in any way err against this, and to levy the aforesaid penalty for the benefit of those at whose suit such delinquents shall have been convicted; and in case that the same mayor and bailiffs shall neglect to carry out the aforesaid, and shall be convicted of this before justices to be assigned by us, then the same mayor and bailiffs shall be compelled through the same justices, to pay to such wronged person or to another prosecuting in his place, the treble of the thing thus sold, and nevertheless, on our part too, they shall be grievously punished.

And because many sound beggars do refuse to labour so long as they can live from begging alms, giving themselves up to idleness and sins, and, at times, to robbery and other crimes – let no one, under the aforesaid pain of imprisonment presume, under colour of piety or alms to give anything to such as can very well labour, or to cherish them in their sloth, so that thus they may be compelled to labour for the necessaries of life.

The law achieved the worst of all worlds. It was enforced with enough vigour to tie up many courts, punish thousands of people and exacerbate poverty, but not with sufficient effect to prevent widespread evasion, corruption or mounting public contempt for the law. (In Essex alone, it has been estimated that one in eight adults – 7,500 people – were fined.) The statute turned out to be a staging post on the journey to the Peasants' Revolt 30 years later. Nevertheless, the Statute of Labourers persisted in some form until it was finally repealed in 1863.

1376–7

'THE AMENDMENT OF SEVERAL ERRORS IN THE GOVERNMENT, AND THE PRESERVATION OF THE REALM'

The 'Good Parliament' of 1376 acquired its name because it stood up to Edward III, now 65 years old and dying, and his fourth son, John of Gaunt, who was England's real ruler at the time. The man who put his head most decisively above the political parapet was Sir Peter de la Mare, the Speaker of the House of Commons. He attacked the royal court's excessive spending; in particular, he accused Alice Perrers, the king's mistress, of taking two thousand to three thousand pounds a year (at a time when a craftsman's wages were around eight pounds a year). On 12 May, speaking as the representative of the Commons, de la Mare told the House of Lords: 'It would be a great profit to the kingdom to remove that lady from the King's company so that the King's treasure could be applied to the war and wardships in the King's gift not be so lightly granted away.'

Parliament decided to banish Alice Perrers from the court and to imprison two members of the court whom it accused of stealing from the treasury. It also appointed a new set of councillors to 'advise' the king. John of Gaunt fought back, dismissing the new councillors a few months later and imprisoning de la Mare in Nottingham Castle. He was released the following year, after the death of Edward III. In the autumn of 1377, de la Mare resumed his place as Speaker of the House of Commons. He set out how the power of the new, ten-year-old king, Richard II, should be constrained. This contemporary account of his speech demonstrates both his belief in the independence of Parliament and the reason why he is regarded as one of the greatest of Commons Speakers.

SIR PETER DE LA MARE'S SPEECH TO THE GOOD PARLIAMENT

That which he had to declare was from their whole body; and therefore required, that if he should happen to speak anything without their consents, that it ought to be amended before his departure from the said place. He commended the feats of chivalry heretofore practised, for which this nation was so renowned; and said that by decay of the same, the honour of the realm did and would daily decrease. That whereas merchants were masters of their own ships, and had the free disposition of them, yet, formerly, one town had more good ships than the whole nation at this time. He therefore prayed that, because the king was then very young and of tender age, for the amendment of several errors in the government, and the preservation of the realm, which was at that time in greater danger than ever, the king and lords of parliament would consider more especially of three things:

First, the appointment of seven sufficient persons, to be selected from the different estates, as continual counsellors to the king, and that their names might be given to the Commons.

Secondly, that good and virtuous men might be appointed for the king's education, and that the charge of his household might be borne by the revenues of the crown, so that what was granted to the wars might be expended that way only;

and, Thirdly, that the common and statute laws might be observed, ratified, and confirmed, and the people governed by them, and not defeated, by any about the king's person, &c.

For the next three years, conflict continued between John of Gaunt and the councillors appointed by Parliament. Gradually, the councillors lost influence and de la Mare's power waned, and the council was finally disbanded in 1380. Yet while this battle for power was being waged, a larger crisis was unfolding.

1381

'ARE WE NOT ALL DESCENDED FROM THE SAME PARENTS, ADAM AND EVE?'

In January 1377, while Sir Peter de la Mare was being held in Nottingham Castle, King Richard II levied a poll tax of 4*d*. a head (i.e. four old pence: roughly a day's pay for a typical labourer). This was unpopular enough, but worse was to follow. A further poll tax was levied in 1379, and another in 1380. This third poll tax was the most severe: at one shilling a head, to be paid by every person aged fifteen or over, it was three times as much as the already extortionate 1377 tax. Evasion, rebellion and lawlessness followed, along with brutal attempts to enforce the law and collect the tax.

Around this time, William Langland wrote *Piers Plowman*, which pleaded cause of the downtrodden.

WILLIAM LANGLAND: *PIERS PLOWMAN*

The needy are our neighbours, if we note rightly;
As prisoners in cells, or poor folk in hovels,
Charged with children and overcharged by landlords.
What they may spare in spinning they spend on rental,
On milk, or on meal to make porridge
To still the sobbing of the children at meal time.
Also they themselves suffer much hunger.

They have woe in wintertime, and wake at midnight
To rise and to rock the cradle at the bedside,
To card and to comb, to darn clouts and to wash them,
To rub and to reel and to put rushes on the paving.
The woe of these women who dwell in hovels
Is too sad to speak of or to say in rhyme.
And many other men have much to suffer
From hunger and from thirst.

◇ ◇ ◇

The uprising that took place in 1381 is wrongly known as the Peasants' Revolt. In fact, it was mainly an uprising of craftsmen and the fourteenth-century equivalent of England's middle classes, including local officials such as bailiffs, constables, jurors and ale-tasters. Faced with the need to accept, evade or enforce the Statute of Labourers, these middle-class subjects regarded the third poll tax as a burden too far. The uprising started in May, in the Essex villages of Fobbing and Brentwood, as a protest against the tax. News spread throughout Essex and Kent, and then to London.

In early June, the leaders of the rebellion, including Wat Tyler, a village blacksmith, met in Barking to decide their next steps. They sought to impose discipline and positive objectives on what had been a disorganised series of protests. They demanded an end to the feudal system, but they did not want to overthrow the monarchy, saying that they stood for 'King Richard and the true Commons'. By 12 June, the insurgents were camped near London on both sides of the Thames, at Blackheath and Mile End.

The Blackheath contingent was addressed by John Ball, a priest whose advocacy of equality put him in conflict with the Church Establishment, especially the Archbishop of Canterbury, who had imprisoned Ball three times for his views. This is one contemporary account of Ball's speech.

JOHN BALL'S SPEECH AT BLACKHEATH

My good friends, things cannot go on well in England, nor ever will until every thing shall be in common; when there shall be neither vassal nor lord, and all distinctions levelled; when the lords shall be no more masters than ourselves. How ill have they used us! And for what reason do they hold us in bondage? Are we not all descended from the same parents, Adam and Eve? And what can they show, or what reasons give, why they should be more the masters than ourselves? Except, perhaps, in making us labour and work, for them to spend.

They are clothed in velvets and rich stuffs, ornamented with ermine and other furs, while we are forced to wear poor cloth. They have wines, spices, and fine bread, when we have only rye and the refuse of the straw; and if we drink, it must be water. They have handsome seats and manors, when we must brave the wind and rain in our labours in the field; but it is from our labour they have wherewith to support their pomp.

We are called slaves; and if we do not perform our services, we are beaten, and we have not any sovereign to whom we can complain, or who wishes to hear us and do us justice. Let us go to the king, who is young, and remonstrate with him on our servitude, telling him we must have it otherwise, or that we shall find a remedy for it ourselves. If we wait on him in a body, all those who come under the appellation of slaves, or are held in bondage, will follow us, in the hopes of being free. When the king shall see us, we shall obtain a favourable answer, or we must then seek ourselves to amend our condition.

On 13 June, the rebellion reached London. Buildings were destroyed – but selectively rather than indiscriminately. In keeping with the revolt leaders' view that they wanted to keep the king but get rid of many of the people and institutions around him, they selected specific targets, such as Lambeth Palace, John of Gaunt's Savoy Palace and a brothel on London Bridge.

The following day, the 14-year-old king and his closest advisers held an initial meeting with Wat Tyler and the other leaders of the revolt at Mile End. Richard offered some concessions, including an end to serfdom. A further and, in the event, decisive encounter took place the following day at Smithfield. This is the account of that meeting, recorded by monks whose Anonimalle Chronicle is regarded as one of the most accurate histories of Mediaeval England. It shows how the king offered to meet most of the insurgents' demands – and how a valet then took matters into his own hands, attacked Tyler and changed the course of history.

THE ANONIMALLE CHRONICLE'S ACCOUNT OF THE PEASANTS' REVOLT

Then the King caused a proclamation to be made that all the commons of the country who were still in London should come to Smithfield, to meet him there; and so they did.

And when the King and his train had arrived there they turned into the Eastern meadow in front of St. Bartholomew's, which is a house of canons: and the commons arrayed themselves on the west side in great battles. At this moment the Mayor of London, William Walworth, came up, and the King bade him go to the commons, and make their chieftain come to him.

Wat Tyler of Maidstone came to the King with great confidence, mounted on a little horse, that the commons might see him. And he dismounted, holding in his hand a dagger. And when he had dismounted he half bent his knee, and then took the King by the hand, and shook his arm forcibly and roughly, saying to him, 'Brother, be of good comfort and joyful, for you shall have, in the fortnight that is to come, praise from the commons even more than you have yet had, and we shall be good companions.'

And the King said to Wat Tyler, 'Why will you not go back to your own country?' But the other answered, with a great oath, that neither he nor his fellows would depart until they had got their charter such as they wished to have it. And he demanded that there should be equality among all men save only the King and there should be no more villeins [peasants who were technically free, but in practice tied to the lord of the manor] in England, and no serfdom or villeinage. And he demanded that there should be only one bishop in England and only one prelate, and all the lands and tenements now held by them should be confiscated, and divided among the commons, only reserving for them a reasonable sustenance. To this the King gave an easy answer, and said that he should have all that he could fairly grant, reserving only for himself the regality of his crown. And then he bade him go back to his home, without making further delay.

Presently Wat Tyler, in the presence of the King, sent for a flagon of water to rinse his mouth, because of the great heat that he was in, and when it was brought he rinsed his mouth in a very rude and disgusting fashion before the King's face. And then he made them bring him a jug of beer, and drank a great draught, and then, in the presence of the King, climbed on his horse again. At this time a certain valet who was among the King's retinue, when he saw him, said aloud that he knew the said Walter for the greatest thief and robber in all Kent. And for these words Wat tried to strike him with his dagger, and would have slain him in the King's presence.

But for his violent behaviour and despite, the Mayor of London, William Walworth, arrested him. And because he arrested him, the said Wat stabbed the Mayor with his dagger in the stomach in great wrath.

But, as it pleased God, the Mayor was wearing armour and took no harm, but like a hardy and vigorous man drew his cutlass, and struck back at the said Wat, and gave him a deep cut on the neck, and then a great cut on the head. And during this scuffle one of the King's household drew his sword, and ran Wat two or three times through the body, mortally wounding him.

Afterwards the King sent out his messengers into divers parts, to capture the malefactors and put them to death. And many were taken and hanged at London, and they set up many gallows around the City of London, and in other cities and boroughs of the south country. At last, as it pleased God, the King seeing that too many of his liege subjects would be undone, and too much blood spilt, took pity in his heart, and granted them all pardon, on condition that they should never rise again. And so finished this wicked war.

On 22 June, a group of rebels met Richard and asked him to restore the initial concessions he had made at Mile End. This time he was in no mood to compromise. His response brought a bloody curtain down on the Peasants' Revolt:

You wretches, detestable on land and sea; you who seek equality with lords are unworthy to live! Give this message to your colleagues: rustics you were, and rustics you are still. You will remain in bondage, not as before, but incomparably harsher. For as long as we live we will strive to suppress you, and your suffering will be an example in the eyes of posterity. However we will spare your lives if you remain faithful. Choose now, which path you want to follow.

1401

'The said lord Benedict shall brand as heretics and cause to be tortured in the usual manner, Henry of Lancaster and his adherents'

Owain Glyn Dŵr, anglicised by Shakespeare to Owen Glendower in *The First Part of King Henry IV*, was not the wild and exotic character portrayed in the play. Nor was he a downtrodden Welsh serf. He was a nobleman and landowner who had served in the English army, and turned to revolt when he lost out in a land dispute with his English neighbour, Baron Grey de Ruthyn. Disgusted by the decision of Henry IV's courts to side with the baron, Glyn Dŵr refused to supply troops to serve under the new king against the Scots. For this, he was labelled a traitor to the English crown.

Glyn Dŵr responded by having himself proclaimed 'Prince of Wales' by his band of followers and leading a revolt against the king. In 1401, the following year, Glyn Dŵr wrote to seek help from Scotland and Ireland.

Owain Glyn Dŵr's letter to the king of Scotland

Most high and mighty and redoubted lord and cousin, I commend me to your most high and royal majesty, humbly as beseemeth me, with all honour and reverence. Most redoubted lord and right sovereign cousin, please it you and your most high majesty to know that Brutus, your most noble ancestor and mine, was the first crowned king who dwelt in this realm of England, which of old times was called Great Britain. The which Brutus begat three sons, to wit Albanact, Locrine and Camber. From which same Albanact you are descended in direct line.

And the issue of the same Camber reigned royally down to Cadwalladar, who was the last crowned king of my people, and from whom I, your simple cousin, am descended in direct line; and after whose decease I and my ancestors and all my said people have been, and still are, under the tyranny and bondage of mine and your mortal foes the Saxons; whereof you, most redoubted lord and right sovereign cousin, have good knowledge. And from this tyranny and bondage the prophecy saith that I shall be delivered by the aid and succour of your royal majesty.

But, most redoubted lord and sovereign cousin, I make grievous plaint to your royal majesty and right sovereign cousinship, that it faileth me much in men at arms. Wherefore, most redoubted lord and right sovereign cousin, I humbly beseech you, kneeling upon my knees, that it may please your royal majesty to send unto me a certain number of men at arms who may aid me and may withstand, with God's help, mine and your foes aforesaid; having regard, most redoubted lord and right sovereign cousin, to the chastisement of this mischief and of all the many past mischiefs which I and my said ancestors of Wales have suffered at the hands of mine and your mortal foes aforesaid. Being well assured, most redoubted lord and right sovereign cousin, that it shall be that, all the days of my life, I shall be bounden to do service and pleasure to your said royal majesty and to repay you.

And in that I cannot send unto you all my businesses in writing, I despatch these present bearers fully informed in all things, to whom it may please you to give faith and credence in what they shall say unto you by word of mouth. From my court. Most redoubted lord and right sovereign cousin, may the Almighty Lord have you in his keeping.

GLYN DŴR'S LETTER TO A LORD IN IRELAND

Greetings and fullness of love, most dread lord and right trusty cousin. Be it known unto you that a great discord or war has arisen between us and our and your deadly foes, the Saxons: which war we have manfully waged now for nearly two years past, and which too, we purport and hope henceforth to wage and to bring to a good and effectual end, by the grace of God our Saviour, and by your help and countenance. But, seeing that it is commonly reported by the prophecy that, before we can have the upper hand in this behalf, you and yours, our well-beloved cousins in Ireland, must stretch forth hereto a helping hand; therefore, most dread lord and right trusty cousin, with heart and soul we pray you that your horsemen and footmen, for the succour of us and our people who now this long while we are oppressed by our said foes and yours, as well as to oppose the treacherous and deceitful will of those same our foes, you do despatch unto us as many as you shall conveniently and honourably be able, saving in all things your honourable estate, as quickly as may seem good to you, bearing in mind our sore need.

Delay not to do this, by the love we bear you and as we put our trust in you, although we may be unknown to your dread person, seeing that, most dread lord and cousin, so long as we shall be able to wage manfully this war in our borders, as doubtless is clear unto you, you and all the other chieftains of your parts of Ireland will be in the mean time have welcome peace and calm repose. And because, my lord cousin, the bearers of these presents shall make things known unto you more fully by word of mouth, may it please you to give credence unto them in all things which they shall say unto you on our behalf, and as it may be your will, to confide in full trust, unto them whatsoever, dread lord and cousin, we your poor cousin may do. Dread lord and cousin, may the almighty preserve your reverence and lordship in long life and good fortune.

Written in North Wales,
on the twenty-ninth day of November

The letters are notable more for their sentiment than their impact: neither Scotland nor the Irish provided much help, though the French did, for a while. By 1404, Glyn Dŵr's forces controlled much of Wales. Along the way they captured Baron Grey de Ruthyn, and released him after a year, on the payment of a large ransom.

In 1406, Glyn Dŵr sent the 'Pennal Letter' to Charles VI, king of France, seeking to cement French support. In order to help achieve this, Glyn Dŵr declared his allegiance to the Pope of Avignon, Benedict XIII. This was significant because two rival popes claimed to lead Europe's Catholics. Charles had originally sided with the Pope of Avignon, while England's King Henry IV recognised the Pope of Rome, Innocent VII. Glyn Dŵr's letter asked Charles VI to forward a series of requests to Pope Benedict. Glyn Dŵr appears to have been unaware that, by the time he wrote his letter, Charles had withdrawn his support for Benedict.

Glyn Dŵr's Pennal Letter

We humbly pray your royal majesty that you will graciously consider it worthy to advance their object, even in the court of the lord Benedict.

First, that all ecclesiastical censures against us, our subjects, or our land, by the aforesaid lord Benedict or Clement his predecessor, by the said Benedict be removed.

Again, that the same lord Benedict shall provide for the metropolitan church of St David's, and other cathedral churches of our principality, prelates, dignitaries, and beneficed clergy and curates, who know our language.

Again, that the same lord Benedict shall revoke and annul all incorporations, unions, annexions, appropriations of parochial churches of our principality made so far, by any authority whatsoever with English monasteries and colleges.

Again, that the said lord Benedict shall concede to us and to our heirs, the princes of Wales, that our chapels etc shall be free, and shall rejoice in the privileges, exemptions and immunities in which they rejoiced in the times of our forefathers the princes of Wales.

Again, that we shall have two universities or places of general study, namely one in North Wales and the other in South Wales, in cities, towns or places to be hereafter decided and determined by our ambassadors and nuncios for that purpose.

Again, that the said lord Benedict shall brand as heretics and cause to be tortured in the usual manner, Henry of Lancaster [Henry IV], the intruder of the kingdom of England, and the usurper of the crown of the same kingdom, and his adherents, in that of their own free will they have burnt or caused to be burnt so many cathedrals, convents and parish churches; that they have savagely hung, beheaded and quartered archbishops, prelates, religious men, as madmen or beggars, or caused the same to be done.

Again, that the same lord Benedict shall grant us, our heirs and adherents, of whatsoever nation that may be, who wage war against the aforesaid intruder and usurper, as long as they hold the orthodox faith, full remission of all our sins, and that the remission shall continue as long as the wars between us, our heirs and our subjects, and the aforesaid Henry, his heirs and subjects, shall endure.

In testimony whereof we make these our letters patent. Given at Pennal on the thirty first day of March, AD 1406, and in the sixth year of our rule.

The Pennal Letter remains the strongest historical statement of Welsh nationhood, but it achieved little at the time. Not only had Charles broken with Benedict; the balance of power within his own court had shifted towards a more conciliatory policy towards England. Far from providing Glyn Dŵr with more help, Charles withdrew the French troops that had been stationed in Wales. In response, Henry IV switched his strategy from outright military confrontation to economic blockade. His patience paid off. Gradually England regained control of Wales. The last confirmed sighting of Glyn Dŵr, reduced to the role of guerrilla leader, was in 1412. In 1415, the revolt finally over, England's new king, Henry V, pardoned Glyn Dŵr. Nobody can be sure whether Glyn Dŵr was still alive or, if he was, knew of the pardon.

1471

'BLESSED BE GOD, THIS LAND IS RULED UNDER A BETTER LAW'

S ir John Fortescue was an English jurist who helped to shape the debate over the role of the monarchy. In *The Difference Between an Absolute and Limited Monarchy*, published in 1471, he compared France and England, arguing that England was a more prosperous country because its limited monarchy allowed the country to reap the practical benefits of the rule of law, as opposed to France, where the monarch had absolute power. At another level, Fortescue's analysis can be read as a critique of the defeat and subsequent murder of Henry VI that year, in England's Civil War. Fortescue supported Henry and the Lancastrian cause, but considered him a poor leader who would have been more successful had he been smarter and less remote in the way he ruled and fought.

SIR JOHN FORTESCUE: *THE DIFFERENCE BETWEEN AN ABSOLUTE AND LIMITED MONARCHY*

There are two kinds of kingdom, of which one is a lordship, called in Latin *dominium regale* and the other is called *dominium politicum et regale*. And they differ in that the first king may rule his people by such laws as he makes himself. And therefore he may set upon them tallages [land taxes] and other impositions such as he wills himself without their assent. The second king may not rule his people by other laws than those that they assent to. And therefore he may set upon them no impositions without their own assent.

Now the French king reigns over his people *dominio regale*; yet neither Louis IX nor any of his progenitors ever set tallages or other impositions upon the people of that land without the assent of the three estates which, when they are assembled, are like the court of the parliament in England. And this order many of his successors kept until recently when Englishmen made such war in France that the three estates dared not come together. And then, for that reason and for the great need which the French king had of supplies for the defence of that land, he took it upon himself to set tallages and other impositions upon the commons without the assent of the three estates; but yet he would not set any such charges, nor has he set any, upon the nobles for fear of rebellion. And the commons there, though they have grouched, have not rebelled.

The French kings have yearly since set such charges upon them and so augmented the same charges that the commons are so impoverished and destroyed that they can scarcely live. They drink water, they eat apples, with bread right brown and made of rye; they eat no flesh unless it be right seldom a little lard, or of the entrails and heads of beasts slain for the nobles and merchants of the land. They wear no woollen [clothing] unless it be a poor coat under their outermost garment, made to great canvas and called a frock. Verily they live in the most extreme poverty and misery and yet they dwell in the most fertile realm in the world. Wherefore the French king has not men of his own realm able to defend it except his nobles who bear no such impositions. By which cause the said king is compelled to make his armies and retinues for the defence of his land of strangers like Scots, Spaniards, men of Germany and of other nations.

If the realm of England, which is an isle and therefore may not lightly get succour from other lands, were ruled under such a law and such a prince, it would then be a prey to all other nations that would conquer, rob or devour it. But, blessed be God, this land is ruled under a better law; and therefore the people thereof are not in such penury nor thereby hurt in their persons but are wealthy and have all things necessary to the sustenance of nature. Wherefore they are mighty and able to resist the adversaries of this realm and to beat other realms that do or would do them wrong.

1516–23

'A CONSPIRACY OF RICH MEN PROCURING THEIR OWN COMMODITIES UNDER THE NAME OF THE COMMONWEALTH'

Sir (subsequently Saint) Thomas More is best known as the Lord Chancellor whose Catholic beliefs compelled him, in 1530, to refuse to support Henry VIII's wish to annul his marriage to Catherine of Aragon. When More refused to attend the wedding of the king to Anne Boleyn, he was charged with treason, tried and executed.

Before all that, More had established himself as a lawyer, a scholar and a Speaker of the House of Commons. In 1516 he invented the word 'utopia', in a book of that name, to describe a perfect, imaginary country run on tolerant and egalitarian principles, without the existence of private property. There were, though, limits to More's liberalism. His Utopia allowed for different religious practices, but not atheism. He favoured an ordered society shaped by religious principles, but not anything that would be recognised centuries later as true liberty. Nevertheless, his critique of the non-utopian societies of Western Europe was one of the most progressive of his day.

SIR THOMAS MORE: *UTOPIA*

> For what justice is this, that a rich goldsmith, or an usurer, or to be short, any of them which either do nothing at all, or else that which they do is such that it is not very necessary to the commonwealth, should have a pleasant and a wealthy living, either by idleness, or by unnecessary business; when in the meantime poor labourers, carters, ironsmiths, carpenters and ploughmen, by so great and continual toil, as drawing and bearing beasts be scant able to sustain, and again so necessary toil, that without it no commonwealth were able to continue and endure one year, do yet get so hard and poor a living, and live so wretched and miserable a life, that the state and condition of the labouring beasts may seem much better and

wealthier? For they be not put to so continual labour, nor their living is not much worse, yea to them much pleasanter, taking no thought in the mean season for the time to come.

But these silly poor wretches be presently tormented with barren and unfruitful labour. And the remembrance of their poor indigent and beggarly old age killeth them up. For their daily wages is so little, that it will not suffice for the same day, much less it yieldeth any overplus, that may daily be laid up for the relief of old age.

Is not this an unjust and an unkind public weal, which giveth great fees and rewards to gentleman, as they call them, and to goldsmiths, and to such other, which be either idle persons, or else only flatterers, and devisers of vain pleasures; and of the contrary part maketh no gentle provision for poor ploughmen, colliers, labourers, carters, ironsmiths, and carpenters: without whom no commonwealth can continue.

But when it hath abused the labours of their lusty and flowering age, at the last when they be oppressed with old age and sickness, being needy, poor, and indigent of all things, then forgetting their so many painful watchings, not remembering their so many and so great benefits, recompenseth and acquitteth them most unkindly with miserable death. And yet besides this the rich men not only by private fraud, but also by common laws, do every day pluck and snatch away from the poor some part of their daily living.

So whereas it seemed before unjust to recompense with unkindness their pains that have been beneficial to the public weal, now they have to this their wrong and unjust dealing (which is yet a much worse point) given the name of justice, yea and that by force of a law. Therefore, when I consider and weigh in my mind all these commonwealths, which nowadays anywhere do flourish, so God help me, I can perceive nothing but a certain conspiracy of rich men procuring their own commodities under the name and title of the commonwealth. They invent and devise all means and crafts, first how to keep safely, without fear of losing, that they have unjustly gathered together, and next how to hire and abuse the work and labour of the poor for as little money as may be. These devices, when the rich men have decreed to be kept and observed for the commonwealth's sake, that is to say for the wealth also of the poor people, then they be made laws.

More became Speaker of the House of Commons in 1523. Tradition dictates that when a new Speaker is elected for the House of Commons, he or she displays reluctance to take the post and has to be dragged to the Speaker's Chair. In More's case, the reluctance was genuine. He did not want the job because he knew that he would have to stand up for his principles, and this would cause trouble. When, at the instigation of Cardinal Wolsey, the Lord Chancellor, More was asked to become Speaker, he asked to be discharged. When the king refused his request, More set out the argument for allowing Members of Parliament to say what they really thought.

SIR THOMAS MORE'S SPEECH TO THE KING ON THE RIGHTS OF MPS

For as much as there be of your Commons here, by your high commandment assembled for your Parliament, a great number which are after the accustomed manner appointed in the Common House to treat and advise of the common affairs among themselves apart: and albeit that hath been as due diligence used in sending up to your Highness' Court of Parliament the most discreet persons out of every quarter, that men could esteem meet thereto, whereby it is not to be doubted but that there is a very substantial assembly of right wise and politic persons: yet since among so many wise men, neither is every man wise alike, nor among so many men like well witted, every man like well spoken; and it often happeneth, that likewise as much folly is uttered with painted polished speeches, so many boisterous and rude in language see deep indeed, and give right substantial counsel: and since also in matters of great importance the mind is often so occupied in the matter, that a man rather studies what to say, than how; by what reason whereof the wisest man might speak in a way that as he would afterward wish to have been uttered otherwise.

Therefore (most Gracious Sovereign) considering that in all your high Courts of Parliament is nothing entreated but of matters of weight and importance concerning your Realm, and your own Royal estate, it could not fail to let and put to silence from the giving of their advice and counsel many of your discreet Commons to the great hindrance of the common affairs, unless they were utterly discharged of all doubt and fear how anything that should happen them: and in this point your well-known benignity puts every man in right good hope.

Yet such is the weight of the matter, such is the reverend dread that the timorous hearts of your natural subjects conceive towards your high Majesty (our most redoubted King and undoubted Sovereign) that they cannot in this point find themselves satisfied, except your gracious bounty herein declared put away the scruple of their timorous minds, and animate and encourage them out of doubt.

It may therefore like your most abundant Grace (our most gracious King) to give to all your Commons here assembled, your most gracious licence and pardon freely, without doubt of your dreadful displeasure, every man to discharge his conscience, and boldly in every thing incident among, declare his advice, and whatsoever any man says, it may like your noble Majesty of your inestimable goodness to take all in good part, interpreting every man's words, how uncunningly so ever they be couched, to proceed yet of a good zeal towards the profit of your Realm and honour of your Royal person, the prosperous estate and preservation whereof (most excellent Sovereign) is the thing which we all your most humble loving subjects, according to the most bounden duty of our natural allegiance, most highly desire and pray for.

Later, Wolsey told the new Speaker: 'Would to God you had been at Rome, Mr More, when I made you Speaker.' More replied: 'Your Grace not offended, so would I too, my Lord.'

As he showed in *Utopia*, More was not a true believer in liberty and free speech for all. When William Tyndale published a Bible in English in 1526, More, now Lord Chancellor, vigorously enforced a century-old law that banned the publishing of Bibles in the vernacular. The fact that Tyndale was a Lutheran added to More's zeal. He held that religion was too important for ordinary people to be allowed to read the Bible for themselves in their mother tongue. Goodness, they might reach their own conclusions, and where could that lead?

1563

'NO PERSON RETAINED SHALL DEPART FROM HIS MASTER, MISTRESS, OR DAME UNLESS IT BE FOR SOME REASONABLE AND SUFFICIENT CAUSE'

The Statute of Artificers set out to address two problems: the shortage of agricultural workers at a time when England's towns and cities were growing rapidly, and the damage being done to the economy by the excessively monopolistic powers of the craft guilds. The statute updated the 1351 Statute of Labourers – and retained some of its harshness. In the summer months, labourers paid by the day had to work from five in the morning until seven in the evening, apart from breakfast, dinner and drinks breaks of up to two hours in total.

However, the statute also took the first steps towards giving workers rights. It stated that no employee should be sacked 'before the end of his or her term' without due cause, and that apprentices should not be mistreated. Indeed, the statute can be regarded as marking the beginning of a nationwide apprenticeship system. It effectively nationalised the basic rules governing apprentices by diminishing the freedom of the craft guilds to do whatever they wanted.

THE STATUTE OF ARTIFICERS

An act containing divers orders for artificers, labourers, etc. Although there remain and stand in force presently a great number of acts and statutes concerning the retaining, departing, wages, and orders of apprentices, servants, and labourers, the said laws cannot conveniently, without the great grief and burden of the poor labourer and hired man, be put in good and due execution; so if the substance of as many of the said laws as are meet to be continued shall be digested and reduced into one sole law and statute, there is good hope that it will come to pass that the same law, being duly executed, should banish idleness, advance husbandry, and yield unto the hired person both in the time of scarcity and in the time of plenty a convenient proportion of wages, be it enacted that:

No person which shall retain any servant shall put away his or her said servant, and that no person retained according to this statute shall depart from his master, mistress, or dame before the end of his or her term, unless it be for some reasonable and sufficient cause or matter to be allowed before two justices of peace, or one at the least, within the said county, or before the mayor or other chief officer of the city, borough, or town corporate.

And be it enacted that if any person after he hath retained any servants, shall put away any such servant at the end of his term without one quarter's warning given before the said end, then every such master, mistress or dame so offending, unless he or they be able to prove by two sufficient witnesses such reasonable and sufficient cause of putting away of their servant during their term be fined 40s.

And be it enacted that all artificers and labourers being hired for wages by the day or week, shall betwixt the midst of the months of March and September, be and continue at their work, at or before five of the clock in the morning, and not to depart until betwixt seven and eight of the clock at night (except it be in the time of breakfast, dinner or drinking, the which time at the most shall not exceed above two hours in the day; and all the said artificers and labourers between the midst of September and the midst of March shall be and continue at their work from the spring of the day in the morning until the night of the same day, except it be in time afore appointed for breakfast and dinner).

And for the declaration and limitation what wages servants, labourers, and artificers, either by the year or day or otherwise, shall have and receive, be it enacted that the justices of peace shall yearly, at every general sessions first to be holden and kept after Easter, assemble themselves together; and conferring together respecting the plenty or scarcity of the time and other circumstances necessary to be considered, shall have authority to limit, rate, and appoint the wages of artificers, handicraftsmen, husbandmen, or any other labourer, servant, or workman.

And be it further enacted that, if any person shall be required by any householder, having and using half a ploughland at the least in tillage, to be an apprentice and to serve in husbandry or in any other kind of art, mystery, or science before expressed, and shall refuse so to do, that then, upon the complaint of such housekeeper made to one justice of peace of the county wherein the said refusal is or shall be made, the said justice or the said mayor shall have power and authority by virtue hereof, if the said person refuse to be bound as an apprentice, to commit him unto ward, there to remain until he be contented and will be bounden to serve as an apprentice should serve, according to the true intent and meaning of this present act.

And if any such master shall misuse or mistreat his apprentice, or the said apprentice shall have any just cause to complain, or the apprentice do not his duty to his master, then the said master or apprentice being grieved and having cause to complain shall repair unto one justice of peace within the said county, or to the mayor of the city, town corporate, market town, or other place where the said master dwelleth, who shall by his wisdom and discretion take such order and direction between the said master and his apprentice as the equity of the cause shall require.

1576

'THERE IS NOTHING SO NECESSARY FOR THE PRESERVATION OF THE PRINCE AND STATE AS FREE SPEECH'

Sir Peter Wentworth was a Puritan critic of Elizabeth I. Entering Parliament as MP for Barnstaple in 1571, he quickly established himself as a defender of the liberties of Parliament. On 8 February 1576, he set out in the clearest terms the moral and practical case for free speech for MPs.

SIR PETER WENTWORTH'S SPEECH TO THE HOUSE OF COMMONS ON FREEDOM OF SPEECH

Mr. Speaker, I find written in a little volume these words: 'Sweet indeed is the name of liberty and the thing itself a value beyond all inestimable treasure.'

In this House which is termed a place of free speech there is nothing so necessary for the preservation of the prince and state as free speech, and without it, it is a scorn and mockery to call it a Parliament house, for in truth it is none, but a very school of flattery and dissimulation and so a fit place to serve the devil and his angels in and not to glorify God and benefit the commonwealth.

Amongst other, Mr. Speaker, two things do great hurt in this place, of the which I do mean to speak: the one is a rumour which runneth about the House and this it is, 'Take heed what you do, the queen's Majesty liketh not such a matter. Whosoever preferreth it, she will be offended with him.' Or the contrary, 'Her majesty liketh of such a matter. Whosoever speaketh against it, she will be much offended with him.' The other: sometimes a message is brought into the House, either of commanding or inhibiting, very injurious to the freedom of speech and consultation. I would to God, Mr. Speaker, that these two were buried in hell, I mean rumours and messages, for wicked they undoubtedly are. The reason is, the devil was the first author of them, from whom proceedeth nothing but wickedness.

Certain it is, Mr. Speaker that none is without fault, no, not our noble Queen. Her Majesty hath committed great faults, yea dangerous faults to herself and the state. It is a dangerous thing in a prince unkindly to entreat and abuse his or her nobility and people as her Majesty did the last Parliament, and it is a dangerous thing in a prince to oppose or bend herself against her nobility and people, and how could any prince more unkindly entreat, abuse and oppose herself against her nobility and people than her Majesty did the last Parliament?

Did she not call it of purpose to prevent traitorous perils to her person and for no other cause? Did not her Majesty send unto us two bills, willing us to make a choice of that we liked best for her safety and thereof to make a law, promising her Majesty's royal consent thereto? And did we not first choose the one and her Majesty refused it, yielding no reason, nay, yielding great reasons why she ought to have yielded to it?

It is a great and special part of our duty and office Mr. Speaker to maintain the freedom of consultation and speech for by this are good laws that do set forth God's glory and are for the preservation of the prince and state made. St. Paul in the same place sayeth, hate that which is evil and cleave unto that which is good; then with St. Paul I do advise you all here present, yea, and heartily and earnestly I desire you from the bottom of your hearts to hate all messengers, tale carriers, or any other thing whatsoever it be that any manner of way infringe the liberties of this honourable council. Yea, hate it or them, I say, as venomous and poison unto our commonwealth, for they are venomous beasts that do use it. Therefore I say again and again, hate that that is evil and cleave to that that is good. And this, loving and faithful hearted, I do wish to be conceived in fear of God, and of love to our prince and state, for we are incorporated into this place to serve God and all England and not to be timeservers and humour feeders.

I have holden you long with my rude speech, the which since it tendeth wholly with pure consciences to seek the advancement of God's glory, our honourable sovereign's safety and to the sure defence of this noble isle of England, and all by maintaining the liberties of this honourable council, the fountain from whence all these do spring, my humble and hearty suit unto you all is to accept my goodwill and that this that I have here spoken of conscience and great zeal unto my prince and state may not be buried in the pit of oblivion and so no good come thereof.

The good news for Wentworth was that his speech was indeed spared 'the pit of oblivion': it was widely reported not just in England but also across Europe. The bad news was that he was arrested the same day his speech was delivered and charged with slander. The next day he was committed to the Tower of London, where he remained until Queen Elizabeth pardoned him one month later.

However, he continued both to cause trouble and to get into it. Finally, in 1593, after campaigning for a change in the rules of succession for the monarchy, he was sent back to the Tower, where he spent the remaining three years of his life.

1602

'O, WHEN DEGREE IS SHAKED,
WHICH IS THE LADDER TO ALL HIGH DESIGNS,
THEN ENTERPRISE IS SICK!'

Shakespeare was a conservative with a lower-case 'c'. A number of his plays – histories, tragedies and comedies – reflect his preference for wise leaders, contented subjects and a common acceptance of the duties that each owes the other, rather than denunciations of the existing order and the need for it to be overthrown. Shakespeare's own political philosophy is most clearly reflected in his work in this speech by Ulysses in *Troilus and Cressida*, which analyses the weaknesses of the Greek army. Ulysses says that it lacks 'degree', which is vital if society is to tick. Without 'degree, priority and place' – that is, without respect for order and authority – anarchy, brute force and evil will reign.

WILLIAM SHAKESPEARE: *TROILUS AND CRESSIDA*

> The heavens themselves, the planets and this centre
> Observe degree, priority and place,
> Insisture, course, proportion, season, form,
> Office and custom, in all line of order;
> And therefore is the glorious planet Sol
> In noble eminence enthroned and sphered
> Amidst the other; whose medicinable eye
> Corrects the ill aspects of planets evil,
> And posts, like the commandment of a king,
> Sans cheque to good and bad: but when the planets
> In evil mixture to disorder wander,
> What plagues and what portents! what mutiny!
> What raging of the sea! shaking of earth!
> Commotion in the winds! frights, changes, horrors,
> Divert and crack, rend and deracinate

The unity and married calm of states
Quite from their fixure! O, when degree is shaked,
Which is the ladder to all high designs,
Then enterprise is sick! How could communities,
Degrees in schools and brotherhoods in cities,
Peaceful commerce from dividable shores,
The primogenitive and due of birth,
Prerogative of age, crowns, sceptres, laurels,
But by degree, stand in authentic place?
Take but degree away, untune that string,
And, hark, what discord follows! each thing meets
In mere oppugnancy: the bounded waters
Should lift their bosoms higher than the shores
And make a sop of all this solid globe:
Strength should be lord of imbecility,
And the rude son should strike his father dead:
Force should be right; or rather, right and wrong,
Between whose endless jar justice resides,
Should lose their names, and so should justice too.
Then every thing includes itself in power,
Power into will, will into appetite;
And appetite, an universal wolf,
So doubly seconded with will and power,
Must make perforce an universal prey,
And last eat up himself. Great Agamemnon,
This chaos, when degree is suffocate,
Follows the choking.
And this neglection of degree it is
That by a pace goes backward, with a purpose
It hath to climb. The general's disdain'd
By him one step below, he by the next,
That next by him beneath; so every step,
Exampled by the first pace that is sick
Of his superior, grows to an envious fever
Of pale and bloodless emulation:
And 'tis this fever that keeps Troy on foot,
Not her own sinews. To end a tale of length,
Troy in our weakness stands, not in her strength.

1606

'HAVE HIS PRIVY PARTS CUT OFF AND BURNT BEFORE HIS FACE'

The Gunpowder Plot is one of the most iconic episodes in Britain's history. Its aim was to depose James I of England (since 1603) and VI of Scotland (since 1567). (Following Queen Elizabeth's death in 1603, the crowns of the two countries were united.) The conspiracy's leader, Robert Catesby, had form: he had been involved in an attempt in 1601 to depose the elderly Elizabeth I. The better-remembered member of Catesby's gang was Guy Fawkes, who had been put in charge of carrying out the plot because he was an explosives expert. Fawkes was caught in the basement of Parliament at midnight on 5 November 1605 as he prepared to set light to 20 barrels of gunpowder. He was taken to the Tower of London, where he was tortured on the instructions of the king: 'The gentler tortures are to be first used unto him, *et sic per gradus ad maiora tenditur* [and thus by steps extended to greater ones], and so God speed your good work.'

Some of the remaining conspirators were caught in Worcestershire, and others were eventually cornered in Staffordshire. Catesby was killed in a shoot-out. The rest were brought to London. This is the official account of the conclusion of their trial.

THE TRIAL OF THE GUNPOWDER PLOT CONSPIRATORS

Sir Edward Coke, the Attorney General said: 'The Conclusion shall be from the admirable Clemency and Moderation of the King, in that howsoever these Traitors have exceeded all others their Predecessors in Mischief; yet neither will the King exceed the usual Punishment of Law, nor invent any new Torture or Torment for them; but is graciously pleased to afford them as well an ordinary Course of Trial, as an ordinary Punishment, much inferior to their Offence. And surely worthy of Observation is the Punishment by Law provided and appointed for High Treason.

'For first, after a Traitor hath had his just Trial, and is convicted and attainted, he shall have his Judgement to be drawn to the place of Execution from his Prison, as being not worthy any more to tread upon the Face of the Earth whereof he was made: Also for that he hath been retrograde to Nature, therefore is he drawn backward at a Horse-Tail. And whereas God hath made the Head of Man the highest and most supreme Part, as being his chief Grace and Ornament; he must be drawn with his Head declining downward, and lying so near the Ground as may be, being thought unfit to take benefit of the common Air. For which Cause also he shall be strangled, being hanged up by the Neck between Heaven and Earth, as deemed unworthy of both, or either; as likewise, that the Eyes of Men may behold, and their Hearts contemn him.

'Then he is to be cut down alive, and to have his Privy Parts cut off and burnt before his Face, as being unworthily begotten, and unfit to leave any Generation after him. His Bowels and inlaid Parts taken out and burnt, who inwardly had conceived and harboured in his heart such horrible Treason. After, to have his Head cut off, which had imagined the Mischief. And lastly, his Body to be quartered, and the Quarters set up in some high and eminent Place, to the View and Detestation of Men, and to become a Prey for the Fowls of the Air.

'And this is a Reward due to Traitors, whose Hearts be hardened: For that it is Physic of State and Government, to let out corrupt Blood from the Heart. But true Repentance is indeed never too late; but late Repentance is seldom found true: Which yet I pray the merciful Lord to grant unto them, that having a Sense of their Offences, they may make a true and sincere Confession both for their Souls Health, and for the Good and Safety of the King and this State. And for the rest that are not yet apprehended, my Prayer to God is that either they may be converted, to the End they perish not, or else confounded, that they hurt not.'

After the reading of their several Examinations, Confessions, and voluntary Declaration as well of themselves, as of some of their dead Confederates, they were all by the Verdict of the Jury found guilty of the Treasons contained in their Indictment.

And then being severally asked, What they could say, wherefore Judgment of Death should not be pronounced against them; there was not one of these (except Rookwood) who would make any continued Speech, either in Defence or Extenuation of the Fact.

Thomas Winter only desired, that he might be hanged both for his Brother and himself.

Guy Fawkes being asked, Why he pleaded Not Guilty, having nothing to say for his Excuse: answered, That he had so done in respect of certain Conferences mentioned in the Indictment, which he said that he knew not of: Which were answered to have been set down according to Course of Law, as necessarily pre-supposed before the Resolution of such a Design.

Keys said, That his Estate and Fortunes were desperate, and as good now as at another time, and for this Cause rather than for another.

Bates craved Mercy.

Robert Winter, Mercy.

John Grant was a good while mute; yet after, submissively said, He was guilty of a Conspiracy intended, but never effected.

But Ambrose Rookwood first excused his denial of the Indictment, for that he had rather lose his Life than give it. Then did he acknowledge his Offence to be so heinous, that he justly deserved the Indignation of the King, and of the Lords, and the Hatred of the whole Commonwealth; yet could he not despair of Mercy at the Hands of a Prince, so abounding in Grace and Mercy: And the rather, because his Offence, tho' it were incapable of any Excuse, yet not altogether incapable of some Extenuation, in that he had been neither Author nor Actor, but only persuaded and drawn in by Catesby, whom he loved above any worldly Man. But howsoever that this was his first Offence, yet he humbly submitted himself to the Mercy of the King, and prayed that the King would herein imitate God, who sometimes doth punish corporally, yet not mortally.

Then the Lord Chief Justice of England, after a grave and prudent Relation and Defence of the Laws made by Queen Elizabeth against Recusants, Priests, and Receivers of Priests, together with the several Occasions, Progresses and Reasons of the same; and having plainly demonstrated and proved that they were all necessary, mild, equal, moderate, and to be justified to all the World; pronounced Judgment.

Upon the rising of the Court, Sir Everard Digby bowing himself towards the Lords, said, 'If I may but hear any of your Lordships say, you forgive me, I shall go more cheerfully to the Gallows.' Whereunto the Lords said, 'God forgive you, and we do.'

And so according to the Sentence, on Thursday following being the 30th of January, Execution was done upon Sir Everard Digby, Robert Winter, John Grant, and Thomas Bates, at the West End of Paul's Church; and on Friday following, upon Thomas Winter, Ambrose Rookwood, Robert Keyes, and Guy Fawkes, within the old Palace-Yard, at Westminster, not far from the Parliament-House.

1607–10

'The king ought not to be under any man, but under God and the Law'

Shortly after the trial of Guy Fawkes and his co-conspirators, Sir Edward Coke was appointed chief justice. Coke had served King James not only in the Gunpowder Plot trial but also by prosecuting Sir Walter Raleigh for treason. However, if the king had hoped that Coke would continue to dance to his tune, he was soon disappointed. Coke presided over the case of Nicholas Fuller, a Puritan barrister who opposed the power of the ecclesiastic (as distinct from civil) courts. On one occasion, Fuller accused the Court of High Commission of being 'popish, under the jurisdiction not of Christ but anti-Christ'. The king, like the Archbishop of Canterbury, wanted Fuller prosecuted for contempt. Coke heard the case, which turned on the division of authority between the ecclesiastical and civil courts, and, implicitly, on the right of the king to intervene in the work of the civil courts. Coke ruled that the civil courts were supreme, and that they had the right to determine the power of the ecclesiastical courts. Moreover, he stated that 'the King cannot take any cause out of any of his Courts, and give Judgment upon it himself'. Coke went further: 'The King ought not to be under any man, but under God and the Law'. These are Coke's notes on his ruling.

SIR EDWARD COKE'S NOTES ON HIS RULING ON THE DIVINE RIGHT OF KINGS

> Note, upon Sunday the 10th of November, in this same Term, the King, upon complaint made to him by Bancroft, the Archbishop of Canterbury, concerning prohibitions, the King was informed [by Bancroft] that when the question was made of what matters the Ecclesiastical Judges have cognizance, either upon the exposition of the Statutes concerning tithes, or any other thing Ecclesiastical, or in any other case in which there is not express authority in Law, the King himself may decide it in his royal person;

and that the Judges are but the delegates of the King, and that the King may take what Causes he shall please to determine, from the determination of the Judges, and may determine them himself. And the Archbishop said, that this was clear in Divinity, that such authority belongs to the King by the Word of God in the Scripture.

To which it was answered by me, in the presence, and with the clear consent of all the Judges of England, and Barons of the Exchequer, that the King in his own person cannot adjudge any case, either criminal, as treason or felony, or betwixt party and party, concerning his inheritance, chattels, or goods, etc; but this ought to be determined and adjudged in some Court of Justice, according to the Law and Custom of England, and always Judgments are given, *Ideo consideratum est per Curiam* [Therefore it is decided by the court], so that the Court gives the Judgment.

The King hath his Court, viz. in the upper house of Parliament, in which he with his Lords is the supreme Judge over all other Judges; for if Error be in the Common Pleas, that may be reversed in the King's Bench: And if the Court of King's Bench err, that may be reversed in the upper house of Parliament, by the King, with the assent of the Lords Spiritual and Temporal, without the Commons. In this respect the King is called the chief Justice. It appears in our Books, that the King may sit in the Star Chamber, but this was to consult with the Justices, upon certain questions proposed to them, and not *in Judicio* [in the way of judgment]; so in the King's Bench he may sit, but the Court gives the Judgment.

It is commonly said in our Books, that the King is always present in Court in the Judgment of Law; and upon this he cannot be non-suit: But the Judgments are always given *Per Curiam* [by the court]; and the Judges are sworn to execute Justice according to Law and Custom of England.

And it appears by Acts of Parliament of that neither by the great Seal, nor by the little Seal, Justice shall be delayed; *ergo*, the King cannot take any cause out of any of his Courts, and give Judgment upon it himself. And the Judges informed the King, that no King after the conquest assumed to himself to give any Judgment in any cause whatsoever, which concerned the administration of Justice within this Realm, but these were solely determined in the Courts of Justice: And the King cannot arrest any man, for the party cannot have remedy against the King; so if the King give any Judgment, what remedy can the party have. Hussey chief Justice, who was Attorney to Edward the fourth reports that Sir John Markham, chief Justice, said to King Edward the fourth that the King cannot arrest a man for suspicion of Treason or Felony, as others of his Lieges may; for that if it be a wrong to the party grieved, he can have no remedy: and it was greatly marvelled that the Archbishop informed the King, that such absolute power and authority, as is aforesaid, belonged to the King by the word of God.

None may be taken by petition or suggestion made to our Lord the King or his Council, unless by Judgment. And no man shall be put to answer without presentment before the Justices, matter of Record, or by due process, according to the ancient Law of the Land: And if any thing be done against it, it shall be void in Law and held for error. A controversy of Land between parties was heard by the King, and sentence given, which was repealed for this, that it did belong to the Common Law: Then the King said, that he thought the law was founded upon reason, and that he and others had reason, as well as the Judges.

To which it was answered by me, that true it was, that God had endowed his Majesty with excellent Science, and great endowments of nature; but his Majesty was not learned in the laws of his Realm of England, and causes which concern the life, or inheritance, or goods, or fortunes of his Subjects; they are not to be decided by natural reason but by the artificial reason and judgment of Law, which Law is an act which requires long study and experience, before that a man can attain to the cognizance of it; the function of judges was not to make but to declare the law, according to the golden mete-wand [gold standard] of the law and not by the crooked cord of discretion. And that the Law was the measure to try the Causes of the Subjects; and which protected his Majesty in safety and peace.

With which the King was greatly offended, and said, that then he should be under the law, which it was treason to affirm. To which I said, *Quod Rex non debet esse sub homine, sed sub Deo et Lege* [the King ought not to be under any man, but under God and the Law].

Nicholas Fuller was no happier than the king with the result of the case. Although Coke ruled that the Church courts could not prosecute Fuller for contempt, they did have the right to try him for specifically ecclesiastical offences, such as schism and heresy. Fuller was so tried, and ended up in prison after all.

For the next nine years, Coke and King James continued to be in conflict. The king variously threatened and cajoled Coke, but did not dare dismiss him until 1616, by which time Coke, whose personal conduct was not always of the highest standard, had made enough enemies for him to be sacked safely. Meanwhile, James continued to argue the case for the divine right of kings, most notably in this speech to Parliament on 21 March 1610.

KING JAMES'S SPEECH TO PARLIAMENT DEFENDING THE DIVINE RIGHT OF KINGS

The state of monarchy is the supremest thing upon earth; for kings are not only God's lieutenants upon earth, and sit upon God's throne, but even by God himself are called gods. There be three principal similitudes that illustrate the state of monarchy: one taken out of the word of God; and the two other out of the grounds of policy and philosophy. In the Scriptures kings are called gods, and so their power after a certain relation compared to the divine power. Kings are also compared to fathers of families: for a king is truly *Parens patriae*, the politique father of his people. And lastly, kings are compared to the head of this microcosm of the body of man.

Kings are justly called gods, for that they exercise a manner or resemblance of divine power upon earth: for if you will consider the attributes to God, you shall see how they agree in the person of a king. God hath power to create or destroy make or unmake at his pleasure, to give life or send death, to judge all and to be judged nor accountable to none; to raise low things and to make high things low at his pleasure, and to God are both souls and body due. And the like power have kings: they make and unmake their subjects, they have power of raising and casting down, of life and of death, judges over all their subjects and in all causes and yet accountable to none but God only. They have the power to exalt low things, and abase high things, and make of their subjects like men at the chess – a pawn to make a bishop or a knight – and to cry up or down any of their subjects as they do their money. And to the king is due both the affections of the soul and the service of the body of his subjects.

A father may dispose of his inheritance to his children at his pleasure, yea, even disinherit the eldest upon just occasions and prefer the youngest, according to his liking; make them beggars or rich at his pleasure; restrain, or banish out of his presence as he finds them give cause of offence; or restore then in favour again with the penitent sinners. So may the king deal with his subjects.

I conclude then this point touching the power of kings with this axiom of divinity, that as to dispute what God may do is blasphemy, so is it sedition in subjects to dispute what a king may do in the height of his power. But just kings will ever be willing to declare what they will do, if they will not incur the curse of God. I will not be content that my power be disputed upon; but I shall ever be willing to make the reason appear of all my doings, and rule my actions according to my laws. I would wish you to be careful to avoid three things in the matter of grievances:

First, that you do not meddle with the main points of government; that is my craft; to meddle with that were to lessen me. I must not be taught my office.

Secondly, I would not have you meddle with such ancient rights of mine as I have received from my predecessors. All novelties are dangerous as well in a politic as in a natural body; and therefore I would be loath to be quarreled in my ancient rights and possessions, for that were to judge me unworthy of that which my predecessors had and left me.

And lastly, I pray you beware to exhibit for grievance anything that is established by a settled law, and whereunto you know I will never give a plausible answer; for it is an undutiful part in subjects to press their king, wherein they know beforehand he will refuse them.

The dispute over the divine right of kings was finally resolved four decades later, by the Civil War. A century after Coke's ruling, another Fuller – the physician and intellectual Thomas Fuller – expanded Coke's view into the proposition, frequently quoted since, that: 'Be you never so high, the law is above you.' The Coke–Fuller doctrine influenced not only the evolution of Britain's legal and democratic system but also the architects of the United States Constitution, who were determined to construct a nation that was governed by laws, not by men.

1628

'RIGHTS AND LIBERTIES, ACCORDING TO THE LAWS AND STATUTES OF THIS REALM'

Demonstrating the occasional truth of the adage that you can't keep a good(ish) man down, Sir Edward Coke gradually rebuilt his career and recovered his influence, especially over the opponents of the king (James until 1625, followed by Charles I). In 1628, at the age of 76, Coke persuaded Parliament to adopt the Petition of Right, which set out the case for people not being taxed or imprisoned except by due process of law and according to Acts of Parliament.

The event that triggered the petition was a botched attack on a French fort, led by one of King Charles's closest allies, the Duke of Buckingham. The attack had been financed by a forced loan, which many parliamentarians considered illegal. The petition was the fullest assertion yet of the rights of the individual. However, the petition was constructed not as a revolutionary document but as a logical extension of what had gone before. For example, it built on the established principles that subjects should not be subject to arbitrary arrests or be forced to pay taxes that had not been agreed by Parliament. 'Take we heed what we yield unto,' Coke said during a later debate on the petition: 'Magna Carta is such a fellow that he will have no sovereign.'

THE PETITION OF RIGHT

To the King's Most Excellent Majesty,

Humbly show unto our Sovereign Lord the King, the Lords Spiritual and Temporal, and Commons in Parliament assembles, that whereas it is declared and enacted by a statute made in the time of the reign of King Edward I, that no tallage or aid shall be laid or levied by the king or his heirs in this realm, without the good will and assent of the archbishops, bishops, earls, barons, knights, burgesses, and other the freemen of the commonalty of this realm; and by authority of parliament holden in the five-and-twentieth year of the reign of King Edward III, it is declared and enacted, that from thenceforth no person should be compelled to make any loans to the king against his will. Your subjects have inherited this freedom, that they should not be compelled to contribute to any tax, tallage, aid, or other like charge not set by common consent, in parliament.

Yet nevertheless of late divers commissions directed to sundry commissioners in several counties, with instructions, have issued; by means whereof your people have been in divers places assembled, and required to lend certain sums of money unto your Majesty, and many of them, upon their refusal so to do, have had an oath administered unto them not warrantable by the laws or statutes of this realm, and others of them have been imprisoned, confined, and sundry other ways molested and disquieted; and divers other charges have been laid and levied upon your people in several counties by lord lieutenants, deputy lieutenants, commissioners for musters, justices of peace and others, by command or direction from your Majesty, or your Privy Council, against the laws and free custom of the realm.

And whereas also that the Magna Carta declares and enacts, that no freeman may be taken or imprisoned or be deprived of his freehold or liberties, or his free customs, or be outlawed or exiled, or in any manner destroyed, but by the lawful judgment of his peers, or by the law of the land.

Nevertheless, divers of your subjects have of late been imprisoned without any cause showed; and when for their deliverance they were brought before your justices, there to undergo and receive as the court should order, and their keepers commanded to certify the causes of their detension, no cause was certified, but that they were detained by your Majesty's special command, signified by the lords of your Privy Council, and yet were returned back to several prisons, without being charged with anything to which they might make answer according to the law.

And whereas also by authority of parliament, in the five-and-twentieth year of the reign of King Edward III, it is declared and enacted, that no man shall be forejudged of life or limb against the form of the Great Charter [Magna Carta] and the law of the land; and by the said Great Charter and other the laws and statutes of this your realm, no man ought to be adjudged to death but by the laws established in this your realm, either by the customs of the same realm, or by acts of parliament: nevertheless of late time divers commissions under your Majesty's great seal have issued forth, by which certain persons have been assigned and appointed commissioners with power and authority to proceed within the land, according to the justice of martial law, against such soldiers or mariners, or other dissolute persons joining with them, as should commit any murder, robbery, felony, mutiny, or other outrage or misdemeanour whatsoever, and by such summary course and order as is agreeable to martial law, and is used in armies in time of war, to proceed to the trial and condemnation of such offenders, and them to cause to be executed and put to death according to the law martial.

They do therefore humbly pray your most excellent Majesty, that no man hereafter be compelled to make or yield any gift, loan, benevolence, tax, or such like charge, without common consent by act of parliament; and that none be called to make answer, or take such oath, or to give attendance, or be confined, or otherwise molested or disquieted concerning the same or for refusal thereof; and that no freeman, in any such manner as is before mentioned, be imprisoned or detained; and that your people may not be so burdened in time to come; and that the aforesaid commissions, for proceeding by martial law, may be revoked and annulled.

All which they most humbly pray of your most excellent Majesty as their rights and liberties, according to the laws and statutes of this realm; and that your Majesty would be also graciously pleased, for the further comfort and safety of your people, to declare your royal will and pleasure, that in the things aforesaid all your officers and ministers shall serve you according to the laws and statutes of this realm, as they tender the honour of your Majesty, and the prosperity of this kingdom.

The petition was read out in Parliament to the king on 7 June. On 26 June, Charles returned to explain why he rejected it. He asserted that his right to raise certain taxes was 'one of the chief maintenances of the crown'; that the House of Commons had no role in interpreting or administering the law, while the House of Lords did so 'only under me'; and that Parliament had no 'power either to make or declare a law without my consent'.

In August, the Duke of Buckingham was assassinated. In a way, this ended the immediate crisis, for Buckingham had been the chief target of the king's critics. But, in the longer term, the petition clarified the issues that led to the Civil War 14 years later.

1641–2

'A MALIGNANT AND PERNICIOUS DESIGN OF SUBVERTING THE FUNDAMENTAL LAWS AND PRINCIPLES OF GOVERNMENT'

Propelled by what they saw as Charles I's continuing intransigence, and enraged by an uprising of Irish Catholics against Protestant settlers, a group of MPs drew up a 'Grand Remonstrance' – a series of more than 200 demands designed to curb the power of the king and enhance that of Parliament. The MPs' leader was John Pym, a Puritan who had risen to prominence partly because of his practical skills, and partly because he had gained the respect of radicals who wanted a republic and those, like himself, who wanted to keep the monarchy, but subject it to the will of Parliament. Charles I accepted a number of measures asserting Parliament's authority, including a law forbidding the dissolution of Parliament without its consent. But when the king insisted on control of the army, Pym's group concluded that he was not serious about surrendering much power. They decided to abandon their strategy of persuasion and replace it with one of coercion. Their document was confrontational, designed to humiliate the king. Pym sought the approval of a House of Commons that was rapidly becoming polarised between the king's supporters and his opponents. This is an edited extract from the Grand Remonstrance, which MPs debated in 1641.

THE GRAND REMONSTRANCE

Most gracious Sovereign,

The Duty which we owe to your Majesty, and our Country cannot but make us very sensible and apprehensive, that the Multiplicity, Sharpness, and Malignity of those Evils under which we have now many years suffered, are fomented and cherished by a corrupt and ill affected Party, who amongst other their mischievous Devices for the alteration of Religion and Government, have sought to blemish and disgrace our Proceedings in this Parliament, and to get themselves a Party and Faction amongst your Subjects, for the better strengthening themselves in their wicked Courses.

The root of all this mischief we find to be a malignant and pernicious design of subverting the fundamental laws and principles of government, upon which the religion and justice of this kingdom are firmly established. The actors and promoters hereof have been: the Jesuit papists, who hate the laws, the Bishops, and the corrupt part of the clergy who cherish formality and superstition as supports of their own ecclesiastical tyranny and usurpation. Such Councillors and courtiers [who] for private ends have engaged themselves to further the interests of some foreign powers.

The Court of Star Chamber hath abounded in extravagant censures whereby His Majesty's subjects have been oppressed by grievous fines, imprisonments, mutilations, whippings, pillories, gags, confinements [and] banishments.

We your most humble and obedient Subjects, do with all faithfulness and humility, beseech your Majesty,

That you will be graciously pleased to concur with the humble Desires of your People in a Parliamentary way, for the preserving the Peace and Safety of the Kingdom, from the malicious Designs of the Popish party.

For depriving the Bishops of their Votes in Parliament, and abridging their immoderate power usurped over the Clergy, and other your good Subjects, which they have perniciously abused, to the hazard of Religion, and great prejudice and oppression of the Laws of the Kingdom, and just liberty of your People.

For the taking away such oppressions in Religion, Church Government, and Discipline as have been brought in and fomented by them.

For uniting all such your Loyal Subjects together, as join in the same fundamental Truths against the Papists, by removing some oppressions and unnecessary Ceremonies, by which divers weak Consciences have been scrupled, and seem to be divided from the rest, and for the due execution of those good Laws, which have been made for securing the liberty of your Subjects.

That your Majesty will likewise be pleased to remove from your Counsel all such as persist to favour and promote any of those pressures and corruptions wherewith your People have been grieved, and that for the future, your Majesty will vouchsafe to employ such persons in your great and public affairs, and to take such to be near you in Places of Trust, as your Parliament may have cause to confide in.

That you will be pleased to forbear to alienate any of the forfeited and escheated Lands in Ireland, which shall accrue to your Crown by reason of this Rebellion, that out of them the Crown may be the better supported, and some satisfaction made to your Subjects of this Kingdom, for the great Expenses they are like to undergo this War.

At the end of an angry debate, the Grand Remonstrance was approved by Parliament by a narrow 11-vote margin (159:148). It was presented to the king at Hampton Court on 1 December. His first instinct was to ignore it, but Parliament had the document printed and widely circulated. Charles had little choice but to answer the charges levelled at him. On 23 December, Charles's written response was sent to Parliament.

Charles I's letter to Parliament

To the petition, we say that although there are divers things in the preamble of it which we are so far from admitting that we profess we cannot at all understand them, we should be as ready to remedy and punish as you to complain of, so that the prayers of your petition are grounded upon such premises as we must in no wise admit; yet notwithstanding, we are pleased to give this answer to you.

For the depriving of the bishops of their votes in parliament, we would have you consider that their right is grounded upon the fundamental law of the kingdom and constitution of parliament.

To the second prayer of the petition, concerning the removal and choice of councillors, we know not any of our Council to whom the character set forth in the petition can belong: there is no man so near to us in place or affection whom we will not leave to the justice of the law, if you shall bring a particular charge and sufficient proofs against him. In the meantime we wish you to forbear such general aspersions as may reflect upon all our Council, since you name none in particular. That for the choice of our councillors and ministers of state, it were to debar us that natural liberty all freemen have; and as it is the undoubted right of the crown of England to call such persons to our secret counsels, to public employment, and our particular service as we shall think fit, so we are and ever shall be very careful to make election of such persons in those places of trust as shall have given good testimonies of their abilities and integrity, and against whom there can be no just cause of exception whereon reasonably to ground a diffidence.

To the third prayer of your petition, concerning Ireland, we understand your desire of not alienating the forfeited lands thereof to proceed from much care and love, and likewise that it may be a resolution very fit for us to take. But whether it may be seasonable to declare resolutions of that nature before the events of a war be seen, that we much doubt of.

There was some prospect that Charles could regain the initiative. The fact that the Remonstrance had been approved by only a narrow margin, the emollient tone of the king's response, the signs of a growing royalist group in Parliament in opposition to Pym: these things, taken together, indicated that Pym could be marginalised without the need for excessively authoritarian measures.

However, just as Pym had chosen confrontation, so now did Charles. He arranged for the Attorney General to impeach Pym and four other MPs: John Hampden, Denzil Holles, Sir Arthur Haselrig and William Strode. On 4 January 1642, the king arrived at Westminster with soldiers to arrest the five men. He addressed the Commons from the Speaker's Chair.

CHARLES I's EXCHANGE WITH SPEAKER LENTHALL

Gentlemen – I am sorry for this occasion of coming unto you. Yesterday I sent a Sergeant at Arms upon a very important occasion to apprehend some that by my command were accused of high treason; whereunto I did expect obedience and not a message. And I must declare unto you here, that albeit no king that ever was in England shall be more careful of your privileges, to maintain them to the uttermost of his power, than I shall be; yet you must know that in cases of treason no person hath a privilege; and therefore I am come to know if any of those persons that were accused are here. For I must tell you, gentlemen, that so long as these persons that I have accused (for no slight crime, but for treason) are here, I can not expect that this House will be in the right way that I do heartily wish it. Therefore I am come to tell you that I must have them wherever I find them.

Charles read out the names of the five men. He received no reply. He then asked the Speaker, William Lenthall, to point out the five MPs. Lenthall replied:

May it please your Majesty, I have neither eyes to see, nor tongue to speak in this place, but as this House is pleased to direct me, whose servant I am; and I humbly beg Your Majesty's pardon that I cannot give any other answer than this to what Your Majesty is pleased to demand of me.

In fact, the five MPs had received advance notice of the king's intentions, and managed to escape by boat. Charles responded:

Well, well! 'Tis no matter. I think my eyes are as good as another's. Since I see the Birds are flown, I do expect from you that you shall send them unto me as soon as they return hither. But I assure you, on the word of a King, I never did intend any force, but shall proceed against them in a legal and fair way, for I never meant any other. I will trouble you no more, but tell you I do expect, as soon as they come to the House, you will send them to me, otherwise I must take my own course to find them.

Two days later, on 6 January, a committee of the House of Commons reviewed the events of the previous three days and asserted that the king's attempt to have the five MPs arrested was illegal.

REPORT OF THE COMMONS COMMITTEE CONSIDERING THE SAFETY OF THE KINGDOM

The Committee met here on 3 January because of the King's Warrant [to arrest Mr Holles, Sir Arthur Haselrig, Mr Pym, Mr Hampden and Mr Strode], which not only against the Privilege of Parliament, but the common liberty of every subject. Serjeant Francis, one of His Majesty's Serjeant at Arms, contrary to all former precedents and privileges of Parliament, demanded of the Speaker to be delivered unto him that he might arrest them for High Treason.

The next day His Majesty came to the said House attended with a great multitude of men armed in a warlike manner, who came up to the very door of the House and placed themselves there, and in other places and passages nearby, to the great terror and disturbance of the Members, then sitting, according their duty, in a peaceable and orderly manner, treating of the great affairs of England and Ireland.

His Majesty, having placed himself in the Speaker's Chair, demanded of them the said Members to be delivered unto him, which is a high breach of the rights and privileges of Parliament. Afterwards His Majesty issued several Warrants for the apprehension of the said Members, which by Law he cannot do, there being no legal charge or accusation, or due process of law, nor any pretence of a charge; all of which are against the fundamental liberties of the subject and the rights of Parliament.

Whereupon we are necessitated, according to our duty, to declare that if any person arrests Mr Holles, Sir Arthur Haselrig, Mr Pym, Mr Hampden or Mr Strode, or any other Member of Parliament, on a Warrant issuing only from the King, he shall be guilty of a Breach of the Liberties of the Subject, and of the privileges of Parliament, and shall be a public enemy of the Commonwealth.

However, we should not endeavour to protect any of our Members that are properly prosecuted for treason, or any other misdemeanour, according to the laws of the Kingdom or the rights and privileges of Parliament. In that event, none shall be more ready and willing than we ourselves to bring them to a speedy and proper trial. It is as important to us to see justice done to criminals, as to defend the just rights and liberties of the subjects and Parliament of England.

The five men remained free. Charles and Parliament were now set on the course to war, and the two sides raised armies to fight their causes.

Pym died of cancer in 1643, when the Civil War was in its early stages. One of the Great Remonstrance's long-term consequences was that no monarch since 1642 has ever been allowed to enter the chamber of the House of Commons. Furthermore, since those days MPs have defended their privilege to say whatever they want (subject to specific restrictions that they have decided and which the Speaker enforces), without the risk of prosecution. And whenever debates about MPs' privileges rage, Lenthall's words – 'neither eyes to see, nor tongue to speak' – are liable to be quoted.

1644

'WHO KILLS A MAN KILLS A REASONABLE CREATURE; BUT HE WHO DESTROYS A GOOD BOOK, KILLS REASON ITSELF'

In 1642, John Milton, the great poet and radical polemicist, married Mary Powell. It was an odd match: Milton was 33 and an active republican while his bride was half his age and the uneducated daughter of a Royalist squire. Milton soon felt he had made a mistake. He wanted a divorce, but the law stymied him. He responded by writing a series of tracts, starting in 1643, deploring the fact that the only legally permitted cause for divorce was adultery. Incompatibility, he argued, was a far more valid reason. Milton's argument offended many people, and there were calls for his tracts to be banned under the Licensing Order of 1643, which had been passed by Parliament in order to wrest the power of censorship from control of the king. (Apart from a brief period leading up to the Civil War, publications in England had been subject to pre-publication 'licensing' since the arrival of printing.)

In general, Milton supported Cromwell; but Milton's brush with censorship prompted him to write one of the finest polemics in favour of free speech. *Areopagitica*, its main title, was the same as that of a 'speech' delivered in Athens in the fifth century BC by Isocrates, one of the city state's finest orators. As with Isocrates, Milton's 'speech' was directed at the legislators of his day, and was published but never spoken. While Milton strongly advocated free speech in *Areopagitica*, he also made it clear that he was no absolutist. He felt that a healthy society should expose people to a wide range of views, including those that dwelt in 'the regions of sin and falsity', but he accepted that a balance must be struck between freedom of speech and the destructive power that could result from abuse of that freedom. He wanted all books to contain the printer's name so that printers as well as authors could be punished afterwards if necessary. What Milton deplored was any system of licensing that operated as pre-publication censorship.

JOHN MILTON: *AREOPAGITICA*

When complaints are freely heard, deeply considered and speedily reformed, then is the utmost bound of civil liberty attained that wise men look for. To which we are already in good part arrived, and it will be attributed first, as is most due, to the strong assistance of God our deliverer, next to your faithful guidance and undaunted wisdom, Lords and Commons of England. Neither is it in God's esteem the diminution of his glory, when honourable things are spoken of good men and worthy magistrates; which if I now first should begin to do, after so fair a progress of your laudable deeds, I might be justly reckoned among the tardiest, and the unwillingest of them that praise ye.

Nevertheless there are three principal things, without which all praising is but courtship and flattery: First, when that only is praised which is solidly worth praise: next, when greatest likelihoods are brought that such things are truly and really in those persons to whom they are ascribed: the other, when he who praises, by showing that such his actual persuasion is of whom he writes, can demonstrate that he flatters not.

For he who freely magnifies what hath been nobly done, and fears not to declare as freely what might be done better, gives ye the best covenant of his fidelity; and that his loyalest affection and his hope waits on your proceedings. His highest praising is not flattery, and his plainest advice is a kind of praising. For though I should affirm and hold by argument, that it would fare better with truth, with learning and the Commonwealth, if one of your published Orders, which I should name, were called in; yet at the same time it could not but much redound to the lustre of your mild and equal government. Lords and Commons, there can no greater testimony appear, than when your prudent spirit acknowledges and obeys the voice of reason from what quarter soever it be heard speaking; and renders ye as willing to repeal any Act of your own setting forth, as any set forth by your predecessors.

If ye be thus resolved, I know not what should withhold me from presenting ye with a fit instance wherein to show both that love of truth which ye eminently profess, and that uprightness of your judgment which is not wont to be partial to yourselves; by judging over again that Order which ye have ordained to regulate printing: that no book, pamphlet, or paper shall be henceforth printed, unless the same be first approved and licensed by such, or at least one of such, as shall be thereto appointed.

This Order avails nothing to the suppressing of scandalous, seditious, and libellous books, which were mainly intended to be suppressed. It will be primely to the discouragement of all learning, and the stop of truth, not only by disexercising and blunting our abilities in what we know already, but by hindering and cropping the discovery that might be yet further made both in religious and civil wisdom.

I deny not, but that it is of greatest concernment in the Church and Commonwealth, to have a vigilant eye how books demean themselves as well as men; and thereafter to confine, imprison, and do sharpest justice on them as malefactors. For books are not absolutely dead things, but do contain a potency of life in them to be as active as that soul was whose progeny they are; nay, they do preserve as in a vial the purest efficacy and extraction of that living intellect that bred them. I know they are as lively, and as vigorously productive, as those fabulous dragon's teeth; and being sown up and down, may chance to spring up armed men. And yet, on the other hand, unless wariness be used, as good almost kill a man as kill a good book. Who kills a man kills a reasonable creature, God's image; but he who destroys a good book, kills reason itself, kills the image of God, as it were in the eye. Many a man lives a burden to the earth; but a good book is the precious life-blood of a master spirit, embalmed and treasured up on purpose to a life beyond life.

We should be wary therefore what persecution we raise against the living labours of public men, how we spill that seasoned life of man, preserved and stored up in books; since we see a kind of homicide may be thus committed, sometimes a martyrdom, and if it extend to the whole impression, a kind of massacre; whereof the execution ends not in the slaying of an elemental life, but strikes at that ethereal and fifth essence, the breath of reason itself, slays an immortality rather than a life.

Good and evil we know in the field of this world grow up together almost inseparably. It was from out the rind of one apple tasted, that the knowledge of good and evil, as two twins cleaving together, leaped forth into the world. He that can apprehend and consider vice with all her baits and seeming pleasures, and yet abstain, and yet distinguish, and yet prefer that which is truly better, he is the true warfaring Christian. Since therefore the knowledge and survey of vice is in this world so necessary to the constituting of human virtue, and the scanning of error to the confirmation of truth, how can we more safely, and with less danger, scout into the regions of sin and falsity than by reading all manner of tractates and hearing all manner of reason?

If we think to regulate printing, thereby to rectify manners, we must regulate all recreation and pastimes, all that is delightful to man. No music must be heard, no song be set or sung, but what is grave and Doric. There must be licensing dancers, that no gesture, motion, or deportment be taught our youth but what by their allowance shall be thought honest. And who shall silence all the airs and madrigals that whisper softness in chambers? Who shall regulate all the mixed conversation of our youth, male and female together, as is the fashion of this country? Who shall still appoint what shall be discoursed, what presumed, and no further? Lastly, who shall forbid and separate all idle resort, all evil company? These things will be, and must be; but how they shall be least hurtful, how least enticing, herein consists the grave and governing wisdom of a state.

In publishing *Areopagitica* as a pamphlet, Milton defied the very system of censorship that he railed against. However, it did him little harm: he went on to work for Cromwell, in 1649, as Secretary for Foreign Tongues in the Council of State. On the other hand, the tract had no immediate effect on Parliament. Licensing continued for another half century.

Meanwhile, Milton's marriage – which triggered the chain of events that led to his writing *Areopagitica* – revived. He and Mary had three daughters and a son (who died in infancy). Mary died shortly after the birth of the third daughter, Deborah, in 1652.

1646

'HAVE YOU SHOOK THIS NATION LIKE AN EARTHQUAKE TO PRODUCE NO MORE THAN THIS?'

The main part of the Civil War lasted three years, until Cromwell's Roundheads finally defeated Charles I's troops at the Battle of Naseby, in June 1645. Yet many who sided with Parliament were dissatisfied with the degree of reform that Cromwell and his allies intended. One Puritan dissident, John Lilburne, complained that MPs lived comfortable lives while soldiers risked their lives fighting on their behalf. He also accused Speaker Lenthall of corresponding with the Royalists and was promptly jailed for slander. Lilburne was released after thousands of Londoners campaigned on his behalf, but he was soon in trouble and in prison again, this time for accusing the Earl of Manchester of being a Royalist sympathiser. Once more, a campaign started for his release.

These campaigners became the Levellers, a group let by John Lilburne, Richard Overton and William Walwyn. They did not decide the group's name for themselves; their opponents did this for them, contemptuously calling them 'levellers' on the (baseless) grounds that the group wanted to abolish private property and so place people on the same level. What the Levellers did demand was complete freedom of speech and religious worship, a written constitution, annual elections to Parliament, free trade and full equality before the law.

In July 1646, the Levellers published their own 'remonstrance'. This argued that the leaders of the Roundheads were too willing to continue acting 'in the name of king and parliament' when the king 'deserved to be excommunicated by all Christian society'. They set out their case for power transferring not just from the king to Parliament, but from Parliament to the people.

THE LEVELLERS: *A REMONSTRANCE OF MANY THOUSAND CITIZENS AND OTHER FREEBORN PEOPLE OF ENGLAND TO THEIR OWN HOUSE OF COMMONS*

> We are well assured ye cannot forget that the cause of our choosing you
> to be parliament-men was to deliver us from all kind of bondage and to

preserve the commonwealth in peace and happiness. We are your principals, and you our agents; it is a truth which you cannot but acknowledge. For if you or any other shall assume or exercise any power that is not derived from our trust and choice thereunto, that power is no less than usurpation and an oppression from which we expect to be freed.

Whatever our forefathers were, or whatever they did or suffered, we are the men of the present age and ought to be absolutely free from all kinds of exorbitances, molestations or arbitrary power; and you we chose to free us from all, without exception or limitation either in respect of persons, officers, degrees, or things; and we were full of confidence that ye also would have dealt impartially on our behalf and made us the most absolute free people in the world.

You cannot fight for our liberties, but it must be in the name of king and parliament; he that speaks of his cruelties must be thrust out of your House and society; your preachers must pray for him – as if he had not deserved to be excommunicated by all Christian society, or as if ye or they thought God were a respecter of the persons of kings in judgement. By this and other your like dealings – your frequent treating and tampering to maintain his honour – we that have trusted you to deliver us from his oppressions and to preserve us from his cruelties are wasted and consumed in multitudes to manifold miseries, whilst you lie ready with open arms to receive him and to make him a great and glorious king.

Have you shook this nation like an earthquake to produce no more than this for us? Is it for this that ye have made so free use and been so bold both with our persons and estates? And do you (because of our readiness to comply with your desires in all things) conceive us so stupid as to be contented with such unworthy returns of our trust and love? No. It is high time we be plain with you. We are not, nor shall not be so contented. We do expect according to reason that ye should in the first place declare and set forth King Charles his wickedness openly before the world, and withal to show the intolerable inconveniences of having a kingly government from the constant evil practices of those of this nation – and so to declare King Charles an enemy, and to publish your resolution never to have any more to do with him.

Ye must also deal better with us concerning the Lords than you have done. Ye only are chosen by us the people; and therefore in you only is the power of binding the whole nation by making, altering, or abolishing of laws. Ye have therefore prejudiced us in acting so as if ye could not make a law without both the royal assent of the king (so ye are pleased to express yourselves) and the assent of the Lords.

What is this but to blind our eyes? If we want a law, we must await till the king and Lords assent; if an ordinance, then we must wait till the Lords assent. Yet ye, knowing their assent to be merely formal do frequently importune their assent, which implies a most gross absurdity. For where their assent is necessary and essential, they must be as free as you to assent or dissent as their understandings and consciences should guide them.

Nor is there any reason that they should in any measure be less liable to any law than the gentry are. Why should any of them assault, strike, or beat any, and not be liable to the law as other men are? Why should not they be as liable to their debts as other men? There is no reason. Yet have ye stood still and seen many of us – and some of yourselves – violently abused without reparation.

We desire you to free us from these abuses *and* their negative voices, or else tell us that it is reasonable we should be slaves – this being a perpetual prejudice in our government neither consulting with freedom nor safety.

Ye know the laws of this nation are unworthy of a free people and deserve from first to last to be considered and seriously debated, and reduced to an agreement with common equity and right reason, which ought to be the form and life of every government – Magna Carta itself being but a beggarly thing containing many marks of intolerable bondage; and the laws that have been made since by parliaments have in very many particulars made our government much more oppressive and intolerable.

Ye have now sat full five years, which is four years longer than we intended; for we could choose you but for (at most) one year. And now we wish ye would publish to all the world the good that you have done for us, the liberty ye have brought us unto. We wish your souls may no further enter into their secret; for God will not be mocked nor suffer such gross hypocrisy to pass without exemplary punishment. And if ye believe there is a God, ye *must* believe it; and if ye *do* believe it, and consider the ways ye have trod and truly repent, *show* it by walking contrary to what ye have done or purposed to do and let us quickly and speedily partake thereof. For God is a God that takes vengeance and will not suffer you to go on to our ruin.

Forsake and utterly renounce all crafty and subtle intentions; hide not your thoughts from us and give us encouragement to be open-breasted unto you. Proclaim aforehand what ye determine to do in establishing anything for continuance; and hear all things that can be spoken with or against the same; and to that intent, let the imprisoned presses at liberty that all men's understandings may be more conveniently informed and convinced as far as is possible by the equity of your proceedings.

◇ ◇ ◇

Over the next few years, the Levellers fought for the arguments put forward in their remonstrance. However, one of Lilburne's passions was not pursued. He was an early advocate of gender equality, arguing that all men and women were 'by nature, equal and alike in power, dignity, authority, and majesty – none of them having (by nature) any authority, dominion or magisterial power, one over or above another'. In the ensuing debates between Levellers and other republicans, however, the arguments for extending the franchise revolved largely around the issue of how many men should have the vote; arguments that ignored the fact that some women property-owners had had the vote in the Middle Ages.

1647

'Every man has a voice by right of nature'

From 28 October until 9 November 1647, an extraordinary series of debates on Britain's future constitution took place in St Mary's Church, Putney. The debate involved Cromwell, officers of his New Model Army, and also civilians. It engaged radicals as well as more cautious reformers. It tackled immediate issues, such as what to do about Charles I (then being held under house arrest at Hampton Court), and more fundamental matters, such as the nature of democracy. Remarkably, a virtually verbatim account of the first three sessions of the debate survives.

One specific dispute concerned the franchise. Thomas Rainsborough, a colonel in Cromwell's army, supported John Lilburne and the Levellers, arguing that all men should have the vote because they could be expected to consent to the authority of a parliament that they had helped to elect. Henry Ireton, Cromwell's son-in-law and an army general, argued that there should continue to be a property qualification, for only people with property could be expected to act responsibly. He wished to preserve the law established by Henry VI in 1429 that restricted the franchise to men who owned property worth 40*s.* a year. (The same Act had stripped the owners of less valuable property of the right to vote on the grounds that 'very great outrageous and excessive numbers of people of small substance and no value' were taking part in elections.)

The argument was introduced by one of the Levellers at the debates, Maximilian Petty. As this extract from the Putney Debates shows, Cromwell sought to cool passions through the time-honoured device of referring the dispute to a committee.

THE PUTNEY DEBATES

> PETTY: We judge that all inhabitants that have not lost their birthright should have an equal voice in elections.

RAINSBOROUGH: I desired that those that had engaged in it might be included. For really I think that the poorest he that is in England hath a life to live, as the greatest he; and therefore truly, sir, I think it's clear, that every man that is to live under a government ought first by his own consent to put himself under that government; and I do think that the poorest man in England is not at all bound in a strict sense to that government that he hath not had a voice to put himself under.

IRETON: We talk of birthright. Truly by birthright there is thus much claim. Men may justly have by birthright, by their very being born in England, that we should not seclude them out of England, that we should not refuse to give them air and place and ground, and the freedom of the highways and other things, to live amongst us. That I think is due to a man by birth. But that by a man's being born here he shall have a share in that power that shall dispose of the lands here, and of all things here, I do not think it a sufficient ground.

It is true, as was said by a gentleman near me, the meanest man in England ought to have a voice in the election of the government he lives under — but only if he has some local interest. I say this: that those that have the meanest local interest — that man that hath but forty shillings a year, he hath as great voice in the election of a knight for the shire as he that hath ten thousand a year.

RAINSBOROUGH: Either it must be the Law of God or the law of man that must prohibit the meanest man in the kingdom to have this benefit as well as the greatest. I do not find anything in the Law of God, that a lord shall choose twenty burgesses, and a gentleman but two, or a poor man shall choose none: I find no such thing in the Law of Nature, nor in the Law of Nations. But I do find that all Englishmen must be subject to English laws, and I do verily believe that there is no man but will say that the foundation of all law lies in the people, and if it lie in the people, I am to seek for this exemption.

IRETON: I wish we may all consider of what right you will challenge that all the people should have right to elections. Is it by the right of nature? If you will hold forth that as your ground, then I think you must deny all property too, and this is my reason. For thus: by that same right of nature whatever it be that you pretend, by which you can say, one man hath an equal right with another to the choosing of him that shall govern him — by the same right of nature, he hath the same equal right in any goods he sees — meat, drink, clothes — to take and use them for his sustenance. He hath a freedom to the land, to take the ground, to exercise it, till it; he hath the same freedom to anything that any one doth account himself to have any propriety in.

RAINSBOROUGH: Sir, to say because a man pleads that every man has a voice by right of nature, that therefore it destroys by the same argument all property – this is to forget the Law of God. That there's a property, the Law of God says it; else why hath God made that law, Thou shalt not steal? I wish you would not make the world believe that we are for anarchy.

CROMWELL: No man says that you have a mind to anarchy, but that the consequence of this rule tends to anarchy, must end in anarchy; for where is there any bound or limit set if you take away this limit, that men that have no interest but the interest of breathing shall have no voice in elections? Therefore I am confident, we should not be so hot one with another.

RAINSBOROUGH: I know that some particular men we debate with believe we are for anarchy.

IRETON: I profess I must clear myself as to that point. I would not desire, I cannot allow myself, to lay the least scandal upon anybody. And truly, for that gentleman that did take so much offence, I do not know why he should take it so.

RAINSBOROUGH: I would fain know what we have fought for. For our laws and liberties? And this is the old law of England – and that which enslaves the people of England – that they should be bound by laws in which they have no voice at all! With respect to the divine law which says *Honour thy father and thy mother* the great dispute is, who is a right father and a right mother? I am bound to know who is my father and mother; and – I take it in the same sense you do – I would have a distinction, a character whereby God commands me to honour them. And for my part I look upon the people of England so, that wherein they have not voices in the choosing of their governors – their civil fathers and mothers – they are not bound to that commandment.

IRETON: Let the question be so: Whether a man can be bound to any law that he doth not consent to? And I shall tell you, that he may and ought to be bound to a law that he doth not give a consent to, nor doth not choose any to consent to; and I will make it clear. If a foreigner come within this kingdom, if that stranger will have liberty to dwell here who hath no local interest here, he, as a man, it's true, hath air, the passage of highways, the protection of laws, and all that by nature; we must not expel him our coasts, give him no being amongst us, nor kill him because he comes upon our land, comes up our stream, arrives at our shore. It is a piece of hospitality, of humanity, to receive that man amongst us. But if that man be received to a being amongst us, I think that man may very well be content to submit himself to the law of the land.

A man ought to be subject to a law, that did not give his consent, but with this reservation, that if this man do think himself unsatisfied to be subject to this law he may go into another kingdom. And so the same reason doth extend, in my understanding, to that man that hath no permanent interest in the kingdom. If he hath money, his money is as good in another place as here; he hath nothing that doth locally fix him to this kingdom. If that man will live in this kingdom, or trade amongst us, that man ought to subject himself to the law made by the people who have the interest of this kingdom in them.

RAINSBOROUGH: Sir, I see that it is impossible to have liberty but all property must be taken away. If it be laid down for a rule, and if you will say it, it must be so. But I would fain know what the soldier hath fought for all this while? He hath fought to enslave himself, to give power to men of riches, men of estates, to make him a perpetual slave.

IRETON: I will tell you what the soldier of the kingdom hath fought for. First, the danger that we stood in was that one man's will must be a law. The people of the kingdom must have this right at least, that they should not be concluded but by the Representative of those that had the interest of the kingdom. Some men fought in this, because they were immediately concerned and engaged in it. Other men who had no other interest in the kingdom but this, that they should have the benefit of those laws made by the Representative, yet fought that they should have the benefit of this Representative. They thought it was better to be concluded by the common consent of those that were fixed men, and settled men, that had the interest of this kingdom in them. 'And from that way,' said they, 'I shall know a law and have a certainty.'

CROMWELL: Let us not spend so much time in such debates as these are, but let us apply ourselves to such things as are conclusive, and that shall be this. I know our debates are endless if we think to bring it to an issue this way. If we may but resolve upon a committee, things may be done.

RAINSBOROUGH: I am not at all against a committee's meeting; and as you say – and I think every Christian ought to do the same – for my part I shall be ready, if I see the way that I am going, and the thing that I would insist on, will destroy the kingdom, I shall withdraw from it as soon as any.

IRETON: I should not speak again, but reflections do necessitate it, do call upon us to vindicate ourselves. I can argue this with a clear conscience: that no man hath prosecuted that with more earnestness, and will stand to that interest more than I do, of having Parliaments successive and not perpetual, and the distribution of elections more equal. I am agreed with you if you insist upon a more equal distribution of elections; I will agree with you, not only to dispute for it, but to fight for it and contend for it. Thus far I shall agree with you.

On the other hand, to those who differ in their terms and say, 'I will not agree with you except you go farther,' I make answer, 'Thus far I can go with you: I will go with you as far as I can.' If you will appoint a committee of some few to consider of that, so as you preserve the equitable part of that constitution that now is, securing a voice to those who are like to be free men, men not given up to the wills of others, and thereby keeping to the latitude which is the equity of constitutions, I will go with you as far as I can. And where I cannot I will sit down, I will not make any disturbance among you.

RAINSBOROUGH: If I do speak my soul and conscience I do think that there is not an objection made but that it hath been answered. There is a great deal of difference between us two. If a man hath all he doth desire, he may wish to sit still; but if I think I have nothing at all of what I fought for, I do not think the argument holds that I must desist as well as he.

IRETON: If you do extend the latitude of the constitution so far that any man shall have a voice in election who has not that interest in this kingdom that is permanent and fixed, who hath not that interest upon which he may have his freedom in this kingdom without dependence, you will put it into the hands of men to choose, not of men desirous to preserve their liberty, but of men who will give it away. If there be anything at all that is a foundation of liberty it is this, that those who shall choose the law-makers shall be men freed from dependence upon others.

CROMWELL: If we should go about to alter these things, I do not think that we are bound to fight for every particular proposition. Servants, while servants, are not included. Then you agree that he that receives alms is to be excluded?

LIEUTENANT-COLONEL THOMAS READE: I suppose it's concluded by all, that the choosing of representatives is a privilege; now I see no reason why any man that is a native ought to be excluded that privilege, unless from voluntary servitude.

PETTY: I conceive the reason why we would exclude apprentices, or servants, or those that take alms, is because they depend upon the will of other men and should be afraid to displease them. For servants and apprentices, they are included in their masters, and so for those that receive alms from door to door; but if there be any general way taken for those that are not so bound to the will of other men, it would be well.

A committee was set up, including both Ireton and Rainsborough, to consider the franchise. However, events intervened to cut its work short. On 11 November, Charles I escaped from Hampton Court. The threat of renewed conflict gave Cromwell an excuse to order his troops back to their regiments, ban further political debate within the army and ignore all reforms he did not like.

1649

'A TYRANT, TRAITOR, MURDERER AND PUBLIC ENEMY'

After escaping from Hampton Court in November 1647, Charles I tried to reach France via the Isle of Wight. But the island's governor supported Cromwell, and Charles was confined to Carisbrooke Castle. He was put on trial in Westminster Hall, London, in January 1649, accused of being a 'tyrant, traitor and murderer; and a public and implacable enemy to the Commonwealth of England'. On 20 January, the Chief Judge, John Bradshaw, read out the charge against Charles:

THE CHARGES AGAINST CHARLES I

That the said Charles Stuart, being admitted King of England, and therein trusted with a limited power to govern by and according to the laws of the land, and not otherwise; and by his trust, oath, and office, being obliged to use the power committed to him for the good and benefit of the people, and for the preservation of their rights and liberties; yet, nevertheless, out of a wicked design to erect and uphold in himself an unlimited and tyrannical power to rule according to his will, and to overthrow the rights and liberties of the people, yea, to take away and make void the foundations thereof, and of all redress and remedy of misgovernment, which by the fundamental constitutions of this kingdom were reserved on the people's behalf in the right and power of frequent and successive Parliaments, or national meetings in Council; he, the said Charles Stuart, for accomplishment of such his designs, and for the protecting of himself and his adherents in his and their wicked practices, to the same ends hath traitorously and maliciously levied war against the present Parliament.

By which cruel and unnatural wars, by him, the said Charles Stuart, levied much innocent blood of the free people of this nation hath been spilt, many families have been undone, the public treasure wasted and exhausted, trade obstructed and miserably decayed, vast expense and damage to the nation incurred, and many parts of this land spoiled, some of them even to desolation.

All which wicked designs, wars, and evil practices of him, the said Charles Stuart, have been, and are carried on for the advancement and upholding of a personal interest of will, power, and pretended prerogative to himself and his family, against the public interest, common right, liberty, justice, and peace of the people of this nation, by and from whom he was entrusted as aforesaid.

By all which it appeareth that the said Charles Stuart hath been, and is the occasioner, author, and continuer of the said unnatural, cruel and bloody wars; and therein guilty of all the treasons, murders, rapines, burnings, spoils, desolations, damages and mischiefs to this nation, acted and committed in the said wars, or occasioned thereby.

Charles declined to defend himself in any conventional sense. Instead he argued that the trial was illegal:

CHARLES I's DEFENCE

The King cannot be tried by any superior jurisdiction on earth. But it is not my case alone – it is the freedom and the liberty of the people of England. And do you pretend what you will, I stand more for their liberties – for if the power without law may make laws, may alter the fundamental laws of the kingdom, I do not know what subject he is in England that can be sure of his life or anything that he calls his own. Therefore, when that I came here I did expect particular reasons to know by what law, what authority, you did proceed against me here.

Charles expanded on this in a written statement. He still maintained the divine right of kings – that 'the King can do no wrong' – citing the Old Testament as saying that this authority came from God. Part of his argument (and he had a point) was that the trial violated the very principle that his opponents had used against him: the need to apply the rule of law and not to act in an arbitrary manner.

Having already made my protestations, not only against the illegality of this pretended Court, but also, that no earthly power can justly call me (who am your King) in question as a delinquent, I would not any more open my mouth upon this occasion, more than to refer myself to what I have spoken, were I in this case alone concerned: but the duty I owe to God in the preservation of the true liberty of my people will not suffer me at this time to be silent: for, how can any free-born subject of England call life or anything he possesseth his own, if power without right daily make new, and abrogate the old fundamental laws of the land.

Wherefore when I came hither, I expected that you would have endeavoured to have satisfied me concerning these grounds which hinder me to answer to your pretended impeachment. But since I see that nothing I can say will move you to it (though negatives are not so naturally proved as affirmatives) yet I will show you the reason why I am confident you cannot judge me, nor indeed the meanest man in England: for I will not (like you) without showing a reason, seek to impose a belief upon my subjects.

There is no proceeding just against any man, but what is warranted, either by God's laws or the municipal laws of the country where he lives. Now I am most confident this day's proceeding cannot be warranted by God's laws; for, on the contrary, the authority of obedience unto Kings is clearly warranted, and strictly commanded in both the Old and New Testament, which, if denied, I am ready instantly to prove.

And for the question now in hand, there it is said, that 'where the word of a King is, there is power; and who may say unto him, what dost thou?' (Ecclesiastes, chapter viii, verse 4). Then for the law of this land, I am no less confident, that no learned lawyer will affirm that an impeachment can lie against the King, they all going in his name: and one of their maxims is, that the King can do no wrong. Besides, the law upon which you ground your proceedings, must either be old or new: if old, show it; if new, tell what authority, warranted by the fundamental laws of the land, hath made it, and when. But how the House of Commons can erect a Court of Judicature, which was never one itself (as is well known to all lawyers) I leave to God and the world to judge. And it were full as strange, that they should pretend to make laws without King or Lords' House, to any that have heard speak of the laws of England.

And admitting, but not granting, that the people of England's commission could grant your pretended power, I see nothing you can show for that; for certainly you never asked the question of the tenth man in the kingdom, and in this way you manifestly wrong even the poorest ploughman it.

Thus you see that I speak not for my own right alone, as I am your King, but also for the true liberty of all my subjects, which consists not in the power of government, but in living under such laws, such a government, as may give themselves the best assurance of their lives, and property of their goods; nor in this must or do I forget the privileges of both Houses of Parliament, which this day's proceedings do not only, violate, but likewise occasion the greatest breach of their public faith that (I believe) ever was heard of.

Besides all this, the peace of the kingdom is not the least in my thoughts; and what hope of settlement is there, so long as power reigns without rule or law, changing the whole frame of that government under which this kingdom hath flourished for many hundred years? The arms I took up were only to defend the fundamental laws of this kingdom against those who have supposed my power hath totally changed the ancient government.

Thus, having showed you briefly the reasons why I cannot submit to your pretended authority, without violating the trust which I have from God for the welfare and liberty of my people, I expect from you either clear reasons to convince my judgment, showing me that I am in an error (and then truly I will answer) or that you will withdraw your proceedings.

The trial continued regardless. On 27 January, Bradshaw responded to Charles's submission. Bradshaw adopted Sir Edward Coke's view that the king was not above the law and therefore could be tried for treason.

BRADSHAW'S RULING AGAINST CHARLES

Sir, the difference has been: who shall be the expositors of this law, sir? Whether you and your party, out of courts of justice, shall take upon them to expound the law, or the courts of justice who are the expounders – nay, the sovereign and highest court of justice, the Parliament of England, that is not only the highest expounder but the sole maker of the law. Sir, for you to set yourself with your single judgment, and those that adhere unto you to set themselves against the resolution of the highest court of justice – that is not law. Sir, as the law is your superior, so truly, sir, there is something that is superior to the law and that is indeed the parent or author of the law – and that is the people of England.

Sir, the term traitor cannot be spared. We shall easily agree it must denote and suppose a breach of trust, and it must suppose it to be done by a superior. And therefore, sir, as the people of England might have incurred that respecting you, if they had been truly guilty of it as to the definition of law, so on the other side when you did break your trust to the kingdom, you did break your trust to your superior. For the kingdom is that for which you were trusted. And therefore, sir, for this breach of trust when you are called to account, you are called to account by your superiors – 'when a king is summoned to judgment by the people, the lesser is summoned by the greater.' And, sir, the people of England cannot be so far wanting to themselves, God having dealt so miraculously and gloriously for them, they having power in their hands and their great enemy, they must proceed to do justice to themselves and to you.

Truly, sir, these are your high crimes – tyranny and treason. And there is a third thing too, if those had not been, and that is murder, which is laid to your charge. All the bloody murders that have been committed since the time that the division was betwixt you and your people must be laid to your charge that have been acted or committed in these late wars.

Bradshaw announced that Charles was guilty, and that 'the said Charles Stuart, as a tyrant, traitor, murderer and public enemy to the good of this nation, shall be put to death by severing of his head from his body'. The execution would take place on 30 January.

The day, when it came, was bitterly cold. Charles wore two thick shirts to stop him shivering. Speaking from the place of execution, the balcony of Whitehall's Banqueting House, Charles addressed the crowd below.

Charles I's speech from the scaffold

Truly I desire the people's liberty and freedom as much as anybody whomsoever; but I must tell you that their liberty and freedom consist in having of government, those laws by which their life and their goods may be most their own. It is not for having share in government, sirs; that is nothing pertaining to them; a subject and a sovereign are clear different things. And therefore until they do that, I mean that you do put the people in that liberty, as I say, certainly they will never enjoy themselves. Sirs, it was for this that now I am come here. If I would have given way to an arbitrary way, for to have all laws changed according to the power of the sword, I needed not to have come here; and therefore I tell you (and I pray God it be not laid to your charge) that I am the martyr of the people.

After brief prayers, Charles said: 'I go from a corruptible to an incorruptible crown; where no disturbance can be, no disturbance in the world.' An eyewitness described the execution itself:

His Majesty stretching forth his hands, the executioner at one blow severed his head from his body; which, being held up and showed to the people, was with his body put into a coffin covered with black velvet and carried into his lodging. His blood was taken up by divers persons for different ends: by some as trophies of their villainy; by others as relics of a martyr; and in some hath had the same effect, by the blessing of God, which was often found in his sacred touch when living.

1649

'The office of King is unnecessary, burdensome, and dangerous to liberty'

During the Civil War, tensions had grown between Cromwell's army and many Members of Parliament. In December 1648, shortly before Charles I's trial and execution, around 370 MPs were effectively purged for being insufficiently loyal to Cromwell. This left fewer than 100 to sit in the House of Commons. One week after Charles's execution, this 'Rump Parliament' voted to abolish the monarchy.

The declaration of Cromwell's Rump Parliament abolishing the monarchy

Whereas Charles Stuart, late King of England, Ireland, and the territories and dominions thereunto belonging, hath by authority derived from Parliament been and is hereby declared to be justly condemned, adjudged to die, and put to death, for many treasons, murders, and other heinous offences committed by him; be it therefore enacted and ordained, and it is enacted, ordained, and declared by this present Parliament, that all the people of England and Ireland, and the dominions and territories thereunto belonging, are discharged of all fealty, homage, and allegiance which is or shall be pretended to be due unto any of the issue and posterity of the said late King, or any claiming under him; and that Charles Stuart, eldest son, and James called Duke of York, second son, and all other issue and posterity of him the said late King, and all and every person and persons pretending title from, by, or under him, are and be disabled to hold or enjoy the said Crown of England and Ireland, and other the dominions thereunto belonging, or any of them; or to have the name, title, style, or dignity of King or Queen of England and Ireland.

And whereas it is and hath been found by experience, that the office of a King in this nation and Ireland, and to have the power thereof in any single person, is unnecessary, burdensome, and dangerous to the liberty, safety, and public interest of the people, and that for the most part, use hath been made of the regal power and prerogative to oppress and impoverish and enslave the subject; and that usually and naturally any one person in such power makes it his interest to encroach upon the just freedom and liberty of the people, and to promote the setting up of their own will and power above the laws, that so they might enslave these kingdoms to their own lust; be it therefore enacted and ordained by this present Parliament, and by authority of the same, that the office of a King in this nation shall not henceforth reside in or be exercised by any one single person; and that no one person whatsoever shall or may have, or hold the office, style, dignity, power, or authority of King of the said kingdoms and dominions.

And it is hereby enacted, that if any person or persons shall endeavour to attempt by force of arms or otherwise, or be aiding, assisting, comforting, or abetting unto any person or persons that shall by any ways or means whatsoever endeavour or attempt the reviving or setting up again of any pretended right of the said Charles, eldest son to the said late King, James called Duke of York, or of any other the issue and posterity of the said late King, or of any person or persons claiming under him or them, to the said regal office, style, dignity, or authority, or to be Prince of Wales; or the promoting of any one person whatsoever to the name, style, dignity, power, prerogative, or authority of King of England and Ireland, and dominions aforesaid, or any of them; that then every such offence shall be deemed and adjudged high treason, and the offenders be subject to the same pains, forfeitures, judgments, and execution as is used in case of high treason.

And whereas by the abolition of the kingly office provided for in this Act, a most happy way is made for this nation (if God see it good) to return to its just and ancient right, of being governed by its own representatives or national meetings in council, from time to time chosen and entrusted for that purpose by the people, it is therefore resolved and declared by the Commons assembled in Parliament, that they will put a period to the sitting of this present Parliament, and dissolve the same so soon as may possibly stand with the safety of the people that hath betrusted them; and that they will carefully provide for the certain choosing, meeting, and sitting of the next and future representatives, with such other circumstances of freedom in choice and equality in distribution of members to be elected thereunto, as shall most conduce to the lasting freedom and good of this Commonwealth.

Six weeks later, on 19 March, the Commons also voted to abolish the House of Lords.

> The Commons of England assembled in Parliament, finding by too long experience that the House of Lords is useless and dangerous to the people of England to be continued, have thought fit to ordain and enact, and be it ordained and enacted by this present Parliament, and by the authority of the same, that from henceforth the House of Lords in Parliament shall be and is hereby wholly abolished and taken away; and that the Lords shall not from henceforth meet or sit in the said House called the Lords' House, or in any other house or place whatsoever, as a House of Lords; nor shall sit, vote, advise, adjudge, or determine of any matter or thing whatsoever, as a House of Lords in Parliament: nevertheless it is hereby declared, that neither such Lords as have demeaned themselves with honour, courage, and fidelity to the Commonwealth, nor their posterities who shall continue so, shall be excluded from the public councils of the nation, but shall be admitted thereunto, and have their free vote in Parliament, if they shall be thereunto elected, as other persons of interest elected and qualified thereunto ought to have.
>
> And be it further ordained and enacted by the authority aforesaid, that no Peer of this land, not being elected, qualified and sitting in Parliament as aforesaid, shall claim, have, or make use of any privilege of Parliament, either in relation to his person, quality, or estate, notwithstanding any law, usage, or custom to the contrary.

On 19 May, the Rump Parliament completed the process by declaring Britain to be a republic.

> Be it declared and enacted by this present Parliament and by the authority of the same that the people of England and of all the Dominions and Territories thereunto belonging are and shall be and are hereby constituted, made, established, and confirmed to be a Commonwealth and free State; and shall from henceforth be governed as a Commonwealth and Free State by the supreme authority of this nation, the representatives of the People in Parliament and by such as they shall appoint and constitute as Officers and Ministers under them for the good of the People and that without any King or House of Lords.

1649

'OUR LIBERTIES AND FREEDOMS, THE TRUE DIFFERENCE AND DISTINCTION BETWEEN MEN AND BEASTS'

On 26 February 1649, less than one month after the execution of Charles I, John Lilburne and the other leaders of the Levellers published a pamphlet, 'England's New Chains', which amounted to a frontal assault on the country's new rulers, accusing them of being just as authoritarian as the monarchy they had fought a civil war to replace. Lilburne sent the pamphlet to Parliament and to Cromwell's Council of State.

JOHN LILBURNE: 'ENGLAND'S NEW CHAINS'

For where is that good, or where is that liberty so much pretended, so dearly purchased? If we look upon what this House [of Commons] hath done since it hath voted it self the Supreme Authority, we find a high Court of Justice erected, to try criminal cases; whereby that great and strong hold of our preservation, the way of trial by 12 sworn men of the neighbourhood, is over-ruled by a Court consisting of persons picked and chosen in an unusual way. This is the first part of our new liberty.

The next is the censuring of a Member of this House, for declaring his judgement in a point of Religion, which is directly opposite to the Reserve in the Agreement concerning Religion.

Then the stopping of our mouths from Printing, is carefully provided for, to gag us from speaking truth, and discovering the tyrannies of bad men, are referred to the care of the General, and by him to his Marshal, to be put in execution; in searching, fining, imprisoning, and other ways corporally punishing all that any ways by guilty of unlicensed Printing.

Those Petitioners that have moved in behalf of the people, how have they been entertained? Sometimes with the compliment of empty thanks, their desires in the mean time not at all considered; at other times meeting with reproaches and threats for their constancy and public affections, and with violent motions, that their petitions be burnt by the common hangman, whilst other are not taken in at all; to so small an account are the people brought, even while they are flattered with notions of being the Original of all just power.

And lastly, for completing this new kind of liberty, a Council of State is hastily erected for Guardians thereof, who to that end are possessed with power to order and dispose all the forces appertaining to England by Sea or Land, to dispose of the public Treasure, to command any person whatsoever before them, to give oath for the discovering of Truth, to imprison any that shall disobey their commands, and such as they shall judge rebellious. What now is become of that liberty that no mans person shall be attached or imprisoned, or otherwise diseased of his freehold, or free Customs, but by lawful judgement of his equals?

Two days later, Lilburne took his argument to Parliament and addressed MPs from the Bar (near the entrance) of the House of Commons. Like MPs then and now, he addressed his remarks through the Speaker (sensibly, Lilburne did not repeat the criticisms of Speaker Lenthall that had landed him in prison four years earlier).

LILBURNE DEFENDS HIMSELF IN PARLIAMENT

Mr Speaker,
I am very glad that without any inconvenience unto my self, and those that are with me, I may freely and cheerfully address my self to this honourable House, as the Supreme Authority of England (time was when I could not) and it much refresh my spirit, to live to see this day, that you have made such a step to the People's Liberties, as to own and declare your selves to be (as indeed you are) the Supreme Authority of this Nation.

Mr Speaker, I am desired by a company of honest men, living in and about London, who in truth do rightly appropriate to themselves, the title of the Contrivers, Promoters, Presenters, and Approvers of the late Large London Petition of the 11th of Sept. last, (which was the first Petition I know of in England, that was presented to this honourable House against the late destructive Personal Treaty with the late King) to present you with their serious apprehensions; And give me leave (I beseech you) for my self and them, to say thus much; That for the most part of us, we are those that in the worst of times durst own our Liberties and Freedoms, in the face of the greatest of our adversaries; and from the beginning of these Wars, never shrunk from the owning of our Freedoms, in the most tempestuous times, nor changed our Principles.

And Mr Speaker, give me leave to tell you, that I am confident our Liberties and Freedoms (the true and just end of all the late Wars) are so dear and precious to us, that we had rather our lives should breath out with them, than to live one moment after the expiration of them.

Mr Speaker, We own this honourable House (as of right) the true Guardian of our Liberties and Freedoms; and we wish and most heartily desire, you would rouse up your spirits (like men of gallantry) and now at last take unto your selves a magnanimous resolution, to acquit your selves (without fear or dread) like the chosen and betrusted Trustees of the People, from whom (as your selves acknowledge and declare) all just power is derived, to free us from all bondage and slavery, and really and truly invest us into the price of all our blood, hazards, and toils; Our Liberties and Freedoms, the true difference and distinction between men and beasts.

Mr Speaker, Though my spirit is full in the sad apprehension of the dying condition of our Liberties and Freedoms: Yet at present I shall say no more, but in the behalf of my self and my friends, I shall earnestly entreat you to read these our serious Apprehensions seriously, and debate them deliberately.

Lilburne cannot have been wholly surprised that Cromwell failed to respond: 'Yes, now you point it out, I can see that I have been a dreadful ogre; I shall change my ways.' Instead, Cromwell had Lilburne and his closest associates arrested for treason and brought before the Council of State, which Lilburne later described as a 'self-appointed junta of the roundheads'. However, it became clear that Cromwell's Council was divided. Some members thought that the arrests might turn Londoners against them. The arrested men waited outside while the Council debated the issue. Lilburne wrote later that he heard Cromwell 'thumping his fist upon the Council table', as he shouted at the council.

CROMWELL TELLS THE COUNCIL OF STATE TO ACT AGAINST LILBURNE AND HIS ALLIES

I tell you, Sir, you have no other way to deal with these men, but to break them in pieces; if you do not break them, they will break you; yea and bring all the guilt of the blood and treasure shed and spent in this kingdom upon your head and shoulders; and frustrate and make void all that work, that with so many years' industry, toil and pains you have done, and so render you to all rational men in the world as the most contemptible generation of silly, low-spirited men in the earth, to be broken and routed by such a despicable, contemptible generation of men as they are; and therefore, Sir, I tell you again, you are necessitated to break them.

Lilburne was brought to trial six months later – six months during which London women, inspired by Lilburne's advocacy of their rights, campaigned for his release; and during which a number of regiments mutinied against Cromwell, their resentments fuelled by their meagre pay. Lilburne used his trial as a platform to attack the judges. The jury evidently warmed to his assertion that they should act independently, and acquitted him. Four years later, he was charged and acquitted again. Cromwell insisted, however, that Lilburne remain in prison. Lilburne subsequently became a Quaker, and after two more years Cromwell released him when he promised to keep quiet. Lilburne died in 1657; he was only in his early 40s.

1651

'THE PASSIONS OF MEN ARE COMMONLY MORE POTENT THAN THEIR REASON'

Thomas Hobbes was already 60 when Britain became a republic. Much of his philosophical thinking was well established. He was neither a republican himself, nor a defender of the divine right of kings. In developing what became known as the concept of the 'social contract', he argued that people had a duty to give allegiance to their rulers, provided that these rulers defended the people's rights to 'peaceable, social and comfortable living'.

Leviathan was written mainly in Paris and published in 1651. It included the oft-used quotation that 'the life of man [is] solitary, poor, nasty, brutish, and short' – though it is not always remembered that Hobbes applied this description to times of conflict, when social disciplines break down because 'men live without a common power to keep them all in awe'. For Hobbes, a powerful government is necessary, but potentially dangerous. It needs to be watched and curbed; hence his description of the state as a 'leviathan'.

In this section of *Leviathan*, Hobbes dissects different kinds of government and the relative advantages of being ruled by a democracy, an aristocracy or a monarchy.

THOMAS HOBBES: *LEVIATHAN*

> Sovereign power is attained in two ways. One, by natural force: as when a man maketh his children to submit themselves, and their children, to his government, as being able to destroy them if they refuse; or by war subdueth his enemies to his will, giving them their lives on that condition. The other, is when men agree amongst themselves to submit to some man, or assembly of men, voluntarily, on confidence to be protected by him against all others. This latter may be called a political Commonwealth, or Commonwealth by Institution; and the former, a Commonwealth by acquisition. And first, I shall speak of a Commonwealth by Institution.

There can be but three kinds of Commonwealth. For the representative must needs be one man, or more; and if more, then it is the assembly of all, or but of a part. When the representative is one man, then is the Commonwealth a monarchy; when an assembly of all that will come together, then it is a democracy, or popular Commonwealth; when an assembly of a part only, then it is called an aristocracy. There be other names of government in the histories and books of policy; as tyranny and oligarchy; but they are not the names of other forms of government, but of the same forms misliked. For they that are discontented under monarchy call it tyranny; and they that are displeased with aristocracy call it oligarchy: so also, they which find themselves grieved under a democracy call it anarchy, which signifies want of government; and yet I think no man believes that want of government is any new kind of government.

It is manifest that men who are in absolute liberty may, if they please, give authority to one man to represent them every one, as well as give such authority to any assembly of men whatsoever; and consequently may subject themselves, if they think good, to a monarch as absolutely as to other representative.

The difference between these three kinds of Commonwealth consists, not in the difference of power, but in the difference of convenience or aptitude to produce the peace and security of the people; for which end they were instituted. And to compare monarchy with the other two, we may observe:

First, that whosoever beareth the person of the people, or is one of that assembly that bears it, beareth also his own natural person. And though he be careful in his politic person to procure the common interest, yet he is more, or no less, careful to procure the private good of himself, his family and friends; and for the most part, if the public interest chance to cross the private, he prefers the private: for the passions of men are commonly more potent than their reason. From whence it follows that where the public and private interest are most closely united, there is the public most advanced.

Now in monarchy the private interest is the same with the public. The riches, power, and honour of a monarch arise only from the riches, strength, and reputation of his subjects. For no king can be rich, nor glorious, nor secure, whose subjects are either poor, or contemptible, or too weak through want, or dissension, to maintain a war against their enemies; whereas in a democracy, or aristocracy, the public prosperity confers not so much to the private fortune of one that is corrupt, or ambitious, as doth many times a perfidious advice, a treacherous action, or a civil war.

Secondly, that a monarch receiveth counsel of whom, when, and where he pleaseth; and consequently may hear the opinion of men versed in the matter about which he deliberates, of what rank or quality soever, and as long before the time of action and with as much secrecy as he will. But when an assembly has need of counsel, none are admitted but such as have a right thereto from the beginning; which for the most part are of those who have been versed more in the acquisition of wealth than of knowledge, and are to give their advice in long discourses which may, and do commonly, excite men to action, but not govern them in it. For the understanding is by the flame of the passions never enlightened, but dazzled: nor is there any place or time wherein an assembly can receive counsel secrecy, because of their own multitude.

Thirdly, that the resolutions of a monarch are subject to no other inconstancy than that of human nature; but in assemblies, besides that of nature, there ariseth an inconstancy from the number. For the absence of a few that would have the resolution, or the diligent appearance of a few of the contrary opinion, undoes today all that was concluded yesterday.

Fourthly, that a monarch cannot disagree with himself, out of envy or interest; but an assembly may; and that to such a height as may produce a civil war.

Fifthly, that in monarchy there is this inconvenience; that any subject, by the power of one man, for the enriching of a favourite or flatterer, may be deprived of all he possesseth; which I confess is a great an inevitable inconvenience. But the same may as well happen where the sovereign power is in an assembly: for their power is the same; and they are as subject to evil counsel, and to be seduced by orators, as a monarch by flatterers; and becoming one another's flatterers, serve one another's covetousness and ambition by turns. And whereas the favourites of monarchs are few, and they have none else to advance but their own kindred; the favourites of an assembly are many, and the kindred much more numerous than of any monarch.

Sixthly, that it is an inconvenience in monarchy that the sovereignty may descend upon an infant, or one that cannot discern between good and evil: and consists in this, that the use of his power must be in the hand of another man, or of some assembly of men, which are to govern by his right and in his name as curators and protectors of his person and authority. But to say there is inconvenience in putting the use of the sovereign power into the hand of a man, or an assembly of men, is to say that all government is more inconvenient than confusion and civil war.

As a child has need of a tutor, or protector, to preserve his person and authority; so also in great Commonwealths the sovereign assembly, in all great dangers and troubles, have need of *custodes libertatis*; that is, of dictators, or protectors of their authority; which are as much as temporary monarchs to whom for a time they may commit the entire exercise of their power; and have, at the end of that time, been oftener deprived thereof than infant kings by their protectors, regents, or any other tutors.

Hobbes's anti-papist views caused the French authorities to turn against him. He returned to England, where he continued to embrace controversy. When the monarchy was restored in 1660, Hobbes found favour with the new king, Charles II, who gave him a pension of one hundred pounds a year (around eight times the wage of a farm labourer). Hobbes lived and argued for another two decades before dying in 1679, four months short of his ninety-second birthday.

1652

'EVERY PERSON OF THE POPISH RELIGION SHALL FORFEIT ONE THIRD PART OF THEIR ESTATES'

In 1641, Ireland's Catholic gentry attempted to seize control of the country from the English and Scottish settlers that ruled it. The rebellion became a factor in both the cause and evolution of England's Civil War, with King Charles backing the Catholics while Parliament backed the settlers. By 1642, the rebellion had become a conventional civil war, with settlers controlling Dublin, Cork and Belfast, and 'Confederate Catholics' most of the rest of Ireland.

After abolishing the monarchy in 1649, Cromwell turned his attention to Ireland, leading an invasion to reconquer the island. A year later, he returned to England (largely to turn his attention to quelling Scotland) and handed control of the army in Ireland to Henry Ireton, his son-in-law and ally in the Putney Debates.

Cromwell and Ireton's forces were exceptionally savage – burning crops, killing civilians and forcing mass movements of population. Tens, perhaps hundreds, of thousands of Irish people were killed, forced into exile, taken as slaves to the West Indies or starved to death. Cromwell's Catholic opponents were also responsible for many atrocities, but it is the genocidal actions of his troops that had, and have, far greater historical resonance.

In August 1652, with Ireland's Catholic gentry destroyed and English rule fully re-established, the English Parliament passed the Act for the Settlement of Ireland, which outlawed Catholicism and divided the Irish people into different groups depending on their loyalty to England and the extent to which they had supported the 1641 rebellion. In effect, it stripped most of the Catholic population of many of their rights and much of their land and property, and threatened many of them with the gallows.

ACT FOR THE SETTLEMENT OF IRELAND 1652

Whereas the Parliament of England, after the expense of much blood and treasure for suppression of the horrid rebellion in Ireland, have by the good hand of God upon their undertakings, brought that affair to such an issue, as that a settlement of that nation may, with God's blessing, be speedily effected, to the end therefore that the people of that nation may know that it is not the intention of the Parliament to extirpate that whole nation, but that mercy and pardon, both as to life and estate, may be extended to all husbandmen, ploughmen, labourers, artificers, and others of the inferior sort, in manner as is hereafter declared:

Be it enacted and declared by this present Parliament, and by the authority of the same, that all and every person and persons of the Irish nation, comprehended in any of the following qualifications, shall be liable unto the penalties and forfeitures therein mentioned and contained, or be made capable of the mercy and pardon therein extended respectively, according as is hereafter expressed and declared; that is to say,

That all and every person and persons, who at any time before the tenth day of November, 1642 (being the time of the sitting of the first General Assembly at Kilkenny in Ireland), have contrived, advised, counselled, promoted, or acted, the rebellion, murders, or massacres done or committed in Ireland, which began in the year 1641; or have at any time before the said tenth day of November, 1642, by bearing arms, or contributing men, arms, horse, plate, money, victual, or other furniture or hablements of war (other than such which they shall make to appear to have been taken from them by mere force and violence), aided, assisted, promoted, acted, prosecuted, or abetted the said rebellion, murders, or massacres, be excepted from pardon of life and estate.

That all and every Jesuit, priest, and other person or persons who have received orders from the Pope or See of Rome, or any authority derived from the same, that have any ways contrived, advised, counselled, promoted, continued, countenanced, aided, assisted, or abetted; or at any time hereafter shall any ways contrive, advise, counsel, promote, continue, countenance, aid, assist, or abet the rebellion or war in Ireland, or any the murders or massacres, robberies, or violences committed against the Protestants, English, or others there, be excepted from pardon for life and estate.

That all and every person and persons (both principals and accessories) who since the first of October, 1641, have or shall kill, slay, or otherwise destroy any person or persons in Ireland, which at the time of their being so killed, slain, or destroyed, were not publicly entertained and maintained in arms as officers or private soldiers, for and on behalf of the English against the Irish.

That all and every person and persons in Ireland, that are in arms or otherwise in hostility against the Parliament of the Commonwealth of England, and shall not within eight and twenty days after publication hereof by the Commissioners for the Parliament, or Commander-in-chief, lay down arms and submit to the power and authority of the said Parliament and Commonwealth, as the same is now established, be excepted from pardon for life and estate.

That all other person and persons (not being comprehended in any of the former qualifications) who have borne command in the war of Ireland against the Parliament of England, be banished during the pleasure of the Parliament of the Commonwealth of England, and their estates forfeited and disposed of as followeth, viz. that two-thirds of their respective estates be had, taken, and disposed of for the use and benefit of the said Commonwealth; and that the other third be respectively had, taken, and enjoyed by the wives and children of the said persons respectively.

That the Commissioners of Parliament and Commander-in-Chief have power to declare, that such person or persons as they shall judge capable of the Parliament's mercy, who have borne arms against the Parliament of England or their forces, and have laid down arms, or shall lay down arms and submit to the power and authority of the said Parliament and Commonwealth, shall be pardoned for their lives, but shall forfeit their estates to the said Commonwealth, to be disposed of as follows, viz. two-thirds thereof for the use, benefit, and advantage of the said Commonwealth, and the other third part of the said respective estates or other lands, to the proportion or value thereof be enjoyed by the said persons, their heirs or assigns respectively.

That all and every person and persons of the Popish Religion, who have resided in Ireland at any time from the first day of October, 1641, to the first of March, 1650, and have not manifested their constant good affection to the interest of the Commonwealth of England (the said persons not being comprehended in any of the former qualifications), shall forfeit one third part of their estates in Ireland to the said Commonwealth: and that all other persons who have resided in Ireland within the time aforesaid, and have not been in actual service for the Parliament, or otherwise manifested their good affection to the interests of the Parliament of England, having opportunity to do the same, shall forfeit one fifth part of their estates to the use of the said Commonwealth.

That all and every person and persons (having no real estate in Ireland, nor personal estate to the value of ten pounds) that shall lay down arms, and submit to the power and authority of the Parliament shall be pardoned for life and estate for any act or thing by them done in prosecution of the war.

Although the Act provided for the execution of very large numbers of the Irish, relatively few were in fact put to death. In the decades that followed, Catholicism was intermittently allowed, and some of the economic rights of Catholics restored. But the power of the Protestant landowners – the 'ascendancy' – gradually became more entrenched.

1653

'GO! GET OUT! MAKE HASTE, YE VENAL SLAVES, BEGONE!'

By 1653, relations between the army and the Rump Parliament had broken down. Each wanted to disband the other. Cromwell sided with the army – and, in particular, with its anger that Parliament had failed to allocate enough money to meet soldiers' claims for decent pay and pensions. For a while, he tried to persuade MPs to agree to a dissolution, so that a new Parliament could be chosen. On 19 April, he believed he had a deal. However, the next day, when he heard that a number of MPs wanted to stay in session, Cromwell and his troops entered the House of Commons, where he made his views on the MPs pungently clear.

CROMWELL'S SPEECH DISSOLVING THE RUMP PARLIAMENT

Ye sordid prostitutes!

It is high time for me to put an end to your sitting in this place, which you have dishonored by your contempt of all virtue, and defiled by your practice of every vice; ye are a factious crew, and enemies to all good government; ye are a pack of mercenary wretches, and would like Esau sell your country for a mess of pottage, and like Judas betray your God for a few pieces of money.

Is there a single virtue now remaining amongst you? Is there one vice you do not possess? Ye have no more religion than my horse; gold is your God; which of you have not barter'd your conscience for bribes? Is there a man amongst you that has the least care for the good of the Commonwealth?

Ye sordid prostitutes have you not defil'd this sacred place, and turn'd the Lord's temple into a den of thieves, by your immoral principles and wicked practices? Ye are grown intolerably odious to the whole nation; you were deputed here by the people to get grievances redress'd, are yourselves become the greatest grievance.

Your Country therefore calls upon me to cleanse the Augean Stable, by putting a final Period to your Iniquitous Proceedings in this House, and which by God's Help, and the strength He has given Me, I now come to do. You have sat too long here for any good you have been doing. Depart, I say, and let us have done with you.

I command ye, therefore, upon the Peril of your Lives, to depart immediately out of this Place.

Go! Get out! Make haste, ye Venal Slaves, begone!

So, take away that shining Bauble there [the mace], and lock up the Doors.

In the name of God, go!

One of Cromwell's generals proceeded to remove the mace. Troops started to clear the chamber. One MP, Alderman Allen, the treasurer of the army, sought to calm things down by asking Cromwell for the mace to be returned, saying: 'It is not too late. The members may yet be called back and the sitting resumed.' Allen was promptly arrested and charged with embezzling army funds. The House of Commons was emptied, and its doors locked.

If Britain has shown other countries how to build a democracy, it has also shown them how to destroy it.

1653

'OLIVER CROMWELL IS HEREBY DECLARED TO BE LORD PROTECTOR FOR LIFE'

The United Kingdom is one of the few democracies without a written constitution. However, it was not always so. In fact, Britain had the world's first written constitution. The Instrument of Government was adopted by Oliver Cromwell's Council of Officers in December 1653. It brought together England, Scotland, Wales and Ireland into a single nation and granted supreme power to Cromwell, as Lord Protector, for life, working with a Council of State and a unicameral Parliament. Parliament would have 460 members: 400 from England and Wales, and 30 each from Scotland and Ireland. Each Parliament would last for up to three years. The franchise was granted to every 'person' (in practice, 'man') who possessed land and/or property totalling £200 or more in value. This was a highly restrictive condition, which gave the vote to only a small minority.

THE INSTRUMENT OF GOVERNMENT

The government of the Commonwealth of England, Scotland, and Ireland, and the dominions thereunto belonging.

I. That the supreme legislative authority of the Commonwealth of England, Scotland, and Ireland, and the dominions thereunto belonging, shall be and reside in one person, and the people assembled in Parliament: the style of which person shall be the Lord Protector of the Commonwealth of England, Scotland, and Ireland.

II. That the exercise of the chief magistracy and the administration of the government over the said countries and dominions, and the people thereof, shall be in the Lord Protector, assisted with a council, the number whereof shall not exceed twenty-one, nor be less than thirteen.

. . .

IV.   That the Lord Protector, the Parliament sitting, shall dispose and order the militia and forces, both by sea and land, for the peace and good of the three nations, by consent of Parliament; and that the Lord Protector, with the advice and consent of the major part of the council, shall dispose and order the militia for the ends aforesaid in the intervals of Parliament.

. . .

VI.   That the laws shall not be altered, suspended, abrogated, or repealed, nor any new law made, nor any tax, charge, or imposition laid upon the people, but by common consent in Parliament, save only as is expressed in the thirtieth article.

VII.   That there shall be a Parliament summoned to meet at Westminster upon the third day of September, 1654, and that successively a Parliament shall be summoned once in every third year, to be accounted from the dissolution of the present Parliament.

VIII.   That neither the Parliament to be next summoned, nor any successive Parliaments, shall, during the time of five months, to be accounted from the day of their first meeting, be adjourned, prorogued, or dissolved, without their own consent.

IX.   That as well the next as all other successive Parliaments shall be summoned and elected in manner hereafter expressed; that is to say, the persons to be chosen within England, Wales, the Isles of Jersey, Guernsey, and the town of Berwick-upon-Tweed, to sit and serve in Parliament, shall be, and not exceed, the number of four hundred. The persons to be chosen within Scotland, to sit and serve in Parliament, shall be, and not exceed, the number of thirty; and the persons to be chosen to sit in Parliament for Ireland shall be, and not exceed, the number of thirty.

. . .

XVII.   That the persons who shall be elected to serve in Parliament, shall be such (and no other than such) as are persons of known integrity, fearing God, and of good conversation, and being of the age of twenty-one years.

XVIII.   That all and every person and persons seised or possessed to his own use, of any estate, real or personal, to the value of £200, and not within the aforesaid exceptions, shall be capable to elect members to serve in Parliament for counties.

. . .

XXIV.   That all Bills agreed unto by the Parliament, shall be presented to the Lord Protector for his consent; and in case he shall not give his consent thereto within twenty days after they shall be presented to him, or give satisfaction to the Parliament within the time limited, that then, upon declaration of the Parliament that the Lord Protector hath not consented nor given satisfaction, such Bills shall pass into and become laws.

. . .

XXVII.   That a constant yearly revenue shall be raised, settled, and established for maintaining of 10,000 horse and dragoons, and 20,000 foot, in England, Scotland and Ireland, for the defence and security thereof, and also for a convenient number of ships for guarding of the seas; besides £200,000 per annum for defraying the other necessary charges of administration of justice, and other expenses of the Government, which revenue shall be raised by the customs, and such other ways and means as shall be agreed upon by the Lord Protector and the Council, and shall not be taken away or diminished, nor the way agreed upon for raising the same altered, but by the consent of the Lord Protector and the Parliament.

XXVIII.   That the said yearly revenue shall be paid into the public treasury, and shall be issued out for the uses aforesaid.

XXIX.   That in case there shall not be cause hereafter to keep up so great a defence both at land or sea, but that there be an abatement made thereof, the money which will be saved thereby shall remain in bank for the public service, and not be employed to any other use but by consent of Parliament, or, in the intervals of Parliament, by the Lord Protector and major part of the Council.

XXX.   That the raising of money for defraying the charge of the present extraordinary forces, both at sea and land, in respect of the present wars, shall be by consent of Parliament, and not otherwise: save only that the Lord Protector, with the consent of the major part of the Council, for preventing the disorders and dangers which might otherwise fall out both by sea and land, shall have power, until the meeting of the first Parliament, to raise money for the purposes aforesaid; and also to make laws and ordinances for the peace and welfare of these nations where it shall be necessary, which shall be binding and in force, until order shall be taken in Parliament concerning the same.

. . .

XXXII.   That the office of Lord Protector over these nations shall be elective and not hereditary; and upon the death of the Lord Protector, another fit person shall be forthwith elected to succeed him in the Government; which election shall be by the Council, who, immediately upon the death of the Lord Protector, shall assemble in the Chamber where they usually sit in Council; and, having given notice to all their members of the cause of their assembling, shall, being thirteen at least present, proceed to the election.

XXXIII.   That Oliver Cromwell, Captain-General of the forces of England, Scotland and Ireland, shall be, and is hereby declared to be, Lord Protector of the Commonwealth of England, Scotland and Ireland, and the dominions thereto belonging, for his life.

. . .

XXXVII.   That such as profess faith in God by Jesus Christ (though differing in judgment from the doctrine, worship or discipline publicly held forth) shall not be restrained from, but shall be protected in, the profession of the faith and exercise of their religion; so as they abuse not this liberty to the civil injury of others and to the actual disturbance of the public peace on their parts: provided this liberty be not extended to Popery or Prelacy, nor to such as, under the profession of Christ, hold forth and practise licentiousness.

Elections were held in the summer of 1654 to elect a new Parliament. The result was not entirely to Cromwell's liking, for the new MPs included Royalists, Presbyterians and other opponents. They tabled amendments to the Instrument of Government, demanding more powers for Parliament. MPs blocked a series of bills that Cromwell had prepared for Parliament to ratify. Eventually, in January 1655, Cromwell dissolved Parliament. Three months later, following a Royalist uprising, Cromwell abandoned the concept of parliamentary government and established an outright military dictatorship. The world's first written constitution was effectively dead.

1660

'THE CIVIL RIGHTS AND ADVANCEMENTS OF EVERY PERSON ACCORDING TO HIS MERIT'

After Cromwell's death in 1658, Britain's system of government broke down. The army reconvened the Rump Parliament – and the antagonisms between the two swiftly resumed. By early 1660, there was a growing clamour for the monarchy to be revived. One of its fiercest opponents was John Milton. Disillusioned with Cromwell, but still a republican, Milton wrote a tract attacking the return of the monarchy.

Published in March 1660, and then in an expanded form the following month, Milton's tract set out the case for a federal democracy, in which majorities had duties as well as rights – not least, the duty to protect the rights of minorities. He likened calls for the return of the monarchy to slaves 'now choosing them back a captain for Egypt'. In this extract, Milton describes his alternative.

JOHN MILTON: *THE READY AND EASY WAY TO ESTABLISH A FREE COMMONWEALTH, AND THE EXCELLENCE THEREOF, COMPARED WITH THE INCONVENIENCIES AND DANGERS OF READMITTING KINGSHIP IN THIS NATION*

> Where is this goodly tower of a commonwealth, which the English boasted they would build to overshadow kings, and be another Rome in the west? The foundation indeed they lay gallantly, but fell into a worse confusion, not of tongues, but of factions, than those at the tower of Babel; and have left no memorial of their work behind them remaining, but in the common laughter of Europe!
>
> Besides this, if we return to kingship, and soon repent, (as undoubtedly we shall, when we begin to find the old encroachments corning on by little and little upon our consciences, which must necessarily proceed from king and bishop united inseparably in one interest,) we may be forced perhaps to fight over again all that we have fought, and spend over again

all that we have spent, but are never like to attain thus far as we are now advanced to the recovery of our freedom.

The happiness of a nation must needs be firmest and certainest in full and free council of their own electing, where no single person, but reason only, sways. And what madness is it for them who might manage nobly their own affairs themselves, sluggishly and weakly to devolve all on a single person; and more like boys under age than men, to commit all to his patronage and disposal, who neither can perform what he undertakes, and yet for undertaking it, though royally paid, will not be their servant, but their lord! How unmanly must it needs be, to count such a one the breath of our nostrils, to hang all our felicity on him, all our safety, our well-being, for which if we were aught else but sluggards or babies, we need depend on none but God and our own counsels, our own active virtue and industry!

I doubt not but all ingenuous and knowing men will easily agree with me, that a free commonwealth without single person or house of lords is by far the best government, if it can be had; but we have all this while, say they, been expecting it, and cannot yet attain it. The cause thereof may be ascribed with most reason to the frequent disturbances, interruptions, and dissolutions, which the parliament hath had, partly from the impatient or disaffected people, partly from some ambitious leaders in the army.

It will be objected, that in those places where they had perpetual senates, they had also popular remedies against their growing too imperious: as in Athens, besides Areopagus, another senate of four or five hundred; in Sparta, the Ephori; in Rome, the tribunes of the people. But the event tells us, that these remedies either little availed the people, or brought them to such a licentious and unbridled democracy, as in fine ruined themselves with their own excessive power. So that the main reason urged why popular assemblies are to be trusted with the people's liberty, rather than a senate of principle men, because great men will be still endeavouring to enlarge their power, but the common sort will be contented to maintain their own liberty, is by experience found false.

The whole freedom of man consists either in spiritual or civil liberty. As for spiritual, who can be at rest, who can enjoy any thing in this world with contentment, who hath not liberty to serve God, and to save his own soul, according to the best light which God hath planted in him to that purpose, by the reading of his revealed will, and the guidance of his Holy Spirit? This liberty of conscience, which above all other things ought to be to all men dearest and most precious, no government more inclinable not to favour only, but to protect, than a free commonwealth;

as being most magnanimous, most fearless, and confident of its own fair proceedings.

The other part of our freedom consists in the civil rights and advancements of every person according to his merit: the enjoyment of those never more certain, and the access to these never more open, than in a free commonwealth. Both which, in my opinion, may be best and soonest obtained, if every county in the land were made a kind of subordinate commonalty or commonwealth, and one chief town or more, according as the shire is in circuit, made cities, if they be not so called already; where the nobility and chief gentry may build houses or palaces befitting their quality, may bear part in the government, make their own judicial laws, or use these that are, and execute them by their own elected judicatures and judges. They shall then have justice in their own hands, law executed fully and finally in their own counties and precincts, long wished and spoken of, but never yet obtained. They shall have none then to blame but themselves, if it be not well administered.

As for controversies that shall happen between men of several counties, they may repair, as they do now, to the capital city, or any other more commodious, indifferent place, and equal judges. They should have here also schools and academies at their own choice, wherein their children may be bred up in their own sight to all learning and noble education; not in grammar only, but in all liberal arts and exercises.

This would soon spread much more knowledge and civility, yea, religion, through all parts of the land, by communicating the natural heat of government and culture more distributively to all extreme parts, which now lie numb and neglected. It would soon make the whole nation more industrious, more ingenious at home; more potent, more honourable abroad.

We have justice done us; nothing can be more essential to the freedom of a people, than to have the administration of justice, and all public ornaments, in their own election, and within their own bounds, without long travelling or depending upon remote places to obtain their right, or any civil accomplishment; so it be not supreme, but subordinate to the general power and union of the whole republic.

1660

'Let all our subjects rely upon the word of a King'

Britain's effective ruler in the spring of 1660 was General George Monck – a Royalist soldier at the start of the Civil War, but subsequently an ally of Cromwell. In March 1660, Monck persuaded the Rump Parliament to dissolve itself. Meanwhile, he was secretly corresponding with the son of Charles I, also called Charles, who was living in Holland. On 4 April, writing from the Dutch town of Breda, Charles set out his terms for returning to London as king – terms devised largely by Monck. Charles promised to allow religious freedom and a free Parliament, to pardon former enemies who accepted him as king, and to pay the arrears owed to General Monck's troops.

The Declaration of Breda

Charles, by the grace of God, King of England, Scotland, France and Ireland, Defender of the Faith, &c. To all our loving subjects, of what degree or quality soever, greeting.

If the general distraction and confusion which is spread over the whole kingdom doth not awaken all men to a desire and longing that those wounds which have so many years together been kept bleeding, may be bound up. All we can say will be to no purpose; however, after this long silence, we have thought it our duty to declare how much we desire to contribute thereunto; and that as we can never give over the hope, in good time, to obtain the possession of that right which God and nature hath made our due, so we do make it our daily suit to the Divine Providence, that He will, in compassion to us and our subjects, after so long misery and sufferings, remit and put us into a quiet and peaceable possession of that our right, with as little blood and damage to our people as is possible; nor do we desire more to enjoy what is ours, than that all our subjects may enjoy what by law is theirs, by a full and entire administration of justice throughout the land, and by extending our mercy where it is wanted and deserved.

And to the end that the fear of punishment may not engage any, conscious to themselves of what is past, to a perseverance in guilt for the future, by opposing the quiet and happiness of their country, in the restoration of King, Peers and people to their just, ancient and fundamental rights, we do, by these presents, declare, that we do grant a free and general pardon, which we are ready, upon demand, to pass under our Great Seal of England, to all our subjects, of what degree or quality soever, who, within forty days after the publishing hereof, shall lay hold upon this our grace and favour, and shall, by any public act, declare their doing so, and that they return to the loyalty and obedience of good subjects; excepting only such persons as shall hereafter be excepted by Parliament, those only to be excepted.

Let all our subjects, how faulty soever, rely upon the word of a King, solemnly given by this present declaration, that no crime whatsoever, committed against us or our royal father before the publication of this, shall ever rise in judgment, or be brought in question, against any of them, to the least endamagement of them, either in their lives, liberties or estates or (as far forth as lies in our power) so much as to the prejudice of their reputations, by any reproach or term of distinction from the rest of our best subjects; we desiring and ordaining that henceforth all notes of discord, separation and difference of parties be utterly abolished among all our subjects, whom we invite and conjure to a perfect union among themselves, under our protection, for the re-settlement of our just rights and theirs in a free Parliament, by which, upon the word of a King, we will be advised.

And because the passion and uncharitableness of the times have produced several opinions in religion, by which men are engaged in parties and animosities against each other (which, when they shall hereafter unite in a freedom of conversation, will be composed or better understood), we do declare a liberty to tender consciences, and that no man shall be disquieted or called in question for differences of opinion in matter of religion, which do not disturb the peace of the kingdom; and that we shall be ready to consent to such an Act of Parliament, as, upon mature deliberation, shall be offered to us, for the full granting that indulgence.

And because, in the continued distractions of so many years, and so many and great revolutions, many grants and purchases of estates have been made to and by many officers, soldiers and others, who are now possessed of the same, and who may be liable to actions at law upon several titles, we are likewise willing that all such differences, and all things relating to such grants, sales and purchases, shall be determined in Parliament, which can best provide for the just satisfaction of all men who are concerned.

And we do further declare, that we will be ready to consent to any Act or Acts of Parliament to the purposes aforesaid, and for the full satisfaction of all arrears due to the officers and soldiers of the army under the command of General Monck; and that they shall be received into our service upon as good pay and conditions as they now enjoy.

Given under our Sign Manual and Privy Signet, at our Court at Breda, this 4th day of April, 1660, in the twelfth year of our reign.

On 15 April, a new parliament, the Convention Parliament, met for the first time. It had a Royalist majority. It also revived the House of Lords. On 25 April, it issued a formal invitation for Charles to return to London as King Charles II. He arrived on 29 May. He was allowed to assert the divine right of kings, but barred from levying taxes without the consent of Parliament. In December 1660, Charles II dissolved the Convention Parliament. It was succeeded by the Cavalier Parliament, which lasted from 1661 until 1679 and did Charles's bidding. The royal 'firm' was back in charge.

One of Charles's first decisions was to restore self-government to Scotland. Yet he remained their monarch – indeed, he had been crowned Scotland's king at Scone in 1651, before fleeing to France and then Holland. (Hence the reference in the Declaration of Breda to 'the twelfth year of our reign'. Charles's 'reign' had begun on the death of his father in 1649.) From 1603 until 1649, and again after 1660, England and Scotland had the same monarch, but they formally remained two separate nations with separate crowns until the Act of Union in 1707. By crowning Charles their king in 1651, the Scots were asserting a right which they considered they had never lost: to determine their own monarch.

1679

'FOR THE SPEEDY RELIEF OF ALL PERSONS IMPRISONED'

By the late 1670s, a group known as the Exclusionists, led by the Earl of Shaftesbury, was campaigning to stop Charles II's brother, James, from succeeding to the throne. They argued that James would be a harsher, less conciliatory ruler than Charles, fearing that he would abolish many hard-won democratic principles. As part of their campaign, the Exclusionists proposed a Habeas Corpus (literally, 'you have the body') bill, to reinforce an earlier Act passed in 1640 which insisted that anyone accused of committing a crime should be brought before a court of law, and not detained indefinitely. These bills codified principles that had first surfaced in the Assize of Clarendon and, more explicitly, Magna Carta.

The bill passed the Commons, but most peers opposed it. The deadlock was eventually broken in the most outrageous way. It took a basic violation of democratic principles to advance democratic rights. Determined to pass the bill before the end of the parliamentary session, the bill's supporters deliberately inflated the numbers passing through the House of Lords lobby on the crucial vote, and declared victory by 57 votes to 55 – even though a total of only 107 peers attended the hearing. Charles, unaware of what had really happened, believed the bill to have been approved legitimately and gave it royal assent.

HABEAS CORPUS ACT 1679

An act for the better securing the liberty of the subject, and for prevention of imprisonments beyond the seas.

WHEREAS great delays have been used by sheriffs, gaolers and other officers, to whose custody, any of the King's subjects have been committed for criminal or supposed criminal matters, in making returns of writs of habeas corpus to them directed, by standing out an alias and pluries habeas corpus, and sometimes more, and by other shifts to avoid their yielding obedience to such writs, contrary to their duty and the known laws of the land, whereby many of the King's subjects have been and hereafter may be long detained in prison, in such cases where by law they are bailable, to their great charges and vexation.

II. For the prevention whereof, and the more speedy relief of all persons imprisoned for any such criminal or supposed criminal matters;

2) be it enacted by the King's most excellent majesty, by and with the advice and consent of the lords spiritual and temporal, and commons, in this present parliament assembled, and by the authority thereof. That whensoever any person or persons shall bring any habeas corpus directed unto any sheriff or sheriffs, gaoler, minister or other person whatsoever, for any person in his or their custody, and the said writ shall be served upon the said officer, or left at the gaol or prison with any of the under-officers, under-keepers or deputy of the said officers or keepers, that the said officer or officers, his or their under-officers, under-keepers or deputies, shall within three days after the service thereof as aforesaid (unless the commitment aforesaid were for treason or felony, plainly and specially expressed in the warrant of commitment) make return of such writ;

3) and bring or cause to be brought the body of the party so committed or restrained, unto or before the lord chancellor, or lord keeper of the great seal of England for the time being, or the judges or barons of the said court from which the said writ shall issue, or unto and before such other person or persons before whom the said writ is made returnable, according to the command thereof;

4) and shall then likewise certify the true causes of his detainer or imprisonment, unless the commitment of the said party be in any place beyond the distance of twenty miles from the place or places where such court or person is or shall be residing; and if beyond the distance of twenty miles, and not above one hundred miles, then within the space of ten days, and if beyond the distance of one hundred miles, then within the space of twenty days, after such delivery aforesaid, and not longer.

III. And to the intent that no sheriff, gaoler or other officer may pretend ignorance of the import of such writ.

2) be it enacted by the authority aforesaid, That all such writs shall be marked in this manner, Per statutum tricesimo primo Caroli secundi Regis, and shall be signed by the person that awards the same;

3) and if any person or persons shall be or stand committed or detained as aforesaid, for any crime, unless for felony or treason plainly expressed in the warrant of commitment, in the vacation-time, and out of term, it shall and may be lawful to and for the person or persons so committed or detained (other than persons convict or in execution of legal process) or any one on his or their behalf, to appeal or complain to the lord chancellor or lord keeper, or any one of his Majesty's justices;

4) and the said lord chancellor, lord keeper, justices or barons or any of them, upon view of the copy or copies of the warrant or warrants of commitment and detainer, upon request made in writing by such person or persons, or any on his, her, or their behalf, attested and subscribed by two witnesses who were present at the delivery of the same, to award and grant an habeas corpus under the seal of such court whereof he shall then be one of the judges,

5) to be directed to the officer or officers in whose custody the party so committed or detained shall be, returnable immediate before the said lord chancellor or lord keeper or such justice, baron or any other justice or baron of the degree of the coif of any of the said courts;

6) and upon service thereof as aforesaid, the officer or officers, his or their under-officer or under-officers, under-keeper or under-keepers, or their deputy in whose custody the party is so committed or detained, shall within the times respectively before limited, bring such prisoner or prisoners before the said lord chancellor or lord keeper, or such justices, barons or one of them,

7) and thereupon within two days after the party shall be brought before them, the said lord chancellor or lord keeper, or such justice or baron before whom the prisoner shall be brought as aforesaid, shall discharge the said prisoner from his imprisonment, taking his or their recognizance, with one or more surety or sureties, in any sum according to their discretions, having regard to the quality of the prisoner and nature of the offence, for his or their

appearance in the court of the King's bench the term following, or at the next assizes, sessions or general gaol-delivery of and for such county, city or place where the commitment was, or where the offence was committed, or in such other court where the said offence is properly cognizable,

8) unless it shall appear unto the said lord chancellor or lord keeper or justice or justices, or baron or barons, that the party so committed is detained upon a legal process, order or warrant, for such matters or offences for the which by the law the prisoner is not bailable.

Although the Act was subsequently amended a number of times, and despite its dubious origins, it remains a cornerstone of individual rights and has inspired similar legislation in many other countries.

1689

'THE BEST MEANS FOR VINDICATING AND ASSERTING THEIR ANCIENT RIGHTS AND LIBERTIES'

James II came to the throne in 1685. His was a short, unhappy reign. His attempts to reassert the primacy of the Catholic Church were fiercely resisted. In July 1688, seven of his leading opponents asked William of Orange – who was James's son-in-law and also nephew – to bring his army from Holland to overthrow James. William landed at Brixham, Devon, in November, and James's forces quickly collapsed. By the end of the year, James had fled. Initially, Parliament offered the throne to Mary, James's daughter. She refused to reign alone, so, for the first and only time, Britain had a job-sharing husband-and-wife monarchy in William and Mary.

In December 1689, Parliament passed the Bill of Rights, which limited the powers of the monarchy. William was unhappy, but had little choice but to accept it. The Bill set out the basic rights of people and Parliament. It also barred Catholics from holding any power as monarch, royal aide or parliamentarian.

THE BILL OF RIGHTS: AN ACT DECLARING THE RIGHTS AND LIBERTIES OF THE SUBJECT AND SETTLING THE SUCCESSION OF THE CROWN

Whereas the Lords Spiritual and Temporal and Commons assembled at Westminster, lawfully, fully and freely representing all the estates of the people of this realm, did upon the thirteenth day of February in the year of our Lord one thousand six hundred eighty-eight [old style date] present unto their Majesties, then called and known by the names and style of William and Mary, prince and princess of Orange, being present in their proper persons, a certain declaration in writing made by the said Lords and Commons in the words following, viz.:

Whereas the late King James the Second, by the assistance of divers evil counsellors, judges and ministers employed by him, did endeavour to subvert and extirpate the Protestant religion and the laws and liberties of this kingdom;

By assuming and exercising a power of dispensing with and suspending of laws and the execution of laws without consent of Parliament;

By committing and prosecuting divers worthy prelates for humbly petitioning to be excused from concurring to the said assumed power;

By issuing and causing to be executed a commission under the great seal for erecting a court called the Court of Commissioners for Ecclesiastical Causes;

By levying money for and to the use of the Crown by pretence of prerogative for other time and in other manner than the same was granted by Parliament;

By raising and keeping a standing army within this kingdom in time of peace without consent of Parliament, and quartering soldiers contrary to law;

By causing several good subjects being Protestants to be disarmed at the same time when papists were both armed and employed contrary to law;

By violating the freedom of election of members to serve in Parliament;

By prosecutions in the Court of King's Bench for matters and causes cognizable only in Parliament, and by divers other arbitrary and illegal courses;

And whereas of late years partial corrupt and unqualified persons have been returned and served on juries in trials, and particularly divers jurors in trials for high treason which were not freeholders;

And excessive bail hath been required of persons committed in criminal cases to elude the benefit of the laws made for the liberty of the subjects;

And excessive fines have been imposed;

And illegal and cruel punishments inflicted;

And several grants and promises made of fines and forfeitures before any conviction or judgment against the persons upon whom the same were to be levied;

All which are utterly and directly contrary to the known laws and statutes and freedom of this realm;

And whereas the said late King James the Second having abdicated the government and the throne being thereby vacant, his Highness the prince of Orange (whom it hath pleased Almighty God to make the glorious instrument of delivering this kingdom from popery and arbitrary power) did (by the advice of the Lords Spiritual and Temporal and divers principal persons of the Commons) cause letters to be written to the Lords Spiritual and Temporal being Protestants, and other letters to the several counties, cities, universities, boroughs and cinque ports, for the choosing of such persons to represent them as were of right to be sent to Parliament, to meet and sit at Westminster upon the two and twentieth day of January in this year one thousand six hundred eighty and eight,* in order to such an establishment as that their religion, laws and liberties might not again be in danger of being subverted, upon which letters elections having been accordingly made;

And thereupon the said Lords Spiritual and Temporal and Commons, pursuant to their respective letters and elections, being now assembled in a full and free representative of this nation, taking into their most serious consideration the best means for attaining the ends aforesaid, do in the first place (as their ancestors in like case have usually done) for the vindicating and asserting their ancient rights and liberties declare:

That the pretended power of suspending the laws or the execution of laws by regal authority without consent of Parliament is illegal;

That the pretended power of dispensing with laws or the execution of laws by regal authority, as it hath been assumed and exercised of late, is illegal;

That the commission for erecting the late Court of Commissioners for Ecclesiastical Causes, and all other commissions and courts of like nature, are illegal and pernicious;

That levying money for or to the use of the Crown by pretence of prerogative, without grant of Parliament, for longer time, or in other manner than the same is or shall be granted, is illegal;

That it is the right of the subjects to petition the king, and all commitments and prosecutions for such petitioning are illegal;

That the raising or keeping a standing army within the kingdom in time of peace, unless it be with consent of Parliament, is against law;

That the subjects which are Protestants may have arms for their defence suitable to their conditions and as allowed by law;

That election of members of Parliament ought to be free;

That the freedom of speech and debates or proceedings in Parliament ought not to be impeached or questioned in any court or place out of Parliament;

That excessive bail ought not to be required, nor excessive fines imposed, nor cruel and unusual punishments inflicted;

---

*   1689 according to today's calendar

That jurors ought to be duly impanelled and returned, and jurors which pass upon men in trials for high treason ought to be freeholders;

That all grants and promises of fines and forfeitures of particular persons before conviction are illegal and void;

And that for redress of all grievances, and for the amending, strengthening and preserving of the laws, Parliaments ought to be held frequently.

And whereas it hath been found by experience that it is inconsistent with the safety and welfare of this Protestant kingdom to be governed by a popish prince, or by any king or queen marrying a papist, the said Lords Spiritual and Temporal and Commons do further pray that it may be enacted, that all and every person and persons that is, are or shall be reconciled to or shall hold communion with the see or Church of Rome, or shall profess the popish religion, or shall marry a papist, shall be excluded and be for ever incapable to inherit, possess or enjoy the crown and government of this realm and Ireland and the dominions thereunto belonging or any part of the same, or to have, use or exercise any regal power, authority or jurisdiction within the same;

And every king and queen of this realm who at any time hereafter shall come to and succeed in the imperial crown of this kingdom shall on the first day of the meeting of the first Parliament next after his or her coming to the crown, sitting in his or her throne in the House of Peers in the presence of the Lords and Commons therein assembled, or at his or her coronation before such person or persons who shall administer the coronation oath to him or her at the time of his or her taking the said oath (which shall first happen), make, subscribe and audibly repeat the declaration mentioned in the statute entitled, An Act for the more effectual preserving the king's person and government by disabling papists from sitting in either House of Parliament.

The restrictions on Catholics entering Parliament were removed in the nineteenth century; otherwise the Bill of Rights remains one of the landmark documents in the evolution of British democracy.

And not just British: it influenced James Madison a century later when he formulated a Bill of Rights for the United States, in the form of amendments to its Constitution. Amendment I repeats the defence of freedom of speech and the right of people to petition their rulers. The principles of habeas corpus are evident in Amendment VI, while Amendment VIII repeats Britain's Bill of Rights virtually word for word: 'Excessive bail shall not be required, nor excessive fines imposed, nor cruel and unusual punishments inflicted.' This amendment provoked one of the most famous US legal controversies of the past half century

– whether execution amounted to 'cruel and unusual punishment' and was therefore unconstitutional.

In another case, the US half-adopted the phraseology of 1689, and some Americans have reason to regret that Madison didn't go the whole hog. Whereas Britain's Bill of Rights allowed people (well, Protestants) to 'have arms for their defence suitable to their conditions and as allowed by law', Amendment II to the US Constitution states that 'a well-regulated Militia, being necessary to the security of a free State, the right of the people to keep and bear Arms shall not be infringed'. Fewer Americans might have guns these days had Madison adopted the qualification, 'suitable to their conditions and as allowed by law'.

1690

'Man hath by nature a power to preserve his life, liberty and estate'

John Locke had hinterland. He was a scientist, engineer and philosopher, but he is best remembered for his contribution to democratic theory. For much of the 1680s he lived in exile in Holland, having been branded a traitor for his radical ideas. He returned to England when William and Mary ascended to the throne.

In his most important work, *Two Treatises of Government*, Locke attacked the concept of the divine right of kings, and went on to demolish the notion that government of any kind should have absolute power. Locke argued that 'nature' had made men fundamentally equal; therefore, they had an equal right to determine who governed them; therefore, to be legitimate, a government required the consent of the majority. By accepting the right of the majority to rule, the individual had a right to expect the state to protect his property, and freedom of speech, thought and worship.

John Locke: *The Second Treatise of Civil Government*

Political power, I take to be a right of making laws, with penalties of death, and consequently all less penalties for the regulating and preserving of property, and of employing the force of the community in the execution of such laws, and in the defence of the commonwealth from foreign injury, and all this only for the public good.

To understand political power aright, and derive it from its original, we must consider what estate all men are naturally in, and that is, a state of perfect freedom to order their actions, and dispose of their possessions and persons as they think fit, within the bounds of the law of Nature, without asking leave or depending upon the will of any other man.

A state also of equality, wherein all the power and jurisdiction is reciprocal, no one having more than another, there being nothing more evident than that creatures of the same species and rank, promiscuously born to all the same advantages of Nature, and the use of the same faculties, should also be equal one amongst another, without subordination or subjection, unless the lord and master of them all should, by any manifest declaration of his will, set one above another, and confer on him, by an evident and clear appointment, an undoubted right to dominion and sovereignty.

Man, being born with a title to perfect freedom, and an uncontrolled enjoyment of all the rights and privileges of the law of nature, equally with any other man, or number of men in the world, hath by nature a power, to preserve his property, that is, his life, liberty and estate, against the injuries and attempts of other men. The community comes to be umpire, by settled standing rules, indifferent, and the same to all parties; and by men having authority from the community, for the execution of those rules, decides all the differences that may happen between any members of that society concerning any matter of right; and punishes those offences which any member hath committed against the society.

Men being, by nature, all free, equal, and independent, no one can be put out of this estate, and subjected to the political power of another, without his own consent. The only way whereby any one divests himself of his natural liberty, and puts on the bonds of civil society, is by agreeing with other men to join and unite into a community for their comfortable, safe, and peaceable living one amongst another, in a secure enjoyment of their properties, and a greater security against any, that are not of it. This any number of men may do, because it injures not the freedom of the rest; they are left as they were in the liberty of the state of nature. When any number of men have so consented to make one community or government, they are thereby presently incorporated, and make one body politic, wherein the majority have a right to act and conclude the rest.

For when any number of men have, by the consent of every individual, made a community, they have thereby made that community one body, with a power to act as one body, which is only by the will and determination of the majority: for that which acts any community, being only the consent of the individuals of it, and it being necessary to that which is one body to move one way; it is necessary the body should move that way whither the greater force carries it, which is the consent of the majority: or else it is impossible it should act or continue one body, one community, which the consent of every individual that united into it, agreed that it should; and so every one is bound by that consent to be concluded by the majority. And therefore we see, that in assemblies, empowered to act by positive laws, where no number is set by that positive law which empowers them, the act of the majority passes for the act of the whole, and of course determines, as having, by the law of nature and reason, the power of the whole.

And thus every man, by consenting with others to make one body politic under one government, puts himself under an obligation, to every one of that society, to submit to the determination of the majority, and to be concluded by it; or else this original compact, whereby he with others incorporates into one society, would signify nothing, and be no compact, if he be left free, and under no other ties than he was in before in the state of nature.

Whosoever therefore out of a state of nature unite into a community, must be understood to give up all the power, necessary to the ends for which they unite into society, to the majority of the community, unless they expressly agreed in any number greater than the majority. And this is done by barely agreeing to unite into one political society, which is all the compact that is, or needs be, between the individuals, that enter into, or make up a commonwealth. And thus that, which begins and actually constitutes any political society, is nothing but the consent of any number of freemen capable of a majority to unite and incorporate into such a society. And this is that, and that only, which did, or could give beginning to any lawful government in the world.

Every man being, as has been shown, naturally free, and nothing being able to put him into subjection to any earthly power, but only his own consent; it is to be considered, what shall be understood to be a sufficient declaration of a man's consent, to make him subject to the laws of any government. There is a common distinction of an express and a tacit consent, which will concern our present case. Nobody doubts but an express consent, of any man entering into any society, makes him a perfect member of that society, a subject of that government.

The difficulty is, what ought to be looked upon as a tacit consent, and how far it binds, i.e. how far any one shall be looked on to have consented, and thereby submitted to any government, where he has made no expressions of it at all. And to this I say, that every man, that hath any possessions, or enjoyment, of any part of the dominions of any government, doth thereby give his tacit consent, and is as far forth obliged to obedience to the laws of that government, during such enjoyment, as any one under it; whether this his possession be of land, to him and his heirs for ever, or a lodging only for a week; or whether it be barely travelling freely on the highway; and in effect, it reaches as far as the very being of any one within the territories of that government.

◇ ◇ ◇

As did the Bill of Rights, Locke influenced democratic ideas in many countries. The opening words of the United States' Declaration of Independence clearly echo his thinking: 'We hold these truths to be self-evident, that all men are created equal, that they are endowed by their Creator with certain unalienable Rights, that among these are Life, Liberty and the pursuit of Happiness.'

1695

'A VOTE WHICH HAS DONE MORE FOR LIBERTY AND FOR CIVILISATION THAN THE MAGNA CARTA OR THE BILL OF RIGHTS'

In the decades leading up to the 1690s, all publications had first to be cleared by the Stationers' Company. By this time, there was growing dissatisfaction with the way censorship operated – partly to do with the principle of free speech, but also to do with the perception that the Stationers' Company was abusing its monopoly for commercial ends. Parliament abolished censorship by deciding not to renew the Licensing Act. More than a century later, in *The History of England*, Thomas Macaulay wrote that this was 'a vote which has done more for liberty and for civilisation than the Magna Carta or the Bill of Rights'.

THE HOUSE OF COMMONS' RESOLUTIONS ON THE LICENSING BILL

The commons cannot agree to the clause marked A:

1. Because it revives and re-enacts a law which in no wise answered the end for which it was made, the title and preamble of that act being to prevent printing seditious and treasonable books, pamphlets, and papers; but there is no penalty appointed for offenders therein, they being left to be punished at common law, as they may be without that act; whereas there are great and grievous penalties imposed by that act for matters wherein neither church nor state is any ways concerned.

2. Because that act gives a property in books to such persons as such books are, or shall be, granted to by letters patents, whether the crown had or shall have any right to grant the same, or not, at the time of such grant.

3. Because that act prohibits printing anything before entry thereof in the register of the Company of Stationers, except proclamations, acts of parliament, and such books as shall be appointed under the sign-manual, or under the hand of a principal secretary of state; whereby both houses of parliament are disabled to order anything to be printed, and the said company are empowered to hinder the printing all innocent and useful books and have an opportunity to enter a title to themselves and their friends for what belongs to and is the labour and right of others.

4. Because that act prohibits any books to be imported without special licence into any port in England, except London; by which means the whole foreign trade of books is restrained to London, unless the lord archbishop of Canterbury, or the lord bishop of London shall, in interruption of their more important affairs in governing the church, bestow their time gratis in looking over catalogues of books and granting licences; whereas the commons think the other ports of the kingdom have as good right as London to trade in books, as well as other merchandises.

5. Because that act leaves it in the power either of the Company of Stationers, or of the archbishop of Canterbury and bishop of London, to hinder any books from being imported, even into the port of London; for if one or more of the Company of Stationers will not come to the custom-house, or that those reverend bishops shall not appoint any learned man to go thither and be present at the opening and viewing books imported, the custom-house officer is obliged to detain them.

6. Because that act appoints no time wherein the archbishop or bishop of London shall appoint a learned man, or that one or more of the Company of Stationers shall go to the custom-house to view imported books; so that they or either of them may delay it till the importer may be undone by having so great a part of his stock lie dead, or the books, if wet, may rot and perish.

7. Because that act prohibits any custom-house officer, under the penalty of losing his office, to open any packet wherein are books until some or one of the Company of Stationers, and such learned man as shall be so appointed, are present; which is impracticable, since he cannot know there are books until he has opened the packet.

8. Because that act confirms all patents of books granted and to be granted —whereby the sole printing of all or most of the classic authors are and have been for many years past, together with a great number of the best books and of most general use, monopolized by the Company of Stationers—and prohibits the importing any such books from beyond sea; whereby the scholars in this kingdom are forced, not only to buy them at the extravagant price they demand, but must be content with their ill and incorrect editions and cannot have the more correct copies which are published abroad, nor the useful notes of foreigners or other learned men upon them.

9. Because that act prohibits anything to be printed till licensed, and yet does not direct what shall be taken by the licenser for such licence; by colour whereof great oppression may be and has been practised.

10. Because that act restrains men bred up in the trade of printing and founding of letters from exercising their trade, even in an innocent and inoffensive way, though they are freemen of the Company of Stationers, either as masters or journeymen—the number of workmen in each of those trades being limited by that act.

11. Because that act compels master-printers to take journeymen into their service, though they have no work or employment for them.

12. Because that act restrains all men who are not licensed by the bishop from selling innocent and inoffensive books, though never so useful, in any part of England, except freemen of the Company of Stationers, who may sell without such licence; so that neither church nor state is taken care of thereby, but the people compelled to buy their freedom of trade in all parts of England from the Company of Stationers in London.

13. Because that act prohibits any one, not only to print books whereof another has entered a claim of property in the register of the Company of Stationers, but to bind, stitch, or put them to sale—and that under a great pecuniary penalty, though it is impossible for a bookbinder, stitcher, or seller to know whether the book brought to him were printed by the proprietor or another.

14. Because that act prohibits smiths to make any ironwork for any printing-press without giving notice to . . . [the] Company of Stationers, under the penalty of £5; whereas he may not know to what use the iron bespoke of him, and forged by him, may be put.

15. Because that act prohibits printing and importing, not only heretical, seditious, and schismatical books, but all offensive books, and doth not determine what shall be adjudged offensive books; so that, without doubt, if the late King James had continued in the throne till this time, books against popery would not have been deemed offensive books.

16. Because that act subjects all men's houses—as well peers' as commoners'—to be searched at any time, either by day or night, by a warrant under the sign-manual, or under the hand of one of the secretaries of state, directed to any messenger, if such messenger shall, upon probable reason, suspect that there are any unlicensed books there; and the houses of all persons free of the Company of Stationers are subject to the like search on a warrant from the master and wardens of the said company or any one of them.

17. Because the penalties for offences against that act are excessive—it being in the power of the judges or justices of the peace to inflict what punishment they please, not extending to life or member.

Within ten years, a range of new newspapers started publication in London and other cities. Literature, dissent and satire all flourished, too. They were constrained by laws punishing sedition; but, crucially, these laws applied after publication: pre-publication censorship had gone.

1701

'A TRUE-BORN ENGLISHMAN'S A CONTRADICTION, IN SPEECH AN IRONY, IN FACT A FICTION'

By his own account, the author of *Robinson Crusoe* and *Moll Flanders* made and lost a fortune at least 13 times. Daniel Defoe's true family name was Foe; he added the 'De' at the beginning to sound more aristocratic. As well as being erratically successful in trade, manufacturing and insurance, he was an active and sometimes impulsive Protestant Dissenter. He joined an ill-fated rebellion against James II and later became a fervent admirer of William III.

In 1701, Defoe responded to attacks on William as a 'foreign' king by writing a sharp satire on the notion that the English can claim superiority based on racial purity. As this extract shows, its basic message is as relevant today as it was 300 years ago.

DANIEL DEFOE: *THE TRUE-BORN ENGLISHMAN*

WHEREVER God erects a house of prayer,
The Devil always builds a chapel there:
And 'twill be found upon examination,
The latter has the largest congregation:
For ever since he first debauched the mind,
He made a perfect conquest of mankind.
With uniformity of service, he
Reigns with a general aristocracy.
No non-conforming sects disturb his reign,
For of his yoke there's very few complain.
He knows the genius and the inclination,
And matches proper sins for every nation.

. . .

Satire, be kind, and draw a silent veil
Thy native England's vices to conceal;
Or, if that task's impossible to do,
At least be just, and show her virtues too—
Too great the first; alas, the last too few!

. . .

The Romans first with Julius Caesar came,
Including all the nations of that name,
Gauls, Greeks, and Lombards, and, by computation,
Auxiliaries or slaves of every nation.
With Hengist, Saxons; Danes with Sueno came,
In search of plunder, not in search of fame.
Scots, Picts, and Irish from the Hibernian shore,
And conquering William brought the Normans o'er.
All these their barbarous offspring left behind,
The dregs of armies, they of all mankind;
Blended with Britons, who before were here,
Of whom the Welsh ha' blessed the character.
From this amphibious ill-born mob began
That vain ill-natured thing, an Englishman.
The customs, surnames, languages, and manners
Of all these nations are their own explainers:
Whose relics are so lasting and so strong,
They ha' left a shibboleth upon our tongue,
By which with easy search you may distinguish
Your Roman-Saxon-Danish-Norman English.

. . .

Thus from a mixture of all kinds began,
That het'rogeneous thing, an Englishman:
In eager rapes, and furious lust begot,
Betwixt a painted Britain and a Scot.
Whose gend'ring off-spring quickly learn'd to bow,
And yoke their heifers to the Roman plough:
From whence a mongrel half-bred race there came,
With neither name, nor nation, speech nor fame.

In whose hot veins new mixtures quickly ran,
Infus'd betwixt a Saxon and a Dane;
While their rank daughters, to their parents just,
Receiv'd all nations with promiscuous lust.
This nauseous brood directly did contain
The well-extracted blood of Englishmen.
Which medly canton'd in a Heptarchy,
A rhapsody of nations to supply,
Among themselves maintain'd eternal wars,
And still the ladies lov'd the conquerors.
The western Angles all the rest subdu'd;
A bloody nation, barbarous and rude:
Who by the tenure of the sword possest
One part of Britain, and subdu'd the rest
And as great things denominate the small,
The conqu'ring part gave title to the whole;
The Scot, Pict, Britain, Roman, Dane, submit,
And with the English-Saxon all unite:
And these the mixture have so close pursu'd,
The very name and memory's subdu'd:
No Roman now, no Britain does remain;
Wales strove to separate, but strove in vain:
The silent nations undistinguish'd fall,
And Englishman's the common name for all.
Fate jumbled them together, God knows how;
What e'er they were, they're true-born English now.
The wonder which remains is at our pride,
To value that which all wise men deride.
For Englishmen to boast of generation,
Cancels their knowledge, and lampoons the nation.
A true-born Englishman's a contradiction,
In speech an irony, in fact a fiction;
A banter made to be a test of fools,
Which those that use it justly ridicules.
A metaphor invented to express
A man a-kin to all the universe.
For as the Scots, as learned men ha' said,
Throughout the world their wand'ring seed ha' spread;
So open-handed England, 'tis believ'd,

Has all the gleanings of the world receiv'd.
Some think of England 'twas our Saviour meant,
The Gospel should to all the world be sent:
Since, when the blessed sound did hither reach,
They to all nations might be said to preach.
'Tis well that virtue gives nobility,
How shall we else the want of birth and blood supply?
Since scarce one family is left alive,
Which does not from some foreigner derive.

The following year, Defoe landed in trouble by writing an even more savage satire, which mocked by exaggeration ways in which High Church Tories might destroy their opponents. For example:

DANIEL DEFOE: *THE SHORTEST WAY WITH DISSENTERS*

If it be a crime of the highest consequence, both against the peace and welfare of the nation, the Glory of God, the good of the Church, and the happiness of the soul: let us rank it among capital offences! And let it receive punishment in proportion to it! We hang men for trifles, and banish them for things not worth naming; but that an offence against God and the Church, against the welfare of the World, and the dignity of Religion shall be bought off for Five Shillings: this is such a shame to a Christian Government, that it is with regret I transmit it to posterity. If men sin against God, affront His ordinances, rebel against His Church, and disobey the precepts of their superiors; let them suffer, as such capital crimes deserve! So will Religion flourish, and this divided nation be once again united.

Neither adherents of the established Church nor Defoe's fellow Dissenters thought this particularly funny. Defoe was charged with seditious libel and, despite pleading guilty in the hope of leniency, ended up in Newgate Prison. He secured his release by doing a deal with Robert Harley, the Speaker of the House of Commons. Defoe agreed to work for Harley as a pamphleteer and spy – though his espionage involved mainly tapping informally into public opinion and privately reporting back.

1701

'Whosoever shall come to the possession of this Crown, shall join in communion with the Church of England'

The death of a child led to an Act that changed the succession to the Crown. Since Mary's death in 1694, William had been the sole monarch. They had no children. Under the Bill of Rights, William's successor would be Mary's sister, Anne. However, only one of Anne's five children lived beyond his second birthday – and he died in 1700, when he was just eleven. As Anne had no other surviving children, there would be no obvious successor to her when she eventually died.

The Act of Settlement, which became law in June 1701, decreed that, after Anne, the next monarch would be Electress Sophia of Hanover, a granddaughter of James I and niece of Charles I; and after her, those descendants who were (a) Protestant and (b) not married to a Catholic. As well as sorting out the succession, the Act tidied up the way England was governed. It barred foreigners from becoming Members of Parliament; protected judges from dismissal, except by a formal decision by Parliament; and barred MPs from being employed by, or having a pension from, the Crown. (This last provision was designed to prevent monarchs buying influence in Parliament.)

Act of Settlement 1701

Whereas in the first year of the reign of Your Majesty, and of our late most gracious sovereign lady Queen Mary (of blessed memory), an Act of Parliament was made, entitled, 'An Act for declaring the rights and liberties of the subject, and for settling the succession of the crown,' wherein it was (amongst other things) enacted, established, and declared that the crown and regal government of the Kingdoms of England, France, and Ireland, and the dominions thereunto belonging, should be and continue to Your Majesty and the said late Queen, during the joint lives of Your Majesty and the said Queen, and to the survivor: and that after the decease of Your Majesty and of the said Queen, the said Crown and regal government should be and remain to the heirs of the body of the said late Queen; and for default of such issue, to Her Royal Highness the Princess Anne of Denmark, and the heirs of her body; and for default of such issue to the heirs of the body of Your Majesty.

And it was thereby further enacted, that all and every person and persons that then were, or afterwards should be reconciled to, or shall hold communion with the see or Church of Rome, or should profess the popish religion, or marry a papist, should be excluded, and are by that Act made for ever incapable to inherit, possess, or enjoy the Crown and government of this realm.

For a further provision of the succession of the Crown in the Protestant line, we Your Majesty's most dutiful and loyal subjects, the Lords Spiritual and Temporal, and Commons, in this present Parliament assembled, do beseech Your Majesty that it may be enacted and declared, and be it enacted and declared by the King's most excellent majesty, by and with the advice and consent of the Lords Spiritual and Temporal, and Commons, in this present Parliament assembled, and by the authority of the same, that the most excellent Princess Sophia, Electress and Duchess Dowager of Hanover, daughter of the most excellent Princess Elizabeth, late Queen of Bohemia, daughter of our late sovereign lord King James the First, of happy memory, be and is hereby declared to be the next in succession, in the Protestant line, to the imperial Crown and dignity of the said Realms of England, France, and Ireland, with the dominions and territories thereunto belonging.

Provided always, and be it hereby enacted, that every King and Queen of this Realm, who shall come to and succeed in the imperial Crown of this Kingdom, by virtue of this act, shall have the coronation oath administered to him, her or them, at their respective coronations, according to the act of Parliament made in the first year of the reign of His Majesty, and the said late Queen Mary, intituled, An act for establishing the coronation oath, and shall make, subscribe, and repeat the declaration in the act first above recited mentioned or referred to, in the manner and form thereby prescribed.

And whereas it is requisite and necessary that some further provision be made for securing our religion, laws and liberties, from and after the death of His Majesty and the Princess Anne of Denmark, and in default of issue of the body of the said Princess, and of His Majesty respectively; be it enacted by the King's most excellent majesty, by and with the advice and consent of the Lords Spiritual and Temporal, and Commons, in Parliament assembled, and by the authority of the same, That whosoever shall hereafter come to the possession of this Crown, shall join in communion with the Church of England, as by law established;

That in case the Crown and imperial dignity of this Realm shall hereafter come to any person, not being a native of this Kingdom of England, this nation be not obliged to engage in any war for the defence of any dominions or territories which do not belong to the Crown of England, without the consent of Parliament;

That no person who shall hereafter come to the possession of this Crown, shall go out of the dominions of England, Scotland, or Ireland, without the consent of Parliament;

That from and after the time that the further limitation by this act shall take effect, all matters and things relating to the well governing of this Kingdom, which are properly cognizable in the Privy Council by the laws and customs of this Realm, shall be translated there, and all resolutions taken thereupon shall be signed by such of the Privy Council as shall advise and consent to the same;

That after the said limitation shall take effect as aforesaid, no person born out of the Kingdoms of England, Scotland, or Ireland, or the dominions thereunto belonging (although he be naturalized or made a denizen, except such as are born of English parents) shall be capable to be of the Privy Council, or a member of either House of Parliament, or to enjoy any office or place of trust, either civil or military, or to have any grant of lands, tenements or hereditaments from the Crown, to himself or to any other or others in trust for him;

That no person who has an office or place of profit under the King, or receives a pension from the Crown, shall be capable of serving as a member of the House of Commons;

That after the said limitation shall take effect as aforesaid, judges commissions be made *quamdiu se bene gesserint*, and their salaries ascertained and established; but upon the address of both Houses of Parliament it may be lawful to remove them;

And whereas the laws of England are the birth-right of the people thereof, and all the Kings and Queens, who shall ascend the throne of this Realm, ought to administer the government of the same according to the said laws, and all their officers and ministers ought to serve them respectively according to the same: the said Lords Spiritual and Temporal, and Commons, do therefore further humbly pray, That all the laws and statutes of this Realm for securing the established religion, and the rights and liberties of the people thereof, and all other laws and statutes of the same now in force, may be ratified and confirmed, and the same are by His Majesty, by and with the advice of the said Lords Spiritual and Temporal, and Commons, and by authority of the same, ratified and confirmed accordingly.

In the event, Electress Sophia of Hanover died before Anne; so when Queen Anne died in 1714, her successor was Sophia's son, who became George I.

Most of the provisions of the 1701 Act remain in force. Today, when an MP wishes to resign from the House of Commons, he or she will usually apply to be either Steward of the Manor of Northstead or Steward of the Chiltern Hundreds: two essentially meaningless titles that are technically 'offices of profit under the crown'. Not for the first time, a constitutional innovation designed to solve one problem (in this case the need to end the monarch's influence with Parliament) has ended up being employed to solve another.

1707

'One Kingdom by the Name of Great Britain'

For a century, the Interregnum apart, England and Scotland had been separate countries with the same monarch. Scotland's Parliament disliked the Act of Settlement and in 1703 voted to choose its own future monarchs. Westminster responded by passing the 1705 Alien Act, which turned Scots into foreign subjects when in England and Wales, and threatened to curb trade with Scotland.

Soon afterwards, discreet negotiations took place. Some Scottish peers, such as the Earl of Glasgow, were bribed with offers of land and money to agree to merge England and Scotland into a single country. Scotland would be allowed to keep its own Church and legal system and in return England's Parliament would vote to give Scottish investors the £398,000 they had lost in an unsuccessful attempt to colonise part of Panama.

All the evidence suggests that most Scots opposed the Union. Posing variously as a fish merchant in Glasgow and a wool manufacturer in Aberdeen, Daniel Defoe reported back to Robert Harley: 'A Scots rabble is the worst of its kind; for every Scot in favour there are ninety-nine against.' However, threats and promises of money counted for more than the popular will. In November 1706, Scotland's Parliament voted for the Union, as Westminster had already done. On 1 May 1707, Great Britain came into being.

Act of Union 1707

Act Ratifying and Approving the Treaty of Union of the Two Kingdoms of SCOTLAND and ENGLAND.

That the Two Kingdoms of Scotland and England shall upon the first day of May next ensuing the date hereof and forever after be United into One Kingdom by the Name of Great Britain And that the Ensigns Armorial of the said United Kingdom be such as Her Majesty shall appoint and the

Crosses of St Andrew and St George be conjoined in such manner as Her Majesty shall think fit and used in all Flags Banners Standards and Ensigns both at Sea and Land.

That the Succession to the Monarchy of the United Kingdom of Great Britain and of the Dominions thereunto belonging after Her Most Sacred Majesty and in default of Issue of Her Majesty be, remain and continue to the Most Excellent Princess Sophia Electress and Duchess Dowager of Hanover and the Heirs of Her body being Protestants upon whom the Crown of England is settled by an Act of Parliament made in England in the twelfth year of the Reign of His late Majesty King William the Third entitled An Act for the further Limitation of the Crown and better securing the Rights and Liberties of the Subject And that all Papists and persons marrying Papists shall be excluded from and for ever incapable to inherit possess or enjoy the Imperial Crown of Great Britain and the Dominions thereunto belonging or any part thereof And in every such case the Crown and Government shall from time to time descend to and be enjoyed by such person being a Protestant as should have inherited and enjoyed the same in case such Papists or person marrying a Papist was naturally dead according to the provision for the Descent of the Crown of England made by another Act of Parliament in England in the first year of the Reign of their late Majesties King William and Queen Mary entitled An Act declaring the Rights and Liberties of the Subject and settling the Succession of the Crown.

That the United Kingdom of Great Britain be Represented by one and the same Parliament to be styled the Parliament of Great Britain.

That all the Subjects of the United Kingdom of Great Britain shall from and after the Union have full Freedom and Intercourse of Trade and Navigation to and from any port or place within the said United Kingdom and the Dominions and Plantations thereunto belonging And that there be a Communication of all other Rights Privileges and Advantages which do or may belong to the Subjects of either Kingdom except where it is otherwise expressly agreed in these Articles.

That all parts of the United Kingdom for ever from and after the Union shall have the same Allowances Encouragements and Drawbacks and be under the same Prohibitions Restrictions and Regulations of Trade and liable to the same Customs and Duties on Import and Export And that the Allowances Encouragements and Drawbacks Prohibitions Restrictions and Regulations of Trade and the Customs and Duties on Import and Export settled in England when the Union commences shall from and after the Union take place throughout the whole United Kingdom.

That all parts of the United Kingdom be for ever from and after the Union liable to the same Excises upon all Excisable Liquors.

That from and after the Union the Coin shall be of the same standard and value throughout the United Kingdom as now in England.

That the Laws concerning Regulation of Trade, Customs and such Excises to which Scotland is by virtue of this Treaty to be liable be the same in Scotland from and after the Union as in England and that all other Laws in use within the Kingdom of Scotland do after the Union and notwithstanding thereof remain in the same force as before (except such as are contrary to or inconsistent with this Treaty) but alterable by the Parliament of Great Britain With this difference betwixt the Laws concerning public Right, Policy and Civil Government and those which concern private Right That the Laws which concern public Right Policy and Civil Government may be made the same throughout the whole United Kingdom but that no alteration be made in Laws which concern private Right except for evident utility of the subjects within Scotland.

That the Court of Session or College of Justice do after the Union and notwithstanding thereof remain in all time coming within Scotland as it is now constituted by the Laws of that Kingdom and with the same Authority and Privileges as before the Union subject nevertheless to such Regulations for the better Administration of Justice as shall be made by the Parliament of Great Britain.

That all heritable Offices, Superiorities, heritable Jurisdictions, Offices for life and Jurisdictions for life be reserved to the Owners thereof as Rights of Property in the same manner as they are now enjoyed by the Laws of Scotland notwithstanding of this Treaty.

That the Rights and Privileges of the Royal Burroughs in Scotland as they now are do Remain entire after the Union and notwithstanding thereof.

That all Peers of Scotland and their successors to their Honours and Dignities shall from and after the Union be Peers of Great Britain and have Rank and Precedence next and immediately after the Peers of the like orders and degrees in England at the time of the Union and before all Peers of Great Britain of the like orders and degrees who may be created after the Union and shall Enjoy all Privileges of Peers as fully as the Peers of England do now or as they or any other Peers of Great Britain may hereafter Enjoy the same.

1726

'THE HIGHEST TAX WAS UPON MEN WHO ARE THE GREATEST FAVOURITES OF THE OTHER SEX'

Like Daniel Defoe, Jonathan Swift was a prolific satirist, as well as being the author of a novel that, in three centuries, has seldom, if ever, been out of print. Unlike Defoe, Swift was a Catholic and a Tory. His best-known work, *Gulliver's Travels*, mocked many of the institutions and ideas of his day from a broadly Tory viewpoint, and also parodied tales of travellers returning from previously undiscovered lands. At the time, Swift said his book was intended 'to vex the world rather than divert it'.

In the extract here, the novel's eponymous traveller, Lemuel Gulliver, observes life in the fictional city of Lagado, which is controlled from above by the tyrannical king of the flying island of Laputa. The word 'Laputa' provides a clue to Swift's purpose in this chapter of the book. In Spanish, *la puta* means 'the whore'; and, two centuries earlier, Martin Luther had famously referred to 'That great whore, Reason'. Swift's brand of satire (like that from the Right in more recent times, such as Peter Simple in the *Daily Telegraph*) is one that does not so much challenge progressive concepts of liberty and democracy head on as mock their possible consequences. Implicitly, such satire challenges supporters of reform to show not only that their ambitions are morally right but also that they are workable in practice – and won't end up doing more harm than good. Swift's target here is a form of reason taken to such extreme lengths that it defies common sense. Swift felt that the Royal Society – which had been founded in 1660 to further scientific discovery and debate – was prone to such failings. In *Gulliver's Travels*, Swift creates the Grand Academy of Lagado as a parody of the Royal Society. Below, Lemuel Gulliver describes what he found there.

JONATHAN SWIFT: *GULLIVER'S TRAVELS*

In the school of political projectors, I was but ill entertained; the professors appearing, in my judgment, wholly out of their senses, which is a scene that never fails to make me melancholy. These unhappy people were proposing schemes for persuading monarchs to choose favourites upon the score of their wisdom, capacity, and virtue; of teaching ministers to consult the public good; of rewarding merit, great abilities, eminent services; of instructing princes to know their true interest, by placing it on the same foundation with that of their people; of choosing for employments persons qualified to exercise them, with many other wild, impossible chimeras, that never entered before into the heart of man to conceive.

But, however, I shall so far do justice to this part of the Academy, as to acknowledge that all of them were not so visionary. There was a most ingenious doctor, who seemed to be perfectly versed in the whole nature and system of government. It is allowed, that senates and great councils are often troubled with redundant, ebullient, and other peccant humours; with many diseases of the head, and more of the heart; with strong convulsions, with grievous contractions of the nerves and sinews in both hands, but especially the right; with spleen, flatus, vertigos, and deliriums; with scrofulous tumours, full of fetid purulent matter; with sour frothy ructations: with canine appetites, and crudeness of digestion, besides many others, needless to mention.

This doctor therefore proposed, 'that upon the meeting of the senate, certain physicians should attend it the three first days of their sitting, and at the close of each day's debate feel the pulses of every senator; after which, having maturely considered and consulted upon the nature of the several maladies, and the methods of cure, they should on the fourth day return to the senate house, attended by their apothecaries stored with proper medicines; and before the members sat, administer to each of them lenitives, aperitives, abstersives, corrosives, restringents, palliatives, laxatives, cephalalgics, icterics, apophlegmatics, acoustics, as their several cases required; and, according as these medicines should operate, repeat, alter, or omit them, at the next meeting.'

This project could not be of any great expense to the public; and might in my poor opinion, be of much use for the despatch of business, in those countries where senates have any share in the legislative power; beget unanimity, shorten debates, open a few mouths which are now closed, and close many more which are now open; curb the petulancy of the young, and correct the positiveness of the old; rouse the stupid, and damp the pert.

Again because it is a general complaint, that the favourites of princes are troubled with short and weak memories; the same doctor proposed, 'that whoever attended a first minister, after having told his business, with the utmost brevity and in the plainest words, should, at his departure, give the said minister a tweak by the nose, or a kick in the belly, or tread on his corns, or lug him thrice by both ears, or run a pin into his breech; or pinch his arm black and blue, to prevent forgetfulness; and at every levee day, repeat the same operation, till the business were done, or absolutely refused.' He likewise directed, 'that every senator in the great council of a nation, after he had delivered his opinion, and argued in the defence of it, should be obliged to give his vote directly contrary; because if that were done, the result would infallibly terminate in the good of the public.'

When parties in a state are violent, he offered a wonderful contrivance to reconcile them. The method is this: You take a hundred leaders of each party; you dispose them into couples of such whose heads are nearest of a size; then let two nice operators saw off the occiput of each couple at the same time, in such a manner that the brain may be equally divided. Let the occiputs, thus cut off, be interchanged, applying each to the head of his opposite party-man. It seems indeed to be a work that requires some exactness, but the professor assured us, 'that if it were dexterously performed, the cure would be infallible.' For he argued thus: 'that the two half brains being left to debate the matter between themselves within the space of one skull, would soon come to a good understanding, and produce that moderation, as well as regularity of thinking, so much to be wished for in the heads of those, who imagine they come into the world only to watch and govern its motion: and as to the difference of brains, in quantity or quality, among those who are directors in faction, the doctor assured us, from his own knowledge, that 'it was a perfect trifle.'

I heard a very warm debate between two professors, about the most commodious and effectual ways and means of raising money, without grieving the subject. The first affirmed, 'the justest method would be, to lay a certain tax upon vices and folly; and the sum fixed upon every man to be rated, after the fairest manner, by a jury of his neighbours.' The second was of an opinion directly contrary; 'to tax those qualities of body and mind, for which men chiefly value themselves; the rate to be more or less, according to the degrees of excelling; the decision whereof should be left entirely to their own breast.' The highest tax was upon men who are the greatest favourites of the other sex, and the assessments, according to the number and nature of the favours they have received; for which, they are allowed to be their own vouchers. Wit, valour, and politeness, were likewise proposed to be largely taxed, and collected in the same manner, by every person's giving his own word for the quantum of what he possessed.

To keep senators in the interest of the crown, it was proposed that the members should raffle for employment; every man first taking an oath, and giving security, that he would vote for the court, whether he won or not; after which, the losers had, in their turn, the liberty of raffling upon the next vacancy. Thus, hope and expectation would be kept alive; none would complain of broken promises, but impute their disappointments wholly to fortune, whose shoulders are broader and stronger than those of a ministry.

Another professor showed me a large paper of instructions for discovering plots and conspiracies against the government. He advised great statesmen to examine into the diet of all suspected persons; their times of eating; upon which side they lay in bed; with which hand they wipe their posteriors; take a strict view of their excrements, and, from the colour, the odour, the taste, the consistence, the crudeness or maturity of digestion, form a judgment of their thoughts and designs; because men are never so serious, thoughtful, and intent, as when they are at stool, which he found by frequent experiment; for, in such conjunctures, when he used, merely as a trial, to consider which was the best way of murdering the king, his ordure would have a tincture of green; but quite different, when he thought only of raising an insurrection, or burning the metropolis.

Gulliver's Travels was an instant bestseller. The first print run sold out within a week. The poet John Gay wrote to Swift to say that 'it is universally read, from the cabinet council to the nursery'. However, Swift's aim to vex the world was never really fulfilled: it seems certain that most of its many millions of readers down the years have been diverted by it instead.

1738

'No man can be so guarded in his expressions, as to wish to see everything he says in this House in print'

Until the end of the eighteenth century, most parliamentarians believed that their debates should be private. All they normally published were the decisions they took, not the words used or the arguments deployed to reach those decisions. With the flowering of the press in the early decades of the eighteenth century came unofficial accounts of what MPs had actually said. On 13 April 1738, they debated the issue. The Speaker introduced the debate, and most speakers (including Sir Robert Walpole, the prime minister) roundly condemned the newspaper reports. Only one MP, Sir William Windham, took a different tack. He argued not that MPs should allow their views to be known at all times, but that Parliament lacked the power to ban reports published during a parliamentary recess.

The House of Commons debate on the legality of reporting parliamentary speeches

THE SPEAKER informed the House, that it was with some concern he saw a practice prevailing, which a little reflected upon the dignity of that House. What he meant was the inserting an account of their proceedings in the printed newspapers, by which means the proceedings of the House were liable to very great misrepresentations. That he had in his hands a printed newspaper, which contained His Majesty's answer to their late Address, before the same had been reported from the Chair, the only way of communicating it to the public. That he thought it his duty to inform the House of these practices, because he had observed them of late to have run into very great abuses; and therefore he hoped that gentlemen would propose some method of stopping it.

SIR WILLIAM WINDHAM: Sir, no gentleman can be more jealous and tender than I have been of the rights and privileges of this House, nor more ready to concur with any measure for putting a stop to any abuses which might affect either of them. But at the same time, Sir, I think we ought to be very cautious how we form a resolution upon this head; and yet I think it is absolutely necessary that some question should be formed.

I say, Sir, we ought to be very cautious in what manner we form a resolution; for it is a question so nearly connected with the liberty of the press, that it will require a great deal of tenderness to form a resolution, which may preserve gentlemen from having their sense misrepresented to the public, and at the same time guard against all encroachments upon the liberty of the press. On the other hand, Sir, I am sensible that there is a necessity of putting a stop to this practice of printing, what are called speeches of this House, because I know that gentlemen's words in this House have been mistaken and misrepresented. Of late, Sir, I have seen such monstrous mistakes in some gentlemen's speeches, as they have been printed in our newspapers, that it is no wonder if gentlemen think it high time to have a stop put to such a practice.

Yet still, Sir, there are two considerations, which I own weigh very much with me upon this occasion. That this House has a right to prohibit the publication of any of its proceedings during the time we are sitting, is past all doubt. But I am not at all so clear as to the right we may have of preventing any of our proceedings from being printed during our recess. If gentlemen are of the opinion, which I do own I am not, that we have a power to prevent any account of our proceedings and debates from being communicated to the public, even during our recess, then they will no doubt think it very proper to come to a resolution against this practice, and to punish it with a very severe penalty; but if we have no such power, Sir, I own I do not see how you can form any resolution upon this head, that will not be liable to very great censure.

The other consideration that weighs very much, Sir, with me upon this occasion, is the prejudice which the public will think they sustain, by being deprived of all knowledge of what passes in this House, otherwise than by the printed Votes, which are very lame and imperfect, for satisfying the curiosity of knowing in what manner their representatives act within doors. They have been long used to be indulged in this, and they may possibly think it a hardship to be deprived of it now.

Nay, Sir, I must go farther: I do not know but they may have a right to know somewhat more of the proceedings of this House than what appears upon your Votes; and if I were sure that the sentiments of gentlemen were not misrepresented, I should be against our coming to any resolution that could deprive them of a knowledge that is so necessary for their being able to judge of the merits of their representatives within doors.

WILLIAM PULTENEY: It is absolutely necessary a stop should be put to the practice which has been so justly complained of. I think no appeals should be made to the public with regard to what is said in this assembly, and to print or publish the speeches of gentlemen in this House, even though they were not misrepresented, looks very much like making them accountable without doors for what they say within. Besides, Sir, we know very well that no man can be so guarded in his expressions, as to wish to see everything he says in this House in print.

As to the question whether we have a right to punish any printer, who shall publish our proceedings, or any part of them, during our recess, which I take to be the only question at present, it may be worthy of consideration. For my part, I am apt to think that we may, because our privileges as a House of Parliament exist during the whole continuance of parliament; and our not sitting never makes any violation of these privileges committed during a recess less liable to censure, the next time we meet as a House.

However, Sir, as it has been long the practice to print some account of our proceedings during our recess, I am against punishing any person for what is past, because very possibly they did not know they were doing amiss; and if any gentlemen think fit to enter into any resolution for the time to come, I dare say it will be sufficient to deter all offenders in that way.

Windham did not pursue his concerns. The House resolved unanimously that to report the proceedings of the House was 'a notorious breach of privilege of the House', including doing so during a recess. The House also resolved to 'proceed with the utmost severity against such offenders'. To get around the law, some editors used the device of reporting the proceedings of such fictional bodies as the 'Robin Hood Society' and the 'Senate of Magna Lilliputia' (in homage to Swift's Lilliput in *Gulliver's Travels*).

Matters came to a head in 1771, when Brass Crosby, a Radical lawyer who was also Lord Mayor of London at the time, dismissed a case against a printer who had been charged with a breach of parliamentary privilege for publishing reports of what MPs had said. Crosby himself was committed to the Tower of London. But such was the public clamour for his release that a number of judges refused to preside over his trial, the case was dropped and Crosby was freed.

After that, further unofficial accounts started to circulate and nobody was punished. In 1803, Parliament allocated space for reporters in the gallery of the House of Commons. William Cobbett, a sharp and perpetual thorn in the flesh of the Establishment, started publishing *Parliamentary Debates* as supplements to his *Political Register*. In 1812, Cobbett, short of cash following a spell in jail for seditious libel, sold *Parliamentary Debates* to his printer, Thomas Hansard. In 1829, Hansard's own name started appearing on the cover of each report, and, ever since, 'Hansard' has been the name by which the verbatim accounts of Parliament have been known. In 1889, Parliament agreed to subsidise Hansard; and, from 1909, took over publication itself. The journey from total censorship to full disclosure was complete.

1741

'HE HAS MONOPOLIZED ALL THE FAVOURS OF THE CROWN. THIS IS A MOST HEINOUS OFFENCE AGAINST OUR CONSTITUTION'

Sir Robert Walpole is generally regarded as Britain's first prime minister, and he was also its longest serving, occupying the post from 1721 until 1742. His official title was First Lord of the Treasury (the name which still adorns the door of 10 Downing Street, of which Walpole was the first tenant, in 1735).

Walpole had held a number of ministerial posts, starting in 1705. He was First Lord of the Treasury from 1715 to 1717. It was when he was reappointed to this post in 1721 that his two decades as 'prime minister' are regarded as having started. The title 'prime minister' was never used, except abusively, during Walpole's career. He acquired his status because of his relationships with George I (king from 1714–27) and his son, George II (Prince of Wales until 1727, then king until 1760). George I spoke little English, and left the day-to-day running of the government to his ministers. Despite taking the Prince of Wales's side in a family feud with George I, Walpole, a Whig, became the dominant figure in the government after the collapse of the South Sea Company in 1720, which ruined the finances and political careers of a number of his fellow ministers. (Walpole himself had sold his shares at a profit shortly before the South Sea Bubble burst.)

By 1741, Walpole was facing mounting criticism triggered by his failure to keep Britain out of a war with Spain, and also by allegations of corruption. On 13 February 1741, Samuel Sandys, who had formerly been close to Walpole, turned on his ally, accusing him of both corruption and undermining Britain's constitution by behaving as a 'prime minister', when – Sandys argued – ministers should have equal status and not face interference from their colleagues.

The House of Commons debate on the removal of Sir Robert Walpole

SAMUEL SANDYS: I believe, there is not a gentleman of this house, who is not sensible, that both the foreign and domestic measures of our government, for several years past, have been dissatisfactory to a great majority of the nation. I believe, there is not a gentleman in this house, if he will freely declare his sentiments, who is not sensible, that one single person in the administration has not only been thought to be, but has actually been the chief, if not the sole adviser and promoter of all those measures. The discontents, the reproaches, and even the curses of the people, are all directed against that single person. They complain of our present measures; they have suffered by past measures; they expect no redress; they expect no alteration or amendment, whilst he has a share in advising or directing our future.

According to our constitution, we can have no sole and prime minister. We ought always to have several prime ministers or officers of state. Every such officer has his own proper department; and no officer ought to meddle in the affairs belonging to the department of another. But it is publicly known, that this minister having obtained a sole influence over all our public councils, has not only assumed the sole direction of all public affairs, but has got every officer of state removed that would not follow his direction, even in the affairs belonging to his own proper department. By this means he has monopolized all the favours of the crown, and engrossed the sole disposal of all places, pensions, titles, and ribbons, as well as of all preferments, civil, military or ecclesiastical.

This, sir, is of itself a most heinous offence against our constitution; but he has greatly aggravated the heinousness of this crime; for having thus monopolized all the favours of the crown, he has made blind loyalty to him at elections and in parliament, the only ground to hope for any honours or preferments, and the only tenure by which any gentleman could preserve what he had.

Can any gentleman who heard this declaration desire a proof of the minister's misconduct, or of his crimes? Was not this openly avowing one of the most heinous crimes that can be committed by a minister in this kingdom? Was it not avowing that he had made use of the favours of the crown for obtaining a corrupt majority in both houses of parliament, and keeping that majority in a slavish dependence upon himself alone? And shall we allow a minister not only to do, but openly to avow, what he ought to be hanged for, should he advise his sovereign to do? It is by means of this crime, sir, that the minister I am speaking of has obtained the authority or approbation of parliament in every step of his conduct.

Suppose this minister had never been guilty of any crime, error, or oversight in his public conduct; suppose the people had all along been perfectly pleased with his administration, yet the very length of it is, in a free country, sufficient cause for removing him. It is a most dangerous thing in a free government, to allow any man to continue too long in the possession of great power. Most commonwealths have been overturned by this very oversight; and in this country, we know how difficult it has often proved, for our parliament to draw an old favourite from behind the throne, even when he has been guilty of the most heinous crimes.

I wish this may not be our case at present; for though I shall not say that the favourite I am now complaining of has been guilty of heinous crimes, yet I will say, that there is a very general suspicion against him, that this suspicion is justified by the present situation of our affairs both at home and abroad, and that it is ridiculous to expect, that any proper discovery should be made, as long as he is in possession of all the proofs, and has the distribution of all the penalties the crown can inflict, as well as of all the favours the crown can bestow.

Therefore I shall conclude with moving, that an humble address be presented to his majesty, that he would be graciously pleased to remove the right honourable Sir Robert Walpole, Knight of the most noble order of the garter, first commissioner for executing the office of treasurer of the exchequer, chancellor and under-treasurer of the exchequer, and one of his majesty's most honourable privy council, from his majesty's presence and councils for ever.

SIR ROBERT WALPOLE: From whence does this attack proceed? From the passions and prejudices of the parties combined against me, who may be divided into three classes, the Boys, the riper Patriots, and the Tories. The Tories I can easily forgive, they have unwillingly come into the measure, and they do me honour in thinking it necessary to remove me, as their only obstacle. My great and principal crime is my long continuance in office, or, in other words, the long exclusion of those who now complain against me.

Can it be fitting in them, who have divided the public opinion of the nation, to share it with those who now appear as their competitors? With the men of yesterday, the boys in politicks, who would be absolutely contemptible did not their audacity render them detestable? With the mock patriots, whose practice and professions prove their selfishness and malignity, who threatened to pursue me to destruction, and who have never for a moment lost sight of their objects?

Sir, if any one instance had been mentioned, if it had been shown, that I ever offered a reward to any member of either house, or ever threatened to deprive any member of his office or employment, in order to influence his vote in parliament, there might have been some ground for this charge; but when it is so generally laid, I do not know what I can say to it, unless it be to deny it as generally and as positively as it has been asserted; and, thank God! till some proof be offered, I have the laws of the land, as well as the laws of charity in my favour.

Some members of both houses have, it is true, been removed from their employments under the crown; but were they ever told, either by me, or by any other of his majesty's servants, that it was for opposing the measures of the administration in parliament? They were removed, because his majesty did not think fit to continue them longer in his service. Would not this reason be approved of by the whole nation, except those who happen to be the present possessors? I cannot, therefore, see how this can be imputed as a crime, or how any of the king's ministers can be blamed for his doing what the public has no concern in: for if the public be well and faithfully served, it has no business to ask by whom.

Has not tranquillity been preserved both at home and abroad, notwithstanding a most unreasonable and violent opposition? Has the true interest of the nation been pursued, or has trade flourished? Have gentlemen produced one instance of this exorbitant power, of the influence which I extend to all parts of the nation, of the tyranny with which I oppress those who oppose, and the liberality with which I reward those who support me? But having first invested me with a kind of mock dignity, and styled me a prime minister, they impute to me an unpardonable abuse of that chimerical authority which they only have created and conferred.

Let me show them that the crown has made no encroachments, that all supplies have been granted by parliament, that all questions have been debated with the same freedom as before the fatal period, in which my counsels are said to have gained the ascendency. What is this unbounded sole power which is imputed to me? How has it discovered itself, or how has it been proved? What have been the effects of the corruption, ambition, and avarice, with which I am so abundantly charged? Have I given any symptoms of an avaricious disposition? Have I obtained any grants from the crown since I have been placed at the head of the treasury? Has my conduct been different from that which others in the same station would have followed? Have I acted wrong in giving the place of auditor to my son, and in providing for my own family? I trust that their advancement will not be imputed to me as a crime, unless it shall be proved that I placed them in offices of trust and responsibility for which they were unfit.

But while I unequivocally deny that I am sole and prime minister, and that to my influence and direction all the measures of government must be attributed, yet I will not shrink from the responsibility which attaches to the post I have the honour to hold; and should during the long period in which I have sat upon this bench, any one step taken by government be proved to be either disgraceful or disadvantageous to the nation, I am ready to hold myself accountable.

To conclude, sir, though I shall always be proud of the honour of any trust or confidence from his majesty, yet I shall always be ready to remove from his, councils and presence, when he thinks fit. I hope all those that have a due regard for our constitution, and for the rights and prerogatives of the crown, without which our constitution cannot be preserved, will be against this motion.

Walpole survived this assault, but was forced to retire a year later, when he lost a vote of no confidence in the House of Commons. A corruption inquiry was launched into the funding of the secret service during Walpole's premiership, but failed to reach a clear conclusion. Elevated to the House of Lords, Walpole continued, until his death in 1745, to advise the king privately.

Samuel Sandys became Chancellor of the Exchequer and Leader of the House of Commons under Walpole's successor, the Earl of Wilmington, but spent only one year in these posts before losing a power struggle with Henry Pelham, a fellow minister and protégé of Walpole. Sandys accepted a peerage as consolation for losing ministerial office.

The title 'prime minister' eventually came to be accepted as an accurate rather than an abusive description of the post's holder, but it was not formally recognised until 1905. Britain's first 'official' prime minister was Sir Henry Campbell-Bannerman, who held the position from 1905 until 1908.

1741

'RIGHT IS OF TWO KINDS, RIGHT TO POWER AND RIGHT TO PROPERTY'

O pinion is divided between those who think David Hume was one of the most important philosophers ever to write in the English language, and those who think he reigns supreme. An atheist who believed in empiricism and scientific method, he irritated the leaders of both religion and academia. However, his ideas contributed significantly to the Age of Enlightenment.

Though Hume was a Radical in terms of intellectual debate, his conclusions on the best form of political arrangement were more conservative. As his 1741 essay 'Of the First Principles of Government' shows, he believed that people's rights would be protected better by a pragmatic monarchy than by a pure republic – that is, a society in which the people have to approve every measure. However, Hume favoured local pure democracy, where, he argued, people would behave rationally and be less swayed by 'popular currents and tides'.

DAVID HUME: 'OF THE FIRST PRINCIPLES OF GOVERNMENT'

NOTHING appears more surprising to those, who consider human affairs with a philosophical eye, than the ease with which the many are governed by the few; and the implicit submission, with which men resign their own sentiments and passions to those of their rulers. When we enquire by what means this wonder is effected, we shall find, that, as FORCE is always on the side of the governed, the governors have nothing to support them but opinion. It is therefore, on opinion only that government is founded; and this maxim extends to the most despotic and most military governments, as well as to the most free and most popular.

Opinion is of two kinds, to wit, opinion of INTEREST, and opinion of RIGHT. By opinion of interest, I chiefly understand the sense of the general advantage which is reaped from government. When this opinion prevails among the generality of a state, or among those who have the force in their hands, it gives great security to any government.

Right is of two kinds, right to *power* and right to *property*. Upon these three opinions, therefore, of public *interest*, of *right to power*, and of *right to property*, are all governments founded, and all authority of the few over the many. There are indeed other principles, which add force to these, and determine, limit, or alter their operation; such as *self-interest*, *fear*, and *affection*: But still we may assert, that these other principles can have no influence alone, but suppose the antecedent influence of those opinions above-mentioned. They are, therefore, to be esteemed the secondary, not the original principles of government.

For, *first*, as to *self-interest*, by which I mean the expectation of particular rewards, distinct from the general protection which we receive from government, it is evident that the magistrate's authority must be antecedently established. Men naturally look for the greatest favours from their friends and acquaintance; and therefore, the hopes of any considerable number of the state would never centre in any particular set of men, if these men had no other title to magistracy.

The same observation may be extended to the other two principles of *fear* and *affection*. No man would have any reason to *fear* the fury of a tyrant, if he had no authority over any but from fear; since, as a single man, his bodily force can reach but a small way, and all the farther power he possesses must be founded either on our own opinion, or on the presumed opinion of others. And though *affection* to wisdom and virtue in a *sovereign* extends very far, and has great influence; yet he must antecedently be supposed invested with a public character, otherwise the public esteem will serve him in no stead, nor will his virtue have any influence beyond a narrow sphere.

A Government may endure for several ages, though the balance of power, and the balance of property do not coincide. This chiefly happens, where any rank or order of the state has acquired a large share in the property; but from the original constitution of the government, has no share in the power. But where the original constitution allows any share of power, though small, to an order of men, who possess a large share of the property, it is easy for them gradually to stretch their authority, and bring the balance of power to coincide with that of property. This has been the case with the House of Commons in ENGLAND.

Most writers, that have treated of the BRITISH government, have supposed, that, as the lower house represents all the commons of GREAT BRITAIN, its weight in the scale is proportioned to the property and power of all whom it represents. But this principle must not be received as absolutely true. For though the people are apt to attach themselves more to the house of commons, than to any other member of the constitution; that house being chosen by them as their representatives, and as the public guardians of their liberty; yet are there instances where the house has not been followed by the people; as we may particularly observe of the *Tory* house of commons in the reign of king WILLIAM.

Were the members obliged to receive instructions from their constituents, like the DUTCH deputies, this would entirely alter the case; and if such immense power and riches, as those of all the commons of GREAT BRITAIN, were brought into the scale, it is not easy to conceive, that the crown could either influence that multitude of people, or withstand that overbalance of property. It is true, the crown has great influence over the collective body in the elections of members; but were this influence, which at present is only exerted once in seven years, to be employed in bringing over the people to every vote, it would soon be wasted; and no skill, popularity, or revenue, could support it.

I must, therefore, be of opinion, that an alteration in this particular would introduce a total alteration in our government, and would soon reduce it to a pure republic. For though the people, collected in a body like the ROMAN tribes, be quite unfit for government, yet when dispersed in small bodies, they are more susceptible both of reason and order; the force of popular currents and tides is, in a great measure, broken; and the public interest may be pursued with some method and constancy. But it is needless to reason any farther concerning a form of government, which is never likely to have place in GREAT BRITAIN, and which seems not to be the aim of any party amongst us. Let us cherish and improve our ancient government as much as possible, without encouraging a passion for such dangerous novelties.

Much of what Hume wrote makes sense a quarter of a millennium later. Much – but not everything. His essay 'Of National Characters' went through various versions. This is part of a footnote to the 1753 version.

David Hume: 'Of National Characters'

I am apt to suspect the Negroes and in general all the other species of men (for there are four or five different kinds) to be naturally inferior to the whites. There never was a civilized nation of any other complexion than white, nor even any individual eminent either in action or speculation. On the other hand, the most rude and barbarous of the Whites, such as the ancient Germans, the present Tartars, have still something eminent about them, in their valour, form of government, or some other particular. Such a uniform and constant difference could not happen, in so many countries and ages, if nature had not made an original distinction between these breeds of men. Not to mention our colonies, there are Negro slaves dispersed all over Europe, of whom none ever discovered the symptoms of ingenuity; though low people, without education, will start up amongst us, and distinguish themselves in every profession. In Jamaica, indeed, they talk of one Negro as a man of parts and learning; but it is likely he is admired for slender accomplishments, like a parrot who speaks a few words plainly.

Hume's 1777 version omitted the word 'species', and targeted his criticism specifically at Negroes rather than all non-whites. It began: 'I am apt to suspect the Negroes to be naturally inferior to the Whites. There scarcely ever was a civilized nation of that complexion, nor even any individual, eminent either in action or speculation.' Can Hume be acquitted on the grounds that he was merely reflecting the racist mores of the eighteenth century? Not entirely. James Ramsay, one of the campaigners for the abolition of slavery, argued at the time that Hume made his remarks 'without any competent knowledge of the subject. Hume might just as well deny intelligence to those who lacked his own corpulence as to those who lacked his white skin.'

1759

'THEY ARE LED BY AN INVISIBLE HAND'

Like David Hume, his friend and fellow Scot Adam Smith helped to shape the Age of Enlightenment. He is best known for *The Wealth of Nations*, published in 1776. But seventeen years earlier, Smith had already introduced one of his most famous nostrums, concerning the way the 'invisible hand' led the aggregate actions of individuals pursuing their self-interests to benefit society as a whole. In *The Theory of Moral Sentiments*, Smith argued that there is an 'inner man' within each of us that regulates our actions: our imagination and sense of sympathy qualify crude material selfishness. Here Smith links imagination to self-interest, prosperity and the political process.

ADAM SMITH: *THE THEORY OF MORAL SENTIMENTS*

Our imagination, which in pain and sorrow seems to be confined and cooped up within our own persons, in times of ease and prosperity expands itself to every thing around us. We are then charmed with the beauty of that accommodation which reigns in the palaces and economy of the great; and admire how every thing is adapted to promote their ease, to prevent their wants, to gratify their wishes, and to amuse and entertain their most frivolous desires.

If we consider the real satisfaction which all these things are capable of affording, by itself and separated from the beauty of that arrangement which is fitted to promote it, it will always appear in the highest degree contemptible and trifling. But we rarely view it in this abstract and philosophical light. We naturally confound it in our imagination with the order, the regular and harmonious movement of the system, the machine or economy by means of which it is produced. The pleasures of wealth and greatness, when considered in this complex view, strike the imagination as something grand and beautiful and noble, of which the attainment is well worth all the toil and anxiety which we are so apt to bestow upon it.

And it is well that nature imposes upon us in this manner. It is this deception which rouses and keeps in continual motion the industry of mankind. It is this which first prompted them to cultivate the ground, to build houses, to found cities and commonwealths, and to invent and improve all the sciences and arts, which ennoble and embellish human life; which have entirely changed the whole face of the globe, have turned the rude forests of nature into agreeable and fertile plains, and made the trackless and barren ocean a new fund of subsistence, and the great high road of communication to the different nations of the earth.

The earth by these labours of mankind has been obliged to redouble her natural fertility, and to maintain a greater multitude of inhabitants. It is to no purpose, that the proud and unfeeling landlord views his extensive fields, and without a thought for the wants of his brethren, in imagination consumes himself the whole harvest that grows upon them. The homely and vulgar proverb, that the eye is larger than the belly, never was more fully verified than with regard to him. The capacity of his stomach bears no proportion to the immensity of his desires, and will receive no more than that of the meanest peasant. The rest he is obliged to distribute among those, who prepare, in the nicest manner, that little which he himself makes use of, among those who fit up the palace in which this little is to be consumed, among those who provide and keep in order all the different baubles and trinkets, which are employed in the economy of greatness; all of whom thus derive from his luxury and caprice, that share of the necessaries of life, which they would in vain have expected from his humanity or his justice.

The produce of the soil maintains at all times nearly that number of inhabitants which it is capable of maintaining. The rich only select from the heap what is most precious and agreeable. They consume little more than the poor, and in spite of their natural selfishness and rapacity, though they mean only their own conveniency, though the sole end which they propose from the labours of all the thousands whom they employ, be the gratification of their own vain and insatiable desires, they divide with the poor the produce of all their improvements. They are led by an invisible hand to make nearly the same distribution of the necessaries of life, which would have been made, had the earth been divided into equal portions among all its inhabitants, and thus without intending it, without knowing it, advance the interest of the society, and afford means to the multiplication of the species.

When Providence divided the earth among a few lordly masters, it neither forgot nor abandoned those who seemed to have been left out in the partition. These last too enjoy their share of all that it produces. In what constitutes the real happiness of human life, they are in no respect inferior to those who would seem so much above them. In ease of body and peace of mind, all the different ranks of life are nearly upon a level, and the beggar, who suns himself by the side of the highway, possesses that security which kings are fighting for.

The same principle, the same love of system, the same regard to the beauty of order, of art and contrivance, frequently serves to recommend those institutions which tend to promote the public welfare. When a patriot exerts himself for the improvement of any part of the public police, his conduct does not always arise from pure sympathy with the happiness of those who are to reap the benefit of it. It is not commonly from a fellow-feeling with carriers and waggoners that a public-spirited man encourages the mending of high roads. When the legislature establishes premiums and other encouragements to advance the linen or woollen manufactures, its conduct seldom proceeds from pure sympathy with the wearer of cheap or fine cloth, and much less from that with the manufacturer or merchant. The perfection of police, the extension of trade and manufactures, are noble and magnificent objects. The contemplation of them pleases us, and we are interested in whatever can tend to advance them. They make part of the great system of government, and the wheels of the political machine seem to move with more harmony and ease by means of them.

We take pleasure in beholding the perfection of so beautiful and grand a system, and we are uneasy till we remove any obstruction that can in the least disturb or encumber the regularity of its motions. All constitutions of government, however, are valued only in proportion as they tend to promote the happiness of those who live under them. This is their sole use and end. From a certain spirit of system, however, from a certain love of art and contrivance, we sometimes seem to value the means more than the end, and to be eager to promote the happiness of our fellow-creatures, rather from a view to perfect and improve a certain beautiful and orderly system, than from any immediate sense or feeling of what they either suffer or enjoy.

Nothing tends so much to promote public spirit as the study of politics, of the several systems of civil government, their advantages and disadvantages, of the constitution of our own country, its situation, and interest with regard to foreign nations, its commerce, its defence, the disadvantages it labours under, the dangers to which it may be exposed, how to remove the one, and how to guard against the other. Upon this account political disquisitions, if just, and reasonable, and practicable, are of all the works of speculation the most useful. Even the weakest and the worst of them are not altogether without their utility. They serve at least to animate the public passions of men, and rouse them to seek out the means of promoting the happiness of the society.

In *The Wealth of Nations*, Smith expanded on the need for free-market competition and small government. Unlike some laissez-faire enthusiasts today, Smith wanted to employ market forces not to entrench wealth but to disperse it. He railed against monopoly. For him, one of the great dangers of a badly regulated economy was that the social benefits of market competition would not be realised. There would be a widening gap between rich and poor, generated by cartels and reinforced by the wrong kind of government action.

ADAM SMITH: *THE WEALTH OF NATIONS*

Wherever there is great property there is great inequality. For one very rich man there must be at least five hundred poor, and the affluence of the few supposes the indigence of the many. The affluence of the rich excites the indignation of the poor, who are often both driven by want, and prompted by envy, to invade his possessions. It is only under the shelter of the civil magistrate that the owner of that valuable property, which is acquired by the labour of many years, or perhaps of many successive generations, can sleep a single night in security. He is at all times surrounded by unknown enemies, whom, though he never provoked, he can never appease, and from whose injustice he can be protected only by the powerful arm of the civil magistrate continually held up to chastise it. The acquisition of valuable and extensive property, therefore, necessarily requires the establishment of civil government. Where there is no property, or at least none that exceeds the value of two or three days' labour, civil government is not so necessary. Civil government, so far as it is instituted for the security of property, is in reality instituted for the defence of the rich against the poor, or of those who have some property against those who have none at all.

1763-75

'THE MOST ABANDONED INSTANCE OF MINISTERIAL EFFRONTERY EVER ATTEMPTED TO BE IMPOSED ON MANKIND'

John Wilkes was a journalist, politician, prankster, spendthrift and pornographer. He was ugly, courageous, witty, corrupt, popular, promiscuous and Radical. Above all, he was a fervent advocate of liberty. He had no respect for the pompous possessors of power and wealth. On one occasion, the Earl of Sandwich said to him: 'Sir, I do not know whether you will die on the gallows or of the pox.' Wilkes replied: 'That, sir, depends on whether I embrace your principles or your mistress.'

Wilkes became a Whig MP for Aylesbury in 1757. In June 1762, he set up a weekly anti-government campaigning paper: *The North Briton*. Although Wilkes wrote as 'the North Briton', his title was a mock reference to the Tory prime minister, the Earl of Bute, who was Scottish; and it was also a dig at a rival pro-Bute weekly, *The Briton*. In issue no. 45 of *The North Briton*, published on 23 April 1763, just after Bute had resigned as prime minister, Wilkes went further than he had before. The Treaty of Paris had just ended the Seven Years War, which had involved much of Europe. There had been much dispute over how the war was waged, and whether Britain had got as much as it should out of the Treaty of Paris. The imposition of excise duty on cider, to help pay for the war, had been especially unpopular.

Wilkes unleashed his invective against Bute, and also against Bute's successor, George Grenville. Wilkes attacked the way they had written the King's Speech, and accused government ministers of undermining liberty. His words set in train events that affected not only Wilkes himself but also the way Britain was governed: the right to free speech, the use of warrants to arrest suspects and the right of local voters to choose who to represent them in Parliament.

JOHN WILKES: *THE NORTH BRITON*

The Scottish minister has indeed retired. Is his influence at an end – or does he still govern by the wretched tools of his power, who to their indelible infamy, have supported the most odious of his measures, the late ignominious Peace, and the wicked extension of the arbitrary mode of Excise? The NORTH BRITON has been steady in his opposition to a single, insolent, incapable, despotic minister; and is equally ready, in the service of his country, to combat the triple-headed serpent-like administration, if the Scot is to assume that motley form. By him every arrangement to this hour has been made, and the notification has been as regularly sent by letter under his hand. It therefore seems clear that he intends only to retire into that situation, which he held before he first took the seals; I mean the dictating to every part of the king's administration.

The King's Speech has always been considered by the legislature, and by the public at large, as the Speech of the [Prime] Minister. It has regularly, at the beginning of every session of parliament, been referred by both houses to the consideration of a committee, and has been generally canvassed with the utmost freedom, when the minister of the crown has been obnoxious to the nation. The ministers of this free country, conscious of the undoubted privileges of so spirited a people, and with the terrors of parliament before their eyes, have ever been cautious, no less with regard to the matter, than to the expressions of speeches, which they have advised the sovereign to make from the throne, at the opening of each session. They well knew that an honest house of parliament, true to their trust, could not fail to detect the fallacious arts, or to remonstrate against the daring acts of violence committed by any minister.

This week has given the public the most abandoned instance of ministerial effrontery ever attempted to be imposed on mankind. The [new Prime Minister's] speech [delivered by the King] last Tuesday is not to be paralleled in the annals of this country. I am in doubt, whether the imposition is greater on the sovereign or on the nation. Every friend of his country must lament that a prince of so many great and amiable qualities, whom England truly reveres, can be brought to give the sanction of his sacred name to the most odious measures, and to the most unjustifiable public declarations, from a throne ever renowned for truth, honour, and unsullied virtue.

I am sure all foreigners, especially the King of Prussia, will hold the Minister in contempt and abhorrence. He has made our Sovereign declare 'My expectations have been fully answered by the happy effects which the several allies of my crown have derived from the salutary measure of the definitive treaty. The powers at war with my good brother the King of Prussia, have been induced to agree to such terms of accommodation, as that great prince has approved; and the success which has attended my negotiation has necessarily and immediately diffused the blessings of peace through every part of Europe.' The infamous fallacy of the whole sentence is apparent to all mankind: for it is known that the King of Prussia did not barely approve, but absolutely dictated, as conqueror, every article of the terms of peace. No advantage of any kind has accrued to that magnanimous prince from our negotiation, but he was basely deserted by the Scottish Prime Minister of England.

A despotic minister will always endeavour to dazzle his prince with high-flown ideas of the prerogative and honour of the crown, which the minister will make a parade of firmly maintaining. I wish as much as any man in the kingdom to see the honour of the crown maintained in a manner truly becoming Royalty. I lament to see it sunk even to prostitution. What a shame was it to see the security of this country in point of military force, complimented away, contrary to the opinion of Royalty itself, and sacrificed to the prejudices and to the ignorance of a set of people, the most unfit, from every consideration, to be consulted on a matter relative to the security of the house of Hanover!

The King of England is only the first magistrate of this country; but is invested by the law with the whole executive power. He is, however, responsible to his people for the due execution of the royal functions, in the choice of ministers, &c. equal with the meanest of his subjects in his particular duty. The personal character of our present amiable sovereign makes us easy and happy that so great a power is lodged in such hands; but the favourite has given too just cause for him to escape the general odium. The prerogative of the crown is to exert the constitutional powers entrusted to it in a way, not of blind favour and partiality, but of wisdom and judgment. This is the spirit of our constitution. The people too have their prerogative, and, I hope, the fine words of DRYDEN will be engraved on our hearts: 'Freedom is the English subject's prerogative.'

On 30 April, Grenville's government issued a 'general warrant' – that is, one that did not name a specific person – for the arrest of 'the authors, printers and publishers of a seditious and treasonable paper, entitled *The North Briton*'. Wilkes and 48 others were arrested. Wilkes managed to secure his freedom on the basis that his arrest was a breach of parliamentary privilege.

Wilkes continued to apply his notion of freedom to the limit. He wrote *An Essay on Women*, an obscene parody of Alexander Pope's *An Essay on Man*. For example, where Pope had written:

> O blindness to the future! kindly given,
> That each may fill the circle marked by Heaven

Wilkes wrote:

> O blindness to the future! kindly given
> That each may enjoy what fucks are marked in Heaven:

The House of Lords voted Wilkes's words as a libel and breach of privilege. Meanwhile, MPs declared issue no. 45 of *The North Briton* as a seditious libel. Wilkes added to the growing chargesheet by taking place in an illegal duel. He avoided further arrest by fleeing to Paris. Wilkes was tried for sedition in his absence and found guilty. On 19 January 1764, he was declared an outlaw.

However, his actions secured one major reform. Two prominent jurists, Lord Camden and Lord Mansfield, ruled that general warrants were 'illegal and void'. Ever since then, arrest warrants have had to name specific suspects.

Wilkes returned to Britain in 1768, fleeing this time from his French creditors. The government, not wishing to inflame his supporters, held back from ordering his arrest. So, although he was formally an outlaw, he was free to stand for Parliament, and was elected as MP for Middlesex, whereupon he surrendered to authorities and went to prison. In February 1769, he was expelled from Parliament, but fought and won the subsequent by-election. He was expelled again in March – and again re-elected. After his third election victory, in April, his defeated opponent, Henry Luttrell, was declared the new MP.

In a debate in the House of Lords, on 9 January 1770, the Earl of Chatham (William Pitt, or Pitt the Elder, as he is more commonly known), the leader of Whig opposition, attacked the House of Commons for repeatedly overturning the decisions of the voters in Middlesex.

WILLIAM PITT'S SPEECH CALLING FOR WILKES TO BE READMITTED TO THE HOUSE OF COMMONS

> We all know what the Constitution is. We all know that the first principle of it is, that the subject shall not be governed by the arbitrium of any one man or body of men, but by certain laws, to which he has virtually given his consent, which are open to him to examine, and not beyond his ability

to understand. Now, my Lords, I affirm, and am ready to maintain, that the late decision of the House of Commons upon the Middlesex election is destitute of every one of those properties and conditions which I hold to be essential to the legality of such a decision.

It is to your ancestors, my Lords, it is to the English barons, that we are indebted for the laws and Constitution we possess. Their virtues were rude and uncultivated, but they were great and sincere. Their understandings were as little polished as their manners, but they had hearts to distinguish right from wrong; they had heads to distinguish truth from falsehood; they understood the rights of humanity, and they had spirit to maintain them.

My Lords, I think that history has not done justice to their conduct, when they obtained from their sovereign that great acknowledgment of national rights contained in Magna Carta: they did not confine it to themselves alone, but delivered it as a common blessing to the whole people.

Great pains have been taken to alarm us with the consequences of a difference between the two houses of Parliament; that the House of Commons will resent our presuming to take notice of their proceedings; that they will resent our daring to advise the Crown, and never forgive us for attempting to save the state. My Lords, I am sensible of the importance and difficulty of this great crisis: at a moment such as this, we are called upon to do our duty, without dreading the resentment of any man. But if apprehensions of this kind are to affect us, let us consider which we ought to respect most, the representative or the collective body of the people. My Lords, five hundred gentlemen are not ten millions; and if we must have a contention, let us take care to have the English nation on our side. The kingdom is in a flame. As mediators between the King and people, it is our duty to represent to him the true condition and temper of his subjects.

My Lords, the character and circumstances of Mr. Wilkes have been very improperly introduced into this question, not only here, but in the House of Commons. With one party he was a patriot of the first magnitude; with the other, the vilest incendiary. For my own part, I consider him merely and indifferently as an English subject, possessed of certain rights which the laws have given him, and which the laws alone can take from him. I am neither moved by his private vices nor by his public merits. In his person, though he were the worst of men, I contend for the safety and security of the best. God forbid, my Lords, that there should be a power in this country of measuring the civil rights of the subject by his moral character, or by any other rule but the fixed laws of the land! I am not now pleading the cause of an individual, but of every freeholder in England. In what manner this House may constitutionally interpose in their defence, and what kind of redress this case will require and admit of, is not at present the subject of our consideration. The amendment, if agreed to, will naturally lead us to such an inquiry.

It is not impossible that the inquiry I speak of may lead us to advise his Majesty to dissolve the present Parliament. His Majesty will then determine whether he will yield to the united petitions of the people of England, or maintain the House of Commons in the exercise of a legislative power, which heretofore abolished the House of Lords, and overturned the monarchy. I willingly acquit the present House of Commons of having actually formed so detestable a design; but they cannot themselves foresee to what excesses they may be carried hereafter; and, for my own part, I should be sorry to trust to their future moderation. Unlimited power is apt to corrupt the minds of those who possess it; and this I know, my Lords, that where law ends, tyranny begins!

In 1774, Wilkes was once again elected MP for Middlesex. This time he was allowed to take his seat. In February 1775, he moved that the decision in February 1769 to expel him from the House of Commons be expunged from the record.

JOHN WILKES'S SPEECH CALLING FOR HIS EXPULSION TO BE EXPUNGED FROM THE RECORD

The motion which I shall have the honour of submitting to the House affects, in my opinion, the very vitals of this Constitution, the great primary sources of the power of the people, whom we represent, and by whose authority only, delegated to us for a time, we are a part of the legislative body of this kingdom. The proceedings of the last Parliament in the business of the Middlesex elections gave a just alarm to almost every elector in the nation. The fatal precedents then attempted to be established were considered as a direct attack on the inalienable rights of the people.

All the great powers of the state at one time appeared combined to pour their vengeance on me. Even imperial Jove pointed his thunderbolts, red with uncommon wrath, at my devoted head. I was scorched, but not consumed. The broad shield of the law protected me. A generous public, and my noble friends, the freeholders of Middlesex, the ever-steady friends of liberty and their country, poured balm into my wounds; they are healed. Scarcely a scar remains: but I feel, I deeply feel, the wounds given to the Constitution; they are still bleeding; this House only can heal them: they only can restore the Constitution to its former state of purity, health, and vigour.

In the first formation of this government, in the original settlement of our Constitution, the people expressly reserved to themselves a very considerable part of the legislative power, which they consented to share jointly with a King and House of Lords. From the great population of our island, this power could not be exercised personally, and therefore the many were compelled to delegate that power to a few; who thus became their deputies and agents only, or their representatives. The freedom of election is the common right of the people, their fair and just share of power; and I hold it to be the most glorious inheritance of every subject of this realm, the noblest and, I trust, the most solid part of that beautiful fabric, the English Constitution.

But, sir, if you can expel whom you please and reject those disagreeable to you, the House will be self-created and self-existing. The original idea of your representing the people will be lost. The consequences of such a principle are to the highest degree alarming. A more forcible engine of despotism cannot be put in the hand of any minister. I wish gentlemen would attend to the plain consequences of such proceedings, and consider how they may be brought home to themselves.

A member hated or dreaded by a minister is accused of any crime; for instance, of having written a pretended libel. No proof whatever is given on oath before you, because you cannot administer an oath. The minister invades immediately the rights of juries. Before any trial, he gets the paper voted a libel, and the member he wishes expelled to be the author – which in fact you are not competent to try. Expulsion means, as is pretended, incapacity. The member is adjudged incapable; he cannot be re-elected, and thus is he excluded from Parliament. A minister by such manoeuvres may garble a House of Commons till not a single enemy of his own, or friend of his country, is left here, and the representation of the people is in a great degree lost.

Corruption had not lent despotism wings to fly so high in the time of Charles I, or the minister of that day would have been contented with expelling Hampden and the four other heroes, because they had immediately been judged incapable, and he would thereby have incapacitated them from thwarting in Parliament the arbitrary measures of a wicked court. Upon all these considerations, in order to quiet the minds of the people, to restore our violated Constitution to its original purity, to vindicate the injured rights of this country in particular, and of all the electors of this kingdom, and that not the least trace of the violence and injustice of the last Parliament may disgrace our records, I humbly move, 'That the resolution of this House of the seventeenth of February, 1769, "That John Wilkes, Esq., having been in this session of Parliament expelled this House, was and is incapable of sitting in the present Parliament," be expunged from the journals of this House, as being subversive of the rights of the whole body of electors of this kingdom.'

Wilkes did not succeed on that occasion, but, in 1782, the House of Commons did decide that its 1769 decision to expel him 'be expunged from the Journals of this House, as being subversive of the Rights of the whole body of Electors of this Kingdom'.

1768

'THE GOOD AND HAPPINESS OF THE MAJORITY IS THE GREAT STANDARD'

Even by the standards of the great polymaths of British history, Joseph Priestley stands out. He was a Presbyterian minister, a social philosopher and a scientist. His discoveries ranged from laughing gas and the ability of India rubber to erase pencil marks to the inverse-square law for the power of an electrical charge. He invented soda water. And he was a pioneer of utilitarianism: the view that the morality of an individual's actions is determined by the wider benefit or harm done to the wider society.

In his *Essay on the First Principles of Government*, Priestley set out the basic case for utilitarianism in determining who should govern a country, what the duties of rulers should be, and when people are justified in using force to overthrow a tyrannical government.

JOSEPH PRIESTLEY: *ESSAY ON THE FIRST PRINCIPLES OF GOVERNMENT*

In countries where every member of the society enjoys an equal power of arriving at the supreme offices, and consequently of directing the strength and the sentiments of the whole community, there is a state of the most perfect political liberty.

It may be said, that no society on earth was ever formed in the manner represented above. I answer, it is true; because all governments whatever have been, in some measure, compulsory, tyrannical, and oppressive in their origin; but the method I have described must be allowed to be the only equitable and fair method of forming a society. And since every man retains, and can never be deprived of his natural right (founded on a regard to the general good) of relieving himself from all oppression, that is, from every thing that has been imposed upon him without his own consent; this must be the only true and proper foundation of all the governments subsisting in the world, and that to which the people who compose them have an unalienable right to bring them back.

It must necessarily be understood, therefore, whether it be expressed or not, that all people live in society for their mutual advantage; so that the good and happiness of the members, that is the majority of the members of any state, is the great standard by which every thing relating to that state must finally be determined.

Let it be observed that I by no means assert, that the good of mankind requires a state of the most perfect political liberty. This, indeed, is not possible, except in exceeding small states. And an ambitious nation could not wish for a fairer opportunity of arriving at extensive empire, than to find the neighbouring countries cantoned out into a number of small governments; which could have no power to withstand it singly, and which could never form sufficiently extensive confederacies, or act with sufficient unanimity, and expedition, to oppose it with success.

Political liberty must, in some measure, be restrained; but *in what manner* a restraint should be put upon it, or *how far* it should extend, is not easy to be ascertained. In general, it should seem, that none but persons of considerable fortune should be capable of arriving at the highest offices in the government; not only because, all other circumstances being equal, such persons will generally have had the best education, and consequently be the best qualified to act for the public good; but because also, they will necessarily have the most property at stake, and will, therefore, be most interested in the fate of their country.

Provided those who make laws submit to them themselves, and, with respect to taxes in particular, so long as those who impose them bear an equal share with the rest of the community, there will be no complaint. But in all cases, when those who lay the tax upon others exempt themselves, there is *tyranny*; and the man who submits to a tax of a penny, levied in this manner, is liable to have the last penny he has extorted from him.

Upon these principles it is evident, that there must have been a gross inattention to the very first principles of liberty, to say nothing worse, in the first scheme of taxing the inhabitants of America in the British parliament.

But if there be any truth in the principles above laid down, it must be a fundamental maxim in all governments, that if any man hold what is called a high rank, or enjoy privileges, and prerogatives in a state, it is because the good of the state requires that he should hold that rank, or enjoy those privileges; and such persons, whether they be called kings, senators, or nobles; or by whatever names, or titles, they be distinguished, are, to all intents and purposes, the *servants of the public*, and accountable to the people for the discharge of their respective offices.

In the largest states, if the abuses of government should, at any time be great and manifest; if the servants, instead of considering that they are made for the people, they should consider the people as made for them; if the oppressions and violations of right should be great, flagrant, and universally resented: if, in consequence of these circumstances, it should become manifest, that the risk, which would be run in attempting a revolution would be trifling, and the evils which might be apprehended from it, were far less than those which were actually suffered, and which were daily increasing; in the name of God, I ask, what principles are those, which ought to restrain an injured and insulted people from asserting their natural rights, and from changing, or even punishing their governors, that is their *servants*, who had abused their trust; or from altering the whole form of their government, if it appeared to be of a structure so liable to abuse?

With respect to large societies, it is very improbable, that the people should be too soon alarmed, so as to be driven to these extremities. In such cases, the power of the government, that is, of the governors, must be very extensive and arbitrary; and the power of the people scattered, and difficult to be united; so that, if a man have common sense, he will see it to be madness to propose, or to lay any measures for a general insurrection against the government, except in case of very general and great oppression.

So obvious are these difficulties, that lie in the way of procuring redress of grievances by force of arms, that I think we may say, without exception, that in all cases of hostile opposition to government, the people must have been in the right; and that nothing but very great oppression could drive them to such desperate measures. The bulk of a people seldom so much as *complain* without reason, because they never think of complaining till they *feel*; so that, in all cases of dissatisfaction with government, it is most probable, that the people are injured.

Priestley was too Radical for many, and not Radical enough for some. He had little sympathy for destitute people, whom he thought should take responsibility for improving their own lives – for example, by keeping out of alehouses. But Priestley's wider influence was considerable. Years later, Jeremy Bentham would say: 'Priestley was the first who taught my lips to pronounce this sacred truth: That the greatest happiness of the greatest number is the foundation of morals and legislation.'

1770-4

'YOUR REPRESENTATIVE OWES YOU HIS JUDGEMENT; AND HE BETRAYS YOU IF HE SACRIFICES IT TO YOUR OPINION'

Edmund Burke's views were a major influence on notions of party and Parliament. He entered Parliament in 1765 as MP for Wendover, a borough effectively owned by Lord Verney. This meant that Burke did not need to do anything as demeaning as campaigning for votes. One of the issues of the day was the power of the king. George III was trying to recover some of the power his predecessors had been forced to cede. Burke wrote an essay that argued that Parliament needed to defend its powers against the king – and this required MPs to work together in political parties, rather than simply following their own personal whims.

EDMUND BURKE: *THOUGHTS ON THE CAUSE OF THE PRESENT DISCONTENTS*

Party is a body of men united for promoting by their joint endeavours the national interest upon some particular principle in which they are all agreed. For my part, I find it impossible to conceive that any one who believes in his own politics, or thinks them to be of any weight, should refuse to adopt the means of having them reduced into practice. It is the business of the speculative philosopher to mark the proper ends of government. It is the business of the politician, who is the philosopher in action, to find out proper means towards those ends, and to employ them with effect. Therefore every honourable connection will avow it as their first purpose, to pursue every just method to put the men who hold their opinions into such a condition as may enable them to carry their common plans into execution, with all the power and authority of the state.

As this power is attached to certain situations, it is their duty to contend for these situations. Without a proscription of others, they are bound to give to their own party the preference in all things; and not to suffer themselves to be led, or to be controlled, or to be overbalanced, in office or in council, by those who contradict the very fundamental principles on which their party is formed, and even those upon which every fair connection must stand.

In order to throw an odium on political connexion, [non-party] politicians suppose it a necessary incident to it, that you are blindly to follow the opinions of your party, when in direct opposition to your own clear ideas; a degree of servitude that no worthy man could bear the thought of submitting to; and such as, I believe, no connexions (except some court factions) ever could be so senselessly tyrannical as to impose.

Men, thinking freely, will in particular instances, think differently. But still, as the greater part of the measures which arise in the course of public business are related to, or dependent on some great *leading general principles in government*, a man must be peculiarly unfortunate in the choice of his political company if he does not agree with them at least nine times in ten.

Of what sort of materials must that man be made, how must he be tempered and put together, who can sit whole years in parliament, with five hundred and fifty of his fellow citizens, amidst the storm of such tempestuous passions, in the sharp conflict of so many wits, and tempers, and characters, in the agitation of such mighty questions, in the discussion of such vast and ponderous interests, without seeing any one sort of men, whose character, conduct, or disposition, would lead him to associate himself with them, to aid and be aided, in any one system of public utility?

By 1774, Lord Verney was down on his luck. He told Burke that he could no longer finance Burke as MP for Wendover. Burke travelled west to Bristol, where he did have to campaign for the votes of the city's freemen to become one of its two MPs. He narrowly defeated Matthew Brickdale, a Tory. At Bristol's Guildhall, on 3 November, on winning the election, Burke delivered a speech that has become a classic statement of the principles of representative (as distinct from direct) democracy. He argued that MPs should be bound by their judgement and conscience – and should not be required to sacrifice those to the instructions or mandates of his constituents.

EDMUND BURKE: SPEECH TO THE ELECTORS OF BRISTOL

I owe myself, in all things, to all the freemen of this city. My particular friends have a demand on me that I should not deceive their expectations. Never was cause or man supported with more constancy, more activity, more spirit. I have been supported with a zeal indeed and heartiness in my friends which (if their object had been at all proportioned to their endeavours) could never be sufficiently commended. They supported me upon the most liberal principles. They wished that the members for Bristol should be chosen for the city, and for their country at large, and not for themselves.

Certainly, gentlemen, it ought to be the happiness and glory of a representative to live in the strictest union, the closest correspondence, and the most unreserved communication with his constituents. Their wishes ought to have great weight with his; their opinion high respect; their business unremitted attention. It is his duty to sacrifice his repose, his pleasures, his satisfactions, to theirs; and, above all, ever, and in all cases, to prefer their interest to his own.

But his unbiased opinion, his mature judgement, his enlightened conscience, he ought not to sacrifice to you – to any man, or to any set of men living. These he does not derive from your pleasure; no, nor from the law and the constitution. They are a trust from Providence, for the abuse of which he is deeply answerable. Your representative owes you, not his industry only, but his judgement; and he betrays, instead of serving, you if he sacrifices it to your opinion.

If government were a matter of will upon any side, yours, without question, ought to be superior. But government and legislation are matters of reason and judgement, and not of inclination; and what sort of reason is that in which the determination precedes the discussion? In which one set of men deliberate, and another decide? And where those who form the conclusion are perhaps three hundred miles distant from those who hear the arguments?

To deliver an opinion is the right of all men; that of constituents is a weighty and respectable opinion, which a representative ought always to rejoice to hear, and which he ought always most serious to consider. But authoritative instructions, mandates issued which the member is bound blindly and implicitly to obey, to vote and to argue for, though contrary to the clearest conviction of his judgement and conscience: these are things utterly unknown to the laws of this land, and which arise from a fundamental mistake of the whole order and tenor of our constitution.

Parliament is not a congress of ambassadors from different and hostile interests, which interests each must maintain, as an agent and advocate, against other agents and advocates; but Parliament is a deliberative assembly of one nation with one interest – that of the whole: where, not local purposes, not local prejudices ought to guide, but the general good, resulting from the general reason of the whole. You choose a member, indeed; but when you have chosen him, he is not a member of Bristol, but he is a member of Parliament. If the local constituent should have an interest or should form a hasty opinion, evidently opposite to the real good of the rest of the community, the member for that place ought to be as far, as any other, from any endeavour to give it effect. I beg pardon for saying so much on this subject. I have been unwillingly drawn into it, but I shall ever use a respectful frankness of communication with you. Your faithful friend, your devoted servant, I shall be to the end of my life; a flatterer you do not wish for.

Burke lost his seat in 1780. He proved too progressive for many Bristol freemen in his sympathy for the American colonies in their battle for independence, his support for Catholic Emancipation and his backing for free trade with Ireland.

1772

'SLAVERY IS SO ODIOUS THAT NOTHING CAN BE SUFFERED TO SUPPORT IT BUT POSITIVE LAW. THEREFORE THE BLACK MUST BE DISCHARGED'

Lord Mansfield was one of Britain's great reforming jurists. He was chief justice of the King's Bench from 1756 until 1788. In 1772, seven years after consigning general warrants to the legal graveyard, he delivered another significant ruling: that anyone who was a slave abroad would be entitled to their freedom if they came to England. This was crucial in two respects: first, it legally acknowledged for the first time that black people were entitled to the same liberty that white people enjoyed; and second, his justification for his decision – that slavery was so 'odious' that it needed specific laws to sanction it – marked a radical extension of the use of common law to protect individual liberty.

Mansfield's ruling came at the end of a case brought on behalf of James Sommersett, a slave who was bought in Virginia and then brought to England by his 'owner', Charles Steuart, in 1769. Sommersett escaped in 1771, but was recaptured after eight weeks, then shackled and imprisoned on a ship, the *Ann and Mary*, due to sail for Jamaica. Before it sailed, three Londoners who opposed slavery and who claimed to be Sommersett's godparents applied for a writ of habeas corpus, which required the ship's captain to bring Sommersett before the court so that his status could be determined.

When Lord Mansfield heard the case, he had to take into account earlier cases overseen by a former Attorney General, Sir Philip Yorke, and two former Lord Chancellors, Talbot and Hardwicke, who had ruled that slaves were items of property: Hardwicke had said they were 'like stock on a farm', and could not achieve freedom either by becoming Christian or coming to England. A month before his final ruling, Mansfield hinted that he would overturn these precedents when he told a court reporter, 'if the parties will have judgment, *"fiat justitia, ruat cælum"* [let justice be done though the heavens may fall]'. He delivered his verdict on 22 June 1772.

LORD MANSFIELD'S RULING ON SOMMERSETT'S CASE

The court now proceeds to give its ruling. The captain of the ship on board of which the Negro was taken, makes his return to the writ in terms signifying that there have been, and still are, slaves to a great number in Africa; and that the trade in them is authorized by the laws and opinions of Virginia and Jamaica; that they are goods and chattels; and, as such, saleable and sold; that James Sommersett is a Negro of Africa, and long before the return of the king's writ was brought to be sold, and was sold to Charles Steuart, esq. then in Jamaica; that Mr Steuart, having occasion to transact business, came over hither, with an intention to return, and to carry him back as soon as the business should be transacted; that such intention has been, and still continues; and that the Negro did remain till the time of his departure in the service of his master Mr Steuart, and quitted it without his consent; and thereupon, before the return of the King's writ, the said Charles Steuart did commit the slave on board the *Ann and Mary*, to safe custody, to be kept till he should set sail, and then to be taken to Jamaica, and there sold as a slave. And this is the cause why he, captain Knowles, commander of the above vessel, detained the said Negro to his custody; and on which he now renders him to the custody of the court.

We pay all due attention to the opinion of Sir Philip Yorke, and Lord Chancellor Talbot, whereby they pledged themselves to the British planters, for all the legal consequences of slaves coming over to this kingdom or being baptized, recognised by Lord Hardwicke: that there was no ground in law in the notion that, if a Negro came over, or became a Christian, he was emancipated.

The only question before us is whether the cause on the return is sufficient? If it is, the Negro must be remanded; if it is not, he must be discharged. Accordingly, the return states that the slave departed and refused to serve; whereupon he was kept, to be sold abroad. So high an act of dominion must be recognised by the law of the country where it is used. The power of a master over his slave has been extremely different, in different countries. The state of slavery is of such a nature, that it is incapable of being introduced on any reasons, moral or political; but only positive law, which preserves its force long after the reasons, occasion, and time itself from whence it was created, is erased from memory: it's so odious, that nothing can be suffered to support it but positive law. Whatever inconveniences, therefore, may follow from a decision, I cannot say this case is allowed or approved by the law of England; and therefore the black must be discharged.

◇ ◇ ◇

The case gave rise to one of the most frequently quoted dictums of British justice: that England has 'too pure an air for a slave to breathe, and so everyone who breathes it becomes free'. This was said not by Mansfield, as is widely believed, but by one of Sommersett's barristers, who cited a case from 1569: 'One Cartwright brought a slave from Russia and would scourge him; for which he was questioned; and it was resolved, that England was too pure an air for a slave to breathe, and so everyone who breathes it becomes free. Everyone who comes to this island is entitled to the protection of English law, whatever oppression he may have suffered and whatever may be the colour of his skin.'

However, Mansfield's ruling did not apply beyond England's shores. For the time being, it remained legal for Britons to buy, own and sell slaves abroad.

1789

'A TRADE FOUNDED IN INIQUITY, AND CARRIED ON AS THIS WAS, MUST BE ABOLISHED'

L ord Mansfield's 1772 ruling in the Sommersett case outlawed slavery in England. In 1778, Edinburgh's Court of Session outlawed it in Scotland. But the slave trade remained legal elsewhere in the British Empire. The campaign for full abolition was led in Parliament by William Wilberforce. A Cambridge-educated tearaway who entered the House of Commons as MP for Hull in 1780, when he was just 21, Wilberforce converted to Christianity in 1784 and changed his lifestyle utterly.

His interest in the slave trade was sparked by Thomas Clarkson, a fellow Cambridge graduate and an early, ardent abolitionist. Wilberforce became convinced by the moral case, but campaigning for its abolition was never going to be easy. It has been estimated that up to 80 per cent of Britain's foreign income was derived from the transport of slaves from Africa to the West Indies, and the supply to Europe of the products of slave labour, such as sugar, cotton and tobacco. On 12 May 1789, following the report of a Privy Council inquiry into the slave trade, Wilberforce made the first of many parliamentary speeches advocating its abolition.

WILLIAM WILBERFORCE'S SPEECH ADVOCATING THE ABOLITION OF THE SLAVE TRADE

I wish exceedingly, in the outset, to guard both myself and the House from entering into the subject with any sort of passion. It is not their passions I shall appeal to – I ask only for their cool and impartial reason; and I wish not to take them by surprise, but to deliberate, point by point, upon every part of this question. I mean not to accuse any one, but to take the shame upon myself, in common, indeed, with the whole parliament of Great Britain, for having suffered this horrid trade to be carried on under their authority. We are all guilty – we ought all to plead guilty, and not to exculpate ourselves by throwing the blame on others.

Having now disposed of the first part of this subject, I must speak of the transit of the slaves in the West Indies. Let any one imagine to himself six or seven hundred of these wretches chained two and two, surrounded with every object that is nauseous and disgusting, diseased, and struggling under every kind of wretchedness! How can we bear to think of such a scene as this? Yet, in this very point (to show the power of human prejudice) the situation of the slaves has been described by Mr [Robert] Norris, one of the Liverpool delegates, in a manner which, I am sure will convince the House how interest can draw a film across the eyes, so thick, that total blindness could do no more; and how it is our duty therefore to trust not to the reasonings of interested men, or to their way of colouring a transaction.

'Their apartments,' says Mr Norris, 'are fitted up as much for their advantage as circumstances will admit. The right ankle of one, indeed is connected with the left ankle of another by a small iron fetter, and if they are turbulent, by another on their wrists. They have several meals a day; some of their own country provisions, with the best sauces of African cookery; and by way of variety, another meal of pulse, &c. according to European taste. After breakfast they have water to wash themselves, while their apartments are perfumed with frankincense and lime-juice. Before dinner, they are amused after the manner of their country. The song and dance are promoted. The men play and sing, while the women and girls make fanciful ornaments with beads, which they are plentifully supplied with.'

Such is the sort of strain in which the Liverpool delegates, and particularly Mr Norris, gave evidence before the Privy Council. What will the House think when, by the concurring testimony of other witnesses, the true history is laid open. The slaves who are sometimes described as rejoicing at their captivity, are so wrung with misery at leaving their country, that it is the constant practice to set sail at night, lest they should be sensible of their departure. The pulse which Mr Norris talks of are horse beans; and the scantiness, both of water and provision, was suggested by the very legislature of Jamaica in the report of their committee, to be a subject that called for the interference of parliament. Mr Norris talks of frankincense and lime juice; when surgeons tell you the slaves are stowed so close, that there is not room to tread among them: and when you have it in evidence from Sir George Yonge, that even in a ship which wanted 200 of her complement, the stench was intolerable.

The song and the dance, says Mr Norris, are promoted. The truth is, that for the sake of exercise, these miserable wretches, loaded with chains, oppressed with disease and wretchedness, are forced to dance by the terror of the lash, and sometimes by the actual use of it. As to their singing, what shall we say when we are told that their songs are songs of lamentation upon their departure which, while they sing, are always in tears, insomuch that one captain (more humane as I should conceive him, therefore, than the rest) threatened one of the women with a flogging, because the mournfulness of her song was too painful for his feelings.

In order, however, not to trust too much to any sort of description, I will call the attention of the House to one species of evidence which is absolutely infallible. Death, at least, is a sure ground of evidence, and the proportion of deaths will not only confirm, but if possible will even aggravate our suspicion of their misery in the transit. It will be found, upon an average of all the ships of which evidence has been given at the Privy Council, that exclusive of those who perish before they sail, not less than 12½ per cent perish in the passage.

Besides these, the Jamaica report tells you, that not less than 4½ per cent die on shore before the day of sale, which is only a week or two from the time of landing. One third more die in the seasoning, and this in a country exactly like their own, where they are healthy and happy as some of the evidences would pretend. Upon the whole, however, here is a mortality of about 50 per cent and this among Negroes who are not bought unless (as the phrase is with cattle) they are sound in wind and limb. How then can the House refuse its belief to the multiplied testimonies before the Privy Council, of the savage treatment of the Negroes in the middle passage? Nay, indeed, what need is there of any evidence? The number of deaths speaks for itself, and makes all such enquiry superfluous.

As soon as ever I had arrived thus far in my investigation of the slave trade, so enormous, so dreadful, so irremediable did its wickedness appear that my own mind was completely made up for the abolition. A trade founded in iniquity, and carried on as this was, must be abolished, let the policy be what it might – let the consequences be what they would, I from this time determined that I would never rest till I had effected its abolition.

Wilberforce's campaign lasted almost half a century. It took another 18 years before Parliament passed the Slave Trade Act 1807, which outlawed trade in new slaves, and a further 26 years before Parliament decreed that all existing slaves must be emancipated. Wilberforce died in July 1833, just one month before the Slavery Abolition Bill became law, which paved the way for most slaves around the British Empire to be freed.

1790–1

'THOSE WHO ATTEMPT TO LEVEL, NEVER EQUALIZE'

The French Revolution, in 1789, saw Edmund Burke break with the more radical Whigs and make common cause with a more conservative group within the party. He put forward his views in *Reflections on the Revolution in France*, published, in 1790, in the form of a letter to a young Parisian man. Burke argued that, far from being a step towards representative democracy, the revolution was a violent and unjustified attack on tradition that would end in tears, and all for an abstract view of a perfect society that ignored the complexities and frailties of human beings and human institutions.

Burke contended that some people were fit to be rulers, while others were more suited to voting for them; therefore it would be dangerous to embrace the concept of pure equality. Within this context, a hereditary monarchy could be a positive asset. Among the targets Burke attacked was the Revolution Society, a London organisation that sided wholeheartedly with France's revolutionaries.

EDMUND BURKE: *REFLECTIONS ON THE REVOLUTION IN FRANCE*

When I see the spirit of liberty in action, I see a strong principle at work; and this, for a while, is all I can possibly know of it. The wild gas, the fixed air, is plainly broke loose; but we ought to suspend our judgment until the first effervescence is a little subsided, till the liquor is cleared, and until we see something deeper than the agitation of a troubled and frothy surface. I must be tolerably sure, before I venture publicly to congratulate men upon a blessing, that they have really received one. Flattery corrupts both the receiver and the giver, and adulation is not of more service to the people than to kings.

I should, therefore, suspend my congratulations on the new liberty of France until I was informed how it had been combined with government, with public force, with the discipline and obedience of armies, with the collection of an effective and well-distributed revenue, with morality and religion, with the solidity of property, with peace and order, with civil and social manners. All these (in their way) are good things, too, and without them liberty is not a benefit whilst it lasts, and is not likely to continue long.

The effect of liberty to individuals is that they may do what they please; we ought to see what it will please them to do, before we risk congratulations which may be soon turned into complaints. Prudence would dictate this in the case of separate, insulated, private men, but liberty, when men act in bodies, is power. Considerate people, before they declare themselves, will observe the use which is made of power and particularly of so trying a thing as new power in new persons of whose principles, tempers, and dispositions they have little or no experience, and in situations where those who appear the most stirring in the scene may possibly not be the real movers.

Believe me, Sir, those who attempt to level, never equalize. In all societies, consisting of various descriptions of citizens, some description must be uppermost. The levellers, therefore, only change and pervert the natural order of things; they load the edifice of society by setting up in the air what the solidity of the structure requires to be on the ground. The association of tailors and carpenters, of which the republic (of Paris, for instance) is composed, cannot be equal to the situation into which by the worst of usurpations—an usurpation on the prerogatives of nature—you attempt to force them.

The Chancellor of France, at the opening of the states, said, in a tone of oratorical flourish, that all occupations were honourable. If he meant only that no honest employment was disgraceful, he would not have gone beyond the truth. But in asserting that anything is honourable, we imply some distinction in its favour. The occupation of a hairdresser or of a working tallow-chandler cannot be a matter of honour to any person—to say nothing of a number of other more servile employments. Such descriptions of men ought not to suffer oppression from the state; but the state suffers oppression if such as they, either individually or collectively, are permitted to rule. In this you think you are combating prejudice, but you are at war with nature.

Whatever kings might have been here or elsewhere a thousand years ago, or in whatever manner the ruling dynasties of England or France may have begun, the king of Great Britain is, at this day, king by a fixed rule of succession according to the laws of his country. Whatever may be the success of evasion in explaining away the gross error of fact, which supposes that his Majesty owes his crown to the choice of his people, yet nothing can evade their full explicit declaration concerning the principle of a right in the people to choose; which right is directly maintained and tenaciously adhered to. Lest the foundation of the king's exclusive legal title should pass for a mere rant of adulatory freedom, the political divine proceeds dogmatically to assert that, by the principles of the Revolution, the people of England have acquired three fundamental rights, all which, with him, compose one system and lie together in one short sentence, namely, that we have acquired a right:

1. to choose our own governors.
2. to cashier them for misconduct.
3. to frame a government for ourselves.

This new and hitherto unheard-of bill of rights, though made in the name of the whole people, belongs to those gentlemen and their faction only. The body of the people of England have no share in it. They utterly disclaim it. They will resist the practical assertion of it with their lives and fortunes. They are bound to do so by the laws of their country made at the time of that very Revolution which is appealed to in favour of the fictitious rights claimed by the Society which abuses its name.

A state without the means of some change is without the means of its conservation. Without such means it might even risk the loss of that part of the constitution which it wished the most religiously to preserve. The two principles of conservation and correction operated strongly at the two critical periods of the Restoration and Revolution, when England found itself without a king. At both those periods the nation had lost the bond of union in their ancient edifice; they did not, however, dissolve the whole fabric.

Burke's arguments split the Whigs, and he became one of the minority 'Old Whigs'. It was his cautious, organic approach to reform that would be adopted by Conservatives in the nineteenth and twentieth centuries, and which gave Burke his place in the pantheon of Conservative heroes.

One of the people that Burke offended was Thomas Paine. Born in Norfolk, he lived in the United States from 1774 until 1787 and was actively involved in the struggle for American independence. In 1776, he wrote a pamphlet, *The American Crisis*, which contained words quoted by President Obama in his inaugural speech in January 2009, to remind his fellow countrymen of how they had been inspired at a time of hardship and uncertainty: 'Let it be told to the future world that in the depth of winter, when nothing but hope and virtue could survive, that the city and the country, alarmed at one common danger, came forth to meet it.'

However, various misfortunes left Paine broke, and he returned to London in 1787. He responded to Burke's attack on the French Revolution by writing *Rights of Man*. In January 1791, he handed the manuscript to his publisher. Shortly afterwards, the government made moves to charge him with seditious libel. To evade arrest, Paine fled abroad. When his book was published in March 1791, Paine was in Paris.

THOMAS PAINE: *RIGHTS OF MAN*

Man did not enter into society to become worse than he was before, nor to have fewer rights than he had before, but to have those rights better secured. His natural rights are the foundation of all his civil rights. But in order to pursue this distinction with more precision, it will be necessary to mark the different qualities of natural and civil rights.

Natural rights are those which appertain to man in right of his existence. Of this kind are all the intellectual rights, or rights of the mind, and also all those rights of acting as an individual for his own comfort and happiness, which are not injurious to the natural rights of others. Civil rights are those which appertain to man in right of his being a member of society. Every civil right has for its foundation some natural right pre-existing in the individual, but to the enjoyment of which his individual power is not, in all cases, sufficiently competent. Of this kind are all those which relate to security and protection.

From this short review it will be easy to distinguish between that class of natural rights which man retains after entering into society and those which he throws into the common stock as a member of society.

A man, by natural right, has a right to judge in his own cause; and so far as the right of the mind is concerned, he never surrenders it. Society grants him nothing. Every man is a proprietor in society, and draws on the capital as a matter of right.

From these premises two or three certain conclusions will follow:

First, that every civil right grows out of a natural right; or, in other words, is a natural right exchanged.

Secondly, that civil power properly considered as such is made up of the aggregate of that class of the natural rights of man, which becomes defective in the individual in point of power, and answers not his purpose, but when collected to a focus becomes competent to the Purpose of every one.

Thirdly, that the power produced from the aggregate of natural rights, imperfect in power in the individual, cannot be applied to invade the natural rights which are retained in the individual, and in which the power to execute is as perfect as the right itself.

The two modes of the Government which prevail in the world, are:

First, Government by election and representation.

Secondly, Government by hereditary succession.

The former is generally known by the name of republic; the latter by that of monarchy and aristocracy.

Those two distinct and opposite forms erect themselves on the two distinct and opposite bases of Reason and Ignorance. As the exercise of Government requires talents and abilities, and as talents and abilities cannot have hereditary descent, it is evident that hereditary succession requires a belief from man to which his reason cannot subscribe, and which can only be established upon his ignorance; and the more ignorant any country is, the better it is fitted for this species of Government.

On the contrary, Government, in a well-constituted republic, requires no belief from man beyond what his reason can give. He sees the rationale of the whole system, its origin and its operation; and as it is best supported when best understood, the human faculties act with boldness, and acquire, under this form of government, a gigantic manliness.

When we survey the wretched condition of man, under the monarchical and hereditary systems of Government, dragged from his home by one power, or driven by another, and impoverished by taxes more than by enemies, it becomes evident that those systems are bad, and that a general revolution in the principle and construction of Governments is necessary.

The romantic and barbarous distinction of men into Kings and subjects, though it may suit the condition of courtiers, cannot that of citizens; and is exploded by the principle upon which Governments are now founded. Every citizen is a member of the Sovereignty, and, as such, can acknowledge no personal subjection; and his obedience can be only to the laws.

All hereditary government is in its nature tyranny. An heritable crown, or an heritable throne, or by what other fanciful name such things may be called, have no other significant explanation than that mankind are heritable property. To inherit a government, is to inherit the people, as if they were flocks and herds.

With respect to the second head, that of being inadequate to the purposes for which government is necessary, we have only to consider what government essentially is, and compare it with the circumstances to which hereditary succession is subject.

Government ought to be a thing always in full maturity. It ought to be so constructed as to be superior to all the accidents to which individual man is subject; and, therefore, hereditary succession, by being subject to them all, is the most irregular and imperfect of all the systems of government.

We have heard the Rights of Man called a levelling system; but the only system to which the word levelling is truly applicable, is the hereditary monarchical system. It is a system of mental levelling. It indiscriminately admits every species of character to the same authority. Vice and virtue, ignorance and wisdom, in short, every quality good or bad, is put on the same level. Kings succeed each other, not as rationals, but as animals.

Hereditary succession is a burlesque upon monarchy. It puts it in the most ridiculous light, by presenting it as an office which any child or idiot may fill. It requires some talents to be a common mechanic; but to be a king requires only the animal figure of man – a sort of breathing automaton. This sort of superstition may last a few years more, but it cannot long resist the awakened reason and interest of man.

In the representative system, the reason for everything must publicly appear. Every man is a proprietor in government, and considers it a necessary part of his business to understand. It concerns his interest, because it affects his property. He examines the cost, and compares it with the advantages; and above all, he does not adopt the slavish custom of following what in other governments are called LEADERS.

Paine admired France's revolutionaries, but not all of them admired him. For, although he abhorred monarchy, Paine deplored vengeance against King Louis XVI, and argued for the king to be banished rather than executed. This angered Robespierre and his Radicals. When they seized power in 1793, they imprisoned Paine, who only narrowly escaped execution. He was not released until Robespierre himself was deposed the following year.

Paine never returned to England, for he had been tried in his absence and found guilty of seditious libel. In a letter to some supporters, he wrote: 'If, to expose the fraud and imposition of monarchy, to promote universal peace, civilization, and commerce, and to break the chains of political superstition, and raise degraded man to his proper rank; if these things be libellous, let the name of libeller be engraved on my tomb.'

1792

'IT IS VAIN TO EXPECT VIRTUE FROM WOMEN TILL THEY ARE, IN SOME DEGREE, INDEPENDENT OF MEN'

Mary Wollstonecraft was a feminist writer who applied the principle of equality to the plight of women. She was part of a circle of Radicals that included Thomas Paine, William Blake and, later, William Wordsworth.

In *A Vindication of the Rights of Woman*, she argued that the lack of women's rights, in everything from property to politics and employment to family life, was not just morally offensive but also harmful in practice, not least to the character of women themselves. If some men regarded women as inferior, this was partly because women were starved of the opportunities that men enjoyed. For Wollstonecraft, emancipation involved educational and social equality as well as formal political equality.

MARY WOLLSTONECRAFT: *A VINDICATION OF THE RIGHTS OF WOMAN*

There is a homely proverb, which speaks a shrewd truth, that whoever the devil finds idle he will employ. And what but habitual idleness can hereditary wealth and titles produce? For man is so constituted that he can only attain a proper use of his faculties by exercising them, and will not exercise them unless necessity, of some kind, first set the wheels in motion. Virtue likewise can only be acquired by the discharge of relative duties; but the importance of these sacred duties will scarcely be felt by the being who is cajoled out of his humanity by the flattery of sycophants. There must be more equality established in society, or morality will never gain ground, and this virtuous equality will not rest firmly even when founded on a rock, if one half of mankind are chained to its bottom by fate, for they will be continually undermining it through ignorance or pride.

It is vain to expect virtue from women till they are, in some degree, independent of men; nay, it is vain to expect that strength of natural affection, which would make them good wives and mothers. Whilst they are absolutely dependent on their husbands they will be cunning, mean, and selfish, and the men who can be gratified by the fawning fondness of spaniel-like affection, have not much delicacy, for love is not to be bought, in any sense of the words, its silken wings are instantly shrivelled up when any thing beside a return in kind is sought. Yet whilst wealth enervates men; and women live, as it were, by their personal charms, how can we expect them to discharge those ennobling duties which equally require exertion and self-denial.

I mean, therefore, to infer that the society is not properly organized which does not compel men and women to discharge their respective duties, by making it the only way to acquire that countenance from their fellow-creatures, which every human being wishes some way to attain.

A truly benevolent legislator always endeavours to make it the interest of each individual to be virtuous; and thus private virtue becoming the cement of public happiness, an orderly whole is consolidated by the tendency of all the parts towards a common centre. But, the private or public virtue of woman is very problematical; for Rousseau, and a numerous list of male writers, insist that she should all her life be subjected to a severe restraint, that of propriety. Why subject her to propriety—blind propriety, if she be capable of acting from a nobler spring, if she be an heir of immortality? Is sugar always to be produced by vital blood? Is one half of the human species, like the poor African slaves, to be subject to prejudices that brutalize them, when principles would be a surer guard, only to sweeten the cup of man? Is not this indirectly to deny woman reason? For a gift is a mockery, if it be unfit for use.

Women are, in common with men, rendered weak and luxurious by the relaxing pleasures which wealth procures; but added to this they are made slaves to their persons, and must render them alluring that man may lend them his reason to guide their tottering steps aright. Or should they be ambitious, they must govern their tyrants by sinister tricks, for without rights there cannot be any incumbent duties. The laws respecting woman make an absurd unit of a man and his wife; and then, by the easy transition of only considering him as responsible, she is reduced to a mere cypher.

I cannot help lamenting that women of a superior cast have not a road open by which they can pursue more extensive plans of usefulness and independence. I may excite laughter, by dropping an hint, which I mean to pursue, some future time, for I really think that women ought to have representatives, instead of being arbitrarily governed without having any direct share allowed them in the deliberations of government.

But, as the whole system of representation is now, in this country, only a convenient handle for despotism, they need not complain, for they are as well represented as a numerous class of hard working mechanics, who pay for the support of royalty when they can scarcely stop their children's mouths with bread. How are they represented whose very sweat supports the splendid stud of an heir apparent, or varnishes the chariot of some female favourite who looks down on shame? Taxes on the very necessaries of life, enable an endless tribe of idle princes and princesses to pass with stupid pomp before a gaping crowd, who almost worship the very parade which costs them so dear.

But what have women to do in society? I may be asked, but to loiter with easy grace; surely you would not condemn them all to suckle fools and chronicle small beer! No. Women might certainly study the art of healing, and be physicians as well as nurses. Business of various kinds, they might likewise pursue, if they were educated in a more orderly manner, which might save many from common and legal prostitution. Women would not then marry for a support, as men accept of places under government, and neglect the implied duties; nor would an attempt to earn their own subsistence sink them almost to the level of those poor abandoned creatures who live by prostitution. The few employments open to women, so far from being liberal, are menial; and when a superior education enables them to take charge of the education of children as governesses, they are not treated like the tutors of sons.

Would men but generously snap our chains, and be content with rational fellowship instead of slavish obedience, they would find us more observant daughters, more affectionate sisters, more faithful wives, more reasonable mothers—in a word, better citizens. We should then love them with true affection, because we should learn to respect ourselves; and the peace of mind of a worthy man would not be interrupted by the idle vanity of his wife, nor the babes sent to nestle in a strange bosom, having never found a home in their mother's.

Mary Wollstonecraft died in 1797, at the age of just 38, due to complications following the birth of her second daughter, Mary Godwin. This daughter would go on to become a major writer in her own right, most famously as the author of *Frankenstein*, which was initially published anonymously in 1818. Only in 1831 was the author revealed to be Mary Shelley (Godwin had married the poet Percy Bysshe Shelley in 1816).

1792

'LET REASON BE OPPOSED TO REASON, AND ARGUMENT TO ARGUMENT, AND EVERY GOOD GOVERNMENT WILL BE SAFE'

Having fled to Paris to escape the government's charges of seditious libel after the publication of *Rights of Man*, Thomas Paine was tried *in absentia* at London's Guildhall in December 1792. Paine's cause was defended by Thomas Erskine, who had become known for fighting cases that overturned old legal nostrums. In one case, his victory effectively ended the doctrine of constructive treason, which had allowed people to be convicted of treason because of the overall effect of their actions, even if no specific action was treasonable. In another, he established the principle that juries, not judges, should determine whether a publication was libellous. He also served as Attorney General to the Prince of Wales, which did not endear Erskine to everyone at the top of British society, for the prince had fallen out with his father, George III. The prince wanted to marry a Catholic and needed the king's permission, which he refused; nevertheless, the wedding went ahead. The marriage was declared null and void, and the king cut off all financial support for the prince. By the time of Paine's trial, Erskine was the obvious choice to defend liberty of opinion. In his speech to the jury, Erskine argued that this liberty was not only right in principle but also provided the best guarantee against the kind of revolution that had erupted in France.

THOMAS ERSKINE'S SPEECH TO THE JURY IN THE TRIAL OF THOMAS PAINE

Other liberties are held under governments, but liberty of opinion keeps governments themselves in due subjection to their duties. The proposition I mean to maintain as the basis for the liberties of the press, and without it is an empty sound, is this: that every man not intending to mislead, but seeking to enlighten others with what his own reason and conscience, however erroneously, had dictated to him as truth, may address himself to the universal reason of a whole nation, either upon the subject of government in general, or upon that of our own particular country; that he may analyze the principles of its constitution, point out its errors and defects, examine and publish its corruptions, warn his fellow-citizens against their ruinous consequences, and exert his whole faculties in pointing out the most advantageous changes in establishments which he considers to be radically defective or sliding from their object by abuse. All this every subject of this country has a right to do, if he contemplates only what he thinks would be for its advantage, and but seeks to change the public mind by the conviction which flows from reasonings dictated by conscience.

Let me not be suspected to be contending, that it is lawful to write a book pointing out defects in the English Government, and exciting individuals to destroy its sanctions, and to refuse obedience. But, on the other hand, I do contend that it is lawful to address the English nation on these momentous subjects; for, had it not been for this unalienable right – thanks be to God and our fathers for establishing it! – how should we have had this constitution which we so loudly boast of? If, in the march of the human mind, no man could have gone before the establishments of the time he lived in, how could our establishment, by reiterated changes, have become what it is? If no man could have awakened the public mind to errors and abuses in our Government, how could it have passed on from stage to stage, through reformation and revolution, so as to have arrived from barbarism to such a pitch of happiness and perfection, that the Attorney General considers it as profanation to touch it farther, or to look for any future amendment?

In this manner power has reasoned in every age: Government, in its own estimation, has been at all times a system of perfection; but a free press has examined and detected its errors, and the people have from time to time reformed them. This freedom has made our government what it is; this freedom alone can preserve it.

Although my arguments upon the liberty of the press may not to-day be honoured with your or the court's approbation, I shall retire not at all disheartened, consoling myself with the reflection that a season may arrive for their reception. The most essential liberties of mankind have been but slowly and gradually received. Gentlemen, I have insisted, at great length, upon the origin of governments, and detailed the authorities which you have heard upon the subject, because I consider it to be not only an essential support, but the very foundation of the liberty of the press.

If Mr. Burke be right in HIS principles of government, I admit that the press, in my sense of its freedom, ought not to be free, nor free in any sense at all; and that all addresses to the people upon the subject of government, and all speculations of amendment, of what kind or nature soever, are illegal and criminal; since, if the people have, without possible recall, delegated all their authorities, they have no jurisdiction to act, and therefore none to think and write upon such subjects; and it would be a libel to arraign Government or any of its acts before those that have no jurisdiction to correct them. But, on the other hand, as it is a settled rule in the law of England that the subject may always address a competent jurisdiction, no legal argument can shake the freedom of the press in my sense of it, if I am supported in my doctrines concerning the great unalienable right of the people to reform or to change their governments.

It is because the liberty of the press resolves itself into this great issue, that it has been, in every country, the last liberty which subjects have been able to wrest from power. This has produced the martyrdom of truth in every age, and the world has been only purged from ignorance with the innocent blood of those who have enlightened it.

When men can freely communicate their thoughts and their sufferings, real or imaginary, their passions spend themselves in air, like gunpowder scattered upon the surface; but pent up by terrors, they work unseen, burst forth in a moment, and destroy every thing in their course. Let reason be opposed to reason, and argument to argument, and every good government will be safe.

Engage the people by their affections, convince their reason, and they will be loyal from the only principle that can make loyalty sincere, vigorous, or rational: conviction that it is their truest interest, and that their government is for their good. Constraint is the natural parent of resistance, and a pregnant proof that reason is not on the side of those who use it. You must all remember Lucian's pleasant story: Jupiter and a countryman were walking together conversing with great freedom and familiarity upon the subject of heaven and earth. The countryman listened with attention and acquiescence, while Jupiter strove only to convince him; but happening to hint a doubt, Jupiter turned hastily round, and threatened him with his thunder. 'Ah! ah!' says the countryman, 'now, Jupiter, I know that you are wrong; you are always wrong when you appeal to your thunder.' This is the case with me. I can reason with the people of England, but I cannot fight against the thunder of authority. Gentlemen, this is my defence for free opinions.

◇ ◇ ◇

Erskine's speech was to no avail. Within moments of him sitting down, the foreman of the jury declared that they need hear no more. They found Paine guilty. Indeed, Erskine suffered a double defeat: as well as losing the case, he lost his position as Attorney General to the Prince of Wales.

Undeterred, Erskine continued to defend the advocates of unpopular causes. In 1794, he defended Thomas Hardy, who, as the Secretary of the London Corresponding Society, belonged to a circle of people who agitated for parliamentary reform. Hardy was one of more than thirty people charged with treason by conspiring to organise a 'pretended general convention of the people, in contempt and defiance of the authority of parliament, and on principles subversive of the existing laws and constitution, and directly tending to the introduction of that system of anarchy and confusion which has fatally prevailed in France'. If he were found guilty, he faced a death sentence. Erskine argued that the crime of treason should apply only to attempts to kill the king, not to attempts to promote wider reforms. This time, he succeeded. The judge instructed the jury to acquit Hardy. Parallel cases against two other men were also dropped. In the end, all the cases collapsed.

However, Erskine's victory was short-lived. William Pitt the Younger's government responded by persuading Parliament to pass two Acts to gag the expression of Radical ideas. The Seditious Meetings Act gave magistrates the power to disperse meetings of more than fifty people, while the Treasonable and Seditious Practices Act allowed the courts to impose heavy punishments (up to seven years' transportation for a second offence) on anyone who 'shall maliciously and advisedly, by writing, printing, preaching, or other speaking, express, publish, utter, or declare any words or sentences to excite or stir up the people to hatred or contempt of the person of his Majesty, his heirs or successors, or the government and constitution of this realm'.

Repression did not end there. Determined to avoid importing to Britain the horrors of the French Revolution and its ugly aftermath, Pitt made the mistake that so many rulers have made down the ages, and continue to make today: he failed to distinguish (or chose to ignore the distinction) between pleas for reform and plans for insurrection. In 1799 and 1800, the Combination Acts outlawed societies of three or more people formed to promote political reform or social demands such as higher wages. These laws were to be enforced by magistrates dispensing summary justice, rather than the slower, more inconvenient attentions of a full trial and jury. These laws were not repealed until 1824.

1795

'NATURAL RIGHTS IS SIMPLE NONSENSE, RHETORICAL NONSENSE — NONSENSE UPON STILTS'

English Radicals towards the end of the eighteenth century were united in their demands for far greater democracy, but divided over the philosophical principles that underpinned their Radicalism. At the heart of this dispute was the concept of 'natural rights'. Thomas Paine had argued for these, and the French Revolution expressly embraced them.

Jeremy Bentham did not. He was an economist, philosopher and jurist. At a time when Britain was a land of oppression – witness the way the law of seditious libel could be used against Paine – Bentham's sympathy for France was not in doubt. Indeed, in 1789, he had proposed a new constitution for France, in which 'the right of election shall be in every French citizen, male or female, being of full age, of sound mind and able to read'. However, when France's actual constitution appeared in 1793, Bentham regarded it as hopelessly muddled in its basic approach to human rights. Bentham's *Anarchical Fallacies*, completed in 1795 but not published until 1816, presented Thomas Paine's pro-Revolutionary words as 'Articles' or 'Sentences', which he then set out to rigorously critique.

Bentham's central point was that rights exist only where there is government to establish those rights and the rule of law to enforce them. In other words, rights exist only in a social context, where competing rights may be traded and balanced. 'Natural rights' outside the state were a recipe for anarchy, for they implied that people had the right to do things irrespective of their impact on others. Such rights were 'figurative', 'sentimental' and, in Bentham's famous phrase, 'nonsense upon stilts'.

JEREMY BENTHAM: *ANARCHICAL FALLACIES*, 'CRITIQUE OF THE DOCTRINE OF INALIENABLE, NATURAL RIGHTS'

ARTICLE II [OF PAINE'S DOCTRINE]

The end in view of every political association is the preservation of the natural and imprescriptible rights of man. These rights are liberty, property, security, and resistance to oppression.

[Bentham's response:] Sentence 1. The end in view of every political association, is the preservation of the natural and imprescriptible rights of man.

More confusion – more nonsense – and the nonsense, as usual, dangerous nonsense. The words can scarcely be said to have a meaning: but if they have, these would be the propositions either asserted or implied: –

1. That there are such things as rights anterior to the establishment of governments.
2. That these rights cannot be abrogated by government: for cannot is implied in the form of the word imprescriptible.
3. That the governments that exist derive their origin from formal associations or what are now called conventions: that all governments that have had any other origin are illegal, that is, no governments at all; resistance to them and subversion of them, lawful and commendable; and so on.

Such are the notions implied in this first part of the article. How stands the truth of things? We know what it is for men to live without government – and living without government, to live without rights: we see it in many savage nations, or rather races of mankind; for instance, among the savages of New South Wales, whose way of living is so well known to us: no habit of obedience, and thence no government – no government, and thence no laws – no laws, and thence no such things as rights.

In proportion to the want of happiness resulting from the want of rights, a reason exists for wishing that there were such things as rights. But reasons for wishing there were such things as rights, are not rights – a reason for wishing that a certain right were established, is not that right – want is not supply – hunger is not bread.

That which has no existence cannot be destroyed – that which cannot be destroyed cannot require anything to preserve it from destruction. Natural rights is simple nonsense: natural and imprescriptible rights, rhetorical nonsense – nonsense upon stilts.

The origination of governments from a contract is a pure fiction, or in other words, a falsehood. It never has been known to be true in any instance; the allegation of it does mischief, by involving the subject in error and confusion, and is neither necessary nor useful to any good purpose.

All governments that we have any account of have been gradually established by habit, after having been formed by force; unless in the instance of governments formed by individuals who have been emancipated, or have emancipated themselves, from governments already formed, the governments under which they were born – a rare case, and from which nothing follows with regard to the rest.

Whence is it, but from government, that contracts derive their binding force? Contracts came from government, not government from contracts. It is from the habit of enforcing contracts, and seeing them enforced that governments are chiefly indebted for whatever disposition they have to observe them.

Sentence 2. These rights [these imprescriptible as well as natural rights,] are liberty, property, security, and resistance to oppression.

Observe the extent of these pretended rights, each of them belonging to every man, and all of them without bounds. Their inconsistency with each other, as well as the inconsistency of them with the existence of government and all peaceable society, will appear still more plainly when we examine them one by one.

1. Liberty. What these instructors as well as governors of mankind appear not to know, is, that all rights are made at the expense of liberty – all laws by which rights are created or confirmed. There is no right without a correspondent obligation. Liberty, as against the coercion of the law, may, it is true, be given by the simple removal of the obligation by which that coercion was applied – by the simple repeal of the coercing law. But as against the coercion applicable by individual to individual, no liberty can be given to one man but in proportion as it is taken from another. All laws creative of liberty are, as far as they go, abrogative of liberty.

Laws creative of rights of property are also struck at by the same anathema. How is property given? By restraining liberty; that is, by taking it away so far as is necessary for the purpose. How is your house made yours? By debarring every one else from the liberty of entering it without your leave.

2. Property. According to this clause, whatever proprietary rights, whatever property a man once has, no matter how, being imprescriptible, can never be taken away from him by any law: or of what use or meaning is the clause? So that the moment it is acknowledged in relation to any article, that such article is my property, no matter how or when it became so, that moment it is acknowledged that it can never be taken away from me: therefore, for example, all laws and all judgments, whereby anything is taken away from me without my free consent – all taxes, for example, and all fines – are void, and, as such call for resistance and insurrection, and so forth, as before.

3. Security. Security for person is the branch that seems here to have been understood: security for each man's person, as against all those hurtful or disagreeable impressions by which a man is affected in his person; loss of life – loss of limbs – loss of the use of limbs – wounds, bruises, and the like. All laws are null and void then, which on any account or in any manner seek to expose the person of any man to any risk – which appoint capital or other corporal punishment – which expose a man to personal hazard in the service of the military power against foreign enemies, or in that of the judicial power against delinquents – all laws which, to preserve the country from pestilence, authorize the immediate execution of a suspected person, in the event of his transgressing certain bounds.

4. Resistance to oppression. Whenever you are about to be oppressed, you have a right to resist oppression. In proportion as a law of any kind is unpleasant to a man, he of course looks upon it as oppression. This article sets itself to work to blow the flame, and urges him to resistance. Submit not to any decree or other act of power, of the justice of which you are not yourself perfectly convinced. If a constable call upon you to serve in the militia, shoot the constable and not the enemy – if the commander of a press-gang trouble you, push him into the sea – if a bailiff, throw him out of the window. If a judge sentences you to be imprisoned or put to death, have a dagger ready, and take a stroke first at the judge.

◇ ◇ ◇

Bentham's alternative approach to 'natural rights' was to build on Joseph Priestley's argument that the aim of legislation should be to secure 'the greatest happiness of the greatest number'. Bentham developed the principle of utilitarianism, which was rooted in the observation that people are motivated by pleasure and pain. The happiest person was one who enjoyed the greatest pleasure and suffered the least pain, and the best society was one that maximised pleasure and minimised pain for the people as a whole. The morality of actions should be judged by how well or how badly they achieved this goal. According to the utilitarians, 'good' and 'bad' had no intrinsic meaning independent of that wider judgement.

In some ways, the debate between Paine and Bentham over natural rights versus utilitarianism inspired the two progressive philosophies of liberalism and social democracy. Their adherents made common cause on many issues, but their approaches to politics remained fundamentally distinct – not least in the arrangement of Britain's political parties after 1900. The difference between the two philosophies always punctured the intermittent dreams of those who wanted the Liberal and Labour parties to merge in order to fight the Conservatives.

1795

'THAT MAN TO MAN, THE WORLD O'ER, SHALL BROTHERS BE FOR A' THAT'

Robert Burns asserted the cause of the underdog at a time when it was risky to express such sentiments. The French Revolution had inspired him when it had terrified most of London's politicians. And for a Scot to pursue the cause of liberty, equality and fraternity looked subversively anti-English – which, to some extent, Burns was. He wanted a republic, but if he couldn't have that, he'd have preferred the monarchy to follow the line of Charles Edward Stuart – 'Bonnie Prince Charlie'. But Burns's Radicalism had a wider resonance and captured the popular imagination, especially in Scotland, which explains why he subsequently became the country's national poet.

ROBERT BURNS: 'A MAN'S A MAN FOR A' THAT'

Is there for honest Poverty
That hings his head, an' a' that;
The coward slave, we pass him by—
We dare be poor for a' that!
For a' that, an' a' that,
Our toils obscure an' a' that,
The rank is but the guinea's stamp,
The Man's the gowd for a' that.

What though on hamely fare we dine,
Wear hoddin grey, an' a that;
Gie fools their silks, and knaves their wine;
A Man's a Man for a' that:
For a' that, an' a' that,
Their tinsel show, an' a' that;
The honest man, tho' e'er sae poor,
Is king o' men for a' that.

Ye see yon birkie, ca'd a lord,
Wha struts, an' stares, an' a' that;
Tho' hundreds worship at his word,
He's but a coof for a' that:
For a' that, an' a' that,
His ribband, star, an' a' that:
The man o' independent mind
He looks an' laughs at a' that.

A prince can mak a belted knight,
A marquis, duke, an' a' that;
But an honest man's aboon his might,
Gude faith, he maunna fa' that!
For a' that, an' a' that,
Their dignities an' a' that;
The pith o' sense, an' pride o' worth,
Are higher rank than a' that.

Then let us pray that come it may,
(As come it will for a' that,)
That Sense and Worth, o'er a' the earth,
Shall bear the gree, an' a' that.
For a' that, an' a' that,
It's coming yet for a' that,
That Man to Man, the world o'er,
Shall brothers be for a' that.

Burns died the following year. He was only 37. Some periodicals had published his poem by then, but his own editor, George Thomson, feared prosecution and did not dare publish 'A Man's a Man For A' That' until 1805.

The song was sung by members of the Scottish Parliament when it met for the first time in 1999, amid widespread demands that the song become Scotland's national anthem.

1800

'ONE KINGDOM, BY THE NAME OF "THE UNITED KINGDOM OF GREAT BRITAIN AND IRELAND"'

The American Revolution inspired a fresh wave of dissent and rebellion in Ireland. In 1782, Britain sought to head off revolt by giving the Irish parliament greater power and allowing Catholics to take part. The move was counterproductive, for the new parliament provided a platform for members who resented the domination of the Protestant Ascendancy that largely ruled the island from Dublin Castle.

The French Revolution had an even greater impact. Many Irish Catholics looked to France to help them eject the British. Waves of French troops arrived between 1796 and 1798 in sufficient numbers to induce uprisings in Ulster in the north and Wexford in the south, but not enough to defeat Britain and secure independence. In 1800, once Britain had largely restored control over Ireland, both the Westminster and Dublin parliaments passed the Act of Union. A century earlier, union with Scotland had created 'Great Britain'; this new Act created the 'United Kingdom'.

ACT OF UNION 1800

> Whereas in pursuance of his Majesty's most gracious recommendation to the two houses of parliament in Great Britain and Ireland respectively, to consider of such measures as might best tend to strengthen and consolidate the connexion between the two kingdoms, the two houses of the parliament of Great Britain and the two houses of the parliament of Ireland have severally agreed and resolved, that, in order to promote and secure the essential interests of Great Britain and Ireland, and to consolidate the strength, power, and resources of the British Empire, it will be advisable to concur in such measures as may best tend to unite the two kingdoms of Great Britain and Ireland into one kingdom, in such manner, and on such terms and conditions, as may be established by the acts of the respective parliaments of Great Britain and Ireland:

And whereas, in furtherance of the said resolution, both houses of the said two parliaments respectively have likewise agreed upon certain articles for effectuating and establishing the said purposes, in the tenor following:

ARTICLE FIRST

That it be the first article of the union of the kingdoms of Great Britain and Ireland, that the said kingdoms of Great Britain and Ireland shall, upon the first day of January which shall be in the year of our lord one thousand eight hundred and one, and for ever after, be united into one kingdom, by the name of 'the United Kingdom of Great Britain and Ireland'; and that the royal style and titles appertaining to the imperial crown of the said united kingdom and its dependencies, and also the ensigns, armorial flags and banners thereof, shall be such as his Majesty, by his royal proclamation under the great seal of the united kingdom, shall be pleased to appoint.

ARTICLE SECOND

That it be the second article of union, that the succession to the imperial crown of the said united kingdom, and of the dominions thereunto belonging, shall continue limited and settled in the same manner as the succession to the imperial crown of the said kingdoms of Great Britain and Ireland now stands limited and settled, according to the existing laws, and to the terms of union between England and Scotland.

ARTICLE THIRD

That it be the third article of union, that the said United Kingdom be represented in one and the same parliament, to be styled 'The parliament of the United Kingdom of Great Britain and Ireland'.

Irish electors would henceforth choose around one fifth of the members of the Westminster parliament – but Catholics (and also Nonconformists) could not serve as MPs. Britain's 'Irish problem' remained a long way from solution.

1809

'Further Provision for preventing corrupt Practices in the procuring of Elections'

At the start of the nineteenth century, not only was Britain's electorate tiny but the practice of buying and selling seats in the House of Commons was also common – especially for those 'close boroughs', where few if any people still lived but which retained the right, established in the Middle Ages, to send representatives to Parliament. ('Open boroughs' were those that had real voters and more or less real elections.)

John Curwen, a Radical Whig, had advocated a wide range of reforms since he had entered Parliament in 1786 as MP for Carlisle. In 1809, he introduced a private member's bill to end the sale of seats in the Commons. The Act that finally emerged was universally known as 'Curwen's Act'. It imposed a fine of £1,000 – roughly £55,000 at today's prices – on those who were convicted of selling seats in Parliament.

Curwen's Act

An Act for better securing the Independence and Purity of Parliament, by preventing the procuring or obtaining of Seats in Parliament by corrupt Practices.

Whereas it is expedient to make further Provision for preventing corrupt Practices in the procuring of Elections and Returns of Members to sit in the House of Commons; Be it declared and enacted

That if any Person or Persons shall, from and after the passing of this Act, give or cause to be given, directly or indirectly, or promise or agree to give any Sum of Money, Gift, or Reward, to any Person or Persons, upon any Engagement, Contract, or Agreement, that such Person or Persons procure or endeavour to procure the Return of any Person to serve in Parliament for any County, Stewartry, City, Town, Borough, Cinque Port, or Place, every Person so having given or promised to give, if not returned himself to Parliament shall for every such Gift or Promise forfeit the sum of One Thousand Pounds; and every Person so returned shall be disabled and incapacitated to serve in that Parliament; and any Person or Persons who shall receive or accept any such Sum of Money, Gift, or Reward, or any such Promise, shall forfeit to His Majesty the Value of such Sum of Money, over and above the Sum of Five Hundred Pounds, which said Sum he shall forfeit to any Person who shall sue for the same.

Provided always, and be it further enacted, That nothing in this Act contained shall extend, or be construed to extend, to any Money paid or agreed to be paid to or by any Person, for any legal Expense *bona fide* incurred at or concerning any Election.

And be it further enacted

That if any Person or Persons shall, from and after the passing of this Act, give or procure to be given, or promise to give or procure to be given, any Office, Place, or Employment, to any Person or Persons whatsoever, or procure or endeavour to procure the Return of any Person to serve in Parliament, such Person so returned shall be and is hereby declared and enacted to be disabled and incapacitated to serve in that Parliament; and any Person holding any Office under his Majesty who shall procure or endeavour to procure the Return of any Person to serve in Parliament, shall forfeit the sum of One Thousand Pounds.

Curwen's Act did not end corruption, but it certainly curtailed it. In September 1812, shortly after he became prime minister, Lord Liverpool wrote to his friend Sir William Scott:

You will, perhaps, be surprised when I tell you that the Treasury have only one seat free of expense, for which our friend Vansittart will be elected. I have two more which personal friends have put at my disposal and this is the sum total free of expenses.

Mr Curwen's bill has put an end to all money transactions between Government and the supposed proprietors of boroughs. Our friends, therefore, who look for the assistance of Government must be ready to start for open boroughs, where the general influence of Government, combined with a reasonable expense on their part, may afford them a chance of success.

1817

'IT IS NOT ANARCHY YE ARE AFRAID OF: WHAT YE ARE AFRAID OF IS GOOD GOVERNMENT'

Jeremy Bentham wrote *Plan of Parliamentary Reform, in the Form of a Catechism* in 1809, but it was not published until 1817, when Bentham wrote a new introduction, which included this defence of universal suffrage against those detractors who said that giving every adult the vote would be dangerous.

JEREMY BENTHAM: *PLAN OF PARLIAMENTARY REFORM, IN THE FORM OF A CATECHISM*

On the topic of supposed or imputed dangerousness, accept the following observations, compressed to that degree of compression which time and place necessitate.

Objection: Universal suffrage, universal hostility and anarchy. *Answer*: No, not the smallest approach to any such evils.

No: it is not in the dangerousness and mischievousness—it is in the undangerousness and beneficialness of this and the other elements of reform, that, in the minds of the ruling and influential few, the opposition has its real ground. Not in the want of light, but in the abundance of it, look for the true object of their fears. In regard to appropriate intellectual aptitude, what is the real, the everlasting fear?—lest it be deficient? No: but lest it be abundant. Yes: on the hemisphere of religion, to delude them with false and political lights—on the political hemisphere, to keep them plunged in the thickest darkness: such, in their 'high situation,' is the policy of 'great characters;' such, in the very nature of things, it is ever destined to be, when vouchsafing to determine the lot of the swinish multitude.

Look on this occasion—if by any means you can endure to look that way—look once more to the American United States. Behold there democracy—behold there pure representative democracy. In the shape in question, any more than in any other shape, what mischief do you see there? In the American United States is there no property? Has it ever been destroyed since the establishment of independence?—has it ever been destroyed there, as it was here, in 1780, by your anti-popery mob; and in 1793, by your Church of England anti-sectarian mobs, with orthodox and loyal justices of the peace to encourage them?

'Oh, but,' says somebody, 'what they have in America is—not the universal-suffrage plan: it is more like the householder plan: only still less popular:—it is actually the property plan.'

True: in individuality, as above, it is not the universal-suffrage plan; but, in principle, look once more, and say once more—where and in what, if in anything, consists the difference? The property—the income there acquired from landed property—there, even as here—consider, even where largest, how small it is, compared with the least amount of what is necessary for, and actually expended on, the means of sustenance.

The Americans—they impose no tax upon the means of political information; you impose an almost prohibitory one. Why impose so enormous an one? Is it for the sake of the money? Yes, surely, in some degree for the money, but in a still greater degree for the sake of the darkness: the same transparent cunning which, in the teeth of all argument, and without the shadow of a pretence, has so recently, yet repeatedly engaged you to deprive them of the use of the press for giving expression to their desires, to keep them in the state of the profoundest ignorance possible, that in the existence of that ignorance you may have a plea for the perpetuation of it.

'Oh, but the information they get, it is, all of it, from Cobbett:—misinformation, all of it:—mischievous information:—a great deal worse than none.'

Well, be it so: what of that? The information you could give—yes, and would give too, if you gave any—what is it that hinders you from giving it? Have you not money enough?—enough at any rate for such a purpose? Know you not of writers enough, who have no objection to the taking of it? Have you not your champions—names with which paper such as this ought not to be defiled? The same hands which circulate your substitutes to the Bible, would they not serve, yea, and suffice, to circulate whatsoever writings it might seem good to you to circulate, for the purpose of serving as antidotes to all such others, by the influence of which good government might, in the fullness of time, be substituted to misrule?

'Oh, but to contend with Jacobins and atheists!—with Jacobins who would substitute the Habeas Corpus act to the abolition of it—atheists, who would substitute the Bible to creeds and catechisms!—to think of contending with such wretches on anything like equal terms!—to think of arguing with miscreants, for whom annihilation would be too mild a destiny!'

Aye—there's the rub! Ever under a monarchy—whether pure and absolute, or mixed and corrupt—everywhere but in that seat of licentiousness, a representative democracy, does excess in force employ itself in the filling up of all deficiencies, in the articles of reason and argument: and, the more palpable the deficiency, the more excessive, the more grinding, the more prostrative, the more irresistible the force.

So much for us of the swinish multitude: so much for us and our ignorance. But you—honourables and right honourables—how is it with you?

Opulence, indolence, intellectual weakness, cowardice, tyranny: Oh yes, these five are naturally in one. From opulence proceeds indolence—from indolence, intellectual weakness—from intellectual weakness, cowardice—from cowardice, tyranny. A phantom of danger presents itself: could he but fix his attention upon it, and look steadily at it, the phantom would vanish; but, being unexercised, his mind is weak: he has no such command over it. Frantic at the thoughts of the danger to himself, he gives his fiat to the cluster of tyrannies by which the security of the whole people is destroyed. And thus it is that, by the very fear—the groundless fear—of its destruction, security may be destroyed.

Yes!—you pillage them: you oppress them: you leave them nothing that you can help leaving them: you grant them nothing, not even the semblance of sympathy: you scorn them: you insult them: for the transgression of scores, or dozens, or units, you punish them by millions; you trample on them, you defame them, you libel them.

No, no:—it is not anarchy ye are afraid of: what ye are afraid of is good government. More and more uncontrovertibly shall this fear be proved upon you;—proved upon you, from the sequel of these pages, even to the very end.

1818

'HE TOSSED AWAY THE RULE AND THE SCALE ALTOGETHER, AND WITHOUT RESTRICTION LET IN ALL: YOUNG OR OLD, MEN OR WOMEN, SANE OR INSANE, ALL MUST VOTE'

On 2 June 1818, Sir Francis Burdett, MP for Westminster, proposed a motion in the House of Commons to provide for universal adult male franchise, annual elections and the secret ballot. A wealthy Radical who had been inspired by the French Revolution, Burdett devised the motion with Jeremy Bentham, and also worked closely with Lord Cochrane, MP for Honiton and another Radical. (Cochrane had been a swashbuckling, somewhat controversial, naval officer, who inspired the character of Horatio Hornblower in C.S. Forester's books, and Patrick O'Brian's character Jack Aubrey.) Their motion was opposed by Henry Brougham, Whig MP for Winchelsea, who was progressive by the general standards of the era, but felt that Burdett and Bentham had gone too far.

The following extracts from the debate are taken from Hansard, which, at that time, recorded speeches in the third person.

THE HOUSE OF COMMONS DEBATE ON THE FRANCHISE AND THE CONDUCT OF ELECTIONS

> **SIR FRANCIS BURDETT:** [In recent years] the question of reform had been greatly agitated: the ablest men of the age had fully discussed it, and sifted it to the bottom. Above all, Mr. Bentham had, with unrivalled ability, proved how easy and safe it was to carry the principles of reform into practical effect.
>
> Annual Parliaments and the most extensive mode of suffrage had been advocated by the late Duke of Richmond, in his famous letter to Colonel Sharman, with a strength of argument quite unanswerable. The same principles had been investigated and maintained with additional force and acuteness and philosophical accuracy, accompanied with complete demonstration of

the safety with which they might be reduced to practice, by Bentham. If any anti-reformer could answer Mr. Bentham's arguments, he would do more efficacious service to reformers and anti-reformers, than could ever be effected by dealing out false imputations and unsubstantiated slander, these being, with a due portion of misrepresentation and exaggeration, the only intellectual weapons hitherto employed by the enemies, against the friends, of reform.

If it could be shown that the most comprehensive suffrage would produce no inconvenience in practice, it ought not in justice to be withheld. Mr. Bentham had, by incontrovertible arguments, demonstrated that no danger whatever would arise from the most extensive suffrage that could be established.

MR. HENRY BROUGHAM: From this charge of inconsistency there was one great authority who was exempt—he meant Mr. Bentham. He had the greatest respect for that gentleman. There existed not a more honest or ingenuous mind than he possessed. He knew no man who had passed a more honourable and useful life. Removed from the turmoil of active life, voluntarily abandoning both emoluments and the power which it held out to dazzle ambitious and worldly minds, he had passed his days in the investigation of the most important truths, and had reached a truly venerable, although, he hoped, not an extreme old age. To him he meant not to impute either inadequate information, or insufficient industry, or defective sagacity.

But he hoped he should not be deemed disrespectful towards Mr. Bentham, if he said that his plan of parliamentary reform showed that he had dealt more with books than with men. He agreed with his honourable friend, the Member for Arundel (Sir Samuel Romilly), who looked up to Mr. Bentham with the almost filial reverence of a pupil for his tutor, in wishing that he had never written that work. But Mr. Bentham was a real advocate for universal suffrage. He was a far more sturdy, and infinitely more consistent reformer than the honourable baronet, as he gave votes not only to all men, but to all women also. He drew no line at all; he weighed not with practical nicety the claims of different classes; he recollected that his principle was universal; he tossed away the rule and the scale altogether, and without restriction let in all: young or old, men or women, sane or insane, all must vote—all must have a voice in electing their representatives. He did not even sanction the exceptions which the honourable baronet seemed inclined to admit with respect to persons of an unsound mind.

The veteran reformer (Major John Cartwright) had lately favoured the world with a plan of suffrage, illustrated by plates, where balloting-boxes, ball-trays, &c. &c. in most accurate array, met the eager gaze of the much-edified inquirer. Now Mr. Bentham was the patron of the ballot, and his doctrine was, that all who can ballot, may enjoy the elective franchise. The moment a person of either sex was able to put a pellet into a box, no matter whether he were insane, and had one of the keepers of a mad-house to guide him, still Mr. Bentham said, that though he did not support the utility of allowing idiots or mad persons to vote for their own sakes, yet rather than make any distinction, he would allow them, as they could not do any harm, and the unbending consistency might do some good. Mr. Bentham had such an invincible objection to lines of every description, that he could not admit of one being drawn, even at the gates of Bedlam. It was not necessary for him to controvert doctrines of this nature, but they were certainly consistent with each other; and he did not think himself uncharitable in saying, that some of the principles promulgated in that House were nearly as chimerical and visionary without being at all consistent.

SIR FRANCIS BURDETT: The learned gentleman (Mr. Brougham), whilst he professed himself friendly to reform, had at the same time attempted to render ridiculous the ablest advocate which reform had ever found—the illustrious and unrivalled Bentham. It was in vain, however, for the learned gentleman to attempt, by stale jokes and misapplied sarcasm, to undervalue the efforts, of a mind the most comprehensive, informed, accurate, acute, and philosophical, that had perhaps in any time or in any country been applied to the subject of legislation, and which, fortunately for mankind, had been brought to bear upon reform, the most important of all political subjects.

The abilities of Bentham, the learned gentleman could not dispute—his disinterestedness he could not deny—his benevolence he could not but admire—and his unremitted labours he would do well to respect, and not to attempt to disparage. The conviction of such a mind after mature investigation, overcoming preconceived prejudice, could not be represented as the result of wild and visionary speculation; and the zealous and honest adherents of the cause of reform might be well contented to rest the question on the foundations, broad and deep, upon which Bentham had placed it. The learned gentleman, therefore, unless he found himself competent at least to attempt to answer the reasons of Bentham, ought, for his own sake, to be more cautious how he endeavoured to misrepresent those reasons, or to effect by mis-statement, what he was unable to accomplish by argument.

Burdett was defeated by 106 votes to nil (i.e. no other MPs supported Burdett and Cochrane, who were tellers). Brougham, who was ennobled in 1830, went on to play an important role, as Lord Chancellor, in persuading the House of Lords to accept what became the Great Reform Act of 1832.

1819

'FROM THIS MOMENT THE YEOMANRY LOST ALL COMMAND OF TEMPER'

By 1819, Lord Liverpool's Tory government faced two sets of grievances that had become intertwined. One was the state of the economy: jobs were scarce and food prices high. The other was that the people who were suffering most had no voice in choosing the people that governed them. A number of political rallies were held to demand reform, culminating in one at St Peter's Field in Manchester on 16 August. It was presided over by Henry Hunt, one of the leaders of the reform movement. The protesters, who included many women and children, were unarmed.

However, local magistrates, alarmed by the size of the gathering, ordered the Manchester and Salford yeomanry to arrest the speakers. The following account of the 'Peterloo Massacre', as it came to be known – an ironic echo of the Battle of Waterloo four years earlier – was published in *The Annual Register*, an independent political review, founded by Edmund Burke in 1758.

THE ANNUAL REGISTER: THE PETERLOO MASSACRE

A little before noon on the 16th August, the first body of reformers began to arrive on the scene of action, which was a piece of ground called St. Peters Field, adjoining a church of that name in the town of Manchester. These persons bore two banners, surmounted with caps of liberty, and bearing the inscriptions, 'no corn laws', 'annual parliaments', 'universal suffrage', 'vote by ballot'. Some of these flags, after being paraded round the field, were planted in the cart on which the speakers stood; but others remained in different parts of the crowd.

Numerous large bodies of reformers continued to arrive from the towns in the neighbourhood of Manchester till about one o' clock, all preceded by flags and many of them in regular marching order, five deep. Two clubs of female reformers advanced, one of them numbering more than 150 members and bearing a white silk banner. One body of reformers timed their steps to the sound of a bugle with much of a disciplined air; another had assumed to itself the motto of the illustrious Wallace; 'God armeth the patriot'. A band of special constables assumed a position on the field without resistance.

The congregated multitude now amounted to a number roundly computed at 80,000, and the arrival of the hero of the day was impatiently expected. At length, Mr. Hunt made his appearance, and after a rapturous greeting, was incited to preside; he signified his assent, and mounting a scaffolding, began to harangue his admirers.

He had not proceeded far, when the appearance of the yeomanry cavalry advancing towards the area in a brisk trot, excited a panic in the outskirts of the meeting. They entered the enclosure, and after pausing a moment to recover their disordered ranks, and breathe their horses, they drew their swords, and brandished them fiercely in the air.

The multitude, by the direction of their leaders, gave three cheers to show that they were undaunted by this intrusion, and the orator had just resumed his speech to assure the people that this was only a trick to disturb the meeting, and to exhort them to stand firm, when the cavalry dashed into the crowd, making for the cart on which the speakers were placed.

The multitude offered no resistance, they fell back on all sides. The commanding officer then approaching Mr. Hunt, and brandishing his sword, told him that he was his prisoner. Mr. Hunt, after enjoining the people to tranquillity, said he would readily surrender to any civil officer on showing his warrant, and Mr. Nadin, the principal police officer, received him in charge. Another person named Johnson, was likewise apprehended, and a few of the mob, some others against whom there were warrants, escaped in the crowd.

A cry now arose among the military of, 'have at their flags' and they dashed down not only those in the cart, but the other dispersed in the field; cutting to right and left to get at them. The people began running in all directions; and from this moment the yeomanry lost all command of temper; numbers were trampled under the feet of men and horses; many, both men and women were cut down by sabres; several, and a peace officer and a female in the number, slain on the spot.

The whole number of persons injured amounted to between three and four hundred. The populace threw a few stones and brick bats in their retreat, but in less than ten minutes, the ground was entirely cleared of its former occupants, and filled by various bodies of military, both horse and foot.

◇ ◇ ◇

Although the numbers attending the rally and the number of casualties have remained matters of dispute, those given by *The Annual Register* are close to the figures that are now most widely accepted: around 60,000 demonstrators, 11 killed and around 500 wounded. Two local journalists were jailed for publishing their accounts of what happened. Henry Hunt served a prison sentence of 30 months. Lord Liverpool's government passed a series of laws, known as the Six Acts, which are the most repressive to have been enacted in the past 200 years. They curtailed the right to demonstrate; and any meeting to promote Radical reform was banned as 'an overt act of treasonable conspiracy'.

In 1821, one witness to the massacre, John Edward Taylor, responded by bringing together a group of local Nonconformist businessmen to launch a new newspaper that promised to 'zealously enforce the principles of civil and religious Liberty [and] warmly advocate the cause of Reform'. Thus was born *The Guardian* (or the *Manchester Guardian*, as it was called until 1959).

1819

'LET A GREAT ASSEMBLY BE
OF THE FEARLESS AND THE FREE'

Percy Bysshe Shelley learned of the Peterloo Massacre on 5 September, three weeks after the event, while living in Italy. He finished 'The Mask of Anarchy' by 18 September, and sent it to Leigh Hunt to be published in Hunt's Radical magazine, the *Examiner*. However, with mounting restrictions on the press, Hunt did not publish the poem until 1832, ten years after Shelley's death.

Shelley's poem refers to Lord Castlereagh (the Foreign Secretary), Lord Eldon (the Lord Chancellor) and Viscount Sidmouth (the Home Secretary).

PERCY BYSSHE SHELLEY: 'THE MASK OF ANARCHY'

As I lay asleep in Italy
There came a voice from over the Sea,
And with great power it forth led me
To walk in the visions of Poesy.

I met Murder on the way –
He had a mask like Castlereagh –
Very smooth he looked, yet grim;
Seven blood-hounds followed him:

All were fat; and well they might
Be in admirable plight,
For one by one, and two by two,
He tossed the human hearts to chew
Which from his wide cloak he drew.

Next came Fraud, and he had on,
Like Eldon, an ermined gown;

His big tears, for he wept well,
Turned to mill-stones as they fell.

And the little children, who
Round his feet played to and fro,
Thinking every tear a gem,
Had their brains knocked out by them.

Clothed with the Bible, as with light,
And the shadows of the night,
Like Sidmouth, next, Hypocrisy
On a crocodile rode by.

And many more Destructions played
In this ghastly masquerade,
All disguised, even to the eyes,
Like Bishops, lawyers, peers, or spies.

Last came Anarchy: he rode
On a white horse, splashed with blood;
He was pale even to the lips,
Like Death in the Apocalypse.

And he wore a kingly crown;
And in his grasp a sceptre shone;
On his brow this mark I saw –
'I AM GOD, AND KING, AND LAW!'

. . .

'What is Freedom? – ye can tell
That which slavery is, too well –
For its very name has grown
To an echo of your own.

'Tis to work and have such pay
As just keeps life from day to day
In your limbs, as in a cell
For the tyrants' use to dwell,

'So that ye for them are made
Loom, and plough, and sword, and spade,
With or without your own will bent
To their defence and nourishment.

'Tis to see your children weak
With their mothers pine and peak,
When the winter winds are bleak, –
They are dying whilst I speak.

. . .

'And at length when ye complain
With a murmur weak and vain
'Tis to see the Tyrant's crew
Ride over your wives and you –
Blood is on the grass like dew.

. . .

'What art thou Freedom? O! could slaves
Answer from their living graves
This demand – tyrants would flee
Like a dream's dim imagery:

'Thou art not, as impostors say,
A shadow soon to pass away,
A superstition, and a name
Echoing from the cave of Fame.

'For the labourer thou art bread,
And a comely table spread
From his daily labour come
In a neat and happy home.

'Thou art clothes, and fire, and food
For the trampled multitude –
No – in countries that are free

Such starvation cannot be
As in England now we see.

'To the rich thou art a check,
When his foot is on the neck
Of his victim, thou dost make
That he treads upon a snake.

'Thou art Justice – ne'er for gold
May thy righteous laws be sold
As laws are in England – thou
Shield'st alike the high and low.

'Thou art Wisdom – Freemen never
Dream that God will damn for ever
All who think those things untrue
Of which Priests make such ado.

'Thou art Peace – never by thee
Would blood and treasure wasted be
As tyrants wasted them, when all
Leagued to quench thy flame in Gaul.

'What if English toil and blood
Was poured forth, even as a flood?
It availed, Oh, Liberty,
To dim, but not extinguish thee.

'Thou art Love – the rich have kissed
Thy feet, and like him following Christ,
Give their substance to the free
And through the rough world follow thee,

'Or turn their wealth to arms, and make
War for thy belovèd sake
On wealth, and war, and fraud – whence they
Drew the power which is their prey.

'Science, Poetry, and Thought
Are thy lamps; they make the lot
Of the dwellers in a cot
So serene, they curse it not.

'Spirit, Patience, Gentleness,
All that can adorn and bless
Art thou – let deeds, not words, express
Thine exceeding loveliness.

'Let a great Assembly be
Of the fearless and the free
On some spot of English ground
Where the plains stretch wide around.

'Let the blue sky overhead,
The green earth on which ye tread,
All that must eternal be
Witness the solemnity.

'From the corners uttermost
Of the bounds of English coast;
From every hut, village, and town
Where those who live and suffer moan,

'From the workhouse and the prison
Where pale as corpses newly risen,
Women, children, young and old
Groan for pain, and weep for cold –

'From the haunts of daily life
Where is waged the daily strife
With common wants and common cares
Which sows the human heart with tares

'Lastly from the palaces
Where the murmur of distress
Echoes, like the distant sound
Of a wind alive around

'Those prison halls of wealth and fashion,
Where some few feel such compassion
For those who groan, and toil, and wail
As must make their brethren pale –

'Ye who suffer woes untold,
Or to feel, or to behold
Your lost country bought and sold
With a price of blood and gold –

'Let a vast assembly be,
And with great solemnity
Declare with measured words that ye
Are, as God has made ye, free.

. . .

'And these words shall then become
Like Oppression's thundered doom
Ringing through each heart and brain,
Heard again – again – again –

'Rise like Lions after slumber
In unvanquishable number –
Shake your chains to earth like dew
Which in sleep had fallen on you –
Ye are many – they are few.'

1820

'DEMOCRATIC REPRESENTATION CANNOT EXIST AS PART OF A MIXED GOVERNMENT'

Following the death of George III in January 1820, Parliament was dissolved and a general election was held in March and April. George Canning was re-elected as Tory MP for Liverpool with an increased majority. As a Cabinet minister, he supported the Six Acts that had been passed after the Peterloo Massacre to curb dissent. On 18 March, shortly after his election victory, he spoke at a meeting of his constituents to explain why he supported the new laws and opposed Radical reform of Parliament. He argued that the 'three branches of the constitution' – the Crown, the House of Lords and the House of Commons – worked well as they were.

Canning's speech is noteworthy for its defence not just of draconian measures but also of 'rotten boroughs' (or, as he called them, 'close boroughs') – parliamentary constituencies with few, if any, residents. These had once been thriving communities, but by the nineteenth century had not been so for many years. Yet dozens of MPs represented these constituencies, and had managed to hold on to them. Canning's speech refers to two such boroughs: the Cornish village of Grampound, and Old Sarum, near Salisbury, which had two MPs despite having had no inhabitants since the seventeenth century; its eleven electors were all landowners who lived elsewhere.

Canning also predicted that a more democratic House of Commons would end up weakening the authority of the House of Lords. In the long run he was, of course, quite right – but not in the assumption, implicit in his speech, that this process would provoke widespread horror.

GEORGE CANNING'S SPEECH TO HIS CONSTITUENTS IN LIVERPOOL OPPOSING WIDENING THE FRANCHISE

Has any country, in any two epochs, ever presented such a contrast with itself as this country in November 1819, and this country in February, 1820? Do I exaggerate when I say, that there was not a man of property who did not tremble for his possessions? That there was not a man of retired and peaceable habits who did not tremble for the tranquillity and security of his home? Was there any man who did not apprehend the Crown to be in danger?

What is the situation of the country now? Is there a man of property who does not feel the tenure by which he holds his possessions has been strengthened? Is there a man of peace who does not feel his domestic tranquillity to have been secured?

What has intervened between the two periods? A calling of that degraded Parliament; a meeting of that scoffed at and derided House of Commons; a concurrence of those three branches of an imperfect Constitution, not one of which, if we are to believe the radical reformers, lived in the hearts or commanded the respect of the nation; but which did restore order, confidence, a reverence for the laws, and a just sense of their own legitimate authority.

Do I deny, then, the general right of the people to meet, to petition, or to deliberate upon their grievances? God forbid! But social right is not a simple, abstract, positive, unqualified term. Rights are, in the same individual, to be compared to duties; and rights in one person are to be balanced with the rights of others.

Let us take this right of meeting in its most absolute sense. The persons who called the meeting at Manchester tell you that they had a right to collect together countless multitudes to discuss the question of parliamentary reform, without reference to the comfort or convenience of the neighbourhood. May not the peaceable, the industrious inhabitant of Manchester say, on the other hand, 'I have a right to quiet in my house; I have a right to be protected in the exercise of my lawful calling; I have a right to be protected against the intimidation or seduction of my workmen?'

Here is a conflict of rights, between which what is the decision? Can any honest man hesitate? Can the decision be other than that the peaceable and industrious shall be protected – the turbulent and mischievous put down?

All power is, or ought to be, accompanied by responsibility. Tyranny is irresponsible power. This definition is equally true, whether the power be lodged in one or many; whether in a despot or in a mob. [The gathering at

St Peter's Fields] was tyranny! And so far as the mobs were under control of a leader, that was despotism! It was against that tyranny, it was against that despotism, that Parliament at length raised its arm.

It has always struck me as extraordinary that there should be persons prepared to entertain radical reform of the House of Commons, without considering in what ways that change must affect the other members of the Constitution, and the action of the Constitution itself. I cannot conceive a Constitution of which one part be an assembly delegated by the people which must not, in a few days' sitting, sweep away every other branch of the Constitution that might attempt to oppose or control it. By what pretension could the House of Lords be maintained in equal authority and jurisdiction with the House of Commons, when once that House of Commons become a direct deputation, speaking the people's will?

I will not consent to take one step, without knowing on what principle I am invited to take it. What more harmless than to disenfranchise a corrupt borough in Cornwall? I have no objection to doing this, but I will *not* do it on the principle of speculative improvement. I will do it on the principle of specific punishment for an offence. And I will take good care that no inference shall be drawn from my consent in this specific case, as to any sweeping concurrence in a scheme of general alteration. I will take away a franchise because it has been practically abused; not because I am at all disposed to inquire into the origin or to discuss the utility of such franchises, any more than I mean to inquire, gentlemen, into your titles or your estates. Disenfranchising Grampound (if that is to be so), I mean to save Old Sarum.

Why is it that I am satisfied with a system which, it is said, no man can support who is not in love with corruption? I will answer for myself. I do verily believe that a complete and perfect democratic representation, such as the reformers aim at, cannot exist as part of a mixed government. My lot is cast under the British monarchy. I am not prepared to sacrifice or to hazard the fruit of centuries of experience, of centuries of struggles, and of more than one century of liberty, as perfect as ever blessed any country upon the earth, for visionary schemes of ideal perfectibility, or for doubtful experiments even of possible improvement.

I would have by choice – if the choice were yet to be made – I would have in this House of Commons a great variety of interests, and I would have them find their way by a great variety of rights of election; satisfied that uniformity of election would produce anything but a just representation of various interests. As to the close boroughs, I know that through them have found their way into the House of Commons men whose talents have been an honour to their kind, and whose names are interwoven with the brightest periods in the history of their country. I cannot think that system altogether vicious which has produced such fruits.

May every man who has a stake in the country, see that the time has come at which his decision must be taken, and, when once taken, steadfastly acted upon – for or against the institutions of the British monarchy!

Canning's argument bears an uncanny resemblance to the case being made today to resist reforming the House of Lords: that the system may not be democratic, but it supplies Parliament with some of its most distinguished members. Among the respresentatives of 'close boroughs' at different times were such major political figures as Henry Brougham, Charles Buller, Edmund Burke, William Pitt the Elder, Sir William Scott and Arthur Wellesley (later the Duke of Wellington).

Canning remained a Cabinet minister, eventually becoming prime minister in April 1827, but he died in office just four months later.

1828–9

'I AM READY TO GO TO PRISON TO PROMOTE THE CAUSE OF THE CATHOLICS, AND OF UNIVERSAL LIBERTY'

Economic inequalities afflicted Ireland as much as the British mainland, but in Ireland the issue was bound up with that of Catholic Emancipation. Catholics could not serve as Members of Parliament or work as civil servants unless they disowned their faith; and relatively few fulfilled the property qualifications that would allow them to vote. However, owing to a legal loophole, they could stand as parliamentary candidates.

In May 1828, William Vesey-Fitzgerald was appointed President of the Board of Trade. At that time, MPs who became government ministers had to resign their seat and seek a fresh mandate from their constituents. So a by-election was held in Vesey-Fitzgerald's Irish constituency of Clare. Daniel O'Connell decided to stand against him. O'Connell, subsequently known as 'The Liberator', was the leading politician of Catholic Ireland in his day.

A successful lawyer, O'Connell argued for peaceful reform – but warned successive British governments that if they refused to reform, the nationalist cause risked being taken over by those who advocated armed insurrection. This was his address to the electors of Clare, in which he considered both the question of his eligibility to serve as MP, and the record of his opponent, who was himself a supporter of Catholic Emancipation.

DANIEL O'CONNELL'S ADDRESS TO THE ELECTORS OF CLARE
ON CATHOLIC EMANCIPATION

TO THE ELECTORS OF THE COUNTY OF CLARE,

Dublin, June 1828

Fellow Countrymen,
Your county wants a representative. I respectfully solicit your suffrages, to raise me to that station.

Of my qualification to fill that station, I leave you to judge. The habits of public speaking, and many, many years of public business, render me, perhaps equally suited with most men to attend to the interests of Ireland in Parliament.

You will be told I am not qualified to be elected: the assertion, my friends, is untrue. I am qualified to be elected, and to be your representative. It is true that as a Catholic, I cannot, and of course never will, take the oaths at present prescribed to members of Parliament; but the authority which created these oaths (the Parliament), can abrogate them: and I entertain a confident hope that, if you elect me, the most bigotted of our enemies will see the necessity of removing from the chosen representative of the people, an obstacle which would prevent him from doing his duty to his King and to his country.

The oath at present required by law is, 'that the sacrifice of the Mass, and the invocation of the blessed Virgin Mary, and other saints, as now practised in the church of Rome, are impious and idolatrous.' Of course, I will never stain my soul with such an oath: I leave that to my honourable opponent, Mr Vesey-Fitzgerald; he has often taken that horrible oath; he is ready to take it again, and asks your votes to enable him so to swear. I would rather be torn limb from limb than take it. Electors of the county of Clare! choose between me, who abominates that oath, and Mr Vesey-Fitzgerald, who has sworn it full twenty times!

Return me to Parliament, and it is probable that such a blasphemous oath will be abolished for ever. As your representative, I will try the question with the friends in Parliament of Mr Vesey-Fitzgerald. They may send me to prison. I am ready to go there to promote the cause of the Catholics, and of universal liberty. The discussion which the attempt to exclude your representative from the House of Commons must excite, will create a sensation all over Europe, and produce such a burst of contemptuous indignation against British bigotry, in every enlightened country in the world, that the voice of all the great and good in England, Scotland, and Ireland, being joined to the universal shout of the nations of the earth, will overpower every opposition, and render it impossible for Peel and Wellington any longer to close the doors of the constitution against the Catholics of Ireland.

Electors of the county of Clare! Mr Vesey-Fitzgerald claims as his only merit, that he is a friend to the Catholics – why, I am a Catholic myself; and if he be sincerely our friend, let him vote for me, and raise before the British empire the Catholic question in my humble person, in the way most propitious to my final success. But no, fellow countrymen, no; he will make no sacrifice to that cause, he will call himself your friend, and act the part of your worst and most unrelenting enemy.

If you return me to Parliament, I pledge myself to vote for every measure favourable to radical reform in the representative system, so that the House of Commons may truly, as our Catholic ancestors intended it should do, represent all the people.

To vote for the repeal of the Vestry bill, the sub-letting act, and the Grand Jury laws.

To vote for the diminution and more equal distribution of the overgrown wealth of the established church in Ireland, so that the surplus may be restored to the sustentation of the poor, the aged, and the infirm.

To vote for every measure of retrenchment and reduction of the national expenditure, so as to relieve the people from the burdens of taxation, and to bring the question of the repeal of the Union, at the earliest possible period, before the consideration of the legislature.

Electors of the county of Clare! choose between me and Mr Vesey-Fitzgerald; choose between him who has so long cultivated his own interest, and one who seeks only to advance yours; choose between the sworn libeller of the Catholic faith, and one who has devoted his early life to your cause; who has consumed his manhood in a struggle for your liberties, and who has ever lived, and is ready to die for the integrity, the honour, the purity, of the Catholic faith, and the promotion of Irish freedom and happiness.

Your faithful servant,

DANIEL O'CONNELL

O'Connell won the election, but was unable to take his seat at Westminster. The election and its outcome made the issue of Catholic Emancipation one of the most urgent political controversies facing the Tory government, now led by the Duke of Wellington.

Wellington, the victor at Waterloo, had entered the Irish Parliament in 1790 and the House of Commons in 1806. On receiving his peerage, in 1809, he transferred to the House of Lords. He became prime minister at the head of a Tory administration in 1828. Although generally opposed to reform, Wellington feared that O'Connell's victory in the Clare by-election could provoke an uprising in Ireland. With Robert Peel, the Home Secretary and Leader of the House of Commons, he persuaded George IV to support the full Emancipation of all Catholics. Wellington set out the case for Emancipation in the second reading of the Roman Catholic Relief Bill on 2 April 1829.

THE DUKE OF WELLINGTON'S SPEECH SUPPORTING CATHOLIC EMANCIPATION

My lords, the point which I shall first bring under your lordships' consideration is the state of Ireland. I know that, by some, it has been considered that the state of Ireland has nothing to do with this question – that it is a subject which ought to be left entirely out of our consideration. My lords, they tell us, that Ireland has been disturbed for the last thirty years – that it is a disturbance we have been accustomed to – and that therefore it does not at all alter the circumstances of the case, as they have hitherto appeared to this House. My lords, it is perfectly true that Ireland has been disturbed during the long period I have stated; but within the last year or two political circumstances have, in no small degree, occasioned that agitation.

My lords, late in the year a considerable town was attacked in the middle of the night by a body of people who came from the neighbouring mountains – the town of Augher. They attacked it with arms, and were driven from it with arms by the inhabitants of the town. This is a state of things which I feel your lordships will admit ought not to exist in a civilized country. Later in the year still, a similar event occurred in Charleville; and, in the course of last autumn, the Roman Catholic Association deliberated upon the propriety of adopting, and the means of adopting, the measure of ceasing all dealings between Roman Catholics and Protestants. My lords, this is the state of society to which I have wished to draw your attention, and for which it is necessary that parliament should provide a remedy.

We might, to be sure, have come and asked parliament to enable us to put down the Roman Catholic Association; but what chance had we of prevailing upon parliament to pass such a bill as that, without being prepared to come forward and state that we were ready to consider the whole condition of Ireland, with a view to apply a remedy to that which parliament had stated to be the cause of the disease? Suppose that parliament had given us the bill to put down the Roman Catholic Association, would it, I ask, do any one thing towards putting down the mischiefs which are the consequences of that organization? Would it do any thing towards giving you the means of getting a better state of things in Ireland, without some further measure to be adopted?

But, my lords, it is said, 'if that will not do, let us proceed to blows.' What, I suppose, is meant by 'proceeding to blows' is coming to civil war. Now, I believe that every government must be prepared to carry into execution the laws of the country by the force placed at its disposition – by the military force, in case that should be necessary; and above all things, to oppose resistance to the law, in case the disaffected or the ill-disposed are inclined to resist the authority or sentence of the law.

But, my lords, even if I had been certain of possessing such means of putting it down, I should certainly have considered it my duty to avoid resorting to those means. I am one of those who have probably passed a longer period of my life engaged in war than most men, and principally, I may say, in civil war; and I must say this – that if I could avoid, by any sacrifice whatever, even one month of civil war in the country to which I am attached, I would sacrifice my life in order to do it *(cheers)*. I say that there is nothing which destroys property and prosperity, and demoralizes character, to the degree that civil war does: by it the hand of man is raised against his neighbour, against his brother, and against his father; the servant betrays his master, and the whole scene ends in confusion and devastation. Yet, my lords, this is the resource to which we must have looked – these are the means to which we must have applied, in order to have put an end to this state of things, if we had not made the option of bringing forward the measures, for which I hold myself responsible.

My lords; the bill is in itself very simple. It concedes to the Roman Catholics the power of holding every office in the state, excepting a few connected with the administration of the affairs of the church; and it also concedes to them the power of becoming members of parliament. I believe it goes further, with respect to the concession of offices, than any former measure which has been introduced into the other House of parliament. I have considered it my duty, in making this act of concession, to make it as large as any reasonable man could expect it to be; seeing clearly, that any thing which remained behind would only give ground for fresh demands, and being convinced, that the settlement of this question would tend to the security of the state, and to the peace and prosperity of the country.

It is the opinion of nearly every considerable man in the country, that the time is now arrived for repealing those laws. Circumstances have been gradually moving to their repeal, ever since the extinction of the House of Stuart; and at last the period is come, when it is quite clear that that repeal cannot with safety be any longer delayed.

There is no doubt that, after this measure shall be adopted, the Roman Catholics can have no separate interest, as a separate sect; for I am sure that neither your lordships nor the other House of parliament will be disposed to look upon the Roman Catholics, nor upon any thing that respects Ireland, with any other eye than that with which you behold whatever affects the interest of Scotland and of this country. For my own part, I will state, that if I am disappointed in the hopes which I entertain, that tranquillity will result from this measure, I shall have no scruple in coming down and laying before parliament the state of the case, and calling upon parliament to enable government to meet whatever danger may arise. I shall act with the same confidence that parliament will support me then, as I have acted in the present case.

The bill, containing a new oath, became law with the support of the Whigs.

1830

'IF REFORM WERE NOT ATTENDED TO IN TIME, THE PEOPLE WOULD LOSE ALL CONFIDENCE IN PARLIAMENT'

I n the general election of July/August 1830 (necessitated by the death of George IV), the Conservatives lost seats but remained the largest party in the House of Commons. The Whigs, led by Earl Grey, proposed a reform of Britain's election system, including widening the franchise and ending the system of 'rotten boroughs'. On 2 November, Grey and Wellington debated the issue in the House of Lords, with Grey defending limited reform as the best way to fend off both revolution and – horror of horrors – universal adult franchise, and Wellington resisting reform altogether. Wellington's reputation as the 'Iron Duke' dates from this period. The label refers not to his military exploits but to his reaction to pro-reform demonstrations outside his London home, Apsley House, which led to bricks being thrown through his windows. He installed iron shutters to prevent further damage.

THE HOUSE OF LORDS DEBATE ON THE REFORM BILL

> **GREY:** Through my whole life I have advocated reform, and I have thought that, if it were not attended to in time, the people would lose all confidence in Parliament, and we must make our minds to witness the destruction of the constitution. I trust that it will not be put off as the Catholic question was put off, but considered in time so that measures may be introduced by which gradual reform can be effected without danger to the institutions of the country.
>
> I have never thought that reform should be insisted on as a matter of popular right, nor have I ever advocated the principle of universal suffrage, which, on the contrary, has always seemed to me to be inconsistent with our institutions. We are now told that every man who pays taxes has a right to participate in the choice of members of the legislature. We are told

more than that – we are told that every man who contributes to the wealth of the country by his labour has a right to vote; we are told, indeed, that every man who has arrived at a full age is entitled to this privilege. These are principles which I deny, and claims which I oppose. The right of the people is to good government; and that is, in my judgement, inconsistent with universal suffrage under our present institutions.

If suffrage be the right of all who pay a certain tax, then I say, that it is in the limit, and not in the extension of that privilege, that such a right consists. I say, my Lords, that preparation ought to be made to revise the constitution, to extend its blessings, and to secure the affection of the people, to ensure their tranquillity, and to confirm their confidence in the legislature, and in a King who only lives for the good of his subjects.

WELLINGTON: The noble Earl has alluded to the propriety of effecting parliamentary reform. The noble Earl has, however, been candid enough to acknowledge that he is not prepared with any measure of reform, and I can have no scruple in saying that his Majesty's government is as totally unprepared with any plan as the noble Lord.

Nay, I, on my own part, will go further, and say, that I have never read or heard of any measure up to the present moment which can in any degree satisfy my mind that the state of the representation can be improved, or be rendered more satisfactory to the country at large than at the present moment. I will not, however, at such an unseasonable time, enter upon the subject, or excite discussion, but I shall not hesitate to declare unequivocally what are my sentiments upon it.

I am fully convinced that the country possesses at the present moment a legislature which answers all the good purpose of legislation, and this to a greater degree than any legislature ever has answered in any country whatever. I will go further, and say, that the legislature and the system of representation possess the full and entire confidence of the country— deservedly possess that confidence—and the discussions in the legislature have a very great influence over the opinions of the country.

I will go still further, and say, that if at the present moment I had imposed upon me the duty of forming a legislature for any country, and particularly for a country like this, in possession of great property of various descriptions, I do not mean to assert that I could form such a legislature as we possess now, for the nature of man is incapable of reaching such excellence at once; but my great endeavour would be to form some description of legislature which would produce the same results.

The representation of the people at present contains a large body of the property of the country, and in which the landed interests have a preponderating influence. Under these circumstances, I am not prepared to bring forward any measure of the description alluded to by the noble Lord. I am not only not prepared to bring forward any measure of this nature, but I will at once declare that as far as I am concerned, as long as I hold any station in the government of the country, I shall always feel it my duty to resist such measures when proposed by others.

Wellington could tell his speech had been badly received. As he sat down, he whispered to his Foreign Secretary, the Earl of Aberdeen, 'What can I have said which seems to have made so great a disturbance?' Aberdeen told him: 'You have announced the fall of your government, that is all.' Aberdeen was right. Whig MPs in the House of Commons were determined to pursue reform, albeit in a limited form. On 15 November, Wellington lost a vote of confidence in the House of Commons and resigned the following day. On 22 November, Earl Grey was appointed prime minister.

1830

'It is no temporary cause that is at work; it is a deep sense of grievous wrongs'

In 1830, a series of riots took place, known as the 'Captain Swing' riots. Agricultural workers complained of low wages and unemployment at a time when new machinery was being introduced in many farms. During the riots, farm machinery was destroyed in many parts of Britain. Around 600 people were imprisoned, 500 transported and 19 executed: punishments that were defended by Earl Grey, leader of the Whig opposition until he became prime minister in November 1830. William Cobbett wrote this article for the *Political Register*, published on 27 November, defending the rioters and linking their struggle to the cause of wider parliamentary reform. It appeared days after Grey became prime minister.

William Cobbett: 'Rural Wars'

Forty-five years ago, the labourers brewed their own beer, and that now none of them do it; that formerly they ate meat, cheese and bread, and they now live almost wholly on potatoes; that formerly it was a rare thing for a girl to be with child before she was married, and that now it is as rare that she is not, the parties being so poor that they are compelled to throw the expense of the wedding on the parish; that the felons in the jails and hulks live better than the honest labouring people, and that these latter commit thefts and robbery, in order to get into the jails and hulks, or to be transported; that men are set to draw wagons and carts like beasts of burden; that they are shut up like Negroes in Jamaica; that married men are forcibly separated from their wives to prevent them from breeding.

It is no *temporary cause*, it is no *new* feeling of discontent that is at work; it is a deep sense of grievous wrongs; it is long harboured resentment; it is an accumulation of revenge for unmerited punishment . . . it is a natural effect of a cause which is as obvious as that ricks are consumed by fire, when fire is put to them.

But if this excite our astonishment, what are we to say of that part of Lord Grey's speech in which he speaks of 'instigators'? What! can these men look at the facts before their eyes; can they see the millions of labourers everywhere rising up, and hear them saying that they will *'no longer starve on potatoes'*; can they see them breaking threshing-machines; can they see them gathering together and demanding an increase of wages; can they see all this, and can they believe that the *fires* do not proceed from the same persons; but that these are the work of some invisible and almost incorporeal agency!

The *motive* of it is, however, evident enough to men who reflect that every tax-eater and tithe-eater, no matter of what sort or size he or she is, is afraid to believe, and wishes the nation not to believe, that *the fires are the work of the labourers*. And *why* are they so reluctant to believe this, and so anxious that it should be believed by nobody? Because the labourers are *the millions* (for mind, *smiths, wheelwrights, collar-makers, carpenters, bricklayers,* are all of one mind); and because, if *the millions be bent upon this work,* who is to stop it?

Then to believe that the labourers are the burners, is to believe that they must have been urged to the deeds by desperation, proceeding from *some grievous wrong,* real or imaginary; and to believe this is to believe that the burnings will continue, until the *wrong be redressed.* To believe this is to believe that there must be such a change of system as will take *from the tax and tithe-eaters a large portion of what they receive, and give it back to the labourers,* and believe this the tax and tithe-eaters never will, until the political Noah *shall enter into the ark!*

[The labourers] look upon themselves as engaged in a *war* with a *just object.* Is this destructive war to go on till all law and all personal safety are at an end? The truth is, that, for many years past, about *forty-five millions a year* have been *withheld from the working-people of England;* about five or six millions have been doled back to them in *poor rates;* and the forty millions have gone to keep up *military academies, dead-weight standing-army, military asylums, pensions, sinecures,* and to give to parsons, and to build new palaces and pull down others, and to pay loan-mongers and all that enormous tribe; and to be expended in various other ways not at all necessary to the well-being of the nation.

These *forty millions* a year must now *remain with the working people* . . . And what is to be the *result* of all this? Why, a violent destruction of the whole fabric of the Government, or a timely, that is, an *immediate* and *effectual* remedy; and there is no remedy but a *radical reform of the Parliament.*

◇ ◇ ◇

In 1831, following the publication of this article, Cobbett was charged with sedition. He refused to engage a barrister, and defended himself – so successfully that the jury declined to convict him, and he went free. In 1832, following the Great Reform Act, Cobbett was finally elected to Parliament at the age of sixty-nine as MP for Oldham, but he died three years later.

1831–2

'THE PRINCIPLE IS TO ADMIT THE MIDDLE CLASS TO A DIRECT SHARE IN THE REPRESENTATION, WITHOUT ANY VIOLENT SHOCK TO THE INSTITUTIONS OF OUR COUNTRY'

While Cobbett argued for radical change, the campaign for more modest reforms was gathering pace. In March 1831, Earl Grey's government introduced a Representation of the People Bill, which standardised the laws on who had the vote. Its intended effect was to double the number of electors; however, even this would leave nine out of ten men over twenty-one years old without the vote. The bill also sought to disenfranchise all the 'rotten boroughs' and to allocate more MPs to fast-growing cities such as Leeds and Manchester.

In the House of Commons, the task of introducing the bill was given to Lord John Russell. He was a relatively junior Cabinet minister, but had been one of Grey's 'Committee of Four' that had drafted the bill. The other three members of the Committee wanted a further reform – secret ballots. Russell alone opposed this, and his view was endorsed by the full Cabinet. He was therefore well placed to make the case for the bill to MPs. He delivered the following speech on 1 March 1831.

THE HOUSE OF COMMONS DEBATE ON THE REFORM BILL

LORD JOHN RUSSELL: No man of common sense pretends that this assembly now represents the commonalty or people of England. If it be a question of right, therefore, right is in favour of reform.

Allow me to imagine, for a moment, a stranger from some distant country, who should arrive in England to examine our institutions. He would have been told that the proudest boast of this celebrated country was its political freedom. If, in addition to this, he had heard that once in six years this country, so wise, so renowned, so free, chose its representatives to sit in the great council where all the ministerial affairs were discussed and determined, he would not be a little curious to see the process by which so important and solemn an operation was effected.

What then would be his surprise if he were taken by his guide, whom he had asked to conduct him to one of the places of election, to a green mound and told that this green mound sent two members to parliament, or to be taken to a stone wall with three niches in it and told that these three niches sent two members to parliament; or, if he were shown a green park with many signs of flourishing vegetable life, but none of human habitation, and told that this green park sent two members to parliament!

But his surprise would increase to astonishment if he were carried into the north of England, where he would see large flourishing towns, full of trade and activity, containing vast magazines of wealth and manufactures, and were told that these places had no representatives in the assembly which was said to represent the people. Suppose him, after all, for I will not disguise any part of the case – suppose him to ask for a specimen of popular election, and to be carried for that purpose to Liverpool; his surprise would be turned into disgust at the gross venality and corruption which he would find to pervade the electors.

After seeing all this, would he not wonder that a nation which had made such progress in every kind of knowledge, and which valued itself for its freedom, should permit so absurd and defective a system of representation any longer to prevail? But whenever arguments of this kind have been urged, it has been replied – and Mr. Canning placed his opposition to reform on this ground – 'We agree that the house of commons is not, in fact, sent here by the people; we agree that, in point of reason, the system by which it is sent is full of anomaly and absurdity; but government is a matter of experience, and so long as the people are satisfied with the actual working of the house of commons, it would be unwise to embark in theoretical change.'

Of this argument, I confess, I always felt the weight, and so long as the people did not answer the appeals of the friends of reform, it was indeed an argument not to be resisted. But what is the case at this moment? The whole people call loudly for reform. The chief grievances of which the people complain are these: first, the nomination of members by individuals; second, the elections by close corporations; third, the expense of elections.

I arrive at last at the objections which may be made to the plan we propose. I shall be told, in the first place, that we overturn the institutions of our ancestors. I maintain that, in departing from the letter, we preserve the spirit of those institutions. Our opponents say our ancestors gave Old Sarum representatives; therefore we should give Old Sarum representatives. We say our ancestors gave Old Sarum representatives because it was a large town; therefore we give representatives to Manchester, which is a large town.

It has been asserted also, if a reform were to be effected, that many men of great talents, who now get into this house for close boroughs, would not be able to procure seats. I have never entertained any apprehensions of the sort, for I believe that no reform that can be introduced will have the effect of preventing wealth, probity, learning, and wit from having their proper influence upon elections. It may be said, too, that one great and injurious effect of the measures I propose will be to destroy the power and privileges of the aristocracy. This I deny. Wherever the aristocracy reside, receiving large incomes, performing important duties, relieving the poor by charity, and evincing private worth and public virtue, it is not in human nature that they should not possess a great influence upon public opinion and have an equal weight in electing persons to serve their country in parliament. Though such persons may not have the direct nomination of members under this bill, I contend that they will have as much influence as they ought to have.

But if by aristocracy those persons are meant who do not live among the people, who know nothing of the people, and who care nothing for them – who seek honours without merit, places without duty, and pensions without service – for such an aristocracy I have no sympathy; and I think the sooner its influence is carried away, with the corruption on which it has thriven, the better for the country.

We propose that every borough which in 1821 had less than 2,000 inhabitants, shall altogether lose the right of sending Members to Parliament. The effect will be, utterly to disfranchise sixty boroughs. But we do not stop here. We find that there are forty-seven boroughs, of only 4,000 inhabitants, and these we shall deprive of the right of sending more than one Member to Parliament. We likewise intend that Weymouth, which at present sends four Members, shall, in future, only elect two. The abolition of sixty boroughs will occasion 119 vacancies, to which are to be added forty-seven for the boroughs allowed to send only one Member, and two of which Weymouth will be deprived, making in the whole 168 vacancies. Such is the extent to which Ministers propose to go in the way of disfranchisement.

We do not mean to allow that the remaining boroughs should be in the hands of select Corporations – that is to say, in the possession of a small number of persons, to the exclusion of the great body of the inhabitants, who have property and interest in the place represented. We therefore propose that the right of voting shall be given to householders paying rates for, or occupying a house of, the yearly value of £10 and upwards. Whether he be the proprietor, or whether he only rent the house, the person rated will have the franchise, upon certain conditions hereafter to be named.

It is my opinion that the whole measure will add to the constituency of the Commons House of Parliament, about half a million of Persons, and these all connected with the property of the country, having a valuable stake amongst us, and deeply interested in our institutions. They are the persons on whom we can depend in any future struggle in which this nation may be engaged, and who will maintain and support Parliament and the Throne in carrying that struggle to a successful termination. I think that those measures will produce a further benefit to the people, by the great incitement which it will occasion to industry and good conduct. For when a man finds, that by industrious exertion, and by punctuality, he will entitle himself to a place in the list of voters, he will have an additional motive to improve his circumstances, and to preserve his character amongst his neighbours. I think, therefore, that in adding to the constituency, we are providing for the moral as well as for the political improvement of the country.

The following day's debate saw this speech in support of the bill from Thomas Macaulay. He was a historian, a Whig politician and an active supporter of limited reform of the British parliament. Macaulay defended the bill against demands for full adult (male) suffrage, and also defended the continuing role of the aristocracy in Parliament. His speech was a classic of its kind – proposing limited measures as the best way both to prevent insurrection and to curb the risk of more radical reform.

THOMAS MACAULAY: I will not, sir, at present express any opinion as to the details of the Bill; but having during the last twenty-four hours given the most diligent consideration to its general principles, I have no hesitation in pronouncing it a wise, noble, and comprehensive measure, skilfully framed for the healing of great distempers, for the securing at once of the public liberties and of the public repose, and for the reconciling and knitting together of all the orders of the State. The principle is plain, rational, and consistent. It is this – to admit the middle class to a large and direct share in the representation, without any violent shock to the institutions of our country.

I believe that there are societies in which every man may safely be admitted to vote. There are countries in which the condition of the labouring-classes is such that they may safely be entrusted with the right of electing members of the Legislature. If the labourers of England were in that state in which I, from my soul, wish to see them; if employment were always plentiful, wages always high, food always cheap; if a large family were considered not as an incumbrance but as a blessing – the principal objections to universal suffrage would, I think, be removed. Universal suffrage exists in the United States without producing any very frightful consequences; and I do not believe that the people of those States, or of any part of the world, are in any good quality naturally superior to our own countrymen. But, unhappily, the lower orders in England, and in all old countries, are occasionally in a state of great distress.

For the sake, therefore, of the whole society, for the sake of the labouring-classes themselves, I hold it to be clearly expedient that, in a country like this, the right of suffrage should depend on a pecuniary qualification. Every argument, sir, which would induce me to oppose universal suffrage, induces me to support the measure which is now before us. I oppose universal suffrage, because I think that it would produce a destructive revolution. I support this measure, because I am sure that it is our best security against a revolution.

I support this measure as a measure of reform; but I support it still more as a measure of conservation. That we may exclude those whom it is necessary to exclude, we must admit those whom it may be safe to admit.

My hon. friend the member of the University of Oxford tells us that, if we pass this law, England will soon be a Republic. The reformed House of Commons will, according to him, before it has sat ten years, depose the King, and expel the Lords from their House. Sir, if my hon. friend could prove this, he would have succeeded in bringing an argument for democracy infinitely stronger than any that is to be found in the works of Paine. His proposition is, in fact, this – that our monarchical and aristocratical institutions have no hold on the public mind of England; that these institutions are regarded with aversion by a decided majority of the middle class.

Now, sir, if I were convinced that the great body of the middle class in England look with aversion on monarchy and aristocracy, I should be forced, much against my will, to come to this conclusion, that monarchical and aristocratic institutions are unsuited to this country. Monarchy and aristocracy, valuable and useful as I think them, are still valuable and useful as means, and not as ends. The end of government is the happiness of the people; and I do not conceive that, in a country like this, the happiness of the people can be promoted by a form of government in which the middle classes place no confidence, and which exists only because the middle classes have no organ by which to make their sentiments known. But, sir, I am fully convinced that the middle classes sincerely wish to uphold the royal prerogatives, and the constitutional rights of the Peers.

Is it possible that gentlemen long versed in high political affairs cannot read these signs? Is it possible that they can really believe that the representative system of England, such as it now is, will last till the year 1860? If not, for what would they have us wait? Would they have us wait merely that we may show to all the world how little we have profited by our own recent experience? Would they have us wait that we may once again hit the exact point where we can neither refuse with authority nor concede with grace? Would they have us wait that the numbers of the discontented party may become larger, its demands higher, its feelings more acrimonious, its organisation more complete?

Have they forgotten how the spirit of liberty in Ireland, debarred from its natural outlet, found a vent by forbidden passages? Have they forgotten how we were forced to indulge the Catholics in all the license of rebels, merely because we chose to withhold from them the liberties of subjects? Let them wait, if this strange and fearful infatuation be indeed upon them, that they should not see with their eyes, or hear with their ears, or understand with their heart.

But let us know our interest and our duty better. Turn where we may – within, around – the voice of great events is proclaiming to us, 'Reform, that you may preserve.' Now, while the heart of England is still sound; now, while the old feelings and the old associations retain a power and a charm which may too soon pass away; now, in this your accepted time; now, in this your day of salvation, take counsel, not of prejudice, not of party spirit, not of the ignominious pride of a fatal consistency, but of history, of reason, of the ages which are past, of the signs of this most portentous time.

Save the multitude, endangered by their own ungovernable passions. Save the aristocracy, endangered by its own unpopular power. Save the greatest, and fairest, and most highly, civilised community that ever existed, from calamities which may lit a few days sweep away all the rich heritage of so many ages of wisdom and glory. The danger is terrible. The time is short. If this Bill should be rejected, I pray to God that none of those who concur in rejecting it may ever remember their votes with unavailing regret, amidst the wreck of laws, the confusion of ranks, the spoliation of property, and the dissolution of social order.

◇ ◇ ◇

On 23 March, the bill was approved by a majority of just one: 302 votes to 301. In the committee stage that followed, the bill's opponents proposed an amendment to scrap the plan to reduce the overall number of MPs from 658 to 596. This amendment was carried by eight votes, effectively wrecking the bill.

Earl Grey responded by calling a snap general election (fought, of course, under the old rules). The Tories lost seats, and the Liberals were returned with a majority of around 130. A new bill was introduced, again widening the franchise and ending the system of 'rotten boroughs', but *not* reducing the overall number of MPs. In a debate on 20 July, Sir Robert Peel opposed the new bill on behalf of the Conservatives:

SIR ROBERT PEEL: [It has been said that the bill's] object was to give to the people a full and fair representation in parliament, and that, as such, it might be justly described as a restoration of the ancient principles of the constitution; for that those principles were that the people should be fully and fairly represented in the commons house of parliament. Now that involved the fallacy that the people of this country ever had the right which it was proposed to give them by this bill.

I would deny that the phrase, the people of England, ever meant the people of England as they were polled by this bill. What was meant by the people of England, when we spoke of the representation of the people of England in ancient times, consisted in the great corporate bodies and those great classes of the community to whom the franchise was entrusted and of whom the members sent to parliament were the representatives. The word 'people' was never used then as it was in the present bill – it was never used so as to mean £10 householders who had never hitherto possessed a right to that franchise which it was now proposed to give them.

The elective franchise, as it had been established in England in former times, had never existed in the form in which the present bill proposed to establish it, but in a much better, more practical, and more beneficial form. So far as [close] boroughs were concerned, they certainly could not be described as any usurpation on the rights of the people.

It was said that the possession of such boroughs could not be advantageous to the aristocracy and, indeed, the lord advocate of Scotland has argued upon a former night that, as the right of returning members from such boroughs was vested in individuals, the possession of such boroughs was disadvantageous to the interests of the aristocracy at large.

Against the government's wishes, an amendment was passed to give the vote to 'tenants at will': people who, at their landowners' discretion, lived in properties worth £50 or more. This was supported as a further extension of the franchise – and opposed as a device that could increase the power of landowners (as, in the absence of a secret ballot, they could see how their tenants voted). Even so, the House of Lords (which still had a large Tory majority) rejected the bill on 8 October. This led to widespread demonstrations, some of which turned ugly: the Duke of Newcastle's castle was burned down, and the windows of the Duke of Wellington's home were broken.

In December 1831, Earl Grey introduced a third Reform Bill, which preserved most of the main characteristics of the second bill. The king agreed to Grey's request that, if necessary, 50 to 60 new peers would be created to help him pass the bill. In the event, the Lords backed off. Enough Tory peers switched sides to approve the bill, in April 1832, by 184 votes to 175.

However, when the peers passed an anti-government amendment in early May, the king, caught between the two sides of the reform dispute, this time refused Grey's request to create more peers. The government immediately resigned, and the king asked the Duke of Wellington to lead a new administration. Wellington failed – there were too few Tory MPs in the Commons. The king had little choice but to reinstate Grey and to create more peers, if necessary, to pass the bill. However, it was not necessary: the Duke of Wellington persuaded 100 Tory MPs to abstain on the bill, which received royal assent on 7 June.

The first general election under the new system was held between 10 December 1832 and 8 January 1833. More than 800,000 men now had the vote, including a substantial section of the middle classes whose ranks had been expanded by the Industrial Revolution. The Liberals won a landslide victory, with a majority of more than 200 in the new House of Commons.

1834

'The whole proceedings were characterised by a shameful disregard of justice and decency'

From 1799 until its repeal in 1824, the Combination Act 1799 made it illegal for workers to come together in trade unions. The story of the Tolpuddle Martyrs is all the more shocking because it starts nine years after trade unions were theoretically allowed. In November 1833, six men from Tolpuddle in Dorset founded the Friendly Society of Agricultural Labourers. They sought to resist their wages being cut from ten shillings (fifty pence) to seven shillings (thirty-five pence) a week. (In today's prices, that is equivalent to a cut from £40 to £28 a week.) If they thought that their actions would be tolerated in a climate of reform, they were mistaken. A local landowner wrote to Lord Melbourne, then Home Secretary, to complain that labourers were being induced to 'enter into combinations of a dangerous and alarming kind, to which they are bound by oaths'. The six men were charged in February 1834 under the 1797 Incitement to Mutiny Act. This Act, designed mainly to prevent mutiny within the navy, prohibited the swearing of secret oaths, as the men had done. One of the accused men, George Loveless, subsequently wrote a book containing this account of his trial.

GEORGE LOVELESS: *VICTIMS OF WHIGGERY*

On the 15th of March, we were taken to the County Hall to await our trial. As soon as we arrived we were ushered down some steps into a miserable dungeon, opened but twice a year, with only a glimmering light; and to make it more disagreeable, some wet and green brushwood was served for firing. The smoke of this place, together with its natural dampness, amounted to nearly suffocation, and in this most dreadful situation we passed nearly three whole days.

As to the trial I need mention but little; the whole proceedings were characterised by a shameful disregard of justice and decency; the most unfair means were resorted to in order to frame an indictment against us; the grand jury appeared to ransack heaven and earth to get some clue against us, but in vain; our characters were investigated from our infancy to the then present moment; our masters were inquired to know if we were not idle, or attended public houses, or some other fault in us; and much as they were opposed to us, they had common honesty enough to declare that we were good labouring servants, and that they had never heard a word against any of us; and when nothing whatever could be raked together, the unjust and cruel judge, John Williams, ordered us to be tried for mutiny and conspiracy, under an act of George III, for the suppression of mutiny amongst the marines and seamen, several years ago, at the Nore.

The greatest part of the evidence against us on our trial, was put into the mouths of the witnesses by the judge; and when he evidently wished them to say any particular thing, and the witness would say: 'I cannot remember,' he would say, 'Now think; I will give you another minute to consider.' Sometimes by charging them to be careful what they said, by way of intimidation, they would merely answer, 'yes;' and the judge would set the words down as proceeding from the witness.

I shall not soon forget his address to the jury, in summing up the evidence: among other things he told them, that if such societies were allowed to exist, it would ruin masters, cause a stagnation in trade, destroy property; and if they should not find us guilty, he was certain that they would forfeit the opinion of the grand jury. I thought to myself, there is no danger but we shall be found guilty, as we have a special jury for the purpose, selected from among those who are most unfriendly towards us – the grand jury, landowners, the petty jury, land renters. Under such a charge, from such a quarter, self interest alone would induce them to say, 'Guilty.'

The judge then inquired if we had anything to say. I instantly forwarded the following short defence, in writing, to him: 'My Lord, if we have violated any law, it was not done intentionally: we have injured no man's reputation person or property: we were uniting together to preserve ourselves, our wives, and our children, from utter degradation and starvation. We challenge any man, or number of men to prove that we have acted, or intend to act different from the above statement.'

The judge asked if I wished it to be read in court. I answered, Yes. It was then mumbled over to a part of the jury, in such an inaudible manner, that although I knew what was there, I could not comprehend it. And here one of the counsel prevented sentence being passed, by declaring that not one charge brought against any of the prisoners was proved, and that if we were found guilty a great number of persons would be dissatisfied; and I shall be for one, said he.

Two days after this we were again placed at the bar to receive sentence, when the judge told us, that not for anything that we had done, or, as he could prove, we intended to do, but for an example to others, he considered it his duty to pass the sentence of seven years' transportation across his Majesty's high seas upon each and every one of us. As soon as the sentence was passed, I got a pencil and a scrap of paper, and wrote the following lines:

God is our guide! from field, from wave,
From plough, from anvil, and from loom;
We come, our country's rights to save,
And speak a tyrant faction's doom:
We raise the watchword liberty;
We will, we will, we will be free!

God is our guide! no swords we draw,
We kindle not war's battle fires;
By reason, union, justice, law,
We claim the birth-right of our sires;
We raise the watchword, liberty,
We will, we will, we will be free!

While we were being guarded back to prison, our hands locked together, I tossed the above lines to some people that we passed; the guard, however, seizing hold of them, they were instantly carried back to the judge; and by some this was considered a crime of no less magnitude than high treason.

On Wednesday, April the 2nd, Mr Woolaston, magistrate, paid me a visit. He said, 'I am sorry, Loveless, to see a man like you in such a situation, but it is your own fault, you are now suffering for your own stubbornness and obstinacy; you have such a proud spirit, you would not pay attention to the cautions of the magistrates; but would rather hearken to idle fellows that were going about the country, who now have deceived you.'

I told him I had not been deceived by any, for I knew of no such persons as he had been describing.

'Yes, you do, for you have hearkened to them rather than pay attention to the magistrate's cautions; for I am certain you saw them, one of them being found on your person when you went to prison.'

'Is Mr. Woolaston in his right mind?' said I.

'What do you mean?'

'The circumstance concerning which the witnesses swore against us, took place on the 9th of December, and the magistrate's cautions did not appear till the 21st of February, following; so that we have been tried for what took place at least nine weeks before the cautions had existence; and yet you say I paid no attention to the magistrates, but listened to idle fellows going about the country; within three days after the cautions appeared I was in the body of the gaol.'

'Ah,' said he, 'it is of no use talking to you.'

'No, Sir, unless you talk more reasonably.'

On Saturday, April the 5th, early in the morning, I was called, to prepare for a journey to Portsmouth; after getting irons on my legs, and locked on the coach, we proceeded to Salisbury, and at the entrance of the town, Mr Glinister, clerk of the prison, who accompanied me, offered to take the irons off my legs. I inquired if he meant to put them on again on leaving Salisbury. He said 'Yes,' but as I should have to walk through some part of the town, I had better have them taken off, as the rattling of the chain would cause people to be looking after us. I told him I did not wish for any such thing, as I was not ashamed to wear the chain, conscious of my innocence.

With the support of the new Home Secretary, Lord John Russell, five of the Tolpuddle Martyrs (including George Loveless) were released in 1836. The sixth man was released the following year. Four of the six returned from Australia to Britain. When they landed at Plymouth, they were hailed as popular heroes.

1834

'THE FIRM MAINTENANCE OF ESTABLISHED RIGHTS, THE CORRECTION OF PROVED ABUSES AND THE REDRESS OF REAL GRIEVANCES'

Battered by divisions within his government, Earl Grey resigned as prime minister in July 1834, to be succeeded by Lord Melbourne. But four months later, William IV, who supported the Tories, sacked Melbourne and invited Sir Robert Peel to lead a Conservative administration. As the Liberals still enjoyed a large majority in the Commons, Peel dissolved Parliament and called a fresh election. His manifesto, sent to his electors in Tamworth on 18 December, is widely regarded as the first statement of Conservative principles. In it, he accepts the reforms of 1832, even though he had opposed them at the time.

SIR ROBERT PEEL: THE TAMWORTH MANIFESTO

To the Electors of the Borough of Tamworth.

Gentlemen,
On the 26th of November last, being then at Rome, I received from His Majesty a summons, wholly unforeseen and unexpected by me, to return to England without delay, for the purpose of assisting His Majesty in the formation of a new government. My acceptance of the first office in the Government terminates, for the present, my political connection with you. In seeking the renewal of it, whenever you shall be called upon to perform the duty of electing a representative in Parliament, I feel it incumbent on me to enter into a declaration of my views of public policy, as full and unreserved as I can make it, consistently with my duty as a Minister of the Crown.

I have the firmest convictions that that confidence cannot be secured by any other course than that of a frank and explicit declaration of principle; that vague and unmeaning professions of popular opinion may quiet distrust for a time, may influence this or that election but that such professions must ultimately and signally fail, if, being made, they are not adhered to, or if they are inconsistent with the honour and character of those who made them.

Now I say at once that I will not accept power on the condition of declaring myself an apostate from the principles on which I have heretofore acted. At the same time, I never will admit that I have been, either before or after the Reform Bill, the defender of abuses, or the enemy of judicious reforms. I appeal with confidence in denial of the charge, to the active part I took in the great question of the currency; in the consolidation and amendment of the Criminal Law; in the revisal of the whole system of Trial by Jury; to the opinions I have professed, and uniformly acted on, with regard to other branches of the jurisprudence of this country – I appeal to this as a proof that I have not been disposed to acquiesce in acknowledged evils, either from the mere superstitious reverence for ancient usages, or from the dread of labour or responsibility in the application of a remedy.

But the Reform Bill, it is said, constitutes a new era, and it is the duty of a Minister to declare explicitly: first, whether he will maintain the Bill itself, secondly whether he will act on the spirit in which it was conceived.

With respect to the Reform Bill itself, I will repeat now the declaration I made when I entered the House of Commons as a member of the Reformed Parliament – that I consider the Reform Bill a final and irrevocable settlement of a great constitutional question – a settlement which no friend to the peace and welfare of this country would attempt to disturb, either by direct or by insidious means.

Then, as to the spirit of the Reform Bill, and the willingness to adopt and enforce it as a rule of government: if, by adopting the spirit of the Reform Bill, it be meant that we are to live in a perpetual vortex of agitation; that public men can only support themselves in public estimation by adopting every popular impression of the day; by promising the instant redress of anything which anybody may call an abuse; by abandoning altogether that great aid of government, more powerful than either law or reason, the respect for ancient rights, and the deference to prescriptive authority; if this be the spirit of the Reform Bill, I will not undertake to adopt it. But if the spirit of the Reform Bill implies merely a careful review of institutions, civil and ecclesiastical, undertaken in a friendly temper combining, with the firm maintenance of established rights, the correction of proved abuses and the redress of real grievances – in that case, I can for myself and colleagues undertake to act in such a spirit and with such intentions.

Such declarations of general principle are, I am aware, necessarily vague: but in order to be more explicit, I will endeavour to apply them practically to some of those questions which have of late attracted the greater share of public interest and attention.

I opposed, and I am bound to state that my opinions in that respect have undergone no change, the admission of Dissenters as a claim of right, into the universities; but I expressly declared that if regulations, enforced by public authorities superintending the professions of law and medicine, and the studies connected with them, had the effect of conferring advantages of the nature of civil privileges on one class of the king's subjects from which another was excluded – those regulations ought to undergo modification, with the view of placing all the King's subjects, whatever their religious creeds, upon a footing of perfect equality with respect to any civil privilege.

Our object will be: the maintenance of peace; the scrupulous and honourable fulfilment of all existing engagements with Foreign Powers; the support of public credit; the enforcement of strict economy; the just and impartial consideration of what is due to all interests – agricultural, manufacturing, and commercial.

Whatever may be the issue of the undertaking in which I am engaged, I feel assured that you will mark, by a renewal of your confidence, your approbation of the course I have pursued in accepting office. I enter upon the arduous duties assigned to me with the deepest sense of the responsibilities they involve, with great distrust of my own qualifications for their adequate discharge, but at the same time with the firm belief that the people of this country will so far maintain the prerogative of the King, as to give to the Ministers of his choice, not an implicit confidence, but a fair trial.

I am, Gentlemen,

With affectionate regard,

Most faithfully yours,

Robert Peel.

Voting took place in January and early February 1835. The Liberals won with a reduced, but still substantial, majority. Peel attempted to continue as prime minister, but resigned in April after a series of defeats in the Commons. Lord Melbourne resumed his role as prime minister, a post he held for the next six years. Peel became prime minister again in 1841, following the Conservatives' victory in that year's election.

1837

'WE HAVE OPENED ALL THE PUBLIC-HOUSES, AND LEFT OUR ADVERSARY NOTHING BUT THE BEER-SHOPS — MASTERLY STROKE OF POLICY THAT, MY DEAR SIR, EH?'

In July 1834, a by-election took place in Sudbury, Suffolk, following the death of its Liberal MP. Charles Dickens spent some time there, and the events inspired this fictional account of the 'Eatanswill' by-election in *The Pickwick Papers*, published three years later. Its depiction of cynical and corrupt behaviour indicates that the Reform Act 1832 had failed to eradicate all the abuses of the system it set out to clean up, not least because the Act had failed to provide for a secret ballot.

CHARLES DICKENS: *THE PICKWICK PAPERS*

The Eatanswill people, like the people of many other small towns, considered themselves of the utmost and most mighty importance, and that every man in Eatanswill, conscious of the weight that attached to his example, felt himself bound to unite, heart and soul, with one of the two great parties that divided the town – the Blues and the Buffs. Now the Blues lost no opportunity of opposing the Buffs, and the Buffs lost no opportunity of opposing the Blues; and the consequence was, that whenever the Buffs and Blues met together at public meeting, Town-Hall, fair, or market, disputes and high words arose between them.

Mr. Pickwick, with his usual foresight and sagacity, had chosen a peculiarly desirable moment for his visit to the borough. Never was such a contest known. The Honourable Samuel Slumkey, of Slumkey Hall, was the Blue candidate; and Horatio Fizkin, Esq., of Fizkin Lodge, near Eatanswill, had been prevailed upon by his friends to stand forward on the Buff interest.

It was late in the evening, when Mr. Pickwick and his companions, assisted by Sam, dismounted from the roof of the Eatanswill coach. They entered the house, the crowd opening right and left to let them pass, and cheering vociferously. The first object of consideration was to secure quarters for the night.

'Can we have beds here?' inquired Mr. Pickwick, summoning the waiter.

'Don't know, sir,' replied the man; 'afraid we're full, sir – I'll inquire, sir.' Away he went for that purpose, and presently returned, to ask whether the gentlemen were 'Blue.'

As neither Mr. Pickwick nor his companions took any vital interest in the cause of either candidate, the question was rather a difficult one to answer. In this dilemma Mr. Pickwick bethought himself of his new friend, Mr. Perker.

'Do you know a gentleman of the name of Perker?' inquired Mr. Pickwick.

'Certainly, sir; honourable Mr. Samuel Slumkey's agent.'

'He is Blue, I think?'

'Oh yes, sir.'

'Then *we* are Blue,' said Mr. Pickwick.

'Ah-ah, my dear sir,' said the little man, advancing to meet him; 'very happy to see you, my dear sir, very. Pray sit down. So you have carried your intention into effect. You have come down here to see an election – eh?'

Mr. Pickwick replied in the affirmative.

'Spirited contest, my dear sir,' said the little man.

'I am delighted to hear it,' said Mr. Pickwick, rubbing his hands. 'I like to see sturdy patriotism, on whatever side it is called forth; – and so it's a spirited contest?'

'Oh yes,' said the little man, 'very much so indeed. We have opened all the public-houses in the place, and left our adversary nothing but the beer-shops – masterly stroke of policy that, my dear sir, eh?' The little man smiled complacently, and took a large pinch of snuff.

'And what are the probabilities as to the result of the contest?' inquired Mr. Pickwick.

'Why doubtful, my dear sir; rather doubtful as yet,' replied the little man. 'Fizkin's people have got three-and-thirty voters in the lock-up coach-house at the White Hart.'

'In the coach-house!' said Mr. Pickwick, considerably astonished by this second stroke of policy.

'They keep 'em locked up there till they want 'em,' resumed the little man. 'The effect of that is, you see, to prevent our getting at them; and even if we could, it would be of no use, for they keep them very drunk on purpose. Smart fellow Fizkin's agent – very smart fellow indeed.'

Mr. Pickwick stared, but said nothing.

'We are pretty confident, though,' said Mr. Perker, sinking his voice almost to a whisper. 'We had a little tea-party here, last night – five-and-forty women, my dear sir – and gave every one of 'em a green parasol when she went away. Five-and-forty green parasols, at seven and sixpence a-piece. All women like finery – extraordinary the effects of those parasols. Secured all their husbands, and half their brothers. My idea, my dear sir, entirely. Hail, rain, or sunshine, you can't walk half a dozen yards up the street, without encountering half a dozen green parasols.'

The noise and bustle which ushered in the morning, were sufficient to dispel from the mind of the most romantic visionary in existence, any associations but those which were immediately connected with the rapidly-approaching election. The beating of drums, the blowing of horns and trumpets, the shouting of men, and tramping of horses, echoed and re-echoed through the streets from the earliest dawn of day; and an occasional fight between the light skirmishers of either party at once enlivened the preparations and agreeably diversified their character.

'Well, Sam,' said Mr. Pickwick, as his valet appeared at his bed-room door, just as he was concluding his toilet; 'all alive today, I suppose?'

'Wery fresh,' replied Sam; 'me, and the two waiters at the Peacock, has been a pumpin' over the independent woters as supped there last night.'

'Pumping over independent voters!' exclaimed Mr. Pickwick.

'Yes,' said his attendant, 'every man slept vere he fell down; we dragged 'em out, one by one, this mornin', and put 'em under the pump, and they're in reg'lar fine order, now. Shillin' a head the committee paid for that 'ere job.'

'Can such things be!' exclaimed the astonished Mr. Pickwick.

'Lord bless your heart, sir,' said Sam, 'why where was you half baptised? That's nothin', that a'nt.'

'Nothing?' said Mr. Pickwick.

'Nothin' at all, sir,' replied his attendant. 'The night afore the last day o' the last election here, the opposite party bribed the bar-maid at the Town Arms, to hocus the brandy and water of fourteen unpolled electors as was a stoppin' in the house.'

'What do you mean by "hocussing" brandy and water?' inquired Mr. Pickwick.

'Puttin' laud'num in it,' replied Sam. 'Blessed if she didn't send 'em all to sleep till twelve hours after the election was over. They took one man up to the booth, in a truck, fast asleep, by way of experiment, but it was no go – they wouldn't poll him; so they brought him back, and put him to bed again.'

'Strange practices, these,' said Mr. Pickwick; half speaking to himself and half addressing Sam.

For three more decades, voting continued to be done openly rather than by secret ballot, and the kinds of practices described by Dickens continued unchecked. Advocates of reform were rebuffed by claims that a secret ballot would be 'unmanly' and 'un-English'. In truth, reform was always going to be hard to achieve when those who had to legislate for it had themselves been elected under a system in which bribery, corruption and intimidation were endemic.

1839

'WE PERFORM THE DUTIES OF FREEMEN; WE MUST HAVE THE PRIVILEGES OF FREEMEN'

In the years following the Reform Act 1832, campaigns sprang up to extend the franchise from middle-class to working-class voters. One of them was the Chartist movement. It was set up in 1837 by six Radical Members of Parliament and six members of the London Working Men's Association, which had been set up by William Lovett, an activist whose causes included the abolition of the stamp tax on newspapers. The Chartists drew up a petition demanding the vote for all adult men. It was signed by 1,280,000 people and presented to Parliament in June 1839.

THE PEOPLE'S CHARTER

Unto the Honourable the Commons of the United Kingdom of Great Britain and Ireland in Parliament assembled, the Petition of the undersigned, their suffering countrymen,

HUMBLY SHEWETH,

For three-and-twenty years we have enjoyed a profound peace. Yet with all these elements of national prosperity, and with every disposition and capacity to take advantage of them, we find ourselves overwhelmed with public and private suffering.

We are bowed down under a load of taxes; our traders are trembling on the verge of bankruptcy; our workmen are starving; capital brings no profit and labour no remuneration; the home of the artificer is desolate, and the warehouse of the pawnbroker is full; the workhouse is crowded and the manufactory is deserted.

It was the fond expectation of the people that a remedy for the greater part, if not for the whole, of their grievances, would be found in the Reform Act of 1832. They were taught to regard that Act as a wise means to a worthy end; as the machinery of an improved legislation, when the will of the masses would be at length potential.

They have been bitterly and basely deceived. The Reform Act has effected a transfer of power from one domineering faction to another, and left the people as helpless as before. Our slavery has been exchanged for an apprenticeship to liberty, which has aggravated the painful feeling of our social degradation, by adding to it the sickening of still deferred hope.

We come before your Honourable House to tell you, with all humility, that this state of things must not be permitted to continue; that it cannot long continue without very seriously endangering the stability of the throne and the peace of the kingdom; and that if by God's help and all lawful and constitutional appliances an end can be put to it, we are fully resolved that it shall speedily come to an end.

We tell your Honourable House that the capital of the master must no longer be deprived of its due reward; that the laws which make food dear, and those which, by making money scarce, make labour cheap, must be abolished; that taxation must be made to fall on property, not on industry; that the good of the many, as it is the only legitimate end, so must it be the sole study of the Government.

Required, as we are universally, to support and obey the laws, nature and reason entitle us to demand that in the making of the laws, the universal voice shall be implicitly listened to. We perform the duties of freemen; we must have the privileges of freemen. Therefore, we demand universal suffrage. The suffrage, to be exempt from the corruption of the wealthy and the violence of the powerful, must be secret.

On 12 July, MPs debated whether to refer the Charter to a committee of the whole House for further consideration. One of the MPs who expressed some sympathy for the Chartists was a thirty-four-year-old Tory, Benjamin Disraeli. This is the account of what he said, as recorded by Hansard, reporting his speech in the third person.

BENJAMIN DISRAELI'S SPEECH TO THE HOUSE OF COMMONS

Mr. Disraeli entirely agreed with the noble Lord [Lord John Russell, Leader of the House of Commons] as to the fallacy he had pointed out, as pervading this petition – that political rights necessarily ensured social happiness. But although they did not approve of the remedy suggested by the Chartists, it did not follow they should not attempt to cure the disease complained of. He did not think they had, up to the present moment, clearly seen what the disease really was. He could not believe, that a movement which, if not national was yet most popular, could have been produced by those common means of sedition to which the noble Lord had referred.

The real cause of this, as all real popular movements, was an apprehension on the part of the people, that their civil rights were invaded. Civil rights partook in some degree of an economical, and in some degree certainly of a political character. They conduced to the comfort, the security, and the happiness of the subject, and at the same time were invested with a degree of sentiment, which mere economical considerations did not involve.

Now, he maintained, that the civil rights of the people of England had been invaded. There had been, undoubtedly, perhaps with no evil intention, perhaps from a foolish desire of following a false philosophy, and applying a system of government not suited to the character of this country, and borrowed from the experience of another – there had been, from whatever motive, an invasion of the civil rights of the English people of late years; and he believed the real cause of this movement was a sentiment on the part of the people of England, that their civil rights had been invaded. That sentiment had doubtless been taken advantage of by trading agitators, but it was participated by much more than agitators, and that discontented minority which must ever exist in all countries.

The origin of this movement in favour of the Charter dated about the same time they had passed their Reform Bill. Its character was not understood by those who assailed it, and perhaps not fully by those who defended it. All would admit this – the old constitution had an intelligible principle, which the present had not. The former invested a small portion of the nation with political rights. Those rights were entrusted to that small class on certain conditions – that they should guard the civil rights of the great multitude.

They had transferred a great part of that political power to a new class, whom they had not invested with those great public duties. For instance, the administration of justice, the regulation of parishes, the building of roads and bridges, the command of the militia and police, the employment of labour, the distribution of relief to the destitute – these were great duties which, ordinarily, had been confined to that body in the nation which enjoyed and exercised political power.

But now they had a class which had attained that great object which all the opulent desired – political power without the conditions annexed to its possession, and without fulfilling the duties which it should impose. What was the consequence? Those who thus possessed power without discharging its conditions and duties were naturally anxious to put themselves to the least possible expense and trouble. Having gained that object, they were anxious to keep it without any appeal to their pocket, and without any cost of their time. To gain their objects, they raised the cry of cheap government – that served the first: to attain the second, they called for the constant interference of the Government. But he contended, they could not have a cheap and centralized Government, and maintain at the same time the civil rights of the people of England. He believed this was the real cause of the Charter; a large body of the people found out that their civil rights had been invaded.

He admitted, that the prayer of the National Petition involved the great fallacy of supposing that social evils would be cured by political rights; but the fallacy was not confined to these poor Chartists. He had never passed an evening in that House that he did not hear some honourable Gentlemen say, that the people were starving, and that the only remedy was household suffrage. Was that proposition less absurd than the prayer of this petition which had been so severely criticized by the noble Lord? The petitioners demanded annual Parliaments; but whether a man called for annual or triennial Parliaments, undoubtedly the change applied for was great in either case, and he did not think the noble Lord [Russell] was justified in speaking in terms of derision.

He was not ashamed to say, however much he disapproved of the Charter, he sympathised with the Chartists. They formed a great body of his countrymen; nobody could doubt they laboured under great grievances, and it would indeed have been a matter of surprise and little to the credit of that House, if Parliament had been prorogued without any notice being taken of what must always be considered a very remarkable social movement.

MPs voted by 235 votes to 46 to reject a proposal to refer the Charter for further debate. Angered by this decision, the Chartists held a convention in Birmingham's Bull Ring, in defiance of a ban by the city council. Police broke up what they described as a 'riot', and several Chartists were arrested. When placards appeared accusing the police of being a 'bloodthirsty and unconstitutional force', Lovett was arrested and charged with seditious libel. He spent 12 months in Warwick jail.

While Lovett was in prison, the remaining Chartists continued his work, publishing their demands in more detail in a circular in October 1839.

THE CHARTISTS' PROPOSED BILL

Being an Outline of an Act to provide for the just Representation of the People of Great Britain and Ireland in the Commons' House of Parliament:

embracing the Principles of Universal Suffrage, no Property Qualification, Annual Parliaments, Equal Representation, Payment of Members, and Vote by Ballot.

Whereas to insure, in as far as it is best possible by human forethought and wisdom, the just government of the people, it is necessary to subject those who have the power of making the laws, to a wholesome and strict responsibility to those whose duty it is to obey them when made:

And, whereas, this responsibility is best enforced through the instrumentality of a body which emanates directly from, and is itself immediately subject to, the whole people, and which completely represents their feelings and their interests:

And, whereas, as the Commons' House of Parliament now exercises in the name and on the supposed behalf of the people, the power of making the laws, it ought, in order to fulfil with wisdom and with honesty the great duties imposed in it, to be made the faithful and accurate representation of the people's wishes, feelings and interests.

Be it therefore Enacted,

That from and after the passing of this Act, every male inhabitant of these realms be entitled to vote for the election of a Member of Parliament, subject however to the following conditions.

That he be a native of these realms, or a foreigner who has lived in this country upwards of two years, and been naturalised.

That he be twenty-one years of age.

That he be not proved insane when the list of voters are revised.

That he be not convicted of felony within six months from and after the passing of this Act.

That his electoral rights be not suspended for bribery at elections, or for personation, or for forgery of election certificates, according to the penalties of this Act . . .

ELECTORAL DISTRICTS

Be it enacted, that for the purpose of obtaining an equal representation of the people in the Commons' House of Parliament, the United Kingdom be divided into 300 electoral districts.

That each such district contain, as nearly as may be, an equal number of inhabitants.

That each electoral district return one representative to sit in the Commons' House of Parliament, and no more.

DURATION OF PARLIAMENT

Be it enacted, that Members of the House of Commons chosen as aforesaid, shall meet on the first Monday in June in each year, and continue their sittings from time to time as they may deem it convenient, till the first Monday in June the following, when the next new Parliament is to be chosen: they shall be eligible to be re-elected. That during an adjournment, they be liable to be called together by the executive, in cases of emergency.

PAYMENT OF MEMBERS

Be it enacted, that every Member of the House of Commons be entitled, at the close of the session, to a writ of expenses on the Treasury, for his legislative duties in the public service, and shall be paid £500 per annum [equivalent to approx £40,000 in 2009].

Subsequent petitions were submitted to Parliament throughout the 1840s, culminating in 1848, when the Chartists claimed to have secured the signatures of 5,700,000 adults – almost half Britain's total adult population. However, the Chartists were accused of massively inflating the true number and also including bogus signatures, such as that of Queen Victoria, and some of the sympathy for the movement ebbed away. Subsequent petitions attracted the signatures of just 54,000 in 1849, and fewer than 12,000 in 1851. The Chartists held their last convention in 1858. Just 41 people turned up.

1842-6

'TO HAVE A USEFUL AND A PROSPEROUS PEOPLE, WE MUST TAKE CARE THAT THEY ARE WELL FED'

F ew domestic policy battles have ever provoked such bitterness as those in the 1840s to repeal the Corn Laws. Laws to curb the import of corn had been in place intermittently since the twelfth century. In 1815, Parliament passed the Importation Act, which barred the import of foreign corn unless the domestic price climbed above £4 per quarter-hundredweight (just under 13 kg). Landowners gained from this law, but working people, the emerging middle class and the rapidly growing number of manufacturers all suffered. From Peterloo on, demonstrations for political reform were generally accompanied by demands for cheap food. Subsequent Acts modified the 1815 law, but retained the principle.

In 1838, a group of Radical Whigs, including Richard Cobden and John Bright, set up the Anti-Corn Law League to campaign for free trade. Cobden, who was elected to Parliament in 1841, delivered the speech below to the House of Commons on 24 February 1842 in favour of a motion to abolish 'all duties payable on the importation of corn, grain, meal, and flour'. Cobden faced not only opposition from the landowning Right but also from some on the Left. Karl Marx was among those who argued that cheap food would be bad for the workers because it would give employers an excuse to force down wages. This was one of the arguments that Cobden sought to counter in his speech.

RICHARD COBDEN'S SPEECH ATTACKING THE CORN LAWS

Not one speaker on the other side of the House has yet grappled with the question so ably propounded by my hon. Friend, which is—How far, how just, how honest, and how expedient it was to have any tax whatever laid upon the food of the people? While I hear herein strong expressions of sympathy for those who have become paupers, I will ask hon. Gentlemen to give some attention to the case of the hard-working man before he reaches that state of abject pauperism in which he can only receive sympathy.

In reading the debates upon the passing of the first stringent Corn law of 1814, I am much struck to find that all parties who took part in that discussion were agreed upon one point—it was that the price of food regulated the rate of wages. But there was one party, that most interested, the working classes, who were not deluded. The great multitude of the nation, without the aid of learning, said—with that intuitive and instructive sagacity which had given rise to the adage, 'The voice of the people is the voice of God'—what the effect of the measure would be upon wages, and therefore it was, that when that law was passed this House was surrounded by the multitudes of London, whom you were compelled to keep from your doors by the point of the bayonet. Yes, and no sooner was the law passed than there arose disturbances and tumults everywhere, and in London bloodshed and murder ensued; for a coroner's jury returned a verdict of wilful murder against the soldiers who were called out and fired upon the people. The same hostility to the measure spread throughout the whole of the north of England; so that then, from the year 1815 down to 1819, when the memorable meeting was held at Peter's field in Manchester, there never was a great public meeting at which there were not borne banners inscribed with the words 'No Corn laws.'

There was no mistake in the minds of the multitude then, and let not hon. Gentlemen suppose that there is any now. The people may not be crying out exclusively for the repeal of the Corn laws, because they have looked beyond that question, and have seen greater evils even than this, which they wish to have remedied at the same time; and, now that the cries for 'Universal Suffrage' and 'The Charter' are heard, let not hon. Gentlemen deceive themselves by supposing that, because the members of the Anti-Corn law League have sometimes found themselves getting into collision with the Chartists, that therefore the Chartists, or the working men generally, were favourable to the Corn laws. If one thing is more surprising than others in the facts which I have mentioned, it is to find in this House, where lecturers of all things in the world are so much decried, the ignorance which prevails upon this question amongst hon. Members on the other side of the House. [Oh! oh!] Yes, I have never seen their ignorance equalled amongst any equal number of working men in the North of England.

I am told that the price of labour in other countries is so low that we must keep up the price of bread here, to prevent wages going down to the same level. But I am prepared to prove, from documents emanating from this

House, that labour is cheaper here than in other countries. I hear a sound of dissent; but I would ask those who dissent, do they consider the quality of the labour? By this test, which is the only fair one, it will be proved that the labour of England is the cheapest labour in the world. The Committee on machinery, last session but one, demonstrated that fact beyond all dispute. They reported that labour on the continent was actually dearer than in England in every branch of industry. Spinners, manufacturers, machine-makers, all agreed that one Englishman on the Continent was worth three native workmen, whether in Germany, France, or Belgium. If they are not, would Englishmen be found in every large town on the Continent?

Have low wages ever proved the prosperity of our manufactures? In every period when wages have dropped, it has been found that the manufacturing interest dropped also; and I hope that the manufacturers will have credit for taking a rather more enlightened view of their own interest than to conclude that the impoverishment of the multitude, who are the great consumers of all that they produce, could ever tend to promote the prosperity of our manufacturers. I will tell the House, that by deteriorating that population, of which they ought to be so proud, they will run the risk of spoiling not merely the animal but the intellectual creature, and that it is not a potato-fed race that will ever lead the way in arts, arms, or commerce. To have a useful and a prosperous people, we must take care that they are well fed.

I perfectly agree with the right hon. Baronet, [Sir Robert Peel, the Conservative Prime Minister] that corn ought only to be admitted free of all restrictions when it is 'wanted.' That is, the particular moment or crisis when it is desirable to open our ports for the admission of foreign corn. But I would ask the House and the Government of the country, who are to decide when the corn is wanted? Is it those who need food and are starving, or those who fare sumptuously every day and roll in all the luxuries of life? What right has the right hon. Baronet to attempt to gauge the appetite of the people? It is an inordinate assumption of power to do so. Such a thing cannot be tolerated under the most monstrous system of despotism which the imagination of man has ever conceived. Do we sit here for the purpose of deciding when the people of this country want food? What do the Members of this House know of want? It is not for them to say when the starving people of this country ought to have food doled out to them. The people are the best judges upon that point.

I will say a word to the noble Lord and his right hon. associates on this [the Opposition] side of the House, who, whilst advocating generally Free-trade principles, have manifested a squeamishness in supporting the motion for a total and immediate repeal of the Corn laws. With all deference to them, that shows too great sympathy with the few, and too little with the many who are suffering.

Cobden was defeated on this occasion, but Peel – a free trader by instinct – did alter the tariff scale on imported corn to help keep down the price of bread.

The event that brought the issue to a head was Ireland's potato famine. The crop failed completely in 1845. By the winter, starvation stalked Ireland and shortages the rest of the United Kingdom. On 4 December 1845, Peel announced that he would lay before Parliament a bill to repeal the Corn Laws. At a Cabinet meeting the following day, Lord Stanley, the Secretary of State for War, led a revolt against Peel's plan. Although Peel knew he could count on the Whigs to help him pass his bill, he promptly announced his intention to resign as prime minister. Queen Victoria summoned Lord John Russell, the Whig leader, to form a government; Peel said he would support Russell over reform of the Corn Laws. Russell, however, failed to form an administration, and Peel rescinded his resignation. His bill to repeal the Corn Laws went before Parliament.

On 12 June 1846, Lord Stanley spoke in the third-reading debate in the Lords to argue against repeal. Stanley spoke immediately after the Bishop of Oxford, who argued that the Corn Laws were wrong because they violated the 'state of nature', to which all legislation should aspire.

LORD STANLEY DEFENDS THE CORN LAWS

There are a great many things in which we cannot approximate to a state of nature. In our clothing, for instance—for if such an approximation were possible, it might not be decent. Voltaire somewhere says—'*Ce n'est pas selon la nature, cependant je porte les culottes.*' We are not in a state of nature—our whole system is artificial. We impose restraints upon personal liberty for the benefit of the community at large. Your Lordships must remember that we are legislating for flesh and blood, not for Utopia. Different countries will have separate, or it may be adverse, interests—they have other laws, interests, and objects; and for you to say we will enter upon a state of nature, but allow everybody else to protect themselves and wear a defensive armour, appears to me to be placing the former in the greatest possible disadvantage towards the latter.

Utopian schemes sounded very well, but they would not work. It was just like the man who invented the most ingenious and beautiful machine on earth, but omitted to provide for the impediments of friction—or like the person who invented a system of projectiles, but forgot to take into account the resistance of air, and the doctrine of gravitation. You must not look to what is good in the abstract, but to what is practically desirable; and as foreign countries will not agree in your scheme, it falls to the ground.

I took the liberty of showing the House a few nights ago, the statement of the Secretary to the Treasury of the United States, in which, so far from holding out any prospect of a relaxation in their tariff, he congratulated his countrymen on the free admission of their bread stuffs into this country, and proved that such a system would more and more exclude English manufactures from American markets. Prussia has not reduced the duties on the cotton and hardware of this country, because our Tariff has been relaxed in favour of her corn and timber. Our Legislature has reduced the duties on timber; but, so far as reciprocity is concerned, we have nothing to congratulate ourselves upon; nothing that can lead us to suppose that the relaxation of protection will lead to that delightful state of nature to which the right rev. Prelate has alluded.

Noble Lords calculate with great confidence on the acquiescence of the Colonies in this measure; but in my opinion you had better wait a little for more certain intelligence. Let us wait until we see the deliberate expression of the people of Canada, and until the opinions of the people of this country are constitutionally expressed. The Government propose a great and a hazardous experiment; they are doubtful of the sentiments of the Canadian people, but yet will not defer the passing of it until the arrival of the next Canadian mail.

As regards the present state of Ireland, I fully agree in opinion with the noble Lord opposite (Lord Monteagle), that the repeal of the Corn Laws will have no effect in healing the distresses that at present exist in that country. The noble Lord gives great credit to the Government for the measures they have taken to supply Ireland with labour and food; but they are temporary and palliative, and not permanent or effective measures. The distress in Ireland does not arise from the dearness of provisions, but from the want of permanent employment; it is the want of employment that causes the great destitution that exists amongst the labouring classes. The greater portion of the landed proprietors of that country are unable to dispose of their estates, they have them so heavily mortgaged; which also prevents their being able to reduce their rents, or give their labourers employment.

I ask your Lordships, then, how can this measure remedy the evils complained of? You are about to introduce a law, which must have the effect, more or less, of reducing the price of corn, and which, I believe, must also tend to increase fluctuation, to cause a great influx at one time, and a great scarcity at another.

What is to be the effect of a reduction in the price of corn by this measure? If the price of corn should fall, then there will be a fall in the prices of other commodities. What is to be the result of that? Why, there will be a great advance in the value of money. There is one interest which will be benefited by it. You are about to confer a boon upon the moneyed interests of this country. Have you considered the effect it will have upon your national debt? If you raise the price of money one-fifth, you will increase the burdens upon the country in the same proportion. I throw out these remarks, in order that your Lordships may not be induced to adopt this measure without thinking of the effect it will have in increasing the burdens upon this country. My opinion is, that the labouring class will be the first to discover that cheap bread is not a blessing but a curse to them, notwithstanding the sweetened hopes that are held out to them to induce them to put the cup to their lips.

Stanley's speech failed to prevent Peel's bill from becoming law. But on 25 June 1846, the day when the bill completed its passage through Parliament, Peel was defeated on the Irish Coercion Bill when pro-Corn Law Tories sided with the Whigs to oppose greater police powers to deal with Irish unrest. Peel promptly resigned. In his resignation speech to MPs on 29 June, he gave generous credit to Richard Cobden for his role in ending the Corn Laws.

SIR ROBERT PEEL'S RESIGNATION SPEECH

In reference to our proposing these measures, I have no wish to rob any person of the credit which is justly due to him for them. But I may say that neither the gentlemen sitting on the benches opposite, nor myself, nor the gentlemen sitting round me—I say that neither of us are the parties who are strictly entitled to the merit. There has been a combination of parties, and that combination of parties together with the influence of the Government, has led to the ultimate success of the measures.

But, Sir, there is a name which ought to be associated with the success of these measures: it is not the name of the noble Lord, the member for London, neither is it my name. Sir, the name which ought to be, and which will be associated with the success of these measures is the name of a man who, acting, I believe, from pure and disinterested motives, has advocated their cause with untiring energy, and by appeals to reason, expressed by an eloquence, the more to be admired because it was unaffected and unadorned—the name which ought to be and will be associated with the success of these measures is the name of Richard Cobden. Without scruple, Sir, I attribute the success of these measures to him.

This time, Lord John Russell did succeed in forming an administration. The impact of these events on the Conservatives was immense. The party split, with free-traders loyal to Peel, such as William Gladstone and the Earl of Aberdeen, becoming 'Peelites'. Peel himself died in 1850, but in 1859 the Peelites joined the Whigs – or, as the party was now known, the Liberals.

In 1851, on the death of his father, Lord Stanley became the Earl of Derby. He was the leader of the Conservative Party for twenty-two years, from 1846 until 1868, but prime minister for only three brief spells, totalling less than four years, in the 1850s and '60s. Following their split over the Corn Laws, the Conservatives did not secure a sustained period in power for almost three decades, until they won the 1874 general election under Benjamin Disraeli.

1843

'I AM HERE THE REPRESENTATIVE OF THE IRISH NATION, AND IN THE NAME OF THAT MORAL, TEMPERATE, VIRTUOUS AND RELIGIOUS PEOPLE, I PROCLAIM THE UNION A NULLITY'

Daniel O'Connell entered Parliament in 1829, shortly after the ban on Catholic MPs was removed. He generally sided with the Whigs; in 1835 he helped them bring down Sir Robert Peel's Tory government. Gradually, however, O'Connell became disillusioned with the Whigs, believing they cared little more than the Tories for the Irish. In 1839, he formed the Repeal Association, which wanted to scrap the 1807 Act of Union and restore full independence to Ireland. He toured Ireland, speaking at mass meetings. This is part of a speech he gave at the Hill of Tara, outside Dublin, on 15 August 1843.

DANIEL O'CONNELL CALLS FOR IRISH INDEPENDENCE

On this spot I have a most important duty to perform. I here protest, in the name of my country and in the name of my God, against the unfounded and unjust Union. My proposition to Ireland is that the Union is not binding on her people. It is void in conscience and in principle, and as a matter of constitutional law I attest these facts.

Yes, I attest by everything that is sacred, without being profane, the truth of my assertions. There is no real union between the two countries, and my proposition is that there was no authority given to anyone to pass the Act of Union. Neither the English nor the Irish Legislature was competent to pass that Act, and I arraign it on these grounds. One authority alone could make that Act binding, and that was the voice of the people of Ireland. The Irish Parliament was elected to make laws and not to make legislatures; and, therefore, it had no right to assume the authority to pass the Act of Union. The Irish Parliament was elected by the Irish people as their trustees; the people were their masters, and the members were their servants, and had no right to transfer the property to any other power on earth.

If the Irish Parliament has transferred its power of legislation to the French Chamber, would any man assert that the Act was valid? Would any man be mad enough to assert it; would any man be insane enough to assert it, and would the insanity of the assertion be mitigated by sending any number of members to the French Chamber? Everybody must admit that it would not. What care I for France? – and I care as little for England as for France, for both countries are foreign to me.

The very highest authority in England has proclaimed us to be aliens in blood, in religion, and in language. I am here the representative of the Irish nation, and in the name of that moral, temperate, virtuous and religious people, I proclaim the Union a nullity. [William] Saurin, [a former Attorney General for Ireland] who had been the representative of the Tory party for twenty years, distinctly declared that the Act of Union was invalid. He said that the Irish House of Commons had no right, had no power to pass the Union, and that the people of Ireland would be justified, the first opportunity that presented itself, in effecting its repeal. So they are. The authorities of the country were charged with the enactment, the alteration, or the administration of its laws. These were their powers; but they had not authority to alter or overthrow the constitution. I therefore proclaim the nullity of the Union.

A few days later, O'Connell, speaking off the cuff, criticised a speech made by Queen Victoria closing that year's parliamentary session. This provoked Peel's government to move against him. It banned a demonstration planned for early October in Clontarf, just north of Dublin, and arrested O'Connell on a charge of seditious conspiracy. He was jailed in 1844, but released on appeal after three months. The following year, the potato famine caused O'Connell's followers to split between those, like him, who believed in non-violent campaigning and those who now argued for violent insurrection. The latter group, Young Ireland, gained the upper hand. O'Connell's influence waned further as his health failed. 'The Liberator' died in Genoa, on his way to Rome, in May 1847.

1845

'Two nations; between whom there is no intercourse and no sympathy'

Disraeli's famous dictum about Britain being 'two nations' – the rich and the poor – appears in the title of his novel *Sybil, or, The Two Nations*. In fact, Disraeli was not the first to make this point. Plato's *Republic* referred to two cities 'warring with each other, one of the poor, the other of the rich'. A decade before *Sybil*, Alexis de Tocqueville wrote of 'two rival nations', again meaning the rich and the poor. And Friedrich Engels, who published *The Condition of the Working Class in England in 1844* in the same year as *Sybil* appeared, argued that the bourgeoisie and the working class were 'two radically dissimilar nations, as unlike as difference of race could make them'.

Yet it is Disraeli's version that is best remembered. *Sybil* was a fictional exploration of working-class conditions at a time when the Industrial Revolution had created a new, large and still rapidly growing population of city dwellers often living not just in poverty but also squalor.

The book's hero is Charles Egremont, a young minor aristocrat and Tory MP who returns to Britain after a period abroad and is shocked by what he finds in northern England. In this passage, Egremont enters the ruins of Marney Abbey and falls into discussion with two strangers.

Benjamin Disraeli: *Sybil, or, The Two Nations*

'You lean against an ancient trunk,' said Egremont, carelessly advancing to the stranger, who looked up at him without any expression of surprise, and then replied. 'They say 'tis the trunk beneath whose branches the monks encamped when they came to this valley to raise their building. And then they were driven out of it, and it came to this. Poor men! Poor men!'

'They would hardly have forfeited their resting-place had they deserved to retain it,' said Egremont.

'They were rich. I thought it was poverty that was a crime,' replied the stranger in a tone of simplicity.

'At any rate, it was a forfeiture which gave life to the community,' said Egremont; 'the lands are held by active men and not by drones.'

'A drone is one who does not labour,' said the stranger; 'whether he wear a cowl or a coronet, 'tis the same to me. Somebody I suppose must own the land; though I have heard say that this individual tenure is not a necessity; but however this may be, I am not one who would object to the lord, provided he were a gentle one. All agree the Monastics were easy landlords; their rents were low; they granted leases in those days. Their tenants too might renew their term before their tenure ran out; so they were men of spirit and property. There were yeomen then, sir: the country was not divided into two classes, masters and slaves; there was some resting place between luxury and misery. Comfort was an English habit then, not merely an English word.'

'And you really think they were easier landlords than our present ones?' said Egremont, inquiringly.

'Human nature would tell us that, even if history did not confess it. The monks were in every district a point of refuge for all who needed succour, counsel and protection; a body of individuals having no cares of their own, with wisdom to guide the inexperienced, with wealth to relieve the suffering, and often with power to protect the oppressed. And now 'tis all over. The monasteries were taken by storm, they were sacked, gutted, battered with warlike instruments, blown up by gunpowder. Never was such a plunder. Nor has England ever lost this character of ravage. I don't know whether the union workhouses will remove it. They are building something for the people at last. After an experiment of three centuries, your gaols being full, and your treadmills losing something of their virtue, you have given us a substitute for the monasteries.'

'You lament the old faith,' said Egremont, in a tone of respect.

'I am not viewing the question as one of faith,' said the stranger. 'It is not as a matter of religion, but as a matter of right, that I am considering it: as a matter, I should say, of private right and public happiness. You had no right to deprive men of their property, and property moreover which under their administration so mainly contributed to the welfare of the community.'

'As for community,' said a voice which proceeded neither from Egremont nor the stranger, 'with the monasteries expired, there is no community in England; there is aggregation, but aggregation under circumstances which make it rather a dissociating, than a uniting, principle.'

It was a still voice that uttered these words, yet one of a peculiar character; one of those voices that instantly arrest attention: gentle and yet solemn, earnest yet unimpassioned. With a step as whispering as his tone, the man who had been kneeling by the tomb, had unobserved joined his associate and Egremont. The fairness of his linen, the neatness of his beard, his gloves much worn, yet carefully mended, intimated that his very faded garments were the result of necessity rather than of negligence.

'You also lament the dissolution of these bodies,' said Egremont.

'There is so much to lament in the world in which we live,' said the younger of the strangers, 'that I can spare no pang for the past.'

'Yet you approve of the principle of their society; if you prefer it, you say, to our existing life.'

'Yes; I prefer association to gregariousness.'

'That is a distinction,' said Egremont, musingly.

'It is a community of purpose that constitutes society,' continued the younger stranger; 'without that, men may be drawn into contiguity, but they still continue virtually isolated.'

'And is that their condition in cities?'

'It is their condition everywhere; but in cities that condition is aggravated. A density of population implies a severer struggle for existence, and a consequent repulsion of elements brought into too close contact. In great cities men are brought together by the desire of gain. They are not in a state of co-operation, but of isolation, as to the making of fortunes; and for all the rest they are careless of neighbours. Christianity teaches us to love our neighbour as ourself; modern society acknowledges no neighbour.'

'Well, we live in strange times,' said Egremont.

'When the infant begins to walk, it also thinks that it lives in strange times,' said his companion.

'Your inference?' asked Egremont.

'That society, still in its infancy, is beginning to feel its way.'

'This is a new reign,' said Egremont, 'perhaps it is a new era.'

'I think so,' said the younger stranger.

'I hope so,' said the older one.

'Well, society may be in its infancy,' said Egremont slightly smiling; 'but, say what you like, our Queen reigns over the greatest nation that ever existed.'

'Which nation?' asked the younger stranger, 'for she reigns over two.'

The stranger paused; Egremont was silent, but looked inquiringly.

'Yes,' resumed the younger stranger after a moment's interval. 'Two nations; between whom there is no intercourse and no sympathy; who are ignorant of each other's habits, thoughts, and feelings, as if they were dwellers in different zones, or inhabitants of different planets; who are formed by a different breeding, are fed by a different food, are ordered by different manners, and are not governed by the same laws.'

'You speak of—' said Egremont, hesitatingly.

'THE RICH AND THE POOR.'

The two strangers turn out to be two Chartists: Walter Gerard, a factory worker, and Stephen Morley, a young journalist. Sybil is Gerard's daughter, with whom Egremont falls in love. Eventually, they marry, but not before Gerard has been shot dead during an assault on Mowbray Castle, of which, it turns out, he was actually the rightful owner. Thus Disraeli makes the daringly radical point for his age that division between rich and poor was a product of circumstance and not of intrinsic merit.

Since *Sybil*, 'one nation' Conservatism has come to represent the more pragmatic and less ideological wing of the party, especially on social policy. It dominated Conservative thinking in the 1950s and '60s, fell out of favour during Margaret Thatcher's premiership and was subsequently revived again. During the party's 2005 leadership election, both main candidates, David Cameron and David Davis, declared that they were 'one nation' Conservatives.

1851–69

'THE DIVISION OF MANKIND INTO TWO CASTES, ONE BORN TO RULE OVER THE OTHER, IS AN UNQUALIFIED MISCHIEF'

Harriet Taylor Mill was one of the most prominent feminist writers and philosophers of the Victorian era. In July 1851, the *Westminster Review*, one of the most prestigious journals of its time, published her essay, 'The Enfranchisement of Women'. Whereas British ideas had influenced the founding fathers of the United States, now it was the turn of American thinking to influence debates about democracy in Britain. Harriet Taylor Mill drew on agitation for women's rights in the US to argue for equality in Britain.

HARRIET TAYLOR MILL: 'THE ENFRANCHISEMENT OF WOMEN'

On the 23rd and 24th of October last, a succession of public meetings was held at Worchester in Massachusetts under the name of a 'Women's Rights Convention,' of which the president was a woman, and nearly all the chief speakers women; numerously reinforced, however, by men, among whom were some of the most distinguished leaders in the kindred cause of negro emancipation. According to the report in the *New York Tribune*, above a thousand persons were present throughout, and 'if a larger place could have been had, many thousands more would have attended.'

The following is a brief summary of the principal demands.

1. *Education* in primary and high schools, universities, medical, legal, and theological institutions.
2. *Partnership* in the labours and gains, risks and remunerations, of productive industry.
3. *A coequal share* in the formation and administration of laws – municipal, state, and national – through legislative assemblies, courts, and executive offices.

As a question of justice, the case seems to us too clear for dispute. As one of expediency, the more thoroughly it is examined the stronger it will appear. That women have as good a claim as men have, in point of personal right, to the suffrage, or to a place in the jury-box, it would be difficult for any one to deny. It cannot certainly be denied by the United States of America, as a people or as a community. Their democratic institutions rest avowedly on the inherent right of every one to a voice in the government.

Their Declaration of Independence, framed by the men who are still their great constitutional authorities – that document which has been from the first, and is now, the acknowledged basis of their polity, commences with this express statement: 'We hold these truths to be self-evident: that all men are created equal'. We do not imagine that any American democrat will evade the force of these expressions by the dishonest or ignorant subterfuge, that 'men,' in this memorable document, does not stand for human beings, but for one sex only.

A like dereliction of the fundamental maxims of their political creed has been committed by the Americans in the flagrant instance of the negroes; of this they are learning to recognise the turpitude. After a struggle which, by many of its incidents, deserves the name of heroic, the abolitionists are now so strong in numbers and in influence that they hold the balance of parties in the United States. It was fitting that the men whose names will remain associated with the extirpation of the aristocracy of colour should be among the originators of the first collective protest against the aristocracy of sex; a distinction as accidental as that of colour, and fully as irrelevant to all questions of government.

Not only to the democracy of America, the claim of women to civil and political equality makes an irresistible appeal, but also to those Radicals and Chartists in the British islands. The Chartist who denies the suffrage to women, is a Chartist only because he is not a lord: he is one of those levellers who would level only down to themselves.

Even those who do not look upon a voice in the government as a matter of personal right, nor profess principles which require that it should be extended to all, have usually traditional maxims of political justice with which it is impossible to reconcile the exclusion of all women from the common rights of citizenship. It is an axiom of English freedom that taxation and representation should be co-extensive. Even under the laws which give the wife's property to the husband, there are many unmarried women who pay taxes. It is one of the fundamental doctrines of the British Constitution, that all persons should be tried by their peers: yet women, whenever tried, are tried by male judges and a male jury. To foreigners the law accords the privilege of claiming that half the jury should be composed of themselves; not so to women. In all things the presumption ought to be on the side of equality. A reason must be given why anything should be permitted to one person and interdicted to another.

We are firmly convinced that the division of mankind into two castes, one born to rule over the other, is in this case, as in all cases, an unqualified mischief; a source of perversion and demoralization, both to the favoured class and to those at whose expense they are favoured; and forming a bar to any really vital improvement, either in the character or in the social condition of the human race.

These propositions it is now our purpose to maintain. But before entering on them, we would endeavour to dispel the preliminary objections which, in the minds of persons to whom the subject is new, are apt to prevent a real and conscientious examination of it. The chief of these obstacles is that most formidable one, custom. Women never have had equal rights with men. Over three-fourths of the habitable world, even at this day, the answer, 'it has always been so,' closes all discussion. But it is the boast of modern Europeans, and of their American kindred, that they know and do many things which their forefathers neither knew nor did; habit is not now the tyrant it formerly was over opinions and modes of action, and the worship of custom is a declining idolatry.

We deny the right of any portion of the species to decide for another portion, or any individual for another individual, what is and what is not their 'proper sphere.' The proper sphere for all human beings is the largest and highest which they are able to attain to. Let every occupation be open to all, without favour or discouragement to any, and employments will fall into the hands of those men or women who are found by experience to be most capable of worthily exercising them. There need be no fear that women will take out of the hands of men any occupation which men perform better than they. Each individual will prove his or her capacities, in the only way in which capacities can be proved – by trial; and the world will have the benefit of the best faculties of all its inhabitants.

Harriet Taylor Mill influenced many people, not least her second husband, John Stuart Mill. She died in 1858, but her husband and her daughter, Helen, from her first marriage, continued her work. Having been elected as MP for City and Westminster in 1865, Mill proposed an amendment to the 1867 Reform Bill to give women the same voting rights as men. He was defeated by 196 votes to 73. Helen helped to found the London Society for Women's Suffrage, which subsequently combined with similar groups in other parts of Britain to form the National Union of Women's Suffrage Societies.

There was one early setback and one early success. The setback arose from a bizarre mistake in 1867 by a local official in Manchester, who included a local shop-owner, Lily Maxwell, on the electoral register, apparently unaware that she was a woman. Maxwell voted, very publicly, in a by-election in November 1867. In the following year, suffragists persuaded a handful of local officials to include property-owning women on the register; as a result, some women voted in the 1868 general election. However, this victory for equality proved short-lived. A test case was heard in 1869 by the eminent judge Sir James Easte Willes. The suffragists' argument was that, although previous legislation had referred to 'man' in granting the right to vote, 'man' had increasingly come to mean a person of either gender. Sir James ruled that this was immaterial, for the vote was granted to men 'not under a legal disability'. It was, Sir James said, this phrase that kept women off the register. He went on to explain why:

SIR JAMES EASTE WILLES'S RULING THAT WOMEN SHOULD NOT HAVE THE RIGHT TO VOTE

> Women are under a legal incapacity to vote at elections. What was the cause of it, it is not necessary to go into: but, admitting that fickleness of judgement and liability to influence have sometimes been suggested as the ground of exclusion, I must protest against its being supposed to arise in this country from any under-rating of the sex either in point of intellect or worth. That would be quite inconsistent with one of the glories of our civilisation – the respect and honour in which women are held. This is not a mere fancy of my own, but it will be found in Selden [a legal historian], in the discussion of the origin of the exclusion of women from judicial and like public functions, where the author gives preference to this reason, that the exemption was founded upon motives of decorum, and was a privilege of that sex.

It took almost half a century for women to gain, or regain, the right to vote in parliamentary elections.

The early, very limited success was the Municipal Franchise Act 1869. This seemed to grant women the right to vote in elections for local councillors on the same terms as men, but a court ruling in 1872 restricted this right to single women and widows: women would lose the vote if and when they married. This restriction was not lifted until 1894.

1854

<u>---</u>

'THE CIVIL SERVICE IS FOR THE UNAMBITIOUS, AND THE INDOLENT OR INCAPABLE'

O ne of the causes of Radicals in the middle of the nineteenth century was reform of the Civil Service. As the role of the government grew, the need for an effective bureaucracy became more urgent. A series of inquiries in the late 1840s and early 1850s culminated in the Northcote–Trevelyan Report. The driving force behind it was William Gladstone, the Chancellor of the Exchequer. Sir Stafford Northcote had been Gladstone's private secretary some years earlier. Sir Charles Trevelyan was one of the Treasury's brightest officials; he had overseen the programme to relieve hunger in Ireland following the potato famine.

Gladstone was shown a draft copy of the report in November 1853. He wanted it to go further. 'This is one of the cases in which a large and bold design is more practicable, as well as more just, than one of narrower limits,' he told Northcote in a letter on 3 December 1853. The final report pulled no punches in describing how the Civil Service recruited the wrong people for the wrong reasons and how its glaring deficiencies should be rectified.

THE 'NORTHCOTE–TREVELYAN REPORT': THE REPORT ON THE ORGANISATION OF THE PERMANENT CIVIL SERVICE

That the permanent civil service, with all its defects, essentially contributes to the proper functions of government, has been repeatedly admitted by those who have successively been responsible for the conduct of our affairs. All, however, who have had occasion to examine its constitution with care, have felt that its organisation is far from perfect.

It would be natural to expect that so important a profession would attract into its ranks the ablest and most ambitious of the youth of the country; that the keenest emulation would prevail among those who had entered it; and that such as were endowed with superior qualifications would rapidly rise to distinction and public eminence. Such, however, is by no means the case. Admission into the civil service is indeed eagerly sought after, but it is for the unambitious, and the indolent or incapable, that it is chiefly desired.

Those whose abilities do not warrant an expectation that they will succeed in the open professions, where they must encounter the competition of their contemporaries, and those whom the indolence of temperament or physical infirmities unfit for active exertions, are placed in the civil service, where they may obtain an honourable livelihood with little labour, and with no risk; where their success depends upon their simply avoiding any flagrant misconduct, and attending with moderate regularity to routine duties; and in which they are secured against the ordinary consequences of old age, or failing health, by an arrangement which provides them with the means of supporting themselves after they have become incapacitated.

It may be noticed in particular that the comparative lightness of the work, and the certainty of provision in the case of retirement owing to bodily incapacity, furnish strong inducements to the parents and friends of sickly youths to endeavour to obtain for them employment in the service of the Government.

The result naturally is, that the public service suffers both in internal efficiency and in public estimation. The character of the individuals influences the mass, and it is thus that we often hear of complaints of official delays, official evasions of difficulty, and official indisposition to improvement. In other professions the able and energetic rise to the top; the dull and inefficient remain at the bottom. In the public establishments, on the contrary, the general rule is that all rise together.

The character of the young men admitted to the public service depends chiefly upon the discretion with which the heads of departments, and others who are entrusted with the distribution of patronage, exercise that privilege. In those cases in which the patronage of departments which it commonly falls to his lot to make are either those of junior clerks, to whom no very important duties are in the first instance to be assigned, or of persons who are to fill responsible and highly paid situations above the rank of ordinary clerkships.

In the first case, as the character and abilities of the new junior clerk will produce but little immediate effect upon the office, the chief of the department is naturally led to regard the selection as a matter of small moment, and will probably bestow the office upon the son or dependant of someone having personal or political claims upon him, or perhaps upon the son of some meritorious public servant, without instituting any very minute inquiry into the merits of the young man himself.

The young man thus admitted is commonly employed upon duties of the merest routine. Many of the first years of his service are spent in copying papers, and other work of an almost mechanical character. In the meantime his salary is gradually advancing till he reaches, by seniority, the top of his class, and on the occurrence of a vacancy in the class above him he is promoted to fill it, as a matter of course, and without any regard to his previous services or his qualifications.

The general principle, then, which we advocate is, that the public service should be carried on by admission into its lower ranks of a carefully selected body of young men, who should be employed from the first upon work suited to their capacities and their education, and should be made constantly to feel that their promotion and future prospects should depend entirely on the industry and ability with which they discharge their duties.

The first step towards carrying this principle into effect should be, the establishment of a proper system of education before appointment. We recommend that a central Board should be constituted for conducting the examination of all candidates for the public service whom it may be thought right to subject to such a test.

The subjects [should be] as numerous as may be found practicable, so as to secure the greatest and most varied amount of talent for the public service. We need hardly allude to the important effect which would be produced upon the general education of the country, if proficiency in history, jurisprudence, political economy, modern languages, political and physical geography, and other matters, besides the staple of classics and mathematics, were made directly conducive to the success of young men entering into the public service. Such an inducement would probably do more to quicken the progress of our universities, for instance, than any legislative measures that could be adopted.

It would probably be right to include in the examination some exercises directly bearing upon official business; to require a précis to be made of a set of papers, or a letter to be written under given circumstances; but the great advantage to be expected from the examinations would be, that they elicit young men of general ability, which is a matter of more moment than their being possessed of any special requirements.

As well as recommending examinations and promotion on merit, the report called for a single Civil Service run by a Civil Service Commission rather than a series of separate organisations, one for each government department. The report is widely regarded as having laid the foundations for the Civil Service of the next century and a half.

However, its recommendations took time to be implemented. Lord Aberdeen, the prime minister, did not share Gladstone's reforming zeal. It took the military disasters of the Crimean War to force the issue. A series of blunders, such as the Charge of the Light Brigade in October 1854, was blamed on the sale of army commissions in particular and the incompetence of British bureaucracy in general. Even then, only limited competition was allowed for entry into the Civil Service. Only when Gladstone became prime minister in 1868 were the Northcote–Trevelyan reforms fully implemented, along with a range of other reforms to modernise the army and abolish the sale of commissions.

As so often happens, a proposal that is radical in one era becomes a treasure of conservatism in another. So it was with Northcote and Trevelyan's wish to recruit civil servants with 'general ability'. Their intention was to find recruits who knew more than Latin, Greek and mathematics. It was a daring idea for its time. A century later, another government inquiry deplored the 'cult of the generalist'. The 1968 Fulton Report said the Civil Service recruited too many generalists and too few people with specialist knowledge of, say, economics or engineering.

1856

'IF YOU ADMIT EVEN ONE LIFE PEERAGE, YOU INTIMATE YOUR READINESS TO ASSENT TO ANYTHING THE HOUSE OF COMMONS MAY DICTATE'

Contrary to popular wisdom, life peerages are not a modern invention. They had been granted intermittently since the fourteenth century. But they had not given their holders the right to sit in the House of Lords since the reign of Henry V – usually because they were (a) women, (b) foreign or (c) members of the House of Lords already – so life peerages simply conferred an extra title.

By the 1850s, pressure was building for a particular reform – not to admit women to the Lords (women were still more than half a century away from having the vote), but to admit more lawyers. The Lords had the ultimate power to rule on certain appeals, and many cases were heard by peers who had little legal knowledge and no formal training. In 1856, Lord Palmerston, the Liberal prime minister, wanted Queen Victoria to appoint a senior judge, Sir James Parke, as a life peer – Lord Wensleydale – with the right to sit in the Lords. It was designed to create a precedent, so that in future a limited number of judges could be made life peers to enable the House of Lords to carry out its judicial function more effectively.

The issue was debated in the House of Lords on 7 February 1856. Much of the debate turned on arguments about whether the royal prerogative on the power to appoint life peers to the House of Lords had been lost through disuse or could be resurrected after 400 years. The most impassioned speech, however, was that of the Earl of Derby, the Conservative leader, who warned that to create even one life peerage would be the thin end of an exceedingly hazardous wedge.

THE EARL OF DERBY'S SPEECH OPPOSING THE CREATION OF LIFE PEERS

I defy noble Lords to deny these two propositions – first, that there has never been, since the constitution was settled – nay, not for 400 years – an attempt to establish such a precedent as this; and, next, I defy you to deny that this precedent being granted would establish a material and serious alteration in the character of the House of Peers. I am prepared to pay it down as a proposition which cannot be controverted, that from the very earliest period the very essence of the peerage has been that it was hereditary. It will not be denied that, originally, the great barons of the realm, holding their privileges by tenure of their lands, to which they had the right of hereditary possession, were in consequence of that tenure hereditarily entitled to sit in Parliament as the Great Council of the nation.

The noble and learned Lord on the woolsack [The Lord Chancellor, who had spoken in favour of admitting life peers] said the danger of a Minister swamping the House was perfectly visionary. But although the House consists of 450 members, of what does a majority of the House consist? Will the noble and learned Lord tell me that no influence might be exercised by the introduction not of 100, not of twenty, but of nine members? Might not twelve or fourteen Peers, introduced with the peculiar qualification of poverty and, therefore, the more under the influence of a minister, altogether alter a decision of this House? Would a minister obtain no undue influence by being able, as one of those peerages dropped off, or as an hereditary peerage became extinct, to supply its place with another peerage for life?

You say there is no danger, because every minister must be guided by public opinion. But that is the greatest of all dangers if, by public opinion, you mean the opinion of the other House of Parliament. Suppose the Lords oppose a measure which a minister desires to carry, and which the Commons have passed by a large majority – what more easy than to create a sufficient number of peers to carry the measure through the Lords? This House would become an absolute cipher in the legislature. My Lords, if you admit the power of a minister to introduce even one life peerage at his discretion, and to keep that peerage dangling from father to son as a bait for further services, I tell you that the hereditary character of this House is gone – its usefulness in legislation is gone – its independence is gone – and you had better abdicate your functions and intimate your readiness to assent to anything the House of Commons may please to dictate.

This is not a visionary apprehension. I am putting a case which must arise, in the struggle of parties, whenever we have either an unscrupulous minister, or a weak minister who, being dependent upon a narrow majority, and wishing to strengthen it, chooses to appeal to the worst feelings of the House and, by overbearing your Lordships, obtain for himself a temporary renewal of power. The precedent must inevitably lead to abuses, the introduction of less worthy individuals, to a serious increase in the power of the Crown, and to the degradation of your Lordships' House.

If you admit the principle that the Crown may create peers for life, but subject to control as to the qualifications and merits of the individuals by the government of the day, then you immediately introduce a doctrine not only dangerous to the prerogative itself, but which will expose the whole monarchical constitution of the country to destruction.

An upper chamber may rest upon one of two great bases. It may rest upon the hereditary character of the House – or you may rest that upper chamber upon the elective principle, but upon an elective principle varying somewhat in its character and in its constituency from the lower House. But between these two constitutional modes of government, there is no alternative.

My Lords, I hope that neither we nor our children are to live to see the time when this great country shall degenerate into a republic, however well suited such an institution may be to other countries; but of this I am sure, that if you desire to maintain an hereditary monarchy with a balanced constitution, to this you must cling as one of its essentials – the hereditary character of the House of Peers.

The House of Lords voted to back the Earl of Derby. Instead, Sir James Parke was made a hereditary peer. In practice, it made no difference, for none of his sons survived him, but the precedent was blocked. Two further attempts to pass life peerages bills failed, but twenty years later the Appellate Jurisdiction Act 1876 was passed, which allowed senior judges to sit as life peers in the House of Lords.

1859–61

'THE ONLY PURPOSE FOR WHICH POWER CAN BE RIGHTFULLY EXERCISED OVER ANY MEMBER OF A CIVILIZED COMMUNITY IS TO PREVENT HARM TO OTHERS'

John Stuart Mill was the leading philosopher of progressive ideas in Victorian Britain. In 1820, as a teenager, he spent a year in France, staying with Sir Samuel Bentham, Jeremy's brother. Mill became a utilitarian himself, developing and modifying Bentham's ideas on the role of the government and citizens' rights and duties. In particular he attacked the notion that property should play any role in determining anyone's democratic rights.

Following the death of his wife, Harriet Taylor Mill, in 1858, he moved to a villa near Avignon in France, where he wrote two of his most influential works: *On Liberty* and *Considerations on Representative Government*. In *On Liberty* Mill set out the principles on which the line should be drawn between individual freedom and collective action. As an ardent, but at the same time wary, democrat, Mill also highlighted the dangers of 'the tyranny of the majority'.

JOHN STUART MILL: ON LIBERTY

The subject of this Essay is not the so-called Liberty of the Will, so unfortunately opposed to the misnamed doctrine of Philosophical Necessity; but Civil, or Social Liberty: the nature and limits of the power which can be legitimately exercised by society over the individual.

The struggle between Liberty and Authority is the most conspicuous feature in the portions of history with which we are earliest familiar, particularly in that of Greece, Rome, and England. But in old times this contest was between subjects, or some classes of subjects, and the government. By liberty, was meant protection against the tyranny of the political rulers. Their power was regarded as necessary, but also as highly dangerous; as a weapon which they would attempt to use against their subjects, no less than against external enemies. To prevent the weaker members of the community from being preyed upon by innumerable vultures, it was needful that there should be an animal of prey stronger than the rest, commissioned to keep them down. But as the king of the vultures would be no less bent upon preying upon the flock than any of the minor harpies, it was indispensable to be in a perpetual attitude of defence against his beak and claws. The aim, therefore, of patriots, was to set limits to the power which the ruler should be suffered to exercise over the community; and this limitation was what they meant by liberty.

A time, however, came in the progress of human affairs, when men ceased to think it a necessity of nature that their governors should be an independent power, opposed in interest to themselves. It appeared to them much better that the various magistrates of the State should be their tenants or delegates, revocable at their pleasure. In that way alone, it seemed, could they have complete security that the powers of government would never be abused to their disadvantage. By degrees, this new demand for elective and temporary rulers became the prominent object of the exertions of the popular party, wherever any such party existed; and superseded, to a considerable extent, the previous efforts to limit the power of rulers. As the struggle proceeded for making the ruling power emanate from the periodical choice of the ruled, some persons began to think that too much importance had been attached to the limitation of the power itself. That (it might seem) was a resource against rulers whose interests were habitually opposed to those of the people. What was now wanted was, that the rulers should be identified with the people; that their interest and will should be the interest and will of the nation. The nation did not need to be protected against its own will. There was no fear of its tyrannizing over itself. Let the rulers be effectually responsible to it, promptly removable by it, and it could afford to trust them with power of which it could itself dictate the use to be made. Their power was but the nation's own power, concentrated, and in a form convenient for exercise.

But, in political and philosophical theories, as well as in persons, success discloses faults and infirmities which failure might have concealed from observation. The notion, that the people have no need to limit their power over themselves, might seem axiomatic, when popular government was a thing only dreamed about, or read of as having existed at some distant period of the past. In time, however, a democratic republic came to occupy a large portion of the earth's surface, and made itself felt as one of the most powerful members of the community of nations; and elective and responsible government became subject to the observations and criticisms which wait upon a great existing fact. It was now perceived that such phrases as 'self-government,' and 'the power of the people over themselves,' do not express the true state of the case. The 'people' who exercise the power, are not always the same people with those over whom it is exercised, and the 'self-government' spoken of, is not the government of each by himself, but of each by all the rest. The will of the people, moreover, practically means, the will of the most numerous or the most active part of the people; the majority, or those who succeed in making themselves accepted as the majority; the people, consequently, may desire to oppress a part of their number; and precautions are as much needed against this, as against any other abuse of power. The limitation, therefore, of the power of government over individuals, loses none of its importance when the holders of power are regularly accountable to the community, that is, to the strongest party therein. This view of things has had no difficulty in establishing itself; and in political speculations 'the tyranny of the majority' is now generally included among the evils against which society requires to be on its guard.

Society can and does execute its own mandates: and if it issues wrong mandates instead of right, or any mandates at all in things with which it ought not to meddle, it practises a social tyranny more formidable than many kinds of political oppression, since, though not usually upheld by such extreme penalties, it leaves fewer means of escape, penetrating much more deeply into the details of life, and enslaving the soul itself. Protection, therefore, against the tyranny of the magistrate is not enough; there needs protection also against the tyranny of the prevailing opinion and feeling. There is a limit to the legitimate interference of collective opinion with individual independence; and to find that limit, and maintain it against encroachment, is as indispensable to a good condition of human affairs, as protection against political despotism.

But though this proposition is not likely to be contested in general terms, the practical question, where to place the limit—how to make the fitting adjustment between individual independence and social control—is a subject on which nearly everything remains to be done.

The object of this Essay is to assert one very simple principle: that the sole end for which mankind are warranted, individually or collectively in interfering with the liberty of action of any of their number, is self-protection. That the only purpose for which power can be rightfully exercised over any member of a civilized community, against his will, is to prevent harm to others. His own good, either physical or moral, is not a sufficient warrant. He cannot rightfully be compelled to do or forbear because it will be better for him to do so, because it will make him happier, because, in the opinions of others, to do so would be wise, or even right. The only part of the conduct of any one, for which he is amenable to society, is that which concerns others. In the part which merely concerns himself, his independence is, of right, absolute. Over himself, over his own body and mind, the individual is sovereign.

Apart from the peculiar tenets of individual thinkers, there is also in the world at large an increasing inclination to stretch unduly the powers of society over the individual, both by the force of opinion and even by that of legislation: and as the tendency of all the changes taking place in the world is to strengthen society, and diminish the power of the individual, this encroachment is not one of the evils which tend spontaneously to disappear, but, on the contrary, to grow more and more formidable. The disposition of mankind, whether as rulers or as fellow-citizens, to impose their own opinions and inclinations as a rule of conduct on others, is so energetically supported by some of the best and by some of the worst feelings incident to human nature, that it is hardly ever kept under restraint by anything but want of power; and as the power is not declining, but growing, unless a strong barrier of moral conviction can be raised against the mischief, we must expect, in the present circumstances of the world, to see it increase.

In *Considerations on Representative Government*, Mill explored the problems with direct democracy and the relative functions of government and Parliament. He argued that the prime job of Parliament was not to run the country but to hold the government of the day to account.

JOHN STUART MILL: *CONSIDERATIONS ON REPRESENTATIVE GOVERNMENT*

There is no difficulty in showing that the ideally best form of government is that in which the sovereignty, or supreme controlling power in the last resort, is vested in the entire aggregate of the community; every citizen not only having a voice in the exercise of that ultimate sovereignty, but being, at least occasionally, called on to take an actual part in the government, by the personal discharge of some public function.

A completely popular government is the only polity which can make out any claim to this character. It is pre-eminent in both the departments between which the excellence of a political constitution is divided. It is both more favourable to present good government, and promotes a better and higher form of national character, than any other polity whatsoever.

But since all cannot, in a community exceeding a single small town, participate personally in any but some very minor portions of the public business, it follows that the ideal type of a perfect government must be representative.

But while it is essential to representative government that the practical supremacy in the state should reside in the representatives of the people, it is an open question what actual functions, what precise part in the machinery of government, shall be directly and personally discharged by the representative body.

There is a radical distinction between controlling the business of government and actually doing it. The same person or body may be able to control everything, but cannot possibly do everything; and in many cases its control over everything will be more perfect the less it personally attempts to do. The commander of an army could not direct its movements effectually if he himself fought in the ranks, or led an assault. It is the same with bodies of men. Some things cannot be done except by bodies; other things cannot be well done by them. It is one question, therefore, what a popular assembly should control, another what it should itself do.

For example, the duty which is considered as belonging more peculiarly than any other to an assembly representative of the people, is that of voting the taxes. Nevertheless, in no country does the representative body undertake, by itself or its delegated officers, to prepare the estimates. Though the supplies can only be voted by the House of Commons, and though the sanction of the House is also required for the appropriation of the revenues to the different items of the public expenditure, it is the maxim and the uniform practice of the Constitution that money can be granted only on the proposition of the Crown. It has, no doubt, been felt, that moderation as to the amount, and care and judgment in the detail of its application, can only be expected when the executive government, through whose hands it is to pass, is made responsible for the plans and calculations on which the disbursements are grounded. Parliament, accordingly, is not expected, nor even permitted, to originate directly either taxation or expenditure. All it is asked for is its consent, and the sole power it possesses is that of refusal.

The principles which are involved and recognised in this constitutional doctrine, if followed as far as they will go, are a guide to the limitation and definition of the general functions of representative assemblies. In the first place, it is admitted in all countries in which the representative system is practically understood, that numerous representative bodies ought not to administer, or to dictate in detail to those who have the charge of administration. Even when honestly meant, the interference is almost always injurious.

The proper duty of a representative assembly in regard to matters of administration is not to decide them by its own vote, but to take care that the persons who have to decide them shall be the proper persons. Even this they cannot advantageously do by nominating the individuals. The qualifications which fit special individuals for special duties can only be recognised by those who know the individuals, or who make it their business to examine and judge of persons from what they have done, or from the evidence of those who are in a position to judge.

Instead of the function of governing, for which it is radically unfit, the proper office of a representative assembly is to watch and control the government: to throw the light of publicity on its acts: to compel a full exposition and justification of all of them which any one considers questionable; to censure them if found condemnable, and, if the men who compose the government abuse their trust, or fulfil it in a manner which conflicts with the deliberate sense of the nation, to expel them from office. This is surely ample power, and security enough for the liberty of the nation. In addition to this, the Parliament has an office, not inferior even to this in importance; to be at once the nation's Committee of Grievances, and its Congress of Opinions; an arena in which not only the general opinion of the nation, but that of every section of it, can produce itself in full light and challenge discussion.

Representative assemblies are often taunted by their enemies with being places of mere talk. There has seldom been more misplaced derision. I know not how a representative assembly can more usefully employ itself than in talk. A place where every interest and shade of opinion in the country can have its cause even passionately pleaded, in the face of the government and of all other interests and opinions, can compel them to listen, and either comply, or state clearly why they do not, is in itself, if it answered no other purpose, one of the most important political institutions that can exist anywhere, and one of the foremost benefits of free government.

Mill returned to Britain in 1865 and became Member of Parliament for City and Westminster. Over the following three years, he embraced a range of radical causes, from women's rights to labour unions and proportional representation to land reform in Ireland. His radicalism proved unpopular with some Liberals and many of his constituents, and he lost his seat in the 1868 general election. Mill returned to France, where he died in 1873.

1864

'HOW CAN WE BEST ADMIT THE WORKING CLASSES TO SOME POWER WITHOUT GIVING THEM THE WHOLE POWER?'

Walter Bagehot, the author of *The English Constitution*, perhaps the most famous of all political textbooks, described himself as a 'conservative Liberal' – that is, somewhere between the two main political parties of his time. From 1860 until his death in 1877, he edited *The Economist*, which had been founded in 1843 by his father-in-law, James Wilson. Bagehot's creed for *The Economist* – that it should embrace pro-market economics and liberal social policies – survives to this day.

Bagehot was a cautious reformer. He wanted more men to have the vote, but not everyone, for this would mean that the majority of electors would be working class, and they might use their collective voting power to take over running the country. He analysed the problem in two articles in *The Economist* in December 1864; in the second of these he proposed his compromise remedy.

WALTER BAGEHOT: 'A SIMPLE PLAN OF REFORM'

We last week showed why the Reform question is so difficult. We showed that people must bend their mind to something new; must accept some anomaly; must admit something out of the way. If they do not, sooner or later democracy is inevitable. The great artisan class is augmenting in numbers, growing in intelligence, intensifying in political tastes. It will have before long some recognised place in the national system. The existing ideas, the common ideas, afford it no place but an exclusive place. Solely founded in all the constituencies on a uniform basis of mere number, it inevitably gives in all constituencies a uniform preponderance to the most numerous class. Throw open the door, admit the working class, and they will be everywhere the most numerous. Some new plan, some additional experiment, some uncommon conception is required, unless we wish to have a worse America, in which the lower orders are equally despotic, but are not equally intelligent. We must choose between anomaly and democracy. There is no third alternative.

We have then to consider what is the minimum of anomaly which will be sufficient for our preservation. How can we best and easiest, in the most effectual way, the most comprehensible way, the most acceptable way, admit the working classes to some power without giving them the whole power? How can we concede to them a share in the Constitution without sacrificing the whole Constitution to them?

We must look carefully at the real world before we try to solve this problem. It is no use upon this subject of all subjects to evade facts, amuse ourselves with theories, spin cobwebs. We must really face the question as it truly stands, or it is of no use facing it at all.

But when we look at the Reform movement as it exists in the world, we immediately perceive that this question of the working men is in practice inseparably associated and confused with a very different question. There is another great interest in this country which conceives itself to be ill represented—which believes that it does not occupy its true place—which thinks that it is kept down, overshadowed, cast into the shade by other interests unequal to itself in value, feebler in intelligence, lower in vigour, and inferior in political capacity. We mean new commercial wealth. It cannot be denied that much of the wealth created in the last thirty years is dissatisfied with the settlement of the Constitution made thirty years since—that it is restless and dissatisfied—that it fancies older, more aristocratic, less energetic classes cast it into the shade.

When the distribution of the English representation was originally made, the Southern part of England was not only the most gentle and agreeable, but the most rich and energetic. Parliamentary boroughs were placed in the South because it was adapted for Parliamentary boroughs: they were not placed in the North, because it was not adapted. Centuries of change and industry have altered all this. The North is now the industrial region, the vigorous member, and we are only carrying out the original design of the English representation, if we take from the parts which were then living but are now dead, and add to the parts which had not been born but now live and thrive.

No one who observes the Reform agitation closely can fail to see how closely this feeling—this sensation of the insufficient representation of commercial wealth and manufacturing industry—is associated with the cry for working-class representation. It is the master manufacturers who agitate for the enfranchisement of their own workmen. The classes whose immediate interests are most clearly opposed, who are constantly and of necessity driving unpleasant bargains with each other, who often are at bitter feud, are on this subject at one. The capitalist heads the movement of the citizen; he is sometime more clamorous for the rights of labour than the labourer himself. The explanation is simple. The capitalist and the labourer have a united interest—a common object—in this matter. When a great manufacturer says at a West Riding meeting, 'I wish to alter the Constitution, so that the working classes around me should be represented,' he means that undoubtedly very sincerely, but he means also, and more sincerely, because half consciously, 'We—I, and such as I—ought to have more power. The stationary South must no longer govern the advancing North.'

Examined by the grave tests of sound philosophy, it cannot be denied that the whole new world of the North has its grievance as well as the artisan part of that world. A good scheme of reform would both increase the power of what we must roughly but intelligibly call 'the North,' at the same time that it gave some power to the whole working classes, though denying them the whole power.

We would propose to effect both these objects by the following means. Transfer a certain considerable number of members from insignificant boroughs—from the well-known boroughs which have uniformly figured in every schedule of proposed disfranchisement—to the great seats of industry, and in those seats of industry, and there only, lower the franchise, so as to admit artisan classes. This would give the necessary representation to the working classes, and it would give them only that necessary representation. Being only possessed of a certain number of seats, they could not rule the country, they could not impose on it their enthusiasms, their prejudices, or their fancied interests. Their members would be only one sort of members out of many sorts.

It may also be objected that this plan is an unjust plan. It gives, it may be said, a vote to an operative in borough A, and denies a vote to a precisely similar operative in borough B. But there is no injustice when we examine the matter. No one has a right to a political power which he will use to impair a better man's political power. The real injustice would be to give votes to all the working classes, for then, in substance, all the better classes, the more instructed classes, the more opulent classes, would have no votes at all.

As we said, we propose this plan—saying that it includes an anomaly, and even because it includes an anomaly. Nothing, as we before proved at length, which does not include an extraordinary uncommon element will achieve the work which there is to do. We concede the exceptional nature of our scheme, but we believe that something exceptional is necessary and that this is the minimum of exception.

Bagehot's proposals were reflected in the Reform Bill introduced to Parliament by Earl Russell's (formerly Lord John Russell) Liberal government in 1866. This proposed the extension of the franchise to another 400,000 people, mostly working-class men in the major cities. However, the bill was voted down by a combination of Conservatives, who felt that the bill went too far, and dissident Liberals, for whom it did not go far enough. In June 1866, following his defeat, Russell resigned and the Liberals went briefly into opposition.

The following year, Bagehot published the first edition of *The English Constitution*. This built on his journalism, including 'A Simple Plan of Reform', and became one of the most enduring analyses of our political system. Bagehot also stood for Parliament for London University. Although he was a clear and vivid writer, he was a poor speaker and failed to be elected.

1865

'ENGLAND IS THE MOTHER OF PARLIAMENTS. WHY SHOULD YOU BE THUS TREATED IN YOUR OWN LAND?'

High on any list of common misquotations is that Britain's Houses of Parliament are 'the mother of parliaments'. What John Bright, the original source of the phrase, actually said was: 'England is the mother of parliaments'. The misquotation invites smugness, but the words that Bright actually used, in the context that he used them, were intended to provoke the opposite reaction: anger.

Bright was one of the most Radical of Liberal MPs in the 1860s. In April 1864, he formed the Reform Union, which advocated triennial parliaments, voting by secret ballot and a big extension of the franchise. The speech in which he coined the phrase about the 'mother of parliaments' was delivered at Birmingham's Town Hall on 18 January 1865. Speaking as America's Civil War was drawing to a close, he praised moves for reform in other countries and warned that Britain, with its proud history of parliamentary rule, was in danger of being left behind in its progress towards democracy. He demanded that the franchise be extended to all adult men, instead of the one in five who owned enough property to have the vote.

The Times' introduction to its verbatim report of Bright's speech provides a telling example of the dictum that 'the past is a foreign country: they do things differently there'. *The Times* plainly told its readers that Bright and his fellow Birmingham MP, William Scholefield, delivered their speeches as they 'paid their annual visit to their constituency'. No present-day MP would get away with visiting his constituency only once a year.

JOHN BRIGHT'S SPEECH ON REFORMING THE FRANCHISE

> Let me remind you of this, that really great questions which affect the true and lasting interests of millions of men can never be laid fast asleep; but that somehow or other they come up again. There is a startling example

of this in what is now taking place in the United States. For 30 years the statesmen of the United States have voted the Negro to be a very great nuisance; they would not talk about him, and they swore each to silence. The Negro's business was to grow rice, sugar and cotton, and not to give trouble to Congress, so they determined to bury that question, and they congratulated themselves that it was buried; but now you see the North and South engaged in deadly conflict, and the Negro standing forth before the world, rubbing the marks of the branding iron from his forehead, while the shackles, which have long oppressed him, are dropping from his limbs, and he is every day becoming more and more a free man.

So here is a question that will not be put to sleep, it is the question of the admission of the people of this country to the rights which are guaranteed by every principle and by everything which is comprehended in the constitution of this United Kingdom. In 1861, this general question of Parliamentary reform was voted a nuisance. It was betrayed. It was slain, and, as they thought, it was buried. But that Bill and that question is not dead, it takes shape again, and somehow or other the Tories, and those Whigs who are like Tories, entertain uncomfortable feelings which approach almost to a shiver.

Now, what is this apparition which alarms them? They are afraid of the five or six millions of grown-up Englishmen, men who are allowed to marry, to keep house, to rear children, men who are expected to earn their living, who pay taxes, who must obey the laws, who must be citizens in all honourable conduct, they are afraid of these five or six million, who by the present system of representation are shut out, and insultingly shut out, from the exercise of the franchise.

We are proud of our country, and there are many things of which we have a right to be proud. We may be proud that England is the ancient country of parliaments. With scarcely any intervening period, parliaments have met constantly for 600 years, and there was something of a parliament before the conquest. England is the mother of parliaments. I ask you men of Birmingham, who are a fair representation of the great mass of the five or six millions, why you should be thus treated in your own land?

You know our boast of what occurs when a Negro slave lands in England; one of our best poets says that:

If their lungs but breathe our air
That moment they are free.

They touch our country and their shackles fall. But what is the case with respect to an Englishman? An Englishman, if he goes to the Cape, can vote; if he goes to Australia he can vote; if he goes to the Canadian Confederation or to our grandest colonies, he can vote; it is only in his own country, on his own soil, where he was born, the very soil which he has enriched with his labour and the sweat of his brow, that he is denied this right which in every other community of Englishmen in the world would be freely accorded to him.

Conservatism, be it Toryism or Whiggism, is the true national peril which we have to face. They may dam the stream, they may keep back the waters, but the volume is ever increasing, and it descends with accelerating force; and the time will come when in all probability – and to a certainty, if wisdom does not take the place of folly – the waters will burst their banks, and these men who fancy they are stemming this imaginary apparition of democracy will themselves be swept away by the resolute will of a united and determined people.

Representation is to be found in Italy, in Austria, even in almost all the German States, in the Northern States, in Belgium, Holland, France, Portugal and Spain. Englishmen everywhere but at home are received in the bosom of this great, permanent, undying constitution and safeguard for human and national freedom; but here they are slandered, they are insulted, they are reviled, they are shut out, they are invited to have a hundred ways of amusing themselves; but if they stand at the House of Commons, or at the poll, and see their richer brethren go up to vote, they are not allowed to register their names in favour of principles for which their fathers before them and themselves have sighed in many a bitter hour of disappointment.

I would change all this. I speak out of no hostility to any class or to any institution, but that man who proposes to exclude permanently five millions of his fellow countrymen from the right which the Constitution of his country makes sacred in his eyes, I say that is the man who separates England into two nations, and makes it impossible we should be wholly and permanently a contented people.

England has long been famous for the enjoyment of personal freedom by her people – they are free to think, they are free to speak, they are free to write, and England has been famed of late years, and is famed now, the world over, for the freedom of her industry and the greatness and freedom of her commerce. Who is there that will meet me on this platform or who will stand on any platform and will dare to say to an open meeting of his fellow countrymen that these millions for whom I am now pleading are too ignorant or too vicious or destructive to be entrusted with the elective franchise?

I, at least, will never thus slander my countrymen. I claim for them the right of admission through their representatives into the most ancient and venerable Parliament which at this hour exists among men, and when they are thus admitted, and not till then, it may be truly said that England, the august mother of free nations, herself is free.

The Times reported that Bright 'resumed his seat amid loud and enthusiastic cheers'.

Bright, however, was not a Radical on all issues to do with widening the franchise. In a letter written in 1882, he set out his reasons against women having the vote.

JOHN BRIGHT OPPOSES WOMEN HAVING THE VOTE

I act from a belief that to introduce women into the strife of political life would be a great evil to them, and that to our sex no possible good could arrive. If women are not safe under the charge and care of fathers, husbands, brothers and sons, it is the fault of our non-civilisation and not of our laws. As civilisation founded upon Christian principle advances, women will gain all that is right for them, although they are not seen contending in the strife of political parties. In my experience I have observed evil results to many women who have entered hotly into political conflict and discussion. I would save them from it. If all the men in a nation do not and cannot adequately express its will and defend its interests, to add all the women will not better the result, and the representative system is a mistake.

'A POLITICAL BETRAYAL WHICH HAS NO PARALLEL IN OUR PARLIAMENTARY ANNALS'

Although he opposed Earl Russell's Reform Bill, the Earl of Derby, prime minister of the incoming Conservative government, decided that change could be delayed no longer. He told Benjamin Disraeli – who, as Leader of the House of Commons, would have to take any new bill through the Commons – that he was 'coming reluctantly to the conclusion that we shall have to deal with the question of reform'.

In the event, Derby's Reform Bill was more radical than Russell's. Derby's calculation was that a wider franchise would actually help his party because the instincts of many householders hitherto denied the vote were instinctively Tory. In the debate in the Commons during the third reading of the bill, on 15 July 1867, Disraeli clashed with Lord Cranborne, one of the most outspoken critics of reform.

Cranborne was then an MP rather than a peer: his was a courtesy title, as the eldest son of the Marquess of Salisbury. (He remained a commoner until his father's death in 1868, when he entered the House of Lords.) He resigned from Derby's Cabinet because of his opposition to the Reform Bill, which he argued was a betrayal of Conservative principles and a surrender to dangerously radical forces. Cranborne's anger increased as Disraeli accepted a series of amendments to widen the franchise more than the original bill had proposed.

LORD CRANBORNE AND BENJAMIN DISRAELI DEBATE THE REFORM BILL

> **LORD CRANBORNE:** I venture to impress this upon the House, because I have heard it said that this Bill is a Conservative triumph. If it be a Conservative triumph to have adopted the principles of your most determined adversary; if it be a Conservative triumph to have introduced a Bill guarded with precautions and securities, and to have abandoned every one of those precautions and securities at the bidding of your opponents,

then in the whole course of your annals I will venture to say the Conservative party has won no triumph so signal as this.

It seems to me that every one who tries to prophesy with respect to this franchise tries to prove that the course you are taking will not have its natural effect. If you gave to 100 men of one class power to outvote fifty of another class, you would naturally conclude, were it a matter in which you had no concern, that the fifty would have no chance whatever. You cannot deny that that would be the natural result. But we hear on all sides that there are peculiar circumstances in this case, and that the influence of rank and position will so modify the natural desires of everybody to get what they can, that the 100 will allow themselves to be guided by the fifty who happen to have a Lord at their head.

I myself do not believe in that influence of wealth and rank. I believe it will operate in quiet times and on ordinary questions. I believe it is very likely that for ordinary purposes you will find members of the upper and middle classes returned to this House, and that where no pressure exists they will be governed by the feelings of the classes to which they belong. But if ever any crisis arises—if there is any stress which draws men into violent action, I believe that then you will find that the upper and middle classes will no longer vote for the class to which they belong, and that those who are elected will care more for their seats than for their class. Depend upon it, if any storm arises, if there is any question of labour against capital, any question of occupation against property, it will be no protection to you that you may have men who belong to the class of proprietors or the class of capitalists in this House. You will see, what has been seen a hundred times, that men will rather vote against their class than peril their own position with their constituents, and will care too much for their own political future to fly in the face of those who elect them.

Upon all questions of foreign policy and of general policy I see no reason to believe that the working classes will come to any other conclusion but what all other sober and reasonable Englishmen come to. But if ever you come to a question between class and class—if ever you come to a question where the interests of one class are, or seem to be, pitted against those of another, you will find that all those securities of rank, wealth, and influence in which you trust are mere feathers in the balance against the solid interest and the real genuine passions of mankind; and you will see that they will use the weapon which you are now putting unreservedly in their hands with a perfect belief that they are in the right.

I entreat hon. Gentlemen opposite not to believe that my feelings on this subject are dictated simply by my hostility to this particular measure, though I object to it most strongly, as the House is aware. But, even if I took a contrary view—if I deemed it to be most advantageous, I still should deeply regret that the position of the Executive should have been so degraded as it has been in the present Session; I should deeply regret to find that the House of Commons has applauded a policy of legerdemain; and I should, above all things, regret that this great gift to the people—if gift you think it—should have been purchased at the cost of a political betrayal which has no parallel in our Parliamentary annals, which strikes at the root of all that mutual confidence which is the very soul of our party Government, and on which only the strength and freedom of our representative institutions can be sustained.

Benjamin Disraeli: Sir, I think it cannot be said that this was a measure which bristled with securities and precautions that have been given up at the bidding of our opponents. That a great many of them have been given up I shall not deny; but they have been given up not always or in the greatest degree at the bidding of our opponents, and some of them have been given up to the general feeling of the House.

Now, Sir, the noble [Lord Cranborne] says that by yielding to these conditions, I have virtually altered the whole character of the Bill. Now, is that true? Is the whole character of the Bill altered? I contend on the contrary, that the Bill, though adapted of course to the requirements of the year in which we are legislating, is at the same time in harmony with the general policy which we have always maintained. [Laughter from the Opposition.] This is a question which cannot be settled by a jeer or a laugh, but by facts, and by facts and results which many of you deprecate and deplore at this moment, and in consequence of which you tell us that you mean to reopen the agitation—a thing which I defy you to do.

The question, therefore, for us practically to consider was—whether we were to accept this settlement of the borough franchise, we will say at £5, or whether we should adhere to the conviction at which we had arrived in 1859—namely, that if you reduced the qualification there was no safe resting-place until you came to a household rating franchise? The noble lord says that immense dangers are to arise to this country because we have departed from the £10 franchise. [Lord Cranbourne: No.] Well, it was something like that, or because you have reduced the franchise. The noble lord is candid enough to see that if you had reduced it after what occurred in 1859, as you ought according to your pledges to have done, you would have had to reduce it again by this time. It is not likely that such a settlement of the difficulty would have been so statesmanlike that you could have allayed discontent or satisfied any great political demands by reducing the electoral qualification by 40s. or so.

Then the question would arise – is there a greater danger from the number who would be admitted by a rating household franchise than from admitting the hundreds of thousands who would come in under a £5 franchise? I think that the danger would be less, that the feeling of the large number would be more national, than by only admitting what I call the Praetorian guard, a sort of class set aside, invested with peculiar privileges, looking with suspicion on their superiors, and with disdain on those beneath them, with no friendly feelings towards the institutions of their country and with great confidence in themselves. I think you would have a better chance of touching the popular heart, of evoking the national sentiment by embracing the great body of those men who occupy houses and fulfil the duties of citizenship by the payment of rates, than by the more limited and, in our opinion, more dangerous proposal.

Sir, the prognostications of evil uttered by the noble lord I can respect, because I know that they are sincere; the warnings and prophecies of the right honourable gentleman I treat in another spirit. For my part, I do not believe that the country is in danger. I think England is safe in the race of men who inhabit her; that she is safe in something much more precious than her accumulated capital – her accumulated experience; she is safe in her national character, in her fame, in the traditions of a thousand years, and in that glorious future which I believe awaits her.

In the event, Cranborne did not insist on a vote (which he knew he would lose), and the bill was passed without a division. The Lords rejected many of the amendments, but the Act that emerged had the effect of doubling the electoral register. Just 1,350,000 men had been entitled to vote in 1865; by 1874, when the full impact of the Act could be felt, the number had risen to 2,750,000 – from around 15 per cent to 30 per cent of all adult men.

1869—86

'WHEN THE HOUSE OF COMMONS IS AT ONE WITH THE NATION, THE VOCATION OF THIS HOUSE HAS PASSED AWAY'

As Britain's electorate grew and the number of seats effectively 'owned' by peers declined, the legitimacy of the House of Lords came under increasing scrutiny. What right did hereditary peers have to reject bills approved by an increasingly democratic House of Commons? The controversy contained two distinct, though interconnected, elements: in what circumstances did the Lords have the right to overrule the Commons, and should the hereditary principle be modified or abandoned?

The central issue in the 1868 election that led to William Gladstone's first Liberal administration was the disestablishment of the Irish Church. A bill to achieve this had been approved by the Commons, but rejected by the Lords before the election. In 1869, Gladstone introduced a new bill to disestablish the Irish Church. Many Conservatives wished to defeat it, and – as for most of the time when the Upper House was dominated by hereditary peers – they had a majority in the Lords.

A further issue was the growing clamour for the secret ballot. Henry Austin Bruce, the Liberal Home Secretary who eventually steered this reform through Parliament, was a reluctant convert to the cause. Until 1869, he had favoured open voting, arguing that it demonstrated the manliness and fearlessness of the democratic process. But, he said, the scale of coercion seen in the 1868 general election had finally persuaded him that the secret ballot was the lesser of two evils. However, this meant that his government wished to implement a reform that they had not proposed in the election that brought them to power; therefore they could not claim a direct popular mandate for this reform.

In June 1869, Lord Salisbury, who had inherited his father's title only the year before, having been an MP for 15 years, set out the basic principles of what became known as the 'Salisbury doctrine', to define the circumstances in which the House of Lords, whatever it felt about a particular measure, should yield to the greater legitimacy of the House of Commons.

LORD SALISBURY'S SPEECH ON THE ROLE OF THE HOUSE OF LORDS

The Object of the existence of a second House of Parliament is to supply the omissions and correct the deficiencies which occur in the proceedings of the first. But it is perfectly true that there may be occasions in our history in which the decision of the House of Commons and the decision of the nation must be taken as practically the same. In ninety-nine cases out of 100 the House of Commons is theoretically the representative of the nation, but it is only so in theory. The constitutional theory has no corresponding basis in fact; because in ninety-nine cases out of 100 the nation, as a whole, takes no interest in our politics, but amuses itself and pursues its usual avocations, allowing the political storm to rage without taking any interest in it. In all these cases I make no distinction – absolutely none – between the prerogative of the House of Commons and the House of Lords.

Again, there is a class of cases small in number, and varying in kind, in which the nation must be called into council and must decide the policy of the Government. It may be that the House of Commons in determining the opinion of the nation is wrong; and if there are grounds for entertaining that belief, it is always open to this House, and indeed it is the duty of this House to insist that the nation shall be consulted, and that one House without the support of the nation shall not be allowed to domineer over the other.

But when once we have come to the conclusion from all the circumstances that the House of Commons is at one with the nation, it appears to me that – save in some very exceptional cases, save in the highest case of morality – in those cases in which a man would not set his hand to a certain proposition, though a revolution should follow from his refusal – it appears to me that the vocation of this House has passed away, that it must devolve the responsibility upon the nation, and may fairly accept the conclusion at which the nation has arrived.

Many peers found Salisbury's argument persuasive; indeed, the next day, an amendment designed to delay the Irish Church bill was defeated by 179 to 146.

However, Salisbury argued that the Lords *should* defeat the 1872 Parliamentary and Municipal Elections Bill, which introduced the secret ballot. Salisbury wrote to Lord Carnarvon outlining his strategy for opposing the bill. Salisbury's letter elaborated on his speech on the Irish Church bill and argued that the 'judgement of the nation' could be known for certain only in the wake of a general election, when the opinions of most voters were 'decidedly expressed'. Otherwise, the House of Lords should decide for itself how best to reflect the 'opinions of the nation'.

LORD SALISBURY'S LETTER TO LORD CARNARVON

I am strongly for rejecting the Bill on the second reading, for this reason. It appears to me of vital necessity that our acceptance of Bills to which we are opposed should be regulated on some principle. If we listen to the Liberals we should accept all important Bills which had passed the House of Commons by a large majority. But that in effect would be to efface the House of Lords.

Another principle – which is, so far as I can gather, what commends itself to Lord Derby – is to watch newspapers, public meetings and so forth, and only to reject when 'public opinion', thus ascertained, growls very loud. This plan gives a premium to bluster and will bring the House into contempt.

The plan which I prefer is frankly to acknowledge that the nation is our Master, though the House of Commons is not, and to yield our own opinion only when the judgement of the nation has been challenged at the polls and decidedly expressed.

This doctrine, it seems to me, has the advantage of being: (1) Theoretically sound. (2) Popular. (3) Safe against agitation, and (4) so rarely applicable as practically to place little fetter upon our independence. It is therefore rather as part of a general principle that because I attach a supreme importance to the question of the Ballot, that I am most earnestly desirous of inducing [the Duke of] Richmond [Leader of the Conservatives in the House of Lords] to resist the second reading.

Salisbury took part in the debate on the bill on 10 June 1872.

LORD SALISBURY'S SPEECH ON THE SECOND READING OF THE PARLIAMENTARY AND MUNICIPAL ELECTIONS BILL

I draw the widest possible distinction between the opinions of the House of Commons and the opinions of the nation. Several of the speakers this evening have admitted what is the fact – namely, that neither this House nor any authority in this State or any other State can resist the deliberate and well-settled opinion of the nation over which it rules. But that the House of Commons is the expression of the opinion of the nation is a constitutional fiction which it is convenient for practical purposes to respect; but which is only literally true on certain occasions and on certain subjects.

It is literally true when a question on which the House of Commons has been elected is under discussion – then it is undoubtedly true that the House of Commons represents the opinion of the nation: – but when four years have gone by, and the memory of all the questions on which the House of Commons was elected has passed away, and when an obvious change has taken place in many opinions of the Government which the House of Commons was elected to support, the House of Commons represents only theoretically and not literally the opinions of the nation.

The members of the Government are not the same as they were when they went to the country – they were then mainly non-Ballot politicians. Therefore, I maintain, the country has never had a fair opportunity of considering whether it likes the Ballot or not.

So far from admitting that because it concerns elections to the House of Commons we ought to obey the behests of that House, I should say, on the contrary, it is rather our duty to regard ourselves in this matter as agents of the nation, and to see that the House of Commons, in thus tampering with the laws under which it was elected, has not transgressed the mandate it received.

This time Salisbury was not successful. That day, the bill (subsequently known generally as the Ballot Act) was approved by the Lords, by 86 votes to 56. Salisbury failed to sway enough peers with his warnings of the grave dangers that secret voting held for democracy. For example, he predicted a sharp increase in the number of Irish MPs who supported Home Rule. He was right. For some politicians, that's the galling thing about the secret ballot: voters are liable to declare their true allegiance.

Meanwhile, Liberals debated how to end the Conservatives' inbuilt majority in the House of Lords. Should they award enough peerages to enable them to outvote the Conservatives? Or take more radical steps and seek to overturn the hereditary principle? Gladstone preferred the former course. In a speech to his constituents in Greenwich, he set out his argument in the wider context of political reform.

Gladstone's speech at Greenwich advocating reform

The enfranchisement, the wide enfranchisement of the working classes, was intended to give the boon of political power not only to the class, but to every individual in the class. We have, therefore, to secure in the case of these persons, many of them to a considerable extent from their temporal circumstances dependent upon others, that the vote which we invite them to give shall be given freely—freely as respects landlord, freely as respects customer, freely as respects employer, freely as respects combination of the working-class itself; and I rejoice to think, gentlemen, that, although the Royal Assent has not yet been given to a bill for secret voting, yet for every practical purpose, after the proceedings of last Session, the question has very nearly reached the stage of final triumph.

There is a question of the future on which we have heard much said of late—I mean the question of the constitution of the House of Lords. [A Voice: 'You had better leave that alone.'] My friend there says, 'Leave the constitution of the House of Lords alone.' I am not prepared quite to agree with my friend, because the constitution of the House of Lords has often been a subject of consideration among the wisest and the most sober-minded men; as, for example, when a proposal—of which my friend disapproves apparently—was made, a few years ago, to make a moderate addition to the House of Lords, of peers holding peerages for life.

I am not going to discuss that particular measure; I will only say that I believe there are various particulars in which the constitution of the House of Lords might, under favourable circumstances, be improved. And I am bound to say that, though I believe there are some politicians, bearing the name of 'Liberal,' who approve of the proceedings of the House of Lords with respect to the Ballot Bill at the close of the last Session, I must own that I deeply lament that proceeding on the part of the House of Lords. It seems to me to have been a great error. After the House of Commons, which had been engaged in other and most serious labours for four or five months, had given some six weeks of the Session—six weeks of very arduous labour—mainly to maturing the Ballot Bill, it appears to me to have been a great and grievous error, I cannot call it anything less, on the part of the House of Lords, in the second week in the month of August, to say that really such was the time at which they had arrived as to render it impossible for them to afford to that measure the number of days—not a very large number of days, according to all precedent and likelihood—that it would have required from them.

But the reform of the House of Lords, which has been recommended in many quarters, is briefly this, that we should eject and expel from the House of Lords what is termed the hereditary principle. Now, gentlemen, I hope I am at least earnest and sincere in my intentions as to being what passes for a Liberal politician; but before I agree, and before I commit myself to expelling from the House of Lords, the hereditary principle, I will think once, I will think twice—nay, I will think even thrice. Before you determine to expel the hereditary principle from the House of Lords, I first ask you, what you will substitute for the hereditary principle? [A Voice—'Five years' election.'] That is a fruitful hint, but yet I have another point to suggest, and it is this: I have a shrewd suspicion in my mind that a very large proportion of the people of England have a sneaking kindness for this hereditary principle.

I do not mean, gentlemen, by these words that a large proportion of the people of England either desire, or intend, or would permit that which I hope that they never will desire, or intend, or permit—namely, that the House of Lords should exercise a paramount control over the legislation of the country. That is quite another matter. But this I do say—that the people of England are not, like the people of France, lovers of naked political equality. England is a great lover of liberty; but of equality she never has been so much enamoured. Gentlemen, in judging of this question, I must say that possibly the observation of the manner in which, for such long periods, and under so many varieties of form, the love of equality in France has proved insufficient to save our generous and distinguished neighbours from the loss of liberty—the observation of these facts may tend to confirm the people of the three kingdoms in the feelings that I think they entertain; but I want to put this to you as a practical question.

The only mode of judging whether an Englishman—and I use the word 'Englishman' for the people of the three kingdoms—is not unfriendly to social inequalities is by watching the working of our institutions in detail. My observation has not been of a very brief term—I wish it had been, for then I should have been younger than I am now—and it is this: that whenever there is anything to be done, or to be given, and there are two candidates for it who are exactly alike—alike in opinions, alike in characters, alike in possessions, and one is a commoner and the other a lord, the Englishman is very apt indeed to prefer the lord.

Under these circumstances, gentlemen, though I hope I shall, while I remain in public life, be able to act zealously and cheerfully with you for the promotion of Liberal opinions, I, for one, have never understood by Liberal opinions either precipitate conclusions or subversive opinions. And I hope we shall well consider, before we commit ourselves to vast changes, to the introduction of new and far-reaching principles, what the results are likely to be.

Gladstone appointed 42 peers during his 1868–74 administration, which diluted the domination of the Conservatives. After Disraeli's 1874–80 administration,

Gladstone returned to office in 1880; battles between the Lords and Commons resumed. Apart from a short spell in opposition, when MPs defeated his government's Budget in June 1885, Gladstone remained prime minister until July 1886. Towards the end of his premiership, agitation for reform began to concern Queen Victoria, who, in one of her exchanges with Gladstone, wrote the following (referring to both Gladstone and herself in the third person):

QUEEN VICTORIA'S LETTER TO GLADSTONE, 7 MARCH 1886

The Queen cannot but think that he might with advantage have dwelt on the following points:

The benefit derived by the nation, in possessing a chamber of the independent nature of the House of Lords; – independent especially, because unlike the House of Commons, its members have not to solicit their seats at the hands of the people by holding out promises which are frequently regretted afterwards by those who made them.

The fact that any attack directed against the House of Lords as an integral part of the constitution cannot fail to affect the stability of the other two, viz: the Sovereign and the House of Commons – a consideration which it strikes the Queen does not seem to have been present to Mr Gladstone's mind.

The great importance (which the Queen is sure Mr Gladstone must himself fully appreciate) of maintaining a power like the House of Lords in order that it may exercise a legitimate and wholesome check upon the greatly increasing radicalism of the present day.

The queen need not have feared: apart from the admission of Law Lords as life peers, which had taken place in 1876, further significant reform of either the formal powers or the composition of the House of Lords was delayed until the twentieth century. And the Salisbury doctrine ended up being updated by Salisbury's grandson, Viscount Cranborne, after the Second World War. A few weeks after Labour's landslide victory in 1945, Cranborne, speaking as Leader of the Conservative opposition in the Lords, promised not to oppose any measure that Labour had explicitly included in its election manifesto. This doctrine has held good for the past six decades.

1886

'CAN ANYTHING STOP A NATION'S DEMAND, EXCEPT ITS BEING PROVED TO BE IMMODERATE AND UNSAFE?'

I n 1886, William Gladstone, prime minister for the third time, introduced the first Irish Home Rule Bill. He had been persuaded of the case for Home Rule by both parliamentary arithmetic and the merits of the case. Charles Stewart Parnell was responsible for both. A Protestant landowner, he sympathised with the nationalist aspirations of Ireland's Catholic majority. He established the Irish Parliamentary Party, which, out of 103 Irish seats in the House of Commons, won 63 in 1880, and 86 in 1885. Gladstone was impressed with both this achievement and the arguments Parnell advanced. He made Irish Home Rule his overriding objective in his later years.

On 7 June 1886, Gladstone put the case for Home Rule to the House of Commons. He also attacked his opponents, such as Joseph Chamberlain, who had resigned from Gladstone's government three months earlier in opposition to Home Rule, and had set up his own party, the Liberal Unionists.

GLADSTONE'S SPEECH TO PARLIAMENT ON IRISH HOME RULE

I do not deny that there may be cases in which legislative incorporation may have been the means of constituting a great country, as in the case of France. But we believe, as proved by history, that where there are those disturbed relations between countries associated, but not incorporated, the true principle is to make ample provision for local independence, subject to Imperial unity. These are propositions of the greatest interest and importance. Gentlemen speak of tightening the ties between England and Ireland as if tightening the tie were always the means to be adopted. Tightening the tie is frequently the means of making it burst, whilst relaxing the tie is very frequently the way to provide for its durability, and to enable it to stand a stronger strain; so that it is true, as was said by the honourable Member for Newcastle [Mr. Joseph Cowen], that the separation of Legislatures is often the union of countries, and the union of Legislatures is often the severance of countries.

It has been asked in this debate, why have we put aside all the other Business of Parliament, and why have we thrown the country into all this agitation for the sake of the Irish Question? ['Hear, hear!'] That cheer is the echo that I wanted. Well, Sir, the first reason is this – because in Ireland the primary purposes of Government are not attained. What said the honourable Member for Newcastle [Mr. J. Cowen] in his eloquent speech? That in a considerable part of Ireland distress was chronic, disaffection was perpetual, and insurrection was smouldering.

I must further say that we have proposed this measure because Ireland wants to make her own laws. It is not enough to say that you are prepared to make good laws. You were prepared to make good laws for the Colonies. You did make good laws for the Colonies according to the best of your light. The Colonists were totally dissatisfied with them. You accepted their claim to make their own laws. Ireland, in our opinion, has a claim not less urgent.

Now, Sir, what is before us? What is before us in the event of the rejection of this Bill? What alternatives have been proposed? Here I must for a moment comment on the fertile imagination of my right honourable Friend the Member for West Birmingham [Mr. Joseph Chamberlain]. He has proposed alternatives, and plenty of them. He has trimmed his vessel and he has touched his rudder in such a masterly way that in whichever direction the winds of Heaven may blow they must fill his sails.

Let me illustrate my meaning. I will suppose different cases. Supposing that at an Election public opinion should be very strong in favour of the Bill. My right honourable Friend would then be perfectly prepared to meet that public opinion, and tell it – 'I declared strongly that I adopted the principle of the Bill.' On the other hand, if public opinion was very adverse to the Bill, my right honourable Friend, again, is in complete armour, because he says – 'Yes, I voted against the Bill.' Supposing, again, public opinion is in favour of a very large plan for Ireland. My right honourable Friend is perfectly provided for that case also. The Government plan was not large enough for him, and he proposed in his speech on the introduction of the Bill that we should have a measure on the basis of federation, which goes beyond this Bill. Lastly – and now I have very nearly boxed the compass – supposing that public opinion should take quite a different turn, and instead of wanting very large measures for Ireland should demand very small measures for Ireland, still the resources of my right honourable Friend are not exhausted, because then he is able to point out that the last of his plans was four Provincial Councils controlled from London.

Under other circumstances I should, perhaps, have been tempted to ask the secret of my right honourable Friend's recipe; as it is, I am afraid I am too old to learn it. When I come to look at these practical alternatives and provisions, I find that they are visibly creations of the vivid imagination born of the hour and perishing with the hour, totally and absolutely unavailable for the solution of a great and difficult problem, the weight of which, and the urgency of which, my right honourable Friend himself in other days has seemed to feel.

What is the case of Ireland at this moment? Have honourable Gentlemen considered that they are coming into conflict with a nation? Can anything stop a nation's demand, except its being proved to be immoderate and unsafe? But here are multitudes, and, I believe, millions upon millions, out-of-doors, who feel this demand to be neither immoderate nor unsafe. In our opinion, there is but one question before us about this demand. It is as to the time and circumstance of granting it. There is no question in our minds that it will be granted, We wish it to be granted in the mode prescribed by Mr. Burke, Mr. Burke said, in his first speech at Bristol:

'I was true to my old-standing invariable principles, that all things which came from Great Britain should issue as a gift of her bounty and beneficence rather than as claims recovered against struggling litigants, or at least, if your beneficence obtained no credit in your concessions, yet that they should appear the salutary provisions of your wisdom and foresight – not as things wrung from you with your blood by the cruel gripe of a rigid necessity.'

The difference between giving with freedom and dignity on the one side, with acknowledgment and gratitude on the other, and giving under compulsion – giving with disgrace, giving with resentment dogging you at every step of your path – this difference is, in our eyes, fundamental, and this is the main reason not only why we have acted, but why we have acted now. This, if I understand it, is one of the golden moments of our history – one of those opportunities which may come and may go, but which rarely return, or, if they return, return at long intervals, and under circumstances which no man can forecast.

Gladstone's bill was defeated by 30 votes because Chamberlain's 93-strong faction of Liberal Unionists voted with the Conservatives. In the general election that followed, the Liberal Unionists and the Conservatives formed an alliance, and together won a clear overall majority. Gladstone returned to power for the last time in 1892, at the age of 82. Again he introduced an Irish Home Rule Bill. This time the Commons passed the bill, but the Conservative and pro-Unionist House of Lords blocked it. Gladstone resigned as prime minister for the last time soon afterwards.

Perhaps the best epitaph for his efforts was provided by King George V, at the time of the violent birth of the Irish Free State three decades later: 'What fools we were not to pass Mr Gladstone's Bill when we had the chance!'

1901

'THE TRUE TEST OF PROGRESS IS NOT THE ACCUMULATION OF WEALTH IN THE HANDS OF A FEW, BUT THE ELEVATION OF A PEOPLE AS A WHOLE'

K eir Hardie was Britain's first Independent Labour Member of Parliament, and the father of the Labour Party. Brought up in Lanarkshire, he was briefly a coalminer. He was first elected to the House of Commons in 1892 for West Ham South, but was defeated three years later, as his views were too radical for many of the Liberals who had voted for him. His campaign for trade unions to work with socialists to send MPs to Parliament finally succeeded when the Trades Union Congress decided to call a conference to 'secure the better representation of labour in the House of Commons'. The conference to establish the Labour Representation Committee was held in London in February 1900.

Eight months later, Hardie returned to Parliament, this time as MP for Merthyr Tydfil in south Wales. He was one of two Labour MPs. The other was Richard Bell, MP for Derby. In April 1901, for the first time, Parliament heard the case for socialism, when Hardie proposed the following motion.

KEIR HARDIE'S MOTION PROMOTING SOCIALISM

> That, considering the increasing burden which the private ownership of land and capital is imposing upon the industrious and useful classes of the community, the poverty and destitution and general moral and physical deterioration resulting from a competitive system of wealth production which aims primarily at profit making, the alarming growth of trusts and syndicates able by reason of their great wealth to influence Governments and plunge peaceful Nations into war to serve their interests, this House is of the opinion that such a condition of affairs constitute a menace to the well-being of the Realm, and calls for legislation designed to remedy the same by inaugurating a Socialist Commonwealth founded upon the common

ownership of land and capital, production for use and not for profit, and equality of opportunity for every citizen.

KEIR HARDIE'S SPEECH

I rise to move the motion that stands in my name. After the discussion to which we have just listened, in which one section of the community has claimed support from the State, and shown that German steamship lines have an advantage over British lines because they are subsidised by the State, I trust the House will listen to the logical outcome of these arguments. I make no apology for bringing the question of Socialism before the House of Commons. It has long commanded the attention of the best minds in the country. It is a growing force in the thought of the world, and whether men agree or disagree with it, they have to reckon with it, and may as well begin by understanding it.

I begin by pointing out that the growth of our national wealth instead of bringing comfort to the masses of the people is imposing additional burdens on them. While our population during the last century increased three and a half times, the wealth of the community increased over six times. But one factor in our national life remained with us all through the century, and is with us still, and that is that at the bottom of the social scale there is a mass of poverty and misery equal in magnitude to that which obtained 100 years ago. I submit that the true test of progress is not the accumulation of wealth in the hands of a few, but the elevation of a people as a whole.

I admit frankly that a considerable improvement was made in the condition of the working people during the last century. At the beginning of the nineteenth century the nation industrially was sick almost unto death. It was at that time passing from the old system of handicraft, under which every man was his own employer and his own capitalist, and traded direct with his customer, to the factory system which the introduction of machinery brought into existence. During these hundred years the wealth of the nation accumulated, and the condition of the working classes as compared with the early years of the century improved, but I respectfully submit to the House that there was more happiness, more comfort and more independence before machinery began to accumulate wealth. I said that an improvement was made during the last century, but I would qualify that statement in this respect—that practically the whole of that improvement was made during the first seventy-five years. During the last quarter of the century the condition of the working classes has been practically stationary. There have been slight increases of wages here and reductions of hours there, but the landlord with his increased rent has more than absorbed any advantage that may have been gained. I could quote figures, if that statement is disputed, showing that in all the industrial parts of the country rents during the past twenty years have been going up by leaps and bounds.

I come now to the causes which have forced thinking people of all ranks of society to reconsider their attitude towards socialism. I refer particularly to the great and alarming growth of what are known as trusts and syndicates in connection with industry. We have hitherto been accustomed to regard a trust as a distinctively American product. That cannot be said any longer. So long as industry is conducted by individuals competing one with another there is a chance of the article produced being supplied at an approximation to its market value, but competition has been found to be destructive of the interests of the owners and possessors of capital in this as in every other country. Three or four firms which formerly entered one market and competed with each other find it conducive to their interests to combine, thereby creating a monopoly which enables them to charge whatever price they like, and to treat their workpeople in any way that seems good to them.

I approach this question of trusts from two points of view: first, from that of the consumer, who is at the mercy of an uncontrolled and, it may be perfectly unscrupulous combination which cares only for dividends; and, secondly—and this is to me of greater concern from that of the worker. The consumer may protect himself, but the worker is helpless. We are rapidly approaching a point when the nation will be called upon to decide between an uncontrolled monopoly, conducted for the benefit and in the interests of its principal shareholders, and a monopoly owned, controlled, and manipulated by the State in the interests of the nation as a whole. This House and the British nation knows to their cost the danger which comes from allowing men to grow rich and permitting them to use their wealth to corrupt the press, to silence the pulpit, to degrade our national life, and to bring reproach and shame upon a great people, in order that a few unscrupulous scoundrels might be able to add to their ill-gotten gains.

Socialism, by placing land and the instruments of production in the hands of the community, eliminates only the idle, useless class at both ends of the scale. Half a million of the people of this country benefit by the present system; the remaining millions of toilers and business men do not. The pursuit of wealth corrupts the manhood of men. We are called upon at the beginning of the twentieth century to decide the question propounded in the Sermon on the Mount as to whether or not we will worship God or Mammon. The present day is a Mammon-worshipping age. Socialism proposes to dethrone the brute-god Mammon and to lift humanity into its place. Just as sure as Radicalism democratised the system of Government politically in the last century so will Socialism democratise the country industrially during the century upon which we have just entered. I beg to move.

Bell seconded the motion formally. As Hardie spoke just before midnight, when the Commons adjourned, there was no vote, or even a debate.

Although Hardie had been virtually ignored in 1901, socialism was not to be sidelined for much longer. In 1906, the Liberals won a landslide victory in the general election, not only winning a majority of 130 but also defeating most Cabinet ministers, including Arthur Balfour, the outgoing prime minister. But as part of their strategy to inflict a crushing defeat on the Conservatives, the Liberals paved the way for their own long-term decline, for they agreed to an electoral pact with Labour, whereby each party would give the other a clear run in different areas. The result was a breakthrough for Labour, which won 30 seats – helped massively by the Liberals' decision to stand aside in 24 of them. Soon after the election, the Labour Representation Committee changed its name to the Labour Party, and Hardie was elected its chairman. Within two decades, Britain had its first Labour government and the Liberals had been relegated to third place.

1908

'It follows that nothing should ever be done for the first time'

F.M. Cornford was a fellow of Trinity College, Cambridge, and a classical scholar specialising in the philosophers of Ancient Greece. However his best-remembered work is a pamphlet, published in 1908, which satirised university politics. He called his pamphlet *Microcosmographia Academica*, which means 'a study of a tiny academic world'.

Its enduring popularity lies in the universal application of his analysis. It applies to the tendency to inertia in any political system in any society at any time. (The *Yes Minister* character Sir Humphrey Appleby reflected precisely the mindset that Cornford set out to debunk.) Even those who have never heard of Cornford or his pamphlet pay unintended homage to him every time they talk of 'the thin end of the wedge', 'a dangerous precedent' or 'the principle of the unripe time': all phrases that first appeared in the same chapter of Cornford's pamphlet.

F.M. Cornford: *Microcosmographia Academica*

There is only one argument for doing something; the rest are arguments for doing nothing.

The argument for doing something is that it is the right thing to do. Even a little knowledge of ethical theory will suffice to convince you that all important questions are so complicated, and the results of any course of action are so difficult to foresee, that certainty, or even probability, is seldom, if ever, attainable. It follows at once that the only justifiable attitude of mind is suspense of judgment; and this attitude, besides being peculiarly congenial to the academic temperament, has the advantage of being comparatively easy to attain. There remains the duty of persuading others to be equally judicious, and to refrain from plunging into reckless courses which might lead them Heaven knows whither. At this point the arguments for doing nothing come in; for it is a mere theorist's paradox that doing nothing has just as many consequences as doing something. It is obvious that inaction can have no consequences at all.

Since the stone-axe fell into disuse at the close of the neolithic age, two other arguments of universal application have been added to the rhetorical armoury by the ingenuity of mankind. They are closely akin; and, like the stone-axe, they are addressed to the Political Motive. They are called the *Wedge* and the *Dangerous Precedent*. Though they are very familiar, the principles, or rules of inaction, involved in them are seldom stated in full. They are as follows.

The *Principle of the Wedge* is that you should not act justly now for fear of raising expectations that you may act still more justly in the future – expectations which you are afraid you will not have the courage to satisfy. A little reflection will make it evident that the Wedge argument implies the admission that the persons who use it cannot prove that the action is not just. If they could, that would be the sole and sufficient reason for not doing it, and this argument would be superfluous.

The *Principle of the Dangerous Precedent* is that you should not now do an admittedly right action for fear you, or your equally timid successors, should not have the courage to do right in some future case, which, *ex hypothesi*, is essentially different, but superficially resembles the present one. Every public action which is not customary, either is wrong, or, if it is right, is a dangerous precedent. It follows that nothing should ever be done for the first time.

It will be seen that both the Political Arguments are addressed to the Bugbear of *Giving yourself away*. Other special arguments can be framed in view of the other Bugbears. It will often be sufficient to argue that a change is a change – an irrefutable truth. If this consideration is not decisive, it may be reinforced by the Fair Trial Argument – '*Give the present system a Fair Trial*'. This is especially useful in withstanding changes in the schedule of an examination. In this connection the exact meaning of the phrase is, 'I don't intend to alter my lectures if I can help it; and if you pass this proposal, you will have to alter yours.' This paraphrase explains what might otherwise be obscure: namely, the reason why a Fair Trial ought only to be given to systems which already exist, not to proposed alternatives.

Another argument is that '*the Time is not Ripe*'. The Principle of Unripe Time is that people should not do at the present moment what they think right at that moment, because the moment at which they think it right has not yet arrived. But the unripeness of the time will, in some cases, be found to lie in the Bugbear, 'What Dr— will say.' Time, by the way, is like the medlar; it has a trick of going rotten before it is ripe.

1909−11

'THEY SAY: "YOU THIEVES!" I SAY THEIR DAY OF RECKONING IS AT HAND'

I n 1909, David Lloyd George, the Chancellor of the Exchequer, unveiled his 'People's Budget'. It was historic both for its content and for the constitutional upheaval it provoked. The Budget was arguably the first to have redistribution of wealth as its explicit goal. It raised money to pay for social reforms, above all the first old-age pension (up to 25p per week – around £23 in today's money – to retired workers over 70). Lloyd George's measures included higher taxes on the highest incomes and new taxes on cars and petrol. However, what caused greatest controversy was his proposal to tax land at a rate of one halfpenny in the pound, so that land worth one thousand pounds would yield just over two pounds in tax revenue per year. Lloyd George faced hostility not because of the size of the proposed tax, which would make only a small dent in landowners' fortunes, but because of the principle of it and the Chancellor's passionate advocacy of redistribution.

Lloyd George knew that he would face opposition from the many Conservative landowners in the House of Lords. So he mounted a crusade to pitch the people against those among the wealthy minority whom he accused of avoiding their social responsibilities. On 30 July 1909, he addressed an audience of four thousand people in Limehouse, one of the poorest parts of London's East End.

LLOYD GEORGE'S SPEECH DEFENDING THE PEOPLE'S BUDGET

The Budget is introduced not merely for the purpose of raising barren taxes, but taxes that are fertile, taxes that will bring forth fruit the security of the country which is paramount in the minds of all. It is rather a shame for a rich country like ours, probably the richest in the world, if not the richest the world has ever seen, that it should allow those who have toiled all their days to end in penury and possibly starvation. It is rather hard that an old workman should have to find his way to the gates of the tomb, bleeding and footsore, through the brambles and thorns of poverty. We cut a new path for him, an easier one, a pleasanter one, through fields of waving corn. We are raising money to pay for the new road, aye, and to widen it, so that 200,000 paupers shall be able to join in the march.

There are so many in the country blessed by Providence with great wealth, and if there are amongst them men who grudge out of their riches a fair contribution towards the less fortunate of their fellow-countrymen they are very shabby rich men. We propose to do more by means of the Budget. We are raising money to provide against the evils and the sufferings that follow from unemployment. We are raising money for the purpose of assisting our great friendly societies to provide for the sick and the widows and orphans. We are providing money to enable us to develop the resources of our own land. I do not believe any fair-minded man would challenge the justice and the fairness of the objects which we have in view in raising this money.

Not far from here, not so many years ago, between the Lea and the Thames you had hundreds of acres of land which was not very useful even for agricultural purposes. In the main it was a sodden marsh. The commerce and the trade of London increased under Free Trade, the tonnage of your shipping went up by hundreds of thousands of tons and by millions; labour was attracted from all parts of the country to cope with all this trade and business which was done here.

What happened? There was no housing accommodation. This Port of London became overcrowded, and the population overflowed. That was the opportunity of the owners of the marsh. All that land became valuable building land, and land which used to be rented at £2 or £3 an acre has been selling within the last few years at £2,000 an acre, £3,000 an acre, £6,000 an acre, £8,000 an acre. Who created that increment? Who made that golden swamp? Was it the landlord? Was it his energy? Was it his brains a very bad look out for the place if it were his forethought? It was purely the combined efforts of all the people engaged in the trade and commerce of the Port of London trader, merchant, shipowner, dock labourer, workman, everybody except the landlord.

It was agricultural land, and because it was agricultural land a munificent Tory Government voted a sum of two millions to pay half the rates of those poor distressed landlords, and you and I had to pay taxes in order to enable those landlords to pay half their rates on agricultural land.

Well, now, that is coming to an end. In future those landlords will have to contribute to the taxation of the country on the basis of the real value only one halfpenny in the pound! Only a halfpenny! And that is what all the howling is about. But there is another little tax called the increment tax. For the future what will happen? We mean to value all the land in the kingdom. And if land goes up in the future by hundreds and thousands an acre through the efforts of the community, the community will get 20 per cent of that increment.

Golders Green is a case in point. A few years ago there was a plot of land there which was sold at £160. Last year I went and opened a Tube railway there. What was the result? This year that very piece of land has been sold for £2,100. £160 before the railway was opened before I was there, £2,100 now. I am entitled to 20 per cent.

I went down a coalmine the other day. We sank into a pit half a mile deep. The earth seemed to be straining around us and above us to crush us in. You could see the pit-props bent and twisted and sundered until you saw their fibres split in resisting the pressure. Sometimes they give way, and then there is mutilation and death. Often a spark ignites, the whole pit is deluged in fire, and the breath of life is scorched out of hundreds of breasts by the consuming flame.

And yet when the Prime Minister and I knock at the door of these great landlords, and say to them: 'Here, you know these poor fellows who have been digging up royalties at the risk of their lives, some of them are old, they have survived the perils of their trade, they are broken, they can earn no more. Won't you give them something towards keeping them out of the workhouse?', they scowl at us, and we say: 'Only a hapenny, just a copper'. They say: 'You thieves!' and they turn their dogs on to us, and you can hear their bark every morning. If this is an indication of the view taken by these great landlords of their responsibility to the people who at the risk of life create their wealth, then I say their day of reckoning is at hand.

All I can say is this: the ownership of land is not merely an enjoyment, it is a stewardship. It has been reckoned as such in the past; and if they cease to discharge their functions, the security and defence of the country, looking after the broken in their villages and in their neighbourhoods then these functions which are part of the traditional duties attached to the ownership of land, and which have given to it its title – if they cease to discharge those functions, the time will come to reconsider the conditions under which the land is held in this country.

We are placing burdens on the broadest shoulders. Why should I put burdens on the people? I am one of the children of the people. I was brought up amongst them. I know their trials; and God forbid that I should add one grain of trouble to the anxieties which they bear with such patience and fortitude. When the Prime Minister did me the honour of inviting me to take charge of the National Exchequer at a time of great difficulty, I made up my mind, in framing the Budget which was in front of me, that at any rate no cupboard should be barer, no lot would be harder. By that test I challenge them to judge the Budget.

In November 1909, peers rejected the Budget by 350 votes to 75. Lloyd George was jubilant. Here was an issue that he could take to the people and, he believed, defeat the House of Lords. Even though more than three years of the seven-year Parliament remained, and although the Liberals enjoyed a big majority in the House of Commons, the prime minister, Herbert Asquith, called an early election for January 1910. He and Lloyd George – and a rising Liberal star, Winston Churchill – campaigned vigorously, turning the election into a referendum on the People's Budget and the Lords.

Their gamble failed. The Liberals lost their majority, and Asquith continued as prime minister of a minority government. In his weakened position, he dropped the land tax as the price to be paid for the House of Lords passing the rest of the Budget. A second general election, in December 1910, produced almost exactly the same result as in January. Asquith remained the leader of a minority government, dependant on the support of the now 42-strong contingent of Labour MPs and 81 Irish Nationalists.

In order to avoid a repetition of the fate of the People's Budget, Asquith proposed a new Parliament Bill to curb the powers of the Lords – effectively removing their power to veto budgets and other money bills, and allowing the House of Commons to overrule the Lords if peers sought to veto a bill approved by the Commons in three successive years. The bill also proposed shortening the maximum life of a parliament from seven years to five.

Of course, for Asquith's bill to become law, it had to be approved by the House of Lords. Asquith persuaded the new king, George V, to be ready to create 250 new Liberal peers to remove the Conservatives' majority in the Upper House. Faced with this prospect, the House of Lords agreed to the new bill and the Parliament Act 1911 passed into law.

PARLIAMENT ACT 1911

Whereas it is expedient that provision should be made for regulating the relations between the two Houses of Parliament:

And whereas it is intended to substitute for the House of Lords as it at present exists a Second Chamber constituted on a popular instead of hereditary basis, but such substitution cannot be immediately brought into operation:

And whereas provision will require hereafter to be made by Parliament in a measure effecting such substitution for limiting and defining the powers of the new Second Chamber, but it is expedient to make such provision as in this Act appears for restricting the existing powers of the House of Lords:

Be it therefore enacted:

If a Money Bill, having been passed by the House of Commons, and sent up to the House of Lords at least one month before the end of the session, is not passed by the House of Lords without amendment within one month after it is so sent up to that House, the Bill shall, unless the House of Commons direct to the contrary, be presented to His Majesty and become an Act of Parliament on the Royal Assent being signified, notwithstanding that the House of Lords have not consented to the Bill.

A Money Bill means a Public Bill which in the opinion of the Speaker of the House of Commons contains only provisions dealing with all or any of the following subjects, namely, the imposition, repeal, remission, alteration, or regulation of taxation; the imposition for the payment of debt or other financial purposes of charges on the Consolidated Fund, or on money provided by Parliament, or the variation or repeal of any such charges; supply; the appropriation, receipt, custody, issue or audit of accounts of public money; the raising or guarantee of any loan or the repayment thereof; or subordinate matters incidental to those subjects or any of them. In this subsection the expressions 'taxation,' 'public money,' and 'loan' respectively do not include any taxation, money, or loan raised by local authorities or bodies for local purposes.

There shall be endorsed on every Money Bill when it is sent up to the House of Lords and when it is presented to His Majesty for assent the certificate of the Speaker of the House of Commons signed by him that it is a Money Bill.

If any Public Bill (other than a Money Bill or a Bill containing any provision to extend the maximum duration of Parliament beyond five years) is passed by the House of Commons in three successive sessions (whether of the same Parliament or not), and, having been sent up to the House of Lords at least one month before the end of the session, is rejected by the House of Lords in each of those sessions, that Bill shall, on its rejection for the third time by the House of Lords, unless the House of Commons direct to the contrary, be presented to His Majesty and become an Act of

Parliament on the Royal Assent being signified thereto, notwithstanding that the House of Lords have not consented to the Bill: Provided that this provision shall not take effect unless two years have elapsed between the date of the second reading in the first of those sessions of the Bill in the House of Commons and the date on which it passes the House of Commons in the third of those sessions.

When a Bill is presented to His Majesty for assent in pursuance of the provisions of this section, there shall be endorsed on the Bill the certificate of the Speaker of the House of Commons signed by him that the provisions of this section have been duly complied with.

CERTIFICATE OF SPEAKER

Any certificate of the Speaker of the House of Commons given under this Act shall be conclusive for all purposes, and shall not be questioned in any court of law.

DURATION OF PARLIAMENT

Five years shall be substituted for seven years as the time fixed for the maximum duration of Parliament under the Septennial Act, 1715.

1913–8

'EITHER WOMEN ARE TO BE KILLED OR WOMEN ARE TO HAVE THE VOTE'

New Zealand was the first country to give women the vote, in 1893. Australia followed nine years later. These examples prompted British suffragettes to step up their campaign. Among the most prominent were Emmeline Pankhurst and her daughters, Christabel and Sylvia. In 1903, Emmeline founded the Women's Social and Political Union (WSPU). She felt, with reason, that traditional campaigning was making no progress and more militant tactics were needed. Members of the WSPU disrupted political meetings, smashed windows, handcuffed themselves to railings and statues, and, when jailed, went on hunger strikes.

In April 1913, Herbert Asquith's Liberal government sought to deal with the prison hunger strikes by passing the Prisoners (Temporary Discharge for Ill Health) Act, universally known as the 'Cat and Mouse Act'. Under this Act, prisoners made weak by hunger strikes were released – and then imprisoned again when they were healthy enough. Emmeline, who had been convicted in 1912 for conspiracy to commit criminal damage, was repeatedly released and re-incarcerated under the Act. In November 1913, during one of her spells of freedom, she travelled to the United States to raise funds for the WSPU. In Hartford, Connecticut, she delivered perhaps her most famous speech, in which she defended her militant strategy.

EMMELINE PANKHURST'S SPEECH TO THE CONNECTICUT WOMEN'S SUFFRAGE ASSOCIATION, 13 NOVEMBER 1913

> It is not at all difficult if revolutionaries come to you from Russia, if they come to you from China, or from any other part of the world, if they are men. But since I am a woman it is necessary to explain why women have adopted revolutionary methods in order to win the rights of citizenship.

Suppose the men of Hartford had a grievance, and they laid that grievance before their legislature, and the legislature obstinately refused to listen to them, or to remove their grievance, what would be the proper and the constitutional and the practical way of getting their grievance removed? Well, it is perfectly obvious at the next general election the men of Hartford would turn out that legislature and elect a new one.

But let the men of Hartford imagine that they were not in the position of being voters at all, that they were governed without their consent being obtained, that the legislature turned an absolutely deaf ear to their demands, what would the men of Hartford do then? They couldn't vote the legislature out. They would have to choose; they would have to make a choice of two evils: they would either have to submit indefinitely to an unjust state of affairs, or they would have to rise up and adopt some of the antiquated means by which men in the past got their grievances remedied.

The great thing is to see that no more damage is done than is absolutely necessary, that you do just as much as will arouse enough feeling to bring about peace, to bring about an honourable peace for the combatants; and that is what we have been doing.

We entirely prevented stockbrokers in London from telegraphing to stockbrokers in Glasgow and vice versa: for one whole day telegraphic communication was entirely stopped. I am not going to tell you how it was done. I am not going to tell you how the women got to the mains and cut the wires; but it was done. It was done, and it was proved to the authorities that weak women, suffrage women, as we are supposed to be, had enough ingenuity to create a situation of that kind. Now, I ask you, if women can do that, is there any limit to what we can do except the limit we put upon ourselves?

When they put us in prison at first, simply for taking petitions, we submitted; we allowed them to dress us in prison clothes; we allowed them to put us in solitary confinement; we allowed them to put us amongst the most degraded of criminals; we learned of some of the appalling evils of our so-called civilisation that we could not have learned in any other way. It was valuable experience, and we were glad to get it.

I have seen men smile when they heard the words 'hunger strike', and yet I think there are very few men today who would be prepared to adopt a 'hunger strike' for any cause. It is only people who feel an intolerable sense of oppression who would adopt a means of that kind. It means you refuse food until you are at death's door, and then the authorities have to choose between letting you die, and letting you go; and then they let the women go.

Now, that went on so long that the government felt that they were unable to cope. It was [then] that, to the shame of the British government, they set the example to authorities all over the world of feeding sane, resisting human beings by force. There may be doctors in this meeting: if so, they know it is one thing to feed by force an insane person; but it is quite another thing to feed a sane, resisting human being who resists with every nerve and with every fibre of her body the indignity and the outrage of forcible feeding. Now, that was done in England, and the government thought they had crushed us. But they found that it did not quell the agitation, that more and more women came in and even passed that terrible ordeal, and they were obliged to let them go.

Then came the legislation – the 'Cat and Mouse Act'. The home secretary said: 'Give me the power to let these women go when they are at death's door, and leave them at liberty under license until they have recovered their health again and then bring them back.' It was passed to repress the agitation, to make the women yield – because that is what it has really come to, ladies and gentlemen. It has come to a battle between the women and the government as to who shall yield first, whether they will yield and give us the vote, or whether we will give up our agitation.

Well, they little know what women are. Women are very slow to rouse, but once they are aroused, once they are determined, nothing on earth and nothing in heaven will make women give way; it is impossible. And so this 'Cat and Mouse Act' which is being used against women today has failed. There are women lying at death's door, recovering enough strength to undergo operations who have not given in and won't give in, and who will be prepared, as soon as they get up from their sick beds, to go on as before. There are women who are being carried from their sick beds on stretchers into meetings. They are too weak to speak, but they go amongst their fellow workers just to show that their spirits are unquenched, and that their spirit is alive, and they mean to go on as long as life lasts.

Now, I want to say to you who think women cannot succeed, we have brought the government of England to this position, that it has to face this alternative: either women are to be killed or women are to have the vote. I ask American men in this meeting, what would you say if in your state you were faced with that alternative, that you must either kill them or give them their citizenship? Well, there is only one answer to that alternative, there is only one way out – you must give those women the vote.

So here am I. I come in the intervals of prison appearance. I come after having been four times imprisoned under the 'Cat and Mouse Act', probably going back to be rearrested as soon as I set my foot on British soil. I come to ask you to help to win this fight. If we win it, this hardest of all fights, then, to be sure, in the future it is going to be made easier for women all over the world to win their fight when their time comes.

Ten months later, Britain was at war with Germany. Within six days of the outbreak of the First World War, the WSPU abandoned its militancy; in return, the government agreed to release all WSPU prisoners and to give the Union £2,000 to organise a 'patriotic rally'.

During the course of the war, women took over many of the jobs normally done by the men sent to the killing fields of France. The changing role of women persuaded increasing numbers of parliamentarians of the absurdity of restricting the franchise to men, but the door to reform was opened by a separate, if related, argument – that, as the law then stood, not all men had the vote, and the disenfranchised included many adult soldiers risking their lives. The time was ripe for a wider look at who should, and who should not, join the electoral register.

In August 1916, Herbert Asquith became the first prime minister to accept the principle that women should have the vote.

HERBERT ASQUITH'S SPEECH TO PARLIAMENT, 14 AUGUST 1916

My record in the matter is clear—I have no special desire or predisposition to bring women within the pale of the franchise, but I have received a great many representations from those who are authorised to speak for them, and I am bound to say that they presented to me not only a reasonable, but, I think, from their point of view, an unanswerable case. They say they are perfectly content, if we do not change the qualification of the franchise, to abide by the existing state of things, but that if we are going to bring in a new class of electors, on whatever ground of State service, they point out—and we cannot possibly deny their claim—that during this War the women of this country have rendered as effective service in the prosecution of the War as any other class of the community.

It is true they cannot fight, in the gross material sense of going out with rifles and so forth, but they fill our munition factories, they are doing the work which the men who are fighting had to perform before, they have taken their places, they are the servants of the State, and they have aided, in the most effective way, in the prosecution of the War. What is more, and this is a point which makes a special appeal to me, they say when the War comes to an end, and when these abnormal and, of course, to a large extent transient, conditions have to be revised, and when the process of industrial reconstruction has to be set on foot, have not the women a special claim to be heard on the many questions which will arise directly affecting their interests, and possibly meaning for them large displacements of labour? I cannot think that the House will deny that, and I say quite frankly that I cannot deny that claim.

Asquith hoped, however, to defer all these issues until the war was over. But the clamour for reform hastened the process. In October 1916, Asquith's Cabinet agreed to set up an all-party Speaker's Conference to consider the electoral system, including the franchise. By the time the meetings of the Conference had finished, in January 1917, Asquith had been replaced as prime minister by David Lloyd George. Asquith, however, remained leader of the Liberal Party and Leader of the Opposition at the head of the segment of his party that opposed Lloyd George's coalition. The Speaker's Conference recommended that all adult men should have the vote – and so should most, but not all, adult women. When the House of Commons debated the recommendations, Asquith opened the debate.

HERBERT ASQUITH'S SPEECH TO PARLIAMENT, 28 MARCH 1917

I come now to the fifth point, upon which the Conference report that they were divided, and that their recommendation represents the majority. The majority decided, first, that some measure of women's suffrage should be conferred, and next, to translate that into concrete form, any woman who possesses herself or is the wife of a man who possesses the proposed new Local Government qualifications – that is to say, six months occupation as owner or tenant of land or premises, and has attained the specified age, say, thirty, or perhaps thirty-five – shall have the Parliamentary franchise.

Here we are upon much more delicate ground. The House will not be unprepared to hear that I myself, and I believe many others, no longer regard this question from the standpoint which we occupied before the War. During the whole of my political life I have opposed the various schemes which have been presented from time to time to Parliament for giving the Parliamentary vote, whether piecemeal or wholesale, to women, while it is only right I should say I have consistently advocated, and done my best to promote, the opening-out to women of other spheres of activity which have been in the past confined exclusively to men.

Why, and in what sense, the House may ask, have I changed my views? There was in ancient Greece a poet named Stesichorus, who was ill-advised enough, in a fit of perverted inspiration, to compose a lampoon upon the character and conduct of Helen, the wife of Menelaus. She was a lady who had the advantage of being connected by relationship with a god. The result was that Stesichorus was smitten with blindness. Thereupon, after consulting the oracle, he conceived the happy idea of writing a Palinode in which he developed the novel theme that it was not Helen at all, but a phantom who had simulated her form. Thereupon, by way of reward, the poet had his sight restored.

I am not going to follow the devious and not very candid procedure of Stesichorus. Some of my Friends may think that, like him, my eyes, which for years in this matter have been clouded by fallacies, and sealed by illusions, at last have been opened to the truth. In point of fact, as far as I am concerned – I do not know what is the case with others – there has been no occasion for the intervention of any supernatural agency.

I am not in the least ashamed – indeed, I am glad to have the opportunity – to disclose the process which has operated in my mind. My opposition to women's suffrage has always been based, and based solely, on considerations of public expediency. Some years ago I ventured to use the expression, 'Let the women work out their own salvation'. Well, Sir, they have worked it out during this War. How could we have carried on the War without them? Short of actually bearing arms in the field, there is hardly a service which has contributed, or is contributing, to the maintenance of our cause in which women have not been at least as active and as efficient as men, and wherever we turn we see them doing, with zeal and success, and without any detriment to the prerogatives of their sex, work which three years ago would have been regarded as falling exclusively within the province of men.

This is not a merely sentimental argument, though it appeals to our feelings as well as our judgement. But what I confess moves me still more in this matter is the problem of reconstruction when the War is over. The questions which will then necessarily arise in regard to women's labour and women's functions and activities in the new ordering of things – for, do not doubt it, the old order will be changed – are questions in regard to which I feel it impossible, consistently with either justice or with expediency, to withhold from women the power and the right of making their voice directly heard.

Let me add that, since the War began, now nearly three years ago, we have had no recurrence of that detestable campaign which disfigured the annals of political agitation in this country, and no one can now contend that we are yielding to violence what we refused to concede to argument.

I therefore believe that some measure of women's suffrage should be conferred.

In regard to the form which their recommendation takes, I understand it has been prompted partly by a desire to prevent a preponderance of female as compared with male voters, and partly by a feeling that a discrimination by way of age was fairer than the setting up of any special class or business qualification.

A very able and energetic lady, a strong advocate of the cause, came to see me the other day and made a counter suggestion that it was the younger women who most needed enfranchisement, and if age was to come into the matter at all it should rather be at the other end of the scale. I do not pronounce any judgement between those two views. I have often said that once you have resolved to ignore the differentia of sex it was difficult to introduce any other discrimination between the case of women and that of men. That is pre-eminently a matter for adjustment and compromise, and I feel confident the proposal will not be allowed to founder upon that rock.

Parliament decided to set the lower age limit for women at 30. It also gave the vote to all men over twenty-one, once they had lived for six months in their constituency. Around 6 million women were expected to meet the age and household qualifications – less than half the 13 million male electors (itself an increase from the 7.7 million men eligible to vote in the previous election in 1910). In fact, 8.5 million women were on the register in time for the general election held on 14 December 1918. This election produced the first victorious woman parliamentary candidate: Sinn Fein's Constance Markievicz in Dublin St Patrick's. However, as an Irish nationalist she refused to take her seat in the House of Commons. The first woman MP to do so was Nancy Astor, who was elected as Conservative MP for Plymouth Sutton in 1919, following the elevation of her husband, the constituency's former MP, to the House of Lords.

In 1928, the voting age for women was lowered to 21 and the householder qualification was removed. Equality of the franchise between men and women was finally achieved.

1921

'IRELAND SHALL BE STYLED AND KNOWN AS THE IRISH FREE STATE'

Following various short-lived attempts to expel Britain from Ireland – most famously the Easter Uprising in 1916, which lasted six days and left four hundred and fifty people dead – a brutal war erupted in 1919 between the Irish Republican Army (IRA) and the 'black and tans': British recruits kitted out with khaki army trousers and dark police tunics. In 1920, David Lloyd George, Britain's prime minister, responded with the Government of Ireland Act. This gave a large degree of self-government to two separate parts of Ireland – the six, mainly Protestant, counties of Northern Ireland and the remaining twenty-six, mainly Catholic, counties.

The fighting did not stop. Negotiations to end the impasse took place in 1921, with the Irish contingent led by Eamon de Valera, and Britain's by Lloyd George. However, de Valera did not attend the final stages of the talks, where the Irish contingent was led by Michael Collins, the IRA's charismatic Director of Intelligence. The final version of the treaty, agreed on 6 December, gave the 26 counties almost complete independence, although it gave Britain access, during times of war or international crisis, to Irish ports 'and other facilities as the British Government may require'. It also required members of the Irish Parliament to swear an oath of allegiance to the king.

ANGLO-IRISH TREATY

Ireland shall have the same constitutional status in the Community of Nations known as the British Empire as the Dominion of Canada, the Commonwealth of Australia, the Dominion of New Zealand, and the Union of South Africa with a Parliament having powers to make laws for the peace order and good government of Ireland and an Executive responsible to that Parliament, and shall be styled and known as the Irish Free State.

The oath to be taken by Members of the Parliament of the Irish Free State shall be in the following form:-

I . . . . . . do solemnly swear true faith and allegiance to the Constitution of the Irish Free State as by law established and that I will be faithful to H.M. King George V., his heirs and successors by law, in virtue of the common citizenship of Ireland with Great Britain and her adherence to and membership of the group of nations forming the British Commonwealth of Nations.

The Government of the Irish Free State shall afford to His Majesty's Imperial Forces

a. In the time of peace such harbour and other facilities as are indicated in the Annex hereto, or such other facilities as may from time to time be agreed between the British Government and the Government of the Irish Free State; and

b. In time of war or of strained relations with a Foreign Power such harbour and other facilities as the British Government may require for the purposes of such defence as aforesaid.

With a view to securing the observance of the principle of international limitation of armaments, if the Government of the Irish Free State establishes and maintains a military defence force, the establishments thereof shall not exceed in size such proportion of the military establishes maintained in Great Britain as that which the population of Ireland bears to the population of Great Britain.

The ports of Great Britain and the Irish Free State shall be freely open to the ships of the other country on payment of the customary port and other dues.

Until the expiration of one month from the passing of the Act of Parliament for the ratification of this instrument, the powers of the Parliament and the Government of the Irish Free State shall not be exercisable as respects Northern Ireland, and the provisions of the Government of Ireland Act 1920, shall, so far as they relate to Northern Ireland remain of full force and effect, and no election shall be held for the return of members to serve in the Parliament of the Irish Free State for constituencies in Northern Ireland, unless a resolution is passed by both Houses of the Parliament of Northern Ireland in favour of the holding of such elections before the end of the said month.

If before the expiration of the said month, an address is presented to

His Majesty by both Houses of the Parliament of Northern Ireland to that effect, the powers of the Parliament and the Government of the Irish Free State shall no longer extend to Northern Ireland, and the provisions of the Government of Ireland Act, 1920, (including those relating to the Council of Ireland) shall so far as they relate to Northern Ireland, continue to be of full force and effect, and this instrument shall have effect subject to the necessary modifications. Provided that if such an address is so presented a Commission consisting of three persons, one to be appointed by the Government of the Irish Free State, one to be appointed by the Government of Northern Ireland, and one who shall be Chairman to be appointed by the British Government shall determine in accordance with the wishes of the inhabitants, so far as may be compatible with economic and geographic conditions the boundaries between Northern Ireland and the rest of Ireland, and for the purposes of the Government of Ireland Act, 1920, and of this instrument, the boundary of Northern Ireland shall be such as may be determined by such Commission.

After the expiration of the said month, if no such address as is mentioned in Article 12 hereof is presented, the Parliament and Government of Northern Ireland shall continue to exercise as respects Northern Ireland the powers conferred on them by the Government of Ireland Act, 1920, but the Parliament and Government of the Irish Free State shall in Northern Ireland have in relation to matters in respect of which the Parliament of Northern Ireland has not the power to make laws under the Act (including matters which under the said Act are within the jurisdiction of the Council of Ireland) the same powers as in the rest of Ireland, subject to such other provisions as may be agreed in manner hereinafter appearing.

Neither the Parliament of the Irish Free State nor the Parliament of Northern Ireland shall make any law so as either directly or indirectly to endow any religion or prohibit or restrict the free exercise thereof or give any preference or impose any disability on account of religious belief or religious status or affect prejudicially the right of any child to attend a school receiving public money without attending the religious instruction at the school or make any discrimination as respects State aid between schools under the management of different religious denominations or divert from any religious denomination or any educational institution any of its property except for public utility purposes and on payment of compensation.

De Valera immediately repudiated the Treaty. As a result, the Irish Free State was born in agony. In June 1922, civil war erupted between Collins's pro-Treaty government forces and de Valera's anti-Treaty Republicans. In August, Collins was killed in an ambush. The Irish government resorted to ever harsher measures to defeat de Valera, who finally agreed, in May 1923, to end his rebellion.

Under the terms of the Treaty, a commission was established to review the boundary between the Irish Free State and Northern Ireland. It recommended only minor changes. In the event, the border remained unchanged. In 1932, de Valera's party, Fianna Fáil, won power. One of his first acts was to abolish the oath of allegiance to the British crown. He also secured Britain's withdrawal from the three naval bases it retained in the west of Ireland.

1931

'FREEDOM FOR THE PIKE IS DEATH FOR THE MINNOWS'

R.H. Tawney was one of the Left's most fertile and original thinkers. A sergeant in the First World War – he refused a commission because of his egalitarian principles – he was badly wounded at the Somme. From 1920 until his retirement three decades later, he taught at the London School of Economics. He was one of the twentieth century's leading proponents of non-Marxist socialism. In *Equality*, published in 1931, he argued that liberty and equality required not just political rights but also a fairer economic system.

R. H. TAWNEY: *EQUALITY*

Liberty and equality have usually in Britain been considered antithetic: and, since fraternity has rarely been considered at all, the famous trilogy has been easily dismissed as a hybrid abortion. Equality implies the deliberate acceptance of social restraints upon individual expansion. It involves the prevention of sensational extremes of wealth and power for the public good. If liberty means, therefore, that every individual shall be free, according to his opportunities, to indulge without limit his appetite for either, it is clearly incompatible, not only with economic and social, but with civil and political, equality, which also prevent the strong exploiting to the full the advantages of their strength, and, indeed, with any habit of life save that of the Cyclops. But freedom for the pike is death for the minnows. It is possible that equality is to be contrasted, not with liberty, but only with a particular interpretation of it.

The test of a principle is that it can be generalised, so that the advantages of applying it are not particular, but universal. Since it is impossible for every individual, as for every nation, simultaneously to be stronger than his neighbours, it is a truism that liberty, as distinct from the liberties of special persons and classes, can exist only in so far as it is limited by rules, which secure that freedom for some is not slavery for others. The spiritual energy of human beings, in all the wealth of their infinite diversities, is the end to which external arrangements, whether political or economic, are merely means. Hence institutions which guarantee to men the opportunity of becoming the best of which they are capable are the supreme political good, and liberty is rightly preferred to equality, when the two are in conflict. The question is whether, in the conditions of modern society, they conflict or not. It is whether the defined and limited freedom, which alone can be generally enjoyed, is most likely to be attained by a community which encourages violent inequalities, or by one which represses them.

Inequality of power is not necessarily inimical to liberty. On the contrary, it is the condition of it. Liberty implies the ability to act, not merely to resist. Neither society as a whole, nor any group within it, can carry out its will except through organs; and, in order that such organs may function with effect, they must be sufficiently differentiated to perform their varying tasks, of which direction is one and execution another. But, while inequality of power is the condition of liberty, since it is the condition of any effective action, it is also a menace to it, for power which is sufficient to use is sufficient to abuse.

Hence, in the political sphere, where the danger is familiar, all civilised communities have established safeguards, by which the advantages of differentiation of function, with the varying degrees of power which it involves, may be preserved, and the risk that power may be tyrannical, or perverted to private ends, averted or diminished. They have endeavoured, for example, in England, to protect civil liberty by requiring that, with certain exceptions, the officers of the State shall be subject to the ordinary tribunals, and political liberty by insisting that those who take decisions on matters affecting the public shall be responsible to an assembly chosen by it. The precautions may be criticised as inadequate, but the need for precautions is not today disputed. It is recognised that political power must rest ultimately on consent, and that its exercise must be limited by rules of law.

The dangers arising from inequalities of economic power have been less commonly recognised. They exist, however, whether recognised or not. For the excess or abuse of power, and its divorce from responsibility, which results in oppression, are not confined to the relations which arise between men as members of a state. They are not a malady which is peculiar to political systems, as was typhus to slums, and from which other departments of life can be regarded as immune. They are a disease, not of political organisations, but of organisation.

The extension of liberty from the political to the economic sphere is evidently among the most urgent tasks of industrial societies. It is evident also, however, that in so far as this extension takes place, the traditional antithesis between liberty and equality will no longer be valid. As long as liberty is interpreted as consisting exclusively in security against oppression by the agents of the State, or as a share in its government, it is plausible, perhaps, to dissociate it from equality; for though experience suggests that, even in this meagre and restricted sense, it is not easily maintained in the presence of extreme disparities of wealth and influence, it is possible to be enjoyed, in form at least, by pauper and millionaire. Such disparities, however, though they do not enable one group to become the political master of another, necessarily cause it to exercise a preponderant influence on the economic life of the rest of society.

Hence, when liberty is construed, realistically, or implying, not merely a minimum of civil and political rights, but securities that the economically weak will not be at the mercy of the economically strong, and that the control of those aspects of economic life by which all are affected will be amenable, in the last resort, to the will of all, a large measure of equality, so far from being inimical to liberty, is essential to it. In conditions which impose co-operative, rather than merely individual, effort, liberty is, in fact, equality in action, in the sense, not that all men perform identical functions or wield the same degree of power, but that all men are equally protected against the abuse of power, and equally entitled to insist that power shall be used, not for personal ends, but for the general advantage.

The truth of the matter is put by Professor [Albert] Pollard in his admirable study, *The Evolution of Parliament*. 'There is only one solution,' he writes, 'to the problem of liberty, and it lies in equality. Every man should have his liberty and no more, to do unto others as he would that they should do unto him; upon that common foundation rest liberty, equality and morality.'

Tawney served on a number of public bodies, most notably the Consultative Committee on Education, chaired by Sir William Henry Hadow, which issued six reports in the 1920s and '30s. Their recommendations formed the basis of the 1944 Education Act, which made secondary schooling free for all pupils.

1939

'HATE, HATE, HATE. LET'S ALL GET TOGETHER AND HAVE A GOOD HATE'

Coming Up for Air is a novel that was published in June 1939 – three months before the Second World War broke out. Written in the first person, its narrator is George (Tubby) Bowling, a 'fat, middle-aged bloke with false teeth and a red face', who sells insurance. In this passage, he goes with his wife, Hilda, to a public meeting organised by the Left Book Club. This was a club founded in 1936 and run by the publisher Victor Gollancz; it sold books only to its members. It warned of the dangers of Hitler, Nazism and fascism, but shied away from criticising Stalin. Orwell was one of its early authors (he wrote *The Road to Wigan Pier* for the Club in 1937), although he never had any sympathy for Soviet Communism.

By 1939, Orwell and the Left Book Club had parted company. Orwell was too free-spirited for Gollancz, who did not break with Britain's Communist Party until after the Nazi–Soviet pact in August 1939. *Coming Up for Air* was published instead by Secker & Warburg. Orwell's account of the various left-wing factions at the meeting, and their ability to ruin a noble cause through empty rhetoric and sectarian prejudice, will be recognised by anyone who has brushed with Britain's far Left at any time in the past 70 years.

GEORGE ORWELL: *COMING UP FOR AIR*

> At the beginning I wasn't exactly listening. The lecturer was rather a mean-looking little chap, but a good speaker. White face, very mobile mouth, and the rather grating voice that they get from constant speaking. Of course he was pitching into Hitler and the Nazis. I wasn't particularly keen to hear what he was saying—get the same stuff in the *News Chronicle* every morning—but his voice came across to me as a kind of burr-burr-burr, with now and again a phrase that struck out and caught my attention.

'Bestial atrocities .... Hideous outbursts of sadism .... Rubber truncheons
.... Concentration camps .... Iniquitous persecution of the Jews ....
Back to the Dark Ages .... European civilization .... Act before it is too
late .... Indignation of all decent peoples .... Alliance of the democratic
nations .... Firm stand .... Defence of democracy .... Democracy ....
Fascism .... Democracy .... Fascism .... Democracy. ...'

You know the line of talk. These chaps can churn it out by the hour.
Just like a gramophone. Turn the handle, press the button, and it starts.
Democracy, Fascism, Democracy. But somehow it interested me to watch
him. A rather mean little man, with a white face and a bald head, standing
on a platform, shooting out slogans.

What's he doing? Quite deliberately, and quite openly, he's stirring up
hatred. Doing his damnedest to make you hate certain foreigners called
Fascists. It's a queer thing, I thought, to be known as 'Mr So-and-so,
the well-known anti-Fascist'. A queer trade, anti-Fascism. This fellow, I
suppose, makes his living by writing books against Hitler. But what did he
do before Hitler came along? And what'll he do if Hitler ever disappears?
Same question applies to doctors, detectives, rat-catchers, and so forth, of
course. But the grating voice went on and on, and another thought struck
me. He MEANS it. Not faking at all—feels every word he's saying. He's
trying to work up hatred in the audience, but that's nothing to the hatred
he feels himself. Every slogan's gospel truth to him. If you cut him open
all you'd find inside would be Democracy-Fascism-Democracy. Interesting
to know a chap like that in private life. But does he have a private life?
Or does he only go round from platform to platform, working up hatred?
Perhaps even his dreams are slogans.

It struck me as I looked round the audience that only about half a dozen
of them had really grasped what the lecturer was talking about, though
by this time he'd been pitching into Hitler and the Nazis for over half an
hour. It's always like that with meetings of this kind. Invariably half the
people come away without a notion of what it's all about. In the front row
Miss Minns was sitting very upright, with her head cocked a little on one
side, like a bird. The lecturer had taken a sheet of paper from under the
tumbler and was reading out statistics about the German suicide-rate. You
could see by the look of Miss Minns's long thin neck that she wasn't feeling
happy. Was this improving her mind, or wasn't it? If only she could make
out what it was all about! The lecturer was describing how the Nazis chop
people's heads off for treason and sometimes the executioner makes a bosh
shot. There was one other woman in the audience, a girl with dark hair,

one of the teachers at the Council School. Unlike the other she was really listening, sitting forward with her big round eyes fixed on the lecturer and her mouth a little bit open, drinking it all in.

Just behind her two old blokes from the local Labour Party were sitting. One had grey hair cropped very short, the other had a bald head and a droopy moustache. Both wearing their overcoats. You know the type. Been in the Labour Party since the year dot. Lives given up to the movement. Twenty years of being blacklisted by employers, and another ten of badgering the Council to do something about the slums. Suddenly everything's changed, the old Labour Party stuff doesn't matter any longer. Find themselves pitchforked into foreign politics—Hitler, Stalin, bombs, machine-guns, rubber truncheons, Rome-Berlin axis, Popular Front, anti-Comintern pact. Can't make head or tail of it. Immediately in front of me the local Communist Party branch were sitting. All three of them very young.

Next to these three another Communist was sitting. But this one, it seems, is a different kind of Communist and not-quite, because he's what they call a Trotskyist. The others have got a down on him. He's even younger, a very thin, very dark, nervous-looking boy. Clever face. Jew, of course. These four were taking the lecture quite differently from the others. You knew they'd be on their feet the moment question-time started. You could see them kind of twitching already. And the little Trotskyist working himself from side to side on his bum in his anxiety to get in ahead of the others.

I'd stopped listening to the actual words of the lecture. But there are more ways than one of listening. I shut my eyes for a moment. The effect of that was curious. I seemed to see the fellow much better when I could only hear his voice.

It was a voice that sounded as if it could go on for a fortnight without stopping. It's a ghastly thing, really, to have a sort of human barrel-organ shooting propaganda at you by the hour. The same thing over and over again. Hate, hate, hate. Let's all get together and have a good hate. Over and over. It gives you the feeling that something has got inside your skull and is hammering down on your brain. But for a moment, with my eyes shut, I managed to turn the tables on him. I got inside HIS skull. It was a peculiar sensation. For about a second I was inside him, you might almost say I WAS him. At any rate, I felt what he was feeling.

1940

'I HAVE NOTHING TO OFFER BUT BLOOD, TOIL, TEARS AND SWEAT'

W inston Churchill's first speech as prime minister took place against as bleak a backdrop as it is possible to imagine. King George VI had invited him to form an administration three days earlier, following Neville Chamberlain's resignation. As Churchill arrived in Downing Street, news was coming through of Germany's invasion of Belgium and Holland. Initially, Churchill's position was precarious. Although Labour and the Liberals welcomed his appointment and joined a coalition government, he was regarded with suspicion by many within his own party – as he had been in the 1930s, when he had been an outspoken rebel. Indeed, although Churchill became prime minister on 10 May, Chamberlain remained the Conservative Party's leader. Moreover, Lord Halifax, whom Churchill felt he had to keep on as Foreign Secretary, wanted to negotiate peace with Hitler rather than fight him to the end.

On the morning of 13 May, Churchill told the Cabinet: 'I have nothing to offer but blood, toil, tears and sweat.' He repeated the phrase that afternoon in the House of Commons when he moved a vote of confidence in his government.

WINSTON CHURCHILL'S SPEECH TO PARLIAMENT

I beg to move,

That this House welcomes the formation of a Government representing the united and inflexible resolve of the nation to prosecute the war with Germany to a victorious conclusion.

On Friday evening last I received His Majesty's commission to form a new Administration. It was the evident wish and will of Parliament and the nation that this should be conceived on the broadest possible basis and that it should include all parties, both those who supported the late Government and also the parties of the Opposition. I have completed the most important part of this task. A War Cabinet has been formed of five Members, representing, with the Opposition Liberals, the unity of the nation. The three party Leaders have agreed to serve, either in the War Cabinet or in high executive office. The three Fighting Services have been filled. It was necessary that this should be done in one single day, on account of the extreme urgency and rigour of events. A number of other positions, key positions, were filled yesterday, and I am submitting a further list to His Majesty to-night. I hope to complete the appointment of the principal Ministers during to-morrow. The appointment of the other Ministers usually takes a little longer, but I trust that, when Parliament meets again, this part of my task will be completed, and that the administration will be complete in all respects.

I considered it in the public interest to suggest that the House should be summoned to meet today. Mr. Speaker agreed, and took the necessary steps, in accordance with the powers conferred upon him by the Resolution of the House. At the end of the proceedings today, the Adjournment of the House will be proposed until Tuesday, 21st May, with, of course, provision for earlier meeting, if need be. The business to be considered during that week will be notified to Members at the earliest opportunity. I now invite the House, by the Motion which stands in my name, to record its approval of the steps taken and to declare its confidence in the new Government.

To form an Administration of this scale and complexity is a serious undertaking in itself, but it must be remembered that we are in the preliminary stage of one of the greatest battles in history, that we are in action at many other points in Norway and in Holland, that we have to be prepared in the Mediterranean, that the air battle is continuous and that many preparations, such as have been indicated by my hon. Friend below the Gangway, have to be made here at home. In this crisis I hope I may be pardoned if I do not address the House at any length today. I hope that any of my friends and colleagues, or former colleagues, who are affected by the political reconstruction, will make allowance, all allowance, for any lack of ceremony with which it has been necessary to act. I would say to the House, as I said to those who have joined this government: 'I have nothing to offer but blood, toil, tears and sweat.'

We have before us an ordeal of the most grievous kind. We have before us many, many long months of struggle and of suffering. You ask, what is our policy? I can say: It is to wage war, by sea, land and air, with all our might and with all the strength that God can give us; to wage war against a monstrous tyranny, never surpassed in the dark, lamentable catalogue of human crime. That is our policy. You ask, what is our aim? I can answer in one word: It is victory, victory at all costs, victory in spite of all terror, victory, however long and hard the road may be; for without victory, there is no survival. Let that be realised; no survival for the British Empire, no survival for all that the British Empire has stood for, no survival for the urge and impulse of the ages, that mankind will move forward towards its goal. But I take up my task with buoyancy and hope. I feel sure that our cause will not be suffered to fail among men. At this time I feel entitled to claim the aid of all, and I say, 'come then, let us go forward together with our united strength.'

Following the debate, Churchill told General Ismay, his Chief of Staff: 'Poor people, poor people. They trust me, and I can give them nothing but disaster for quite a long time.'

Over the following weeks the military news got far worse, as Belgium, Holland and France all fell to Germany, but Churchill's political position strengthened. He secured a Cabinet majority to end all talk of compromise with Hitler. By the end of the year, Churchill had replaced Lord Halifax as Foreign Secretary with Anthony Eden, who shared Churchill's determination to fight to the end, and he had also taken over as leader of the Conservative Party when Chamberlain resigned due to ill health, shortly before his death in November.

1941

'THAT SOCIETY IS BEST WHICH CAN MAKE THE MOST PROGRESS WITH THE LEAST RESTRAINT'

One of the sharpest conundrums for an open society is when, if ever, it is right to curb liberty in order to defend democracy. On 21 January 1941, Herbert Morrison, the (Labour) Home Secretary in Churchill's wartime coalition, banned the *Daily Worker*, the newspaper of Britain's Communist Party. He also banned *The Week*, a left-wing paper edited by Claud Cockburn, a former *Times* journalist who had covered the Spanish Civil War for the *Daily Worker*. At the time of the ban, Germany had yet to invade the Soviet Union; Stalin was still at peace with Hitler. The *Daily Worker* loyally reflected the view that Britain was engaged in a war to protect capitalism, not to advance the interests of the people.

On 12 January 1941, a 'People's Convention' had been held in London, attended by around 2,000 people, including many Communists. The convention demanded 'friendship with the Soviet Union', the establishment of a 'People's Government' and 'a People's Peace to enable people of all countries to determine their own future'. As a result, Morrison decided that the war effort was in danger of being undermined and so banned the *Daily Worker* and *The Week*. The day after he imposed the ban, he explained his decision to the House of Commons.

HERBERT MORRISON'S SPEECH DEFENDING HIS BAN OF THE *DAILY WORKER* AND *THE WEEK*

> This action has been taken because it is and has been for a long period the settled and continuous policy of those papers to try to create in their readers a state of mind in which they will refrain from co-operating in the national war effort and may become ready to hinder that effort.
>
> It is my firm conviction that freedom of the press should be maintained even at the risk that it may sometimes be abused. If in newspapers which share the national determination to win the war there is occasionally

published matter which, though not intended to be harmful to the national interest, may nevertheless have a prejudicial effect, I recognise that the inestimable advantage of maintaining a free press far outweighs the risks which such freedom may sometimes entail.

There is, however, a wide difference between accepting such occasional risks and allowing the continuous publication of newspapers of which the deliberate purpose is to weaken the will of our people to achieve victory in this the greatest and most momentous struggle in our history. Since the end of September 1939, when the *Daily Worker* reversed its policy, it has refrained from publishing anything calculated to encourage co-operation in the struggle which this country is waging against Nazi and Fascist tyranny and aggression; and has by every device of distortion and misrepresentation sought to make out that our people have nothing to gain by victory, that the hardships and sufferings of warfare are unnecessary and are imposed upon them by a callous Government carrying out a selfish contest in the interests of a privileged class.

The object of this propaganda is to bring about the downfall of democratic and constitutional government, regardless of the consequences to the fate of Great Britain and her Allies in the present war. All other considerations are subordinated to the fantastic hope that the weakening of democratic institutions may provide an opportunity for the substitution of a Communist dictatorship.

Small as may be the prospect of such propaganda making headway in this country, the Government would be failing in their duty if in time of war – when all liberties and the whole future of democracy are at stake – they failed to exercise the powers with which they have been entrusted against papers which are conducted for the purpose of weakening our war effort.

Supporters of Morrison's ban included many liberals. The *Manchester Guardian* said in an editorial on 22 January that:

Recently the *Daily Worker* has largely devoted its columns to derogatory accounts of Service conditions on the one hand and to the encouragement of agitation among munition workers on the other. This might be excusable if the motive were honest, if it were really desired to help the country in its struggle to keep democracy alive in Europe. But the *Daily Worker* did not believe either in the war or in democracy; its only aim was to confuse and weaken. We can well spare it.

However, a minority of MPs opposed the ban, and secured a debate on 28 January. They were led by Aneurin Bevan, one of the most eloquent parliamentarians that the Left produced in the twentieth century.

ANEURIN BEVAN'S SPEECH TO PARLIAMENT OPPOSING THE BAN

It is perfectly clear to everyone who has thought about the matter for a moment that in any community, whether in peace or war, the amount of liberty to be accorded to any minority or any individual must necessarily be under some restraint. Therefore, there is an element of expediency in all liberty, although that society is best which can make the most progress with the least restraint.

I accept also that in time of war restrictions upon liberty must be greater than they are in times of peace. It is expedient to give less liberty because society is in greater jeopardy. I am, therefore, not concerned to argue the abstract principle that anyone has a right to absolute liberty. That would be a foolish position to take up. What I am contending is that it was not expedient to suppress the *Daily Worker* because we could still afford the amount of liberty which the newspaper was enjoying.

It is, therefore, my first contention that that there has been an unnecessary deprivation of the liberty of the subject by the suppressing of the *Daily Worker*. What influence did the *Daily Worker* exercise? It would have had to exercise such influence as to be undermining the war effort, before the right hon. Gentleman would have been justified in taking away its liberty. What evidence is there that the war effort of the country and the morale of the population were being affected?

We have stood up against the worst bombardment that any civil population has ever had, and we have been called upon to bear trials which no other population has been called upon to bear. We have sustained them to the admiration of the world. In fact so negligible, so unimportant, so uninfluential was the circulation of the *Daily Worker* that it was unable to undermine the morale of the country when it was exposed to the greatest bombardment in its history. It seems to me quite unnecessary, in circumstances of that description, to take away a liberty which can be shown not to have affected the national war effort.

If there is any case at all against the *Daily Worker*, the best thing is to state it – to argue it. When the *Daily Worker* was coming out, morning by morning, and its articles could be discussed, and they were discussed, the answer to it arose spontaneously in the minds of its readers, and it was by the atmosphere of public discussion, by the full utilisation of democratic institutions, that its power was kept within bounds. Now that it has been suppressed its views will be disseminated in places where they cannot be replied to.

That is the vicious part of the suppression. It is not merely that, but taking away the voice from subversive opinion you take away the opportunity for effective answer to that voice and the people will be denied the opportunity of hearing in public the case that they will hear whispered to them in private. It seems to me that, on those grounds alone, the action of the Home Secretary was extremely unwise.

Take the second ground. A minority has not the right in any society, especially in time of war, to withhold from the Government, from the majority, the instruments of executive action. It is entitled to conduct its propaganda, but is not entitled to take its propaganda to the point where it performs, acts or persuades other people to perform acts which frustrate the will of the majority. That is an abuse of minority rights.

In other words, if the *Daily Worker* in an article called upon engineers to refuse to make shells or incited people directly to sabotage the war effort, action could be taken against it for that act alone, because it would be an attempt on the part of the minority to deny to the majority the effective instrument for carrying out the people's will. Can the right hon. Gentleman say that the *Daily Worker* has been guilty of that? If so, the Home Secretary has his remedy in the courts. He has his powers. He has been given power since the beginning of the war to take action in the courts against on specific charges against individuals or collections of individuals of that kind, but he has not done so.

There is nothing which will provoke a greater sense of dissatisfaction among the industrial population than the belief, which will now be distributed among them independent of the merits of the *Daily Worker*, that a newspaper has been suppressed by a police act of the Home Secretary because it was expressing an unpopular point of view.

The other day I had an argument with some prominent Communists about the People's Convention. I was opposing it. One of the objects of the Convention was the promotion and defence of democratic and trade union rights in Great Britain. I pointed out that there were no greater evidences of the vitality of democratic rights in this country than the publication of the *Daily Worker* and the holding of the People's Convention.

I cannot say that today. The right hon. Gentleman has taken that reply away from me; he has taken the defence from me and given the case to our opponents quite unnecessarily. When a meeting is held in Great Britain today in support of democratic rights one name will spring to the lips of every person, namely the *Daily Worker*, and people will say, 'Your democracy is so weak you could not afford the voice of opposition.' The right hon. Gentleman has done a real disservice to the cause of democracy by the action he has taken.

Bevan's motion to oppose the ban was defeated by 297 votes to 11. The 11 included Willie Gallacher, Britain's lone Communist MP. Less than five months later, on 22 June 1941, Germany invaded the Soviet Union. Britain's Communist Party instantly did a U-turn and supported the war against Hitler. On 24 July, the Labour MP George Strauss asked Morrison if he would lift the ban on the *Daily Worker*. Morrison replied:

> No, Sir. At this critical period of the war, the government would not feel justified in relaxing a safeguard against a newspaper which systematically fomented opposition to the war effort. If the British Communist party are now prepared to aid our Russian ally by giving to the war effort assistance which they previously were not willing to give to their own country, I welcome this change so far as it goes. In view, however, of the changes in the professions of the leaders of the party, it would be premature and rash to treat the latest of these sudden conversions as proof of a lasting change of heart.

As German troops penetrated Russia, almost reaching Moscow, and Churchill and Stalin put aside decades of enmity to become firm allies, pressure grew on Morrison to change policy. In May 1942, the Labour Party's annual conference defied its executive and called for the ban to be lifted. Four bishops supported this call. Finally, on 26 August 1942, Morrison allowed both the *Daily Worker* and *The Week* to resume publication.

1941-2

'A REVOLUTIONARY MOMENT IN THE WORLD'S HISTORY IS A TIME FOR REVOLUTIONS, NOT FOR PATCHING'

The Second World War provided a great impulse for the view that liberty had an economic and social dimension, and not just a legal and constitutional one. Even when Britain stood alone and many cities were being battered by the Blitz, a lively debate took place about how society should be ordered after the war. There was general recognition that governments had made a hash of the aftermath of the First World War, with hardship and high unemployment at home, and a viciously counterproductive strategy of bleeding Germany dry. In January 1941, the radical weekly news magazine *Picture Post* devoted a whole issue to 'A Plan for Britain'. It argued for and foreshadowed many of the reforms that were implemented after the war.

In May 1941, Anthony Eden, the Foreign Secretary, set out, for the first time, the coalition government's objectives. His was a bold, idealistic vision in the spirit of the 'one nation' Conservatism espoused by Benjamin Disraeli almost a century earlier.

ANTHONY EDEN'S SPEECH AT THE MANSION HOUSE ON BRITAIN'S WAR AIMS

> Hitler has destroyed the bases of political and social co-operation throughout Europe and he is destroying her economic structure. The future of Europe will depend on how moral and material reconstruction is brought about throughout the world.
>
> While all our efforts are concentrated on winning the war, H. M. Government has naturally been giving careful thought to this all-important matter which has been equally in the mind of the President of the United States of America.
>
> We have found in President Roosevelt's message to Congress in 1941 the keynote of our own purposes. On that occasion the President said:

In the future days which we seek to make secure, we look forward to a world founded upon four essential human freedoms.

The first is freedom of speech and expression – everywhere in the world.

The second is freedom of every person to worship God in his own way – everywhere in the world.

The third is freedom from want, which, translated into world terms, means economic understandings which will secure to every nation a healthy peacetime life for its inhabitants – everywhere in the world.

The fourth is freedom from fear, which, translated into world terms, means a world-wide reduction of armaments to such a point and in such a thorough fashion that no nation will be in a position to commit an act of physical aggression against any neighbour – anywhere in the world.

That is no vision of a distant millennium. It is a definite basis for a kind of world attainable in our own time and generation. That kind of world is the very antithesis of the so-called 'New Order' of tyranny which the dictators seek to create with the crash of a bomb. To that new order we oppose the great conception – the 'moral order.'

Today I wish to put before you certain practical ways in which 'freedom from want' may be applied to Europe.

We have declared that social security must be the first object of our domestic policy after the war. And social security will be our policy abroad not less than at home. It will be our wish to work with others to prevent the starvation of the post-armistice period, the currency disorders throughout Europe, and the wide fluctuations of employment, markets and prices which were the cause of so much misery in the twenty years between the two wars. We shall seek to achieve this in many ways which will interfere as little as possible with the proper liberty of each country over its own economic fortunes.

Let no one suppose, however, that we for our part intend to return to the chaos of the old world. To do so would bankrupt us no less than others. When peace comes we shall make such relaxations of our war-time financial arrangements as will permit the revival of international trade on the widest possible basis. We shall hope to see the development of a system of international exchange in which the trading of goods and services will be the central feature.

No one can suppose that the economic reorganization of Europe after the Allied victory will be an easy task. But we shall not shirk our opportunity and our responsibility to bear our share of the burdens. The peaceful brotherhood of nations, with due liberty to each to develop its own balanced economic life and its characteristic culture, will be the common object. But it is the transition to this end which presents the problem. It is the establishment of an international economic system, capable of translating the technical possibilities of production into actual plenty, and maintaining the whole population in a continuous fruitful activity, which is difficult. The world cannot expect to solve the economic riddle easily or completely. But the free nations of America, the Dominions and ourselves alone possess a command of the material means.

And, what is perhaps more important, these nations clearly have the will and the intention to evolve a post-war order which seeks no selfish national advantage; an order where each member of the family shall realise its own character and perfect its own gifts in liberty of conscience and person. We have learnt the lesson of the interregnum between the two wars. We know that no escape can be found from the curse which has been lying on Europe except by creating and preserving economic health in every country.

Under a system of free economic co-operation Germany must play a part. But here I draw a distinction. We must never forget that Germany is the worst master Europe has yet known. Five times in the last century she has violated the peace. She must never be in a position to play that role again. Our political and military terms of peace will be designed to prevent a repetition of Germany's misdeeds.

We cannot now foresee when the end will come. But it is in the nature of a machine so rigid as the German to break suddenly and with little warning. When it comes, the need of succour to the European peoples will be urgent.

The right economic outcome after the war requires on our part no exceptional unselfishness but will require constructive imagination. It is obvious that we have no motive of self-interest prompting us to the economic exploitation either of Germany or of the rest of Europe. This is not what we want nor what we could perform. The lasting settlement and internal peace of the Continent as a whole is our only aim. The fact that at the bottom of his heart every combatant knows this is the ultimate source of our strength. To every neutral, satellite or conquered country, it is obvious that our victory is, for the most fundamental and unalterable reasons, to their plain advantage. But that victory stands also for something greater still. Only our victory can restore, both to Europe and to the world, that freedom which is our heritage from centuries of Christian civilization, and that security which alone can make possible the betterment of man's lot upon the earth.

Two weeks later, Arthur Greenwood, the (Labour) Minister without Portfolio, announced the establishment of an inter-departmental committee 'to undertake, with special reference to the inter-relation of the schemes, a survey of the existing national schemes of social insurance and allied services, including workmen's compensation, and to make recommendations'.

This dry Whitehall language heralded the start of a social revolution. The man appointed to chair the committee was William Beveridge. More than 30 years earlier, as a young civil servant, he had run Britain's system of labour exchanges; his ideas influenced the then Chancellor, David Lloyd George, and the young, radical rising star of the Liberal Party, Winston Churchill. By the late 1930s, Beveridge had become Master of University College, Oxford. He was regarded as the ideal man – an outsider, but with an insider's understanding – to chair the committee.

When the Beveridge Committee reported in November 1942, it caused a sensation – for its radical language as much as for its radical ideas.

The 'Beveridge Report': the Report of the Inter-Departmental Committee on Social Insurance and Allied Services

Three guiding principles may be laid down at the outset.

The first principle is that any proposals for the future, while they should use to the full the experience gathered in the past, should not be restricted by consideration of sectional interests established in the obtaining of that experience. Now, when the war is abolishing landmarks of every kind, is the opportunity for using experience in a clear field. A revolutionary moment in the world's history is a time for revolutions, not for patching.

The second principle is that organisation of social insurance should be treated as one part only of a comprehensive policy of social progress. Social insurance fully developed may provide income security; it is an attack upon Want. But Want is one only of five giants on the road of reconstruction and in some ways the easiest to attack. The others are Disease, Ignorance, Squalor and Idleness.

The third principle is that social security must be achieved by co-operation between the State and the individual. The State should offer security for service and contribution. The State in organising security should not stifle incentive, opportunity, responsibility; in establishing a national minimum, it should leave room and encouragement for voluntary action by each individual to provide more than that minimum for himself and his family.

The Plan for Social Security set out in this Report is built upon these principles. It uses experience but is not tied by experience. It is put forward as a limited contribution to a wider social policy, though as something that could be achieved now without waiting for the whole of that policy. It is, first and foremost, a plan of insurance – of giving in return for contributions benefits up to subsistence level, as of right and without means test, so that individuals may build freely upon it.

Abolition of want requires, first, improvement of State insurance, that is to say provision against interruption and loss of earning power. All the principal causes of interruption or loss of earnings are now the subject of schemes of social insurance. If, in spite of these schemes, so many persons unemployed or sick or old or widowed are found to be without adequate income for subsistence according to the standards adopted in the social surveys, this means that the benefits amount to less than subsistence by those standards or do not last as long as the need, and that the assistance which supplements insurance is either insufficient in amount or available only on terms which make men unwilling to have recourse to it. To prevent interruption or destruction of earning power from leading to want, it is necessary to improve the present schemes of social insurance in three directions: by extension of scope to cover persons now excluded, by extension of purposes to cover risks now excluded, and by raising the rates of benefit.

Abolition of want requires, second, adjustment of incomes, in periods of earning as well as in interruption of earning, to family needs, that is to say, in one form or another it requires allowances for children. Without such allowances as part of benefit – or added to it, to make provision for large families, no social insurance against interruption of earnings can be adequate.

By a double re-distribution of income through social insurance and children's allowances, want, as defined in the social surveys, could have been abolished in Britain before the present war. The income available to the British people was ample for such a purpose. The Plan for Social Security set out in this Report takes abolition of want after this war as its aim. It includes as its main method compulsory social insurance, with national assistance and voluntary insurance as subsidiary methods. It assumes allowances for dependent children, as part of its background. The plan assumes also establishment of comprehensive health and rehabilitation services and maintenance of employment, that is to say avoidance of mass unemployment, as necessary conditions of success in social insurance.

The provision to be made for old age represents the largest and most growing element in any social insurance scheme. The proposal is to introduce for all citizens adequate pensions without means test by stages over a transition period of twenty years, while providing immediate assistance pensions for persons requiring them.

The main feature of the Plan for Social Security is a scheme of social insurance against interruption and destruction of earning power and for special expenditure arising at birth, marriage or death. The scheme embodies six fundamental principles: flat rate of subsistence benefit; flat rate of contribution; unification of administrative responsibility; adequacy of benefit; comprehensiveness; and classification. Based on them and in combination with national assistance and voluntary insurance as subsidiary methods, the aim of the Plan for Social Security is to make want under any circumstances unnecessary.

For the limited number of cases of need not covered by social insurance, national assistance subject to a uniform means test will be available.

Medical treatment covering all requirements will be provided for all citizens by a national health service organised under the health departments and post-medical rehabilitation treatment will be provided for all persons capable of profiting by it.

A Ministry of Social Security will be established, responsible for social insurance, national assistance and encouragement and supervision of voluntary insurance and will take over, so far as necessary for these purposes, the present work of other Government Departments and of local Authorities in these fields.

The report was an instant hit. More than 600,000 copies were sold – far more than any other government report before or since. It caught the mood of a nation that was celebrating German defeats at Stalingrad and El Alamein (a much smaller battle, but it marked a turning point for Britain's army in North Africa). A national insurance plan to 'abolish want' and a national health service to provide care for all were ideas that proved massively popular.

Churchill supported the report's objectives, but fretted about the costs. He warned that Beveridge's ideas would take time and money to implement. In February 1943, Churchill circulated a note to the Cabinet saying that 'we cannot initiate the legislation now or commit ourselves to the expenditure involved. That can only be done by a responsible government and a House of Commons refreshed by contact with the people' – in other words, after Britain's voters had chosen a new government. In retrospect, we can see that Churchill had a point. Britain would end the war with its finances in dire shape; would it be right to bind the hands of a post-war government with expensive long-term commitments? Yet the public was impatient. 'Beveridge now' was a popular cry, and Churchill's caution would gain him few votes when he faced the electorate in 1945.

1945

'No Socialist Government could afford to allow free expressions of public discontent. They would have to fall back on some form of Gestapo'

Britain's unwritten constitution can be summed up in six words: 'The Crown in Parliament is supreme.' In theory, Parliament can do whatever it wants. When Parliament decided to extend its own life in the First and Second World Wars, no constitutional obstacle blocked its path.

In practice, though, such extreme measures require consensus. Following Germany's defeat in May 1945, Labour rejected Churchill's wish to sustain the wartime coalition until the defeat of Japan. So Parliament was dissolved and polling day set for 5 July. In those pre-television days, radio played a vital role in the election. However, it was not BBC news or current affairs that mattered – indeed, until 1959, the BBC broadcast no news whatsoever about general election campaigns beyond such technical information as the close of nominations and the hours when polling stations would be open. What voters could listen to were the party election broadcasts. These took the form of speeches by leading politicians after the 9 p.m. news each evening; they had huge audiences. The series opened on 4 June with an address by Winston Churchill, who assaulted the Labour Party with startling vitriol, given that its leading members had been members of his Cabinet only days earlier. The following night, Clement Attlee (who had been deputy prime minister in the wartime coalition) replied on behalf of the Labour Party.

WINSTON CHURCHILL'S ELECTION BROADCAST

My sincere hope was that we could have held together until the war against Japan was finished. I know that many of my Labour colleagues would have been glad to carry on. On the other hand, the Socialist Party as a whole had been for some time eager to set out upon the political warpath, and when large numbers of people feel like that it is not good for their health to deny them the fight they want. We will therefore give it to them to the best of our ability.

Party, my friends, has always played a great part in our affairs. Party ties have always been considered honourable bonds, and no one could doubt that when the German war was over and the immediate danger to this country, which had led to the Coalition, had ceased, conflicting loyalties would arise. Our Socialist and Liberal friends felt themselves forced, therefore, to put party before country. They have departed, and we have been left to carry the nation's burden.

My friends, I must tell you that a socialist policy is abhorrent to British ideas on freedom. Although it is now put forward in the main by people who have a good grounding in the Liberalism and Radicalism of the early part of this century, there can be no doubt that Socialism is inseparably interwoven with Totalitarianism and the abject worship of the State. It is not alone that property, in all its forms, is struck at, but that liberty, in all its forms, is challenged by the fundamental conceptions of Socialism.

Look how even today they hunger for controls of every kind, as if these were delectable foods instead of wartime inflictions and monstrosities. There is to be one State, to which all are to be obedient in every act of their lives. This State is to be the arch-employer, the arch-planner, the arch-administrator and ruler, and the arch-caucus-boss.

How is an ordinary citizen or subject of the King to stand up against his formidable machine which, once it is in power, will prescribe for every one of them where they are to work, what they are to work at; where they may go and what they may say; what views they are to hold and within what limits they may express them; where their wives are to go to queue up for the State ration; and what education their children are to receive to mould their views of human liberty and conduct in the future?

A Socialist State once thoroughly completed in all its details and its aspects – and that is what I am speaking of – could not afford to suffer opposition. Here in old England, in Great Britain, of which old England forms no inconspicuous part, in this glorious Island, the cradle and citadel of free democracy throughout the world, we do not like to be regimented and ordered about and have every action of our lives prescribed for us. In fact we punish criminals by sending them to Wormwood Scrubs and Dartmoor, where they get full employment, and whatever board and lodging is appointed by the Home Secretary.

Socialism is, in its essence, an attack not only upon British enterprise, but upon the right of the ordinary man or woman to breathe freely without having a harsh, clumsy, tyrannical hand clapped across their mouth and nostrils. A free parliament – look at that – a free parliament is odious to the Socialist doctrinaire. Have we not heard Mr Herbert Morrison descant upon his plans to curtail parliamentary procedure and pass laws simply by resolutions of broad principle in the House of Commons, afterwards to be left by Parliament to the executive and to the bureaucrats to elaborate and enforce by departmental regulations? As for Sir Stafford Cripps on 'Parliament in the Socialist State', I have not time to read to you what he said, but perhaps it will meet the public eye during the election campaign.

But I will go farther. I declare to you, from the bottom of my heart, that no socialist system can be established without a political police. Many of those who are advocating Socialism or voting Socialist today will be horrified at this idea. That is because they are short-sighted, that is because they do not see where their theories are leading them.

No Socialist Government conducting the entire life and industry of the country could afford to allow free, sharp, or violently-worded expressions of public discontent. They would have to fall back on some form of Gestapo, no doubt very humanely directed in the first instance. And this would nip opinion in the bud; it would stop criticism as it reared its head; and it would gather all the power to the supreme party and the party leaders, rising like stately pinnacles above their vast bureaucracies of civil servants, no longer servants and no longer civil. And where would the ordinary simple folk – the common people, as they like to call them in America – where would they be, once this mighty organism had got them in its grip?

I stand for the sovereign freedom of the individual within the laws which freely elected parliaments have freely passed. I stand for the rights of the ordinary man to say what he thinks of the government of the day, however powerful, and to turn them out, neck and crop, if he thinks he can better his temper or his home thereby, and if he can persuade enough others to vote with him.

CLEMENT ATTLEE'S ELECTION BROADCAST

When I listened to the Prime Minister's speech last night, in which he gave such a travesty of the policy of the Labour Party, I realized at once what was his object. He wanted the electors to understand how great was the difference between Winston Churchill, the great leader in war of a united nation, and Mr Churchill, the party leader of the Conservatives. He feared lest those who had accepted his leadership in war might be tempted out of gratitude to follow him further. I thank him for having disillusioned them so thoroughly. The voice we heard last night was that of Mr. Churchill, but the mind was that of Lord Beaverbrook.

I am also addressing you tonight on the wireless for the first time for five years as a party leader. But before turning to the issues that divide parties, I would like to pay my tribute to my colleagues in the late Government, of all parties or of none, with whom I have had the privilege of serving under a great leader in war, the Prime Minister. No political differences will efface the memory of our comradeship in this tremendous adventure, of the anxieties shared, of the tasks undertaken together, and of the spirit of friendly cooperation in a great cause which prevailed. The fact that men of diverse political views, backed by the continuous support of Parliament and the country, were able to work together for five years is a great testimony to British democracy and to the political maturity of this country.

It was, however, inevitable that, when an approach was made to long-term policy in relation to the economic organization of the country, there would be a divergence of view on the principles to be applied, which necessitate an appeal to the country. The issues involved had sooner or later to be put to the people by the rival parties in order that they might be decided.

The Prime Minister spent a lot of time painting to you a lurid picture of what would happen under a Labour Government in pursuit of what he called a Continental conception. He has forgotten that Socialist theory was developed by Robert Owen in Britain long before Karl Marx. He has forgotten that Australia, New Zealand, whose peoples have played so great a part in the war, and the Scandinavian countries have had Socialist governments for years, to the great benefit of their peoples, with none of these dreadful consequences.

When he talks of the danger of a secret police and all the rest of it he forgets that these things were actually experienced in this country only under the Tory Government of Lord Liverpool in the years of repression when the British people who had saved Europe from Napoleon were suffering deep distress. He has forgotten many things, including, when he talks of the danger of Labour mismanaging finance, his own disastrous record at the Exchequer over the gold standard.

The Conservative Party believe that the basis of our economic activities must be what they call private enterprise, inspired by the motive of private profit. They would reduce direction by and for the nation to the minimum. They seem to hold that, if every individual seeks his own interest, somehow or other the interests of all will be served. It is a pathetic faith resting on no foundation of experience. The Labour Party, on the contrary, believes that if you want certain results you must plan to secure them – that, in peace as in war, the public interest must come first, and that if in war we were able to provide food, clothing, and employment for all our people it is not impossible to do the same in peace provided the Government has the will and the power to act.

My Labour colleagues have shown that they can administer great departments, accept heavy responsibilities and plan and carry out far-reaching polices. Forty years ago the Labour Party might with some justice have been called a class party, representing almost exclusively the wage-earners. It is still based on organized labour, but has steadily become more and more inclusive. In the ranks of the Parliamentary Party and among our candidates you will find numbers of men and women drawn from every class and occupation in the community. Wage and salary earners form the majority, but there are many from other walks of life, from the professions, and from the business world, giving a wide range of experience. More than 120 of our candidates come from the fighting services, so that youth is well represented.

The Conservative Party remains as always a class Party. In 23 years in the House of Commons I cannot recall more than half a dozen Conservatives from the ranks of the wage-earners. It represents today as in the past, the forces of property and privilege. The Labour Party is, in fact, the one party which most nearly reflects in its representation and composition all the main streams which flow into the great river of our national life.

Our appeal to you, therefore, is not narrow or sectional. We have to plan the broad lines of our national life so that all may have the duty and the opportunity of rendering service to the nation, every one in his or her own sphere, and that all may help to create and share in an increasing material prosperity free from the fear of want. We have to preserve and enhance the beauty of our country, to make it a place where men and women may live finely and happily, free to worship God in their own way, free to speak their minds, free citizens of a great country.

Whether Attlee was right or wrong to attribute Churchill's aggression to Lord Beaverbrook, a controversial right-wing newspaper owner and one of Churchill's closest confidants, it is clear that the Canadian-born press baron welcomed Churchill's attack on the Labour Party. Beaverbrook's *Daily Express* was Britain's biggest-selling newspaper at the time; its front-page headline on 5 June was: GESTAPO IN BRITAIN IF SOCIALISTS WIN.

However, many people, including some Conservatives, thought Churchill had gone too far. So, evidently, did the British public. Although polling day was 5 July, the votes were not counted until 26 July, to give time for the votes of service personnel to reach Britain from all over the world. During this three-week period, talks began at Potsdam, near Berlin, on the post-war shape of Europe. Churchill took Attlee with him on the constitutionally correct grounds that nobody could be certain who would be prime minister after 26 July. However, Churchill never expected that he would be ejected from office. Nor did many people. The one clear sign that Labour might win came from opinion polls for the *News Chronicle*, but most, including the *News Chronicle* itself, disbelieved the figures.

In fact, the polls were right and almost all the pundits wrong. Labour won with a landslide majority, and Attlee, who had returned to London with Churchill for the results, became prime minister on the evening of 27 July. The next day, Attlee returned to Potsdam alone.

1946

'THE NINETEENTH-CENTURY LIBERAL EXPONENTS OF OUR CONSTITUTIONAL SYSTEM GRIEVOUSLY MISLED THE OUTSIDE WORLD'

Leo Amery was a rare beast: a lifelong politician and a serious thinker on the character of Britain's constitution. First elected to Parliament in 1911 for the Liberal Unionists, shortly before they merged with the Conservative Party, he remained an MP until 1945. With Churchill, he was one of the few Tory MPs to oppose appeasement in the 1930s. When the House of Commons met on 2 September 1939, following Germany's invasion of Poland, Amery was unhappy with the speech of Neville Chamberlain, the prime minister. When Arthur Greenwood rose to reply for the Labour Party, Amery called out, 'Speak for England, Arthur'. Eight months later, Amery delivered the most devastating attack on Chamberlain in a debate on the conduct of the war. Amery echoed Cromwell's words to the Rump Parliament in 1653: 'You have sat too long here for any good you have been doing. Depart, I say, and let us have done with you. In the name of God, go!' The next day Chamberlain was, indeed, gone.

Following Amery's defeat in the 1945 election, he delivered a series of lectures at All Souls College, Oxford, on the British constitution. These were the Chichele Lectures, named after Henry Chichele, the founder of the college in the fifteenth century. In this extract, Amery argued that the essential decision that voters made at election time was which party was to form the government, and it was therefore better to have an election system that clarified that choice, rather than a more proportional voting system.

LEO AMERY'S CHICHELE LECTURE: 'THE ESSENTIAL NATURE OF THE CONSTITUTION'

The starting point and mainstream of action has always been the Government. It is the Prime Minister who, in the name of the Crown, makes appointments and confers honours without consulting Parliament. It is the Prime Minister, in the name of the Crown, who summons Parliament. It is the Government which settles the programme of parliamentary business and directs and drives Parliament in order to secure that programme. If Parliament fails to give sufficient support it is the Government, or an alternative government, which, in the name of the Crown, dissolves Parliament.

At a general election the voter is not in a position to choose either the kind of representative or the kind of government he would like if he had a free choice. There is a Government in being which he can confirm or else reject in favour of the alternative team. The candidates before him – the only candidates worth taking seriously – are either supporters of the team in office or of its rivals for office. It is within those narrow limits that his actual power is exercised. He may be influenced by the personality of the candidates, still more by that of the leaders of the parties, by a Government's record or by its opponents' promises, by sheer party loyalty or light-hearted desire for change. No doubt, too, he has had his continuous share in the making of that public opinion which helps to shape parties and influence governments. But by the time it comes to an actual decision his function is the limited and essentially passive one of accepting one of the two alternatives put before him.

Our whole political life, in fact, turns round the issue of government. The two-party system is often referred to as if it were the happy result of an accidental historical development, or as the consequence of a natural division between two types of mind. Both statements contain a substantial element of truth. But the decisive and continuous influence has been the fact that a governing team with a majority in Parliament can normally only be displaced by another team capable of securing an alternative majority. The two-party system is the natural concomitant of a political tradition in which government, as such, is the first consideration, and in which the views and preferences of voters or of members of Parliament are continuously limited to the simple alternatives of 'for' or 'against'. It is, indeed, only under the conditions created by such a tradition that there can be any stability in a government dependent from day to day on the support of a majority in Parliament.

It is precisely on that issue that the nineteenth-century Liberal exponents of our constitutional system so grievously misled the outside world. They created the belief that it was possible successfully to combine the British form of Constitution with the prevalent continental conception, derived from the French Revolution, of political power as a delegation from the individual citizen through the legislature to an executive dependent on that legislature.

That conception naturally involves the widest freedom in the citizen's choice of party regarded as the end in itself. In many countries it has led to the almost indefinite multiplication of parties. Another consequence has been the adoption of systems of proportional representation, usually based on party lists, in order to secure for the individual voter or individual party their fair share of the composition of the legislature.

Such a system of government, not in and with Parliament, but by Parliament, is bound, by its very nature, to be weak and unstable, subject to the continual shifting and reshuffling of coalition ministries and to the influence of personal ambitions. Face to face with the growing need of the age for more governmental action and more definite leadership, it has almost everywhere broken down. The rise of dictatorships and of one-party governments has been the almost inevitable consequence of the ineffectiveness of constitutions which reproduced the outward form of the British Constitution, without that spirit of strong and stable government which is of its essence.

Democratic government based, in principle, at least, on delegation from below can, no doubt, be made to work. But in order to do so, the Government, however chosen, must enjoy a real measure of independence and for a reasonably long period. What cannot work, as Mill himself admitted, and as Cromwell decided somewhat more forcibly before him, is government by an elected assembly or subject to continual direct dictation and interference by such an assembly. In any case that is not the kind of government under which we live ourselves. Our system is one of democracy, but of democracy by consent and not by delegation, of government of the people, for the people, with, but not by, the people.

1948

'DESPITE OUR FINANCIAL ANXIETIES, WE ARE STILL ABLE TO DO THE MOST CIVILISED THING IN THE WORLD'

Aneurin Bevan built the greatest monument of Labour's post-war government by turning the dream of a 'national health service' into reality. Clement Attlee's decision to appoint him as Minister of Health was as inspired as it was unexpected, given Bevan's rebellious past (as with his protest over the banning of the *Daily Worker* in 1941). In fighting for the NHS to be born, Bevan battled against not only the Conservatives but also the British Medical Association (BMA), in those days a citadel of reactionary views, at a time when Britain was broke and money for ambitious social reforms was in short supply.

The Act creating the NHS passed into law in November 1946, but the doctors' leaders continued to oppose its implementation. When Bevan announced that the NHS would come into being on 5 July 1948, the BMA decided to conduct a referendum amongst its members. Bevan chose to fight the BMA and its Conservative supporters with words. He staged a debate in Parliament on 9 February 1948, at which, according to Michael Foot, his biographer, he delivered one of his 'most coruscating speeches'.

ANEURIN BEVAN'S SPEECH TO THE HOUSE OF COMMONS ON THE NATIONAL HEALTH SERVICE

I beg to move:

> That this House takes note that the appointed day for the National Health Service has been fixed for July 5th; welcomes the coming into force on that date of this measure which offers to all sections of the community comprehensive medical care and treatment and lays for the first time a sound foundation for the health of the people; and is satisfied that the conditions under which all the professions concerned

are invited to participate are generous and fully in accord with their traditional freedom and dignity.

The House will recollect that this Debate was requested from this side of the House, and not by the Opposition. There is some significance in that fact. During the last six months to a year there has been a sustained propaganda in the newspapers supporting the party opposite, which has resulted in grave misrepresentation of the nature of the Health Service and of the conditions under which the medical profession are asked to enter the Health Service. There has been even worse misrepresentation, sustained by a campaign of personal abuse, from a small body of spokesmen who have consistently misled the great profession to which they are supposed to belong.

I would like to make one personal reference. It has been suggested that one of the reasons why the medical profession are so stirred up at the moment is because of personal deficiencies of my own. I am very conscious of these. They are very great. Absence of introspection was never regarded as part of a Celtic equipment; therefore, I am very conscious of my limitations.

But it can hardly be suggested that conflict between the British Medical Association and the Minister of the day is a consequence of any deficiencies that I possess, because we have never been able yet to appoint a Minister of Health with whom the B.M.A. agreed. My distinguished fellow country-man had quite a little difficulty with them. He was a Liberal, and they found him an anathema. Then there was Mr. Ernest Brown who was a Liberal National, whatever that might mean, representing a Scottish constituency. They found him abominable. As for Mr. Willink, a Conservative representing an English constituency, they found him intolerable.

I am a Welshman, a Socialist representing a Welsh constituency, and they find me even more impossible. Yet we are to assume that one of the reasons why the doctors are taking up this attitude is because of unreasonableness on my part. It is a quality which I appear to share in common with every Minister of Health whom the British Medical Association have met.

If I may be allowed to make a facetious transgression, they remind me of a famous argument between Chesterton and Belloc. They were arguing about the cause of drunkenness, and they decided to apply the principles of pure logic. They met one night and drank nothing but whisky and water, and they got drunk. They met the next evening and drank nothing but brandy and water, and they got drunk. They met the third night and drank nothing but gin and water, and again they got drunk. They decided that as the constant factor was water it was obviously responsible – a conclusion which was probably most agreeable to Bacchic circles.

I would warn hon. Members opposite that it is not only the British working class, the lower income groups, which stands to benefit by a free health service. Consider very seriously the tradition of the professional classes. Consider that social class which is called the 'middle class'. Their entrance into the scheme, and their having a free doctor and a free hospital service, is emancipation for many of them. There is nothing that destroys the family budget of the professional worker more than heavy hospital bills and doctors' bills. There is no doubt about that at all, and if hon. Members do not know it, they are really living in another world. I know of middle-class families who are mortgaging their future because of heavy surgeons' bills and doctors' bills.

Therefore, it is absolutely vital, not only for the physical good health of the community, but in the interests of all social groups, that they should all be put in the system on 5 July and that there should not be some in and some out of the scheme. That is why I deplore the letter today in *The Times* from a distinguished orthopaedist, who talked about private practice as though it should be the glory of the profession. What should be the glory of the profession is that a doctor should be able to meet his patients with no financial anxiety.

I now come to the Amendment on the Paper, and may I say at once that the Government are prepared to add the Amendment to this Motion. If hon. Members look at the Amendment, they will see that it is one to which all Members of the House can subscribe. It:

declines to prejudice in any way the right of individuals in all the professions concerned to express their opinions freely, according to their traditions, and in the interest of their patients, upon the terms and conditions of service under the proposed National Health Scheme.

Who disagrees with that? A more innocuous collection of bromides I have never heard of or seen.

May I say this in conclusion? I think it is a sad reflection that this great Act, to which every party has made its contribution, in which every section of the community is vitally interested, should have so stormy a birth. I should have thought, and we all hoped, that the possibilities contained in this Act would have excited the medical profession, that they would have realised that we are setting their feet on a new path entirely, that we ought to take pride in the fact that, despite our financial and economic anxieties, we are still able to do the most civilised thing in the world – put the welfare of the sick in front of every other consideration.

I, therefore, deplore the fact that the best elements in the profession have been thrust on one side by the medical politicians, who are not really concerned about the welfare of the people or of their own profession, but are seeking to fish in these troubled waters. I hope the House will not hesitate to tell the British Medical Association that we look forward to this Act starting on 5th July, and that we expect the medical profession to take their proper part in it because we are satisfied that there is nothing in it that any doctor should be otherwise than proud to acknowledge.

The BMA referendum went ahead, and produced an overwhelming vote against the NHS. But through a mixture of charm and aggression, and threats and bribes (Bevan himself said of hospital consultants that he had to 'stuff their mouths with gold'), Bevan persuaded 90 per cent of all doctors to accept the new service.

On 4 July, the eve of the birth of the NHS, Bevan spoke at a Labour Party rally in Manchester, where he accused the Conservatives of being 'lower than vermin' – a remark as sharp and controversial as Churchill's accusation three years earlier that a Labour government would lead to the creation of a British version of the Gestapo. Bevan recalled the hardships of his own childhood; he said that poverty was caused mainly by poor social organisation:

That is why no amount of cajolery, and no attempts at ethical or social seduction, can eradicate from my heart a deep burning hatred for the Tory Party that inflicted those bitter experiences on me. So far as I am concerned they are lower than vermin. They condemned millions of first-class people to semi-starvation. Now the Tories are pouring out money in propaganda of all sorts and are hoping by this organised sustained mass suggestion to eradicate from our minds all memory of what we went through. But, I warn you young men and women, do not listen to what they are saying now. Do not listen to the seductions of Lord Woolton [Chairman of the Conservative Party]. He is a very good salesman. If you are selling shoddy stuff you have to be a good salesman. But I warn you they have not changed, or if they have they are slightly worse than they were.

The NHS was an instant success with the public. Its future was assured when the Conservatives abandoned their opposition. Less than two years after the birth of the NHS, the Conservatives' 1950 general election manifesto stated unambiguously: 'We pledge ourselves to maintain and improve the Health Service.'

1948

'NOW IS THE TIME TO RESTORE THE SENSE OF THE ULTIMATE VALUE OF EVERY HUMAN BEING'

Sydney Silverman has a special place in the pantheon of awkward-squad heroes. He led the fight for almost 20 years to abolish capital punishment in Britain. For the first half of his life, he was a pacifist; he went to prison three times during the First World War for refusing to join the army. He abandoned his pacifism in the face of Hitler's persecution of Europe's Jews, but did not abandon his belief in the sanctity of human life.

When Labour won the 1945 election, Silverman, who had then been an MP for ten years, was widely expected to join the government. However, Attlee regarded him as too radical. So Silverman devoted himself to a number of passionate causes, of which the abolition of capital punishment was, eventually, his most successful. His first parliamentary foray into this issue came on 14 April 1948, when he proposed an amendment to the Criminal Justice Bill.

SYDNEY SILVERMAN'S SPEECH TO PARLIAMENT PROPOSING AN END TO THE DEATH PENALTY

> What we desire to get decided by the House is the general question of principle whether the capital penalty can be inflicted any longer, by this country at this date, in cases of murder in peacetime. It is not only the melodrama and sensationalism with which these proceedings are surrounded; it is not only the squalor, every detail of which spreads into the newspapers in every one of these crimes; it is not only the relentless finality of this penalty, that once it has been inflicted there is no room for rectification if there were an error or miscarriage of justice. Above all these things, there is the sense which we all have that this penalty, of itself, denies the very principle on which we claim the right to inflict it – namely, the sanctity of human life.
>
> In spite of all these things – and they are weighty matters – I think almost everyone would retain the penalty if they were convinced that, with its

retention, there would be fewer murders than if it were removed. Ultimately, the justification, and the sole justification if there be one for the retention of this penalty is that it is necessary to protect society and that, unless we do inflict it, society cannot protect itself from murderers. No one can prove that is true; no one can prove that it is untrue. It is a speculation either way, but we may compare it and draw inferences from the comparison both with our previous legal history and with the state of affairs in other countries in which this penalty has been abolished.

It has been abolished in many European countries, and in a number of American countries, and it has been abolished a very long time. If we compare it, first, with our own legal and judicial history, and remember how many crimes to which this penalty has been attached within a not very long period, it will be seen that the removal of the death penalty from any crime has at no time been followed by an increase in the incidence of that crime. There is no ground whatever for saying, and the facts are all against it, that in any of the other offences to which the death penalty has produced any deleterious consequences of any kind.

In those countries which have abolished it, the figures show that its abolition has not caused an increase in crimes of violence and has not caused an increase in the incidence of murder. It is possible that this country is different. No one can prove that it is not, but I should have thought that a reasonable inference was that, this country's civilisation being of no lower standard than the civilisation of all those other countries, a barbaric penalty with which they have been able to dispense without harm to their community or to their society, can be dispensed in our case with no greater harm than in theirs.

In his Second Reading Speech, the Home secretary said that the Government had not put this matter into the Bill because they thought public opinion was not ripe for it. I concede that if that were correct, they would be justified in leaving it out, and this House would not be justified in putting it in, because these matters cannot be judged intrinsically in a vacuum. Penalties are not right or wrong in themselves. They must be seen against the background of the social morality of the time in which they are being discussed, and must not be either too far ahead or too far behind the level of morality of civilisation.

How is that public opinion to be ascertained? It cannot be done by going down to a constituency and counting heads going into a club or a cinema or a theatre, posing the question, counting the answers and saying that is the public opinion of this country. If we wish to obtain the public opinion of this country on such a matter we must only do it, and can only do it, by getting a cross-section of our citizens, by giving them the facts as we know them, by putting forward the arguments of both sides, and by relying on their good sense, good judgment and moral integrity.

Where can we find a better cross-section of the community than this House of Commons? We are not delegates; we are not bound to ascertain exactly what a numerical majority of our constituents would wish and then to act accordingly without using our own judgment. Edmund Burke long ago destroyed any such theory. We are not delegates. We are representatives. Our business is to act according to our consciences, honestly looking at the facts and coming to as right a judgment as we may.

I suppose that after we have had two world wars with infinite loss of human life, after we have had the bombardment of cities and the wiping out of whole populations, after we have had new crimes committed against whole peoples for which we have had to invent new names, after such incidents as those of Hiroshima and Nagasaki – I suppose it may seem a very small matter whether half a dozen worthless human beings, who have themselves taken human life, should live or die.

But, surely, it is the duty of all of us who value our civilisation not to depress still further those moral and spiritual values, but to seek to raise them, and to seek to raise them at precisely this moment when they are most in danger. Now is the time to restore the sense of the ultimate value of every human being. I say that this new Clause ought to be overwhelmingly passed by this House because it represents, in the last analysis, those moral and spiritual values on which, really, society is founded.

The government allowed a free vote on Silverman's amendment; that is, it did not instruct Labour MPs on how to vote. But James Chuter Ede, the Home Secretary, advised MPs to reject it. He argued that without the death penalty more murders would be committed. Most Labour MPs sided with Silverman. His amendment was passed by MPs by 245 to 222. However, the Lords rejected it and the amendment fell.

Silverman carried on campaigning and bringing the issue before Parliament. Eventually, with the support of Harold Wilson's new government in 1964, Silverman introduced a new private member's bill. It passed both Houses and received the royal assent in October 1965. Seventeen people who had been sentenced to death automatically had their sentences commuted to life imprisonment. The last two executions in Britain had taken place over a year earlier, in August 1964.

1948–50

'IN THE CENTRE OF OUR MOVEMENT STANDS THE IDEA OF A CHARTER OF HUMAN RIGHTS, GUARDED BY FREEDOM AND SUSTAINED BY LAW'

Winston Churchill was no sudden post-war convert to the cause of European unity. As early as 1930, he had written in an American magazine, the *Saturday Evening Post*, that:

> The conception of a United States of Europe is right. Every step taken to that end which appeases the obsolete hatreds and vanished oppressions, which makes easier the traffic and reciprocal services of Europe, which encourages nations to lay aside their precautionary panoply, is good in itself.

However, he made it clear he was thinking about the other side of the Channel, not including Britain: 'We have our own dreams. We are with Europe but not of it. We are linked but not compromised.'

The Second World War caused Churchill to revise his thinking. During the war itself, he started to set out his ideas for the pooling of sovereignty with the aim of building a more peaceful and prosperous world. He continued to flesh out these ideas in opposition after 1945. In Zurich, in September 1946, he said: 'We must recreate the European family in a regional structure called, as it may be, the United States of Europe.' On 7 May 1948, he addressed the Congress of Europe in The Hague and set out his goal of a world government, with large regional groups to be formed as stepping stones along the way. This time there was no suggestion of Britain standing aside.

WINSTON CHURCHILL'S SPEECH TO THE CONGRESS OF EUROPE, THE HAGUE

This Congress has brought together leaders of thought and action from all the free countries of Europe. Statesmen of all political parties, leading figures from all the Churches, eminent writers, leaders of the professions, lawyers, chiefs of industry and prominent trade-unionists are gathered here. In fact a representative grouping of the most essential elements in the political, industrial, cultural and spiritual life of Europe is now assembled in this ancient hall. And although everyone has been invited in his individual capacity, nevertheless this Congress, and any conclusions it may reach, may fairly claim to be the voice of Europe.

It is time indeed that that voice should be raised upon the scene of chaos and prostration, caused by the wrongs and hatreds of the past, and amid the dangers which lie about us in the present and cloud the future. We shall only save ourselves from the perils which draw near by forgetting the hatreds of the past, by letting national rancours and revenges die, by progressively effacing frontiers and barriers which aggravate and congeal our divisions, and by rejoicing together in that glorious treasure of literature, of romance, of ethics, of thought and toleration belonging to all, which is the true inheritance of Europe, the expression of its genius and honour, but which by our quarrels, our follies, by our fearful wars and the cruel and awful deeds that spring from war and tyrants, we have almost cast away.

The Movement for European Unity must be a positive force, deriving its strength from our sense of common spiritual values. It is a dynamic expression of democratic faith based upon moral conceptions and inspired by a sense of mission. In the centre of our movement stands the idea of a Charter of Human Rights, guarded by freedom and sustained by law. It is impossible to separate economics and defence from the general political structure. Mutual aid in the economic field and joint military defence must inevitably be accompanied step by step with a parallel policy of closer political unity. It is said with truth that this involves some sacrifice or merger of national sovereignty. But it is also possible and not less agreeable to regard it as the gradual assumption by all the nations concerned of that larger sovereignty which can alone protect their diverse and distinctive customs and characteristics and their national traditions all of which under totalitarian systems, whether Nazi, Fascist, or Communist, would certainly be blotted out for ever.

Nothing that we do or plan here conflicts with the paramount authority of a world organisation of the United Nations. On the contrary I have always believed, as I dared in the war, that a Council of Europe was a subordinate but necessary part of the world organisation. I thought at that time, when I had great responsibility, that there should be several regional councils, august but subordinate, that these should form the massive pillars upon which the world organisation would be founded in majesty and calm. This was the direction in which my hopes and thought lay three or four years ago. To take an example from the military sphere, with which our hard experiences have made us all familiar, the design for world government might have followed the system of three or more groups of armies – in this case armies of peace – under one supreme headquarters. Thus I saw the vast Soviet Union forming one of these groups. The Council of Europe, including Great Britain linked with her Empire and Commonwealth, would be another. Thirdly, there was the United States and her sister republics in the Western Hemisphere with all their great spheres of interest and influence.

To some extent events have moved in this direction, but not in the spirit or the shape that was needed. The western hemisphere already presents itself as a unit. Here at The Hague we are met to help our various Governments to create the new Europe. But we are all grieved and perplexed and imperilled by the discordant attitude and policy of the third great and equal partner, without whose active aid the world organisation cannot function, nor the shadow of war be lifted from the hearts and minds of men and nations. We must do our best to create and combine the great regional unities which it is in our power to influence, and we must endeavour by patient and faithful service, to prepare for the day when there will be an effective world government resting upon the main groupings of mankind.

Thus for us and for all who share our civilisation and our desire for peace and world government, there is only one duty and watchword: Persevere. That is the command which should rule us at this Congress. Persevere along all the main lines that have been made clear and imprinted upon us by the bitter experiences through which we have passed. Persevere towards those objectives which are lighted for us by all the wisdom and inspiration of the past.

We are here to lay the foundations upon which the statesmen of the western democracies may stand, and to create an atmosphere favourable to the decisions to which they may be led. We must here and now resolve that in one form or another a European Assembly shall be constituted which will enable that voice to make itself continuously heard and we trust with ever-growing acceptance through all the free countries of this Continent.

A high and a solemn responsibility rests upon us here this afternoon in this Congress of a Europe striving to be reborn. If we allow ourselves to be rent and disordered by pettiness and small disputes, if we fail in clarity of view or courage in action, a priceless occasion may be cast away for ever. But if we all pull together and pool the luck and the comradeship – and we shall need all the comradeship and not a little luck if we are to move together in this way – and firmly grasp the larger hopes of humanity, then it may be that we shall move into a happier sunlit age, when all the little children who are now growing up in this tormented world may find themselves not the victors nor the vanquished in the fleeting triumphs of one country over another in the bloody turmoil of destructive war, but the heirs of all the treasures of the past and the masters of all the science, the abundance and the glories of the future.

One of Churchill's ambitions was realised. In November 1950, the Council of Europe adopted the European Convention on Human Rights and established the European Court of Human Rights. The Convention itself was, and remains, firmly in the British tradition of liberty, which is not surprising as the key member of the committee that crafted it was a British lawyer and Conservative politician, David Maxwell Fyfe.

THE EUROPEAN CONVENTION ON HUMAN RIGHTS

Everyone's right to life shall be protected by law. No one shall be deprived of his life intentionally save in the execution of a sentence of a court following his conviction of a crime for which this penalty is provided by law.

No one shall be subjected to torture or to inhuman or degrading treatment or punishment.

No one shall be held in slavery or servitude.

No one shall be required to perform forced or compulsory labour.

Everyone has the right to liberty and security of person. No one shall be deprived of his liberty save in the following cases and in accordance with a procedure prescribed by law:

a. the lawful detention of a person after conviction by a competent court;

b. the lawful arrest or detention of a person for non-compliance with the lawful order of a court or in order to secure the fulfilment of any obligation prescribed by law;

c. the lawful arrest or detention of a person effected for the purpose of bringing him before the competent legal authority of reasonable suspicion of having committed an offence or when it is reasonably considered necessary to prevent his committing an offence or fleeing after having done so;

d. the detention of a minor by lawful order for the purpose of educational supervision or his lawful detention for the purpose of bringing him before the competent legal authority;

e. the lawful detention of persons for the prevention of the spreading of infectious diseases, of persons of unsound mind, alcoholics or drug addicts, or vagrants;

f. the lawful arrest or detention of a person to prevent his effecting an unauthorized entry into the country or of a person against whom action is being taken with a view to deportation or extradition.

Everyone who is arrested shall be informed promptly, in a language which he understands, of the reasons for his arrest and the charge against him.

Everyone arrested or detained shall be brought promptly before a judge or other officer authorized by law to exercise judicial power and shall be entitled to trial within a reasonable time or to release pending trial. Release may be conditioned by guarantees to appear for trial.

Everyone who is deprived of his liberty by arrest or detention shall be entitled to take proceedings by which the lawfulness of his detention shall be decided speedily by a court and his release ordered if the detention is not lawful.

In the determination of his civil rights and obligations or of any criminal charge against him, everyone is entitled to a fair and public hearing within a reasonable time by an independent and impartial tribunal established by law. Judgement shall be pronounced publicly by the press and public may be excluded from all or part of the trial in the interest of morals, public order or national security in a democratic society, where the interests of juveniles or the protection of the private life of the parties so require, or the extent strictly necessary in the opinion of the court in special circumstances where publicity would prejudice the interests of justice.

Everyone charged with a criminal offence shall be presumed innocent until proved guilty according to law.

Everyone charged with a criminal offence has the following minimum rights:

a. to be informed promptly, in a language which he understands and in detail, of the nature and cause of the accusation against him;

b. to have adequate time and the facilities for the preparation of his defence;

c. to defend himself in person or through legal assistance of his own choosing or, if he has not sufficient means to pay for legal assistance, to be given it free when the interests of justice so require;

d. to examine or have examined witnesses against him and to obtain the attendance and examination of witnesses on his behalf under the same conditions as witnesses against him;

e. to have the free assistance of an interpreter if he cannot understand or speak the language used in court.

Everyone has the right to respect for his private and family life, his home and his correspondence.*

Everyone has the right to freedom of thought, conscience and religion; this right includes freedom to change his religion or belief, and freedom, either alone or in community with others and in public or private, to manifest his religion or belief, in worship, teaching, practice and observance.*

Freedom to manifest one's religion or beliefs shall be subject only to such limitations as are prescribed by law and are necessary in a democratic society in the interests of public safety, for the protection of public order, health or morals, or the protection of the rights and freedom of others.

Everyone has the right to freedom of expression. This right shall include freedom to hold opinions and to receive and impart information and ideas without interference by public authority and regardless of frontiers.*

Everyone has the right to freedom of peaceful assembly and to freedom of association with others, including the right to form and to join trade unions for the protection of his interests.*

Men and women of marriageable age have the right to marry and to found a family, according to the national laws governing the exercise of this right.

Everyone whose rights and freedoms as set forth in this Convention are violated shall have an effective remedy before a national authority notwithstanding that the violation has been committed by persons acting in an official capacity.

The enjoyment of the rights and freedoms set forth in this Convention shall be secured without discrimination on any ground such as sex, race,

---

* The Convention allows Governments to limit these rights by law in certain defined circumstances, for example 'in the interests of public safety, for the protection of public order, health or morals, or the protection of the rights and freedoms of others'.

colour, language, religion, political or other opinion, national or social origin, association with a national minority, property, birth or other status.

One year later, Churchill was back in power. Britain was, and remained, a member of the Council of Europe and a signatory to the European Convention on Human Rights. But, more broadly, Churchill had lost his enthusiasm for British involvement in a 'United States of Europe'. Although he attacked the refusal in 1950 of the Attlee government to join the European Coal and Steel Community (the forerunner of the Common Market and, later, the European Union), Churchill did nothing to reverse this decision when he won the 1951 general election. In a strategy paper he wrote shortly after resuming the premiership, he made it clear that his two main international priorities were the Commonwealth and the 'English-speaking peoples' (i.e. the United States). Europe came third.

Churchill was far from alone in declining to hold a fixed view on Europe. At different times, the leaderships of both Labour and the Conservatives have been both strongly pro-European and stridently sceptical. This lack of a consistent national consensus reflected the views of a divided public. It helps to explain why the UK did not join the Common Market until 1973, and why it retained the pound long after most of the rest of the European Union adopted a single currency, the euro.

1957

'A MAN'S JUDGMENT IS GENERALLY MORE LOGICAL AND LESS TEMPESTUOUS THAN THAT OF A WOMAN'

By the 1950s, criticism was mounting of hereditary peerages both in principle and in the way they excluded women from the House of Lords. The government proposed a Life Peerages Bill, which would allow both men and women to be made peers for life. One of the peers who spoke in the debate on 3 December 1957 was the twenty-eight-year-old Earl Ferrers, who had inherited his title three years earlier on the death of his father.

Earl Ferrers's speech on the Life Peerages Bill

I hope very strongly that this provision will not become law because, in my humble opinion, I think it would be an unmitigated disaster to have women in this House. It is fashionable to deride and laugh at people who consider that the introduction of women into the House of Lords would be a mistake. Indeed, there was a good example of that last Sunday in the *Sunday Dispatch* newspaper. There was an article headed, 'What is wrong with women milords?' I feel it is important simply because I do not wish any observations that I have to make against the introduction of women to be taken in the same vein as articles such as this attempt to portray. It said: 'It is not only the House of Lords that needs reform. It is their Lordships' state of mind. There they sit over their pheasant and port, busily cutting their own throats.'

I do not believe the criterion of rebellion should be age or a desire for port. I feel that there are many people, not only old people, not only noble Lords, but many people throughout the country, who distinctly feel that the introduction of women would be a mistake.

Of course, if it ever looks as if the House of Lords will not give its consent to a rather extreme piece of legislation, it is the fashionable thing to say that the House is putting a rope round its own neck, and that if it does not agree to such a measure it will rot on its own feet. But the great merit of your Lordships' House is that it has always done what it considers right, despite all the threats that are from time to time put forward, and I therefore hope that your Lordships will do what your Lordships consider is right over this particular clause of the Bill. I fail, I must say, to see any sound reason why women should be made Members of your Lordships' House.

I do not believe it is universally accepted that the introduction of women into another place has been a roaring success, and I suggest that we should profit by our failures. Members of another place are, of course, delighted at the thought, because they can elevate their more rumbustious female elements to this House. I hate the idea of your Lordships' House becoming a repository of over-exuberant female politicians, and unfortunately we are unable to elevate them further, for that prerogative rests with the Almighty.

Frankly, I find women in politics highly distasteful. In general, they are organising, they are pushing and they are commanding. Some of them do not even know where their loyalty to their country lies. I disagree with those who say that women in your Lordships' House would cheer up our Benches. If one looks at a cross-section of women already in Parliament I do not feel that one could say that they are an exciting example of the attractiveness of the opposite sex.

I believe that there are certain duties and certain responsibilities which nature and custom have decreed men are more fitted to take on; and some responsibilities which nature and custom have decreed women should take on. It is generally accepted that the man should bear the major responsibility for life. It is generally accepted, for better or worse, that a man's judgment is generally more logical and less tempestuous than that of a woman. Why then should we encourage women to eat their way, like acid into metal, into positions of trust and responsibility which previously men have held?

If we allow women into this House where will this emancipation end? Shall we in a few years' time be referring to 'the noble and learned Lady, the Lady Chancellor'? I find that a horrifying thought. But why should we not? Shall we follow the rather vulgar example set by Americans of having female ambassadors? Will our judges, for whom we have so rich and well-deserved respect, be drawn from the serried ranks of the ladies? If that is so, I would offer to the most reverend Primate the humble and respectful advice that he had better take care lest he find himself out of a job.

Those examples may sound a little excessive, but I fail to see any reason whatever why, if one allows women to become Peers, this form of emancipation should not extend into those other positions of trust and responsibility which in the past have been carried out, and to such good effect, by men.

There is another reason: in this age of science and statistics, where everything has to be accounted for and tabulated, where even the atom and the molecule are no longer a mass of red and green balls attached by pieces of wire which no well-intentioned student could ever understand, there are nevertheless three virtues which evade such tabulation: common sense, intuition and judgement; and I do not believe that the common sense, intuition and judgement of the public will allow women to be taken into those positions of trust of which I have spoken.

I hope, therefore, that your Lordships' judgment and logic will be such that women will not find their way here. If it should come to pass that there was a vote upon this matter, I trust that the outcome would portray the feeling that I feel sure nine out of ten noble Lords have in their heart – namely, that we like women; we admire them; sometimes we even grow fond of them; but we do not like them here.

Ferrers's speech failed to sway his fellow peers. The bill was passed into law in 1958. Since the 1960s, almost all new peerages have been life peerages. On the rare occasion that a theoretically hereditary peerage has been created, it has generally been to honour men with no male heir, such as William Whitelaw (deputy prime minister under Margaret Thatcher) and George Thomas (Speaker of the House of Commons in the late 1970s and early '80s), both of whom were made viscounts.

As for Earl Ferrers, he served as a minister in a number of Conservative governments, including that of Britain's first woman prime minister, Margaret Thatcher. At the time of writing this book, Earl Ferrers remains an active peer – one of the minority who were elected to continue to serve by his fellow hereditaries in the House of Lords when the majority of hereditary peers were expelled in 1999.

1957

'There must remain a realm of private morality and immorality which is not the law's business'

In 1954, the government set up a committee, chaired by Sir John Wolfenden, to inquire into whether the law should be changed with regard to homosexuality and prostitution. The committee itself had a clear Establishment bias – Wolfenden himself was a former public-school head teacher – so when the report was published, on 3 September 1957, its recommendation that homosexual relations between consenting adults be legalised caused something of a sensation. The first print run was sold out within hours.

The 'Wolfenden Report': the Report of the Departmental Committee on Homosexual Offences and Prostitution

It will be apparent from our terms of reference that we are concerned throughout with the law and offences against it. We clearly recognise that the laws of society must be acceptable to the general moral sense of the community if they are to be respected and enforced. But we are not charged to enter into matters of private moral conduct except in so far as they directly affect the public good.

In considering whether homosexual acts between consenting adults in private should cease to be criminal offences we have examined the more serious arguments in favour of retaining them as such. We now set out these arguments and our reasons for disagreement with them. In favour of retaining the present law, it has been contended that homosexual behaviour between adult males, in private no less than in public, is contrary to the public good on the grounds that –

it menaces the health of society;

it has damaging effects on family life;

a man who indulges in these practices with another man may turn his attention to boys.

As regards the first of these arguments, it is held that conduct of this kind is a cause of the demoralisation and decay of civilisations, and that therefore, unless we wish to see our nation degenerate and decay, such conduct must be stopped, by every possible means. We have found no evidence to support this view, and we cannot feel it right to frame the laws which should govern this country in the present age by reference to hypothetical explanations of history of other peoples in ages distant in time and different in circumstances from our own.

In so far as the basis of this argument can be precisely formulated, it is often no more than the expression of revulsion against what is regarded as unnatural, sinful or disgusting. Many people feel this revulsion, for one or more of these reasons. But moral conviction or instinctive feeling, however strong, is not a valid reason for over-riding the individual's privacy and for bringing within the ambit of the law private sexual behaviour of this kind.

The second contention, that homosexual behaviour between males has a damaging effect on family life, may well be true. Indeed, we have had evidence that it often is; cases in which homosexual behaviour on the part of the husband has broken up a marriage are by no means rare, and there are also cases in which a man in whom the homosexual component is relatively weak nevertheless derives such satisfaction from homosexual outlets that he does not enter upon a marriage which might have been successfully and happily consummated.

We deplore this damage to what we regard as the basic unit of society; but cases are also frequently encountered in which a marriage has been broken up by homosexual behaviour on the part of the wife, and no doubt some women, too, derive sufficient from homosexual outlets to prevent their marrying. We have had no reasons shown to us which would lead us to believe that homosexual behaviour between males inflicts any greater damage on family life than adultery, fornication or lesbian behaviour. These practices are all reprehensible from the point of view of harm to the family, but it is difficult to see why on this ground male homosexual behaviour alone should be a criminal offence.

We have given anxious consideration to the third argument, that an adult male who has sought as his partner another adult male may turn from such a relationship and seek as his partner a boy or succession of boys. In this matter we have been much influenced by our expert witnesses. They are in no doubt that whatever may be the origins of the homosexual condition, there are two recognisably different categories among adult male homosexuals. There are those who seek as partners other adult males, and there are paedophiles, that is to say men who seek as partners boys who have not reached puberty.

We are authoritatively informed that a man who has homosexual relations with an adult partner seldom turns to boys, and *vice versa*, though it is apparent from the police reports we have seen and from other evidence submitted to us that such cases do happen. But paedophiliacs, together with the comparatively few who are indiscriminate, will continue to be liable to the sanctions of criminal law, exactly as they are now. It would be paradoxical if the making legal of an act at present illegal were to turn men towards another kind of act which is, and would remain, contrary to the law.

Indeed it has been put to us that to remove homosexual behaviour between adult males from the listed crimes may serve to protect minors; with the law as it is there may be some men who would prefer an adult partner but who at present turn their attention to boys because they consider that this course is less likely to lay them open to prosecution or to blackmail than if they sought other adults as their partners.

We have outlined the arguments against a change in the law, and we recognise their weight. We believe, however, that they have been met by the counter-arguments we have already advanced. There remains one additional counter-argument which we believe to be decisive, namely, the importance which society and the law ought to give to individual freedom of choice and action in matters of private morality.

Unless a deliberate attempt is made by society, acting through the agency of the law, to equate the sphere of crime with that of sin, there must remain a realm of private morality and immorality which is, in brief and crude terms, not the law's business. To say this is not to condone or encourage private immorality. On the contrary, to emphasise the personal and private nature of moral and immoral conduct is to emphasise the personal and private responsibility of the individual for his own actions, and that is a responsibility which a mature agent can properly be expected to carry for himself without the threat of punishment from the law.

We accordingly recommend that homosexual behaviour between consenting adults in private should no longer be a criminal offence.

Wolfenden's proposal to repeal the law banning homosexuality was supported by, among others, *The Times*, *The Spectator*, *The Economist* and the Archbishop of Canterbury – but not by the government. When the issue was debated in the House of Commons on 26 November 1958, one Conservative MP named James Dance argued against any change in the law.

JAMES DANCE'S SPEECH OPPOSING THE LEGALISATION OF
HOMOSEXUALITY

I should like to refer in particular to Part Two of the Report, which deals
with homosexual practices. I oppose this section of the Report. We hear a
lot these days of the potential danger to future generations from the fall-out
of strontium. I believe that these homosexual practices are not a potential
danger but are a present danger to the youth of our country.

One only has to look back into history to find that it was the condoning
of this sort of offence which led to the downfall of the Roman Empire.
I feel that it was the condoning of these offences which led to the fall of
Nazi Germany. [Laughter.] Yes, that is perfectly true. I believe that here
at home if these offences are allowed to continue unchecked our moral
standards will be lowered.

I should like to make a practical suggestion. I do not think it would
necessarily work now, but when a cure is available I suggest that in the
same way as one sees those venereal disease posters in male public urinals,
similar notices should be put up advising homosexuals that there is a cure
and mentioning the nearest clinic where they can get that cure. I would
go even further than that. When we have this cure and its availability
publicised—free, if need be—the full severity of the law should come down
on homosexuals who carry on these practices.

In the meantime, we must not take away any powers from the law. I do
not say that we should increase them; let us leave them as they are now. We
can always change the powers of the law in the future if desirable. I sincerely
hope that, by keeping the law as it is and by encouraging our scientists to
pursue their research, the beastly and horrible problem which faces us today
will gradually minimise itself so that the law enforcing punishment will no
longer be necessary.

Gay sex among men over 21 was not legalised in England and Wales until
1967 – and in Scotland, not until 1980. It took until 1994 to lower the age
of consent to 18, and until 2000 to equalise the age of consent for gay and
straight sex to 16.

In 1988, Parliament passed the Local Government Act, whose Section 28
stated that local authorities 'shall not intentionally promote homosexuality or
publish material with the intention of promoting homosexuality' or 'promote
the teaching in any maintained school of the acceptability of homosexuality
as a pretended family relationship'. Rightly or wrongly, that was regarded by
many people, and not just gay men and women, as government endorsement of

homophobia. Following a long campaign, Section 28 was repealed in 2000, after Labour returned to power. Other reforms followed. In 2004, the Civil Partnership Act gave gay couples the chance to go through a legal ceremony that provided most of the same rights as marriage. Finally, in 2006, the Equality Act brought together laws outlawing discrimination: for the first time, gay men and women had the same legal protection as those seeking equal treatment on grounds of gender, race and disability (and religion, which the 2006 Act also brought into the scope of discrimination law).

1959

'WE CANNOT, WE DARE NOT, IN AFRICA OF ALL PLACES, FALL BELOW OUR OWN HIGHEST STANDARDS'

Kenya was a British colony until it achieved independence in 1963. During the 1950s, British troops faced the Mau Mau rebellion, fought by guerrillas seeking independence. Some of the captured guerrillas were held at the Hola detention camp in Coast Province. On 3 March 1959, 85 detainees refused to work. Guards beat them up, killing 11 of them and seriously injuring around 60. Prison officials said initially that the prisoners had died as a result of drinking contaminated water. Eventually, the truth emerged from a magistrate's inquest. The affair raised important questions about the nature of Britain's role, and the morality of its actions, in the post-war world. In a Commons debate on 27 July, the Conservative MP Enoch Powell spoke movingly, and at times in tears, about the Hola scandal.

ENOCH POWELL'S SPEECH IN THE HOLA CAMP DEBATE

The affair of Hola Camp was a great administrative disaster, and to that administrative disaster there were three aspects. There was the authorisation of an operation which in its nature was likely to have fatal results; there was the failure to see that that operation, such as it was, was at least carried out with the minimum of risk; and, finally, there was the incident, which it is difficult to find a word to describe, of the water cart communiqué. The new documents show that the responsibility for all three aspects of this administrative disaster goes higher than can be discharged by the premature retirement of the officer in charge of the camp or by the retirement, accelerated by a few weeks, of the Commissioner of Prisons.

The responsibility here lies not only with Sullivan and Lewis [the camp's commandant and deputy], but at a level above them. It lies with those to whom they actually appealed for help, whom they warned of the danger, from whom they received indeed a decision which transferred responsibility upwards, but no other help or guidance. That responsibility, transcending Sullivan and Lewis, has not been recognised; but it cannot be ignored, it cannot be burked, it will not just evaporate into thin air if we do nothing about it.

I am as certain of this as I am of anything, that my right hon. Friend the Secretary of State [Alan Lennox-Boyd] from the beginning to the end of this affair is without any jot or tittle of blame for what happened in Kenya, that he could not be expected to know, that it could not be within the administrative conventions that these matters should be brought to his attention before or during the execution. When I say my right hon. Friend was in this matter utterly and completely blameless, that is of a piece with his administration of his high office generally, which has been the greatest exercise of the office of Colonial Secretary in modern times. It is in the name of that record, it is in the name of his personal blamelessness, that I beg of him to ensure that the responsibility is recognised and carried where it properly belongs, and is seen to belong.

I have heard it suggested that there were circumstances surrounding this affair at Hola Camp which, it is argued, might justify the passing over of this responsibility—which might justify one in saying, 'Well, of course, strictly speaking, that is quite correct; but then here there were special circumstances.'

It has been said—and it is a fact—that these eleven men were the lowest of the low; sub-human was the word which one of my hon. Friends used. So be it. But that cannot be relevant to the acceptance of responsibility for their death. I know that it does not enter into my right hon. Friend's mind that it could be relevant, because it would be completely inconsistent with his whole policy of rehabilitation, which is based upon the assumption that whatever the present state of these men, they can be reclaimed. No one who supports the policy of rehabilitation can argue from the character and condition of these men that responsibility for their death should be different from the responsibility for anyone else's death. In general, I would say that it is a fearful doctrine, which must recoil upon the heads of those who pronounce it, to stand in judgment on a fellow human-being and to say, 'Because he was such-and-such, therefore the consequences which would otherwise flow from his death shall not flow.'

It is then said that the morale of the Prison Service, the morale of the whole Colonial Service, is above all important and that whatever we do, whatever we urge, whatever we say, should have regard to that morale. 'Amen' say I. But is it for the morale of the Prison Service that those who executed a policy should suffer—whether inadequately or not is another question—and those who authorised it, those to whom they appealed, should be passed over? I cannot believe that that supports the morale of a service.

Going on beyond that, my hon. Friend the Member for Leicester, South-East (Mr. Peel) reminded the House how proud the Colonial Service is of the integrity of its administration and its record. Nothing could be more damaging to the morale of such a service than that there should be a breath or a blemish left upon it. No, Sir; that argument from the morale of the Prison Service and the Colonial Service stands on its head if what we mean is that therefore the consequences of responsibility should not follow in this case as they would in any other similar case.

Finally it is argued that this is Africa, that things are different there. Of course they are. The question is whether the difference between things there and here is such that the taking of responsibility there and here should be upon different principles. We claim that it is our object—and this is something which unites both sides of the House—to leave representative institutions behind us wherever we give up our rule. I cannot imagine that it is a way to plant representative institutions to be seen to shirk the acceptance and the assignment of responsibility, which is the very essence of responsible Government.

Nor can we ourselves pick and choose where and in what parts of the world we shall use this or that kind of standard. We cannot say, 'We will have African standards in Africa, Asian standards in Asia and perhaps British standards here at home.' We have not that choice to make. We must be consistent with ourselves everywhere. All Government, all influence of man upon man, rests upon opinion. What we can do in Africa, where we still govern and where we no longer govern, depends upon the opinion which is entertained of the way in which this country acts and the way in which Englishmen act. We cannot, we dare not, in Africa of all places, fall below our own highest standards in the acceptance of responsibility.

Harold Macmillan, the prime minister, rejected Lennox-Boyd's offer to resign over the scandal, but replaced him as Colonial Secretary three months later. His successor, Iain Macleod, closed the detention camps and released all Mau Mau prisoners.

1961

'IN PARLIAMENT TRADITION HAS ALWAYS SERVED
AS A VALUED LINK, REMINDING US OF OUR HISTORY,
NEVER AS A CHAIN BINDING US TO THE PAST'

When Viscount Stansgate died in November 1960, his title passed to his eldest surviving son, Tony Benn. Under the law as it stood, Benn had to give up his seat as Labour MP for Bristol South-East. But Benn wanted to remain in the Commons instead of going to the Lords. He argued people should have the right to renounce their peerages – a cause he had advocated for some years and for which he had enlisted the support of, among others, Sir Winston Churchill.

On 13 April 1961, following a report from the Committee of Privileges, which ruled against Benn, the writ was due to be moved in the House of Commons to hold a by-election in Bristol to elect Benn's successor. Benn asked the Speaker, Sir Harry Hylton-Foster, for permission to address MPs from the Bar of the Commons – a small area just inside the door to the chamber. The precedent for a peer addressing MPs from the Bar had been established when the Duke of Wellington reported on the victory at Waterloo. Benn wrote the following speech, which he hoped to deliver.

TONY BENN'S CASE FOR BEING ALLOWED TO REMAIN AN MP

Mr Speaker,

I am most grateful to you, Sir, and to the House as a whole for permitting me to attend and speak before reaching a decision on my petition. I am very conscious that the issues to be raised today are of the highest constitutional importance as compared to which my own fate must be counted as of little importance. I shall not, therefore, weary Members with the special circumstances of my case but will address myself to the major questions now before the House. However I ask for indulgence to make three personal references.

First I make no apology for wishing to remain a Member of Parliament. Service in this House of Commons is the highest service to which any man can aspire and ought to be upheld as such. The fount of our honour is the ballot box and it would be a bad day for this House if its Members secretly cherished a preference for the other place.

Secondly I must express my thanks for the unfailing support of those who sent me to this place to represent them. Many years ago Edmund Burke, who also represented Bristol, made clear what loyalty an MP owes to his constituents. I have been sustained in these lonely months by the touching loyalty of constituents for their MP.

The Lord Mayor, Aldermen and Burgesses of Bristol have petitioned both Houses and the Great Seal of the City. Yesterday a fresh petition was presented, signed by over 10,000 of my electors. If the House made it necessary to consult them more formally I have no doubt what their answer would be.

My third and final personal point is this. Whatever Parliament may ultimately decide about it I am asking that the Stansgate peerage which was created for a special purpose, having now served that purpose, should be allowed to lapse completely and for all time – preserving no privileges for the future. This is the united view of the whole family including my wife, my eldest son, my brother, my mother and was shared by my beloved father.

I now turn to the report of the Committee of Privileges. The Committee delved deeply into the customs of Parliaments going back to 1299. In its report it chose to rest upon two very ancient precedents.

The first was the opinion of Mr Justice Doddridge in 1626 that a peerage is 'a personal dignity annexed to posterity and fixed in the blood'. The Second was Mr Speaker Onslow's opinion in 1760 that 'Attendance in both Houses is considered a service and the two services are incompatible with each other'. I should like to point out that neither of these rulings have ever been laid down in Statute nor judicially determined. From these precedents all subsequent decisions flow. The Committee did not feel called upon to 'express any view as to whether a change in the law is desirable'.

In considering the report the House is not obliged to interpret its duties so narrowly. Indeed the main question today is what the law should be. Is it right to endorse decisions made in 1626 and 1760 in the totally different circumstances of 1961? In the intervening years there have been fundamental changes in the composition, powers and indeed the whole character of both Houses.

Today the Commons, strengthened by the Reform Acts, the Parliament Acts and the establishment of universal franchise, enjoys unquestioned supremacy: where there is a conflict of duty between willing elected membership of this House and unwilling hereditary membership of the House of Lords can there be any doubt which should take precedence?

The phraseology of the Writ of Summons to the Lords was described as being 'archaic' by the present Attorney-General in evidence he submitted to a Committee of the House of Lords in 1955. The Lords endorsed this view in June 1958 when a Standing Order was passed providing that any peer who does not answer his Writ of Summons within 35 days shall be automatically given leave of absence for the remainder of the Parliament.

If therefore the Lords themselves attach so little importance to the Writ of Summons why should this House rank it above the duties we perform as servants of our constituents? This House has throughout its history always protected its Members against those who sought to interfere with them. And in the process it has never shrunk from conflict with the Lords and even the Crown.

Does it make sense now, when those battles have long since been won, to disqualify a Member who wants to serve here and to deliver him in response to an 'archaic' Writ of Summons that the Lords do not enforce? There is here a simple contradiction between the common law and common sense. It should surely be resolved by legislation that will permit all who renounce the privileges of peerage to enjoy the rights of commoners.

What are the objections raised against this simple proposal? First it is said that constitutional changes should not be made to suit the convenience of one person. There is no argument about that. This case must stand or fall on its general merits. Parliament did not remove the disqualification on Catholics because it liked O'Connell or atheists because it sympathised with Bradlaugh. It did so because it was right. The man concerned was only the occasion for change.

Secondly it is said that this will breach the hereditary basis of the House of Lords. Yet four years ago the Life Peerages Bill provided for recruitment on an entirely non-hereditary basis which involves far more fundamental changes.

Thirdly it is said that this will cut off an important source of recruitment to the Lords as if young men ritually sacrificed could somehow revitalise the ageing peers. It is an argument more appropriate to Mau Mau than to the Mother of Parliaments.

Fourthly it is believed by some that this change would undermine the Throne itself. But such a proposition has only to be stated openly for its manifest absurdity to be apparent. It would indeed be a poor outlook for the monarchy if its maintenance were to depend on the insecure reputation and uncertain future of the House of Peers.

All these arguments and objections rest upon the assumption that our constitution is so precariously balanced on a pedestal of tradition that any change will threaten its stability. But to believe that is totally to misread the whole history of Parliament – rich with examples of brilliant innovations and studded with new precedents that have shaped our destiny.

If Mr Speaker Lenthall had been bound by tradition when Charles I forced an entry to arrest the five Members he would not have returned his famous answer to the King asserting the supremacy of the Commons.

Our ancient pageantry is but a cloak covering the most flexible and adaptable system of Government ever devised by man. It has been copied all over the world just because it is such a supreme instrument of peaceful change. In Parliament tradition has always served as a valued link, reminding us of our history, never as a chain binding us to the past. To misunderstand that would be to misunderstand everything that this House has achieved over the centuries.

The Speaker refused to let Benn deliver his speech. The by-election went ahead. Benn stood – and more than doubled his majority. However, as his peerage disqualified him from serving in the Commons, Benn's Conservative opponent, Malcolm St Clair, became the new MP. Two years later, Parliament passed a bill to allow members of the House of Lords to renounce their peerages. Benn did so immediately, St Clair resigned as MP, and a further by-election was held. Benn duly won and took his seat once more in the Commons.

Later the same year, the Earl of Home and Lord Hailsham used the new law to renounce their peerages in order to compete for the leadership of the Conservative Party, following Harold Macmillan's resignation as prime minister. Home emerged victorious from the secretive process (the last Conservative to become party leader before the decision was thrown open to a formal election) and, as Sir Alec Douglas-Home, became an MP when he won a by-election in Kinross and West Perthshire.

1963

'THIS IS YOUR LIFE, HENRY BROOKE
– AND WAS THEIRS'

The BBC did not create the satire boom of the 1960s: it was already under way with the stage review *Beyond the Fringe*, and the new fortnightly magazine *Private Eye*. But by commissioning *That Was the Week That Was*, or *TW3* as it became widely known, the BBC expanded the audience for satire dramatically. Broadcast live on Saturday nights at a time when Britain had only two television channels, *TW3* had 12 million viewers at its peak – the kind of audience figures that are reserved today for unusually tense episodes of *Coronation Street* or *EastEnders*.

The following sketch about the Conservative Home Secretary, Henry Brooke, took the form of a parody of *This Is Your Life*, the weekly show then presented by Eamonn Andrews. *TW3*'s presenter, David Frost, played the part of Andrews. The sketch, which Frost co-wrote with Christopher Booker, was based on an attack on Brooke that Booker had written for *Private Eye*. The sketch provides one example of why Edward Heath, who later became prime minister, blamed (or credited) *TW3* for the 'death of deference' in Britain.

CHRISTOPHER BOOKER AND DAVID FROST: *THAT WAS THE WEEK THAT WAS*

'ANDREWS': This is Your Life, Henry Brooke. You were born Home Secretary a few short months ago, on Friday 13th July 1962. Of all the many tributes that have been paid to you for your work on behalf of your fellow-man, perhaps the best-known and most sincere came from Mr Marcus Lipton, Labour MP for Brixton:

'LIPTON': You are the most hated man in Britain.

'ANDREWS': Henry – you had only been born Home Secretary for six days when – do you remember this voice?

VOICE: Henry wanted me to be the first to be emigrated under the new Immigration Act.

'ANDREWS': Yes, Henry, that was the voice of Carmen Bryan, whom you haven't seen in the flesh – ever.

'BRYAN': The first time I heard of Henry was when I was put in prison for six weeks. I'd stolen goods worth £2 but it was my first offence and Henry thought it was very serious. So he said he was going to deport me.

'ANDREWS': Can you remember what you said to the House of Commons, Henry?

'BROOKE': 'I think it would be a great act of injustice if I were to stand in the way of her returning to Jamaica.'

'ANDREWS': Did you really? Anything else?

'BROOKE': 'I am not prepared to look at this case again.'

'ANDREWS': And for four days, Henry, you stood firm. And then, on July 23rd, do you remember what you said?

'BROOKE': 'I am certain it would be wrong to impose on a person convicted of shoplifting both the experience of six weeks in prison and the penalty of deportation against her will.'

'ANDREWS': Your word, Henry, isn't very eloquent, is it? Hardly worth keeping at all. But you were going to deport her?

'BROOKE': Yes, we were going to send her back where she came from.

'ANDREWS': And where was that?

'BROOKE': Brixton.

'ANDREWS': But you did it all, Henry, to protect the nation's interest.

'BROOKE': Oh yes – my country – white and wrong.

'ANDREWS': And then, on July 29th this voice was heard in a field in Gloucestershire:

VOICE: Sieg Heil.

'**ANDREWS**': Yes, the voice of George Lincoln Rockwell, the American Nazi leader, recorded in Britain on July 29. Two days later you announced that George Lincoln Rockwell would be officially banned from entering Britain. But August 1962 was a busy time for you, Henry. Do you remember this voice?

VOICE: Save me, save me.

'**ANDREWS**': Yes, you have a broad back, Henry, and you turned it on Robert Soblen. Unfortunately Dr Soblen cannot be with us tonight – but, you remember, Henry – he was a convicted spy and a dying man. The Americans demanded his return, and he fled here from Israel and asked for the traditional right of political asylum. But to you, Henry, there were more important things than tradition.

'**BROOKE**': Yes, I am sure that when the full facts are revealed, you will agree that I was acting in the best interests of this country. By acting in the best interests of the United States.

'**ANDREWS**': You decided not only that he couldn't stay but even where he'd got to go. You told the House of Commons:

'**BROOKE**': 'Directions have been given to the airline for Dr Soblen's removal to the United States. He is fit to travel and I must act as I have said I will.'

'**ANDREWS**': Alas, Henry, Dr Soblen took an overdose of drugs – and let you down. Now, do you remember this voice?

VOICE: Defense de gate-crasher.

'**ANDREWS**': Yes, it's the voice of George Bidault. What was it you said about him to the House of Commons, do you remember?

'**BROOKE**': 'I have no grounds for thinking that Mr Bidault is now in this country.'

Enter 'Bidault'

'**ANDREWS**': Well, Henry, it's happened again. And what was it you said last time M. Bidault was here?

'**BROOKE**': 'My permission for him to enter the country was neither sought nor granted.'

'**Bidault**': Understandable, huh?

'**Andrews**': And so, Henry, to this week and the case of Chief Enaharo, the Nigerian opposition leader who has asked for asylum but whom you are sending back into danger. He got in without you noticing him – like Rockwell and Bidault. You've changed your mind – as you did with Carmen Bryan. And you've ignored the spirit of British tradition to please another Government – like Soblen. Your policy, Mr Brooke, has been one of trial and error. Their trials. Your errors. On behalf of us all – particularly Dr Soblen and Chief Enaharo – THIS IS YOUR LIFE, HENRY BROOKE – and was theirs.

'**Brooke**': Just shows. If you're Home Secretary, you can get away with murder.

TW3 was taken off the air at the end of 1963, after just 37 editions. The stated reason was that 1964 would be an election year, and the BBC feared that the programme would be unduly influential.

1966—8

'LIKE THE ROMAN, I SEEM TO SEE "THE RIVER TIBER FOAMING WITH MUCH BLOOD"'

Two speeches during the 1960s shaped the arguments about race, immigration and identity in Britain. The first came from Roy Jenkins, who became Home Secretary in Harold Wilson's Labour government in December 1965. He was arguably Britain's most effectively liberal Home Secretary of the twentieth century, not only defending liberal values but also legislating for them. Race was one area of special concern to him. He instigated three Race Relations Acts, in 1965, 1968 and, in a subsequent government, 1976; these progressively toughened measures to outlaw practising or inciting racial discrimination. On 23 May 1966, he delivered this speech to the National Committee for Commonwealth Immigrants.

ROY JENKINS'S SPEECH ON RACIAL INTEGRATION

Integration is perhaps rather a loose word. I do not regard it as meaning the loss, by immigrants, of their own national characteristics and culture. I do not think we need in this country a 'melting pot', which will turn everybody out in a common mould, as one of a series of carbon copies of someone's misplaced version of the stereotyped Englishman.

It would be bad enough if that were to occur in the relatively few in this country who happen to have pure Anglo-Saxon blood in their veins. If it were to happen to the rest of us, to the Welsh (like myself), to the Scots, to the Irish, to the Jews, to the mid-European, and to still more recent arrivals, it would be little short of a national disaster. It would deprive us of most of the positive advantages of immigration which, as I shall develop in a moment, I believe to be very great indeed.

I define integration, therefore, not as a flattening process of assimilation but as equal opportunity, accompanied by cultural diversity, in an atmosphere of mutual tolerance. This is the goal. We may fall a little short of its full attainment, as have other communities both in the past and in the present. But if we are to maintain any sort of world reputation for civilised living and social cohesion, we must get far nearer to its achievement than is the case today.

In so far as this is something which can be brought about by government action, this is now a Home Office responsibility. I welcome this. We have traditionally had the responsibility for the control of admission – of aliens for many years past, and more recently of Commonwealth citizens. I regard this as a distasteful but necessary duty. My instincts are all against the restriction of free movement, whether for work or education or pleasure, from one country to another. Distasteful though it may be, however, it remains a duty.

In present circumstances we are bound, as almost everyone now recognises, to contain the flow of immigrants within the economic and social capacity of the country to absorb them – the social factor being for the moment, I believe, more restrictive than the economic. There are of course differing views about absorptive capacity, but the Government has a clear responsibility to see that it is not put so high as to create a widespread resistance to effective integration policies. Equally it must not be so unreasonably low as to create an embittered sense of apartness in the immigrant community itself. But this will depend, in my view, not only on the numerical decisions but on the way these decisions are administered; and it is my firm intention to do so as sympathetically as I possibly can, especially when dealing with hard borderline cases.

There are some people, many of them by no means illiberal, who believe that if everybody would only stay at home in their own countries, the world would be a much easier and better place. From this view I firmly dissent. Easier it might conceivably be, but certainly not better or more civilizing or innovating.

For centuries past this and every other country which has played a part in the mainstream of world events has benefited immensely from its immigrants. Some of them came in much more aggressive ways than those we are discussing today, but at least from the Norman Conquest, to the wave of German and Austrian and Czechoslovak refugees in the thirties, we have been constantly stimulated and jolted out of our natural island lethargy by a whole series of immigrants.

Those who came were always made unwelcome by some people, but they have rarely failed to make a contribution out of proportion to their numbers. If anyone doubts this let them look at British business today, and at the phenomenal extent to which the more successful companies have been founded – or rejuvenated – by men whose origin was outside these islands.

But this is not merely a matter of business. Where in the world is there a university which could preserve its fame, or a cultural centre which would keep its eminence, or a metropolis which could hold its drawing power if it were to turn inwards and serve only its own hinterland and its own racial group? To live apart, for a person, a city, a country, is to lead a life of declining intellectual stimulation.

Nor should we underestimate the special contribution which has been made by the recent immigrants from the West Indies, from India and Pakistan, and from other Commonwealth countries. Some are highly gifted with outstanding talents in a wide variety of human activities. They and many others are making a major contribution to our national welfare and prosperity. They work in our hospitals as doctors and nurses, they build houses and run transport services in our cities. They help to fill the many labour shortages, particularly in urban areas, particularly in vital but undermanned public services which go with a full employment society.

Let there be no suggestion therefore that immigration, in reasonable numbers, is a cross we have to bear, and no pretence that if only those who have come could find jobs back at home, our problems could be at an end. So far from being the case, our doctor shortage would become still more chronic; many of our hospitals and institutions, particularly those performing tasks (like the care of the aged) which are medically unglamorous but socially essential, would have to close down; and our urban public transport systems would be reduced to skeleton services with mounting public inconvenience and a disastrous effect upon private car road congestion.

There is therefore no overall rational basis for resentment of the coloured population in our midst. Far from hindering our successful national development, they positively help it. But resentment does not always spring from rational causes, particularly when, as is the case with coloured immigrants, their skin and their cultural differences make them natural targets for those who are looking for scapegoats.

A few people, whether out of political opportunism or personal inadequacy, have deliberately whipped up prejudice, playing on fear and ignorance, and blaming the immigrants for problems which were none of their making – but which stemmed from previous parsimony in housing, schools and welfare services. Of course there are some who have legitimate individual grievances against an immigrant, just as white men can have against white men, or black men against black men. But this is not the root of the problems. The root is community prejudice, and it is that which, whether it springs from fear and inadequacy or less reputable motives, we have to deal.

For three centuries we have softened civil conflicts and adjusted our political system to the demands of a constantly changing economic and class structure. The problem we are discussing today makes less demands upon our capacity for tolerance and change than many which we have successfully surmounted in the past. But the way in which we face it, particularly in the next few years, can have a great effect upon our future. If we overcome we shall have a new message to offer the world. If we fail we shall be building up, both inside and outside the country, vast difficulties for future generations of English people.

Two years later, on April 20 1968, a rather different speech was delivered by Enoch Powell. The Conservative Party, now led by Edward Heath, was in opposition. Powell was shadow defence secretary, but did not confine his speeches to defence matters. His 'rivers of blood' speech, delivered to the Conservative Political Centre in Birmingham, was intended to generate immense controversy. To ensure this, Powell gave an advance copy of his speech to Associated TeleVision, a regional ITV company, which sent a film crew to record him delivering it.

ENOCH POWELL'S 'RIVERS OF BLOOD' SPEECH

A week or two ago I fell into conversation with a constituent, a middle-aged, quite ordinary working man employed in one of our nationalised industries. After a sentence or two about the weather, he suddenly said: 'If I had the money to go, I wouldn't stay in this country. I have three children, all of them been through grammar school and two of them married now, with family. I shan't be satisfied till I have seen them all settled overseas. In this country in 15 or 20 years' time the black man will have the whip hand over the white man.'

Here is a decent, ordinary fellow Englishman, who in broad daylight in my own town says to me, his Member of Parliament, that his country will not be worth living in for his children. What he is saying, thousands and hundreds of thousands are saying and thinking – not throughout Great Britain, perhaps, but in the areas that are already undergoing the total transformation to which there is no parallel in a thousand years of English history.

It almost passes belief that at this moment 20 or 30 additional immigrant children are arriving from overseas in Wolverhampton alone every week –

and that means 15 or 20 additional families a decade or two hence. Those whom the gods wish to destroy, they first make mad. We must be mad, literally mad, as a nation to be permitting the annual inflow of some 50,000 dependants, who are for the most part the material of the future growth of the immigrant-descended population. It is like watching a nation busily engaged in heaping up its own funeral pyre.

In the hundreds upon hundreds of letters I received when I last spoke on this subject two or three months ago, there was one striking feature which was largely new and which I find ominous. All Members of Parliament are used to the typical anonymous correspondent; but what surprised and alarmed me was the high proportion of ordinary, decent, sensible people, writing a rational and often well-educated letter, who believed that they had to omit their address because it was dangerous to have committed themselves to paper to a Member of Parliament agreeing with the views I had expressed, and that they would risk penalties or reprisals if they were known to have done so. The sense of being a persecuted minority which is growing among ordinary English people in the areas of the country which are affected is something that those without direct experience can hardly imagine.

I am going to allow just one of those hundreds of people to speak for me:

Eight years ago in a respectable street in Wolverhampton a house was sold to a Negro. Now only one white (a woman old-age pensioner) lives there. This is her story. She lost her husband and both her sons in the war. So she turned her seven-roomed house, her only asset, into a boarding house. She worked hard and did well, paid off her mortgage and began to put something by for her old age. Then the immigrants moved in. With growing fear, she saw one house after another taken over. The quiet street became a place of noise and confusion. Regretfully, her white tenants moved out.

The day after the last one left, she was awakened at 7am by two Negroes who wanted to use her 'phone to contact their employer. When she refused, as she would have refused any stranger at such an hour, she was abused and feared she would have been attacked but for the chain on her door. Immigrant families have tried to rent rooms in her house, but she always refused. Her little store of money went, and after paying rates, she has less than £2 per week. She went to apply for a rate reduction and was seen by a young girl, who on hearing she had a seven-roomed house, suggested she should let part of it. When she said the only people she could get were Negroes, the girl said, 'Racial prejudice won't get you anywhere in this country.' So she went home.

The telephone is her lifeline. Her family pay the bill, and help her out as best they can. Immigrants have offered to buy her house - at a price which the prospective landlord would be able to recover from his tenants in weeks, or at most a few months. She is becoming afraid to go out. Windows are broken. She finds excreta pushed through her letter box. When she goes to the shops, she is followed by children, charming, wide-grinning piccaninnies. They cannot speak English, but one word they know. 'Racialist,' they chant. When the new Race Relations Bill is passed, this woman is convinced she will go to prison. And is she so wrong? I begin to wonder.

Now, at all times, where there are marked physical differences, especially of colour, integration is difficult though, over a period, not impossible. There are among the Commonwealth immigrants who have come to live here in the last fifteen years or so, many thousands whose wish and purpose is to be integrated and whose every thought and endeavour is bent in that direction.

But to imagine that such a thing enters the heads of a great and growing majority of immigrants and their descendants is a ludicrous misconception, and a dangerous one. We are on the verge here of a change. Now we are seeing the growth of positive forces acting against integration, of vested interests in the preservation and sharpening of racial and religious differences, with a view to the exercise of actual domination, first over fellow-immigrants and then over the rest of the population.

For these dangerous and divisive elements the legislation proposed in the Race Relations Bill is the very pabulum they need to flourish. Here is the means of showing that the immigrant communities can organise to consolidate their members, to agitate and campaign against their fellow citizens, and to overawe and dominate the rest with the legal weapons which the ignorant and the ill-informed have provided. As I look ahead, I am filled with foreboding; like the Roman, I seem to see 'the River Tiber foaming with much blood.'

That tragic and intractable phenomenon which we watch with horror on the other side of the Atlantic but which there is interwoven with the history and existence of the United States itself, is coming upon us here by our own volition and our own neglect. Only resolute and urgent action will avert it even now. Whether there will be the public will to demand and obtain that action, I do not know. All I know is that to see, and not to speak, would be the great betrayal.

The following day Heath sacked Powell from the Shadow Cabinet. On Monday, 22 April, Heath was interviewed on BBC TV's *Panorama*. He said:

I dismissed Mr Powell because I believed his speech was inflammatory and liable to damage race relations. I am determined to do everything I can to prevent racial problems developing into civil strife. I don't believe the great majority of the British people share Mr Powell's way of putting his views in his speech.

Many Britons did, however, back Powell: 74 per cent, according to one survey.

Hostility between Heath and Powell persisted through Heath's premiership from 1970 to 1974. In 1972, Idi Amin expelled Asians from Uganda. Heath announced that all British passport-holding Ugandan Asians would be admitted to Britain. Around 30,000 came to the UK. When Powell challenged Heath's handling of this issue at the party's annual conference that autumn, Heath responded that the British people 'have refused to be scared into supporting the attitude of meanness and bad faith towards the refugees. They have responded in accordance with our traditions of honouring our obligations and holding out a friendly hand to people in danger and distress'.

Powell also opposed the UK's entry into the European Community, which took place on 1 January 1973. Just over a year later, Powell exacted his revenge by resigning from the Conservative Party and advising electors to vote Labour in the February 1974 general election. With an exceptionally large swing to Labour in the West Midlands, Powell's own heartland, the party won just four more seats across Britain than the Conservatives and ended Heath's four-year tenure as prime minister.

1967

'WHO BREAKS A BUTTERFLY ON A WHEEL?'

O n 29 June 1967, Mick Jagger was sentenced to three months in prison for 'possessing a highly dangerous and harmful drug' – in fact, just four amphetamine tablets. After one night in Brixton prison, Jagger was released on bail, pending an appeal. The day after that, *The Times* published one of its most celebrated editorials on liberty and the rule of law. Its editor, William Rees-Mogg, chose for the headline a phrase from Alexander Pope's poem 'Epistle to Dr Arbuthnot': 'Who breaks a butterfly upon a wheel?' Rees-Mogg did not explain the literary allusion; presumably he expected his readers to be familiar with it. He presumably also expected that most *Times* readers would not be too sympathetic towards Jagger's lifestyle or, for that matter, his music; which is one reason why the editorial jolted many people.

TIMES EDITORIAL ON *MICK JAGGER*'S ARREST FOR POSSESSING DRUGS

Mr Jagger has been sentenced to imprisonment for three months. He is appealing against conviction and sentence, and has been granted bail until the hearing of the appeal later in the year. In the meantime, the sentence of imprisonment is bound to be widely discussed by the public. And the circumstances are sufficiently unusual to warrant such discussion in the public interest.

Mr Jagger was charged with being in possession of four tablets containing amphetamine sulphate and methyl amphetamine hydrochloride; these tablets had been bought, perfectly legally, in Italy, and brought back to this country. They are not a highly dangerous drug, or in proper dosage a dangerous drug at all. They are of the benzedrine type and the Italian manufacturers recommend them both as a stimulant and as a remedy for travel sickness.

In Britain it is an offence to possess these drugs without a doctor's prescription. Mr Jagger's doctor says that he knew and had authorized their use, but he did not give a prescription for them as indeed they had already been purchased. His evidence was not challenged. This was therefore an offence of a technical character, which before this case drew the point to public attention any honest man might have been liable to commit. If after his visit to the Pope the Archbishop of Canterbury had bought proprietary airsickness pills on Rome airport, and imported the unused tablets into Britain on his return, he would have risked committing precisely the same offence. No one who has ever travelled and bought proprietary drugs abroad can be sure that hc has not broken the law.

Judge Block directed the jury that the approval of a doctor was not a defence in law to the charge of possessing drugs without a prescription, and the jury convicted. Mr Jagger was not charged with complicity in any other drug offence that occurred in the same house. They were separate cases, and no evidence was produced to suggest that he knew that Mr Fraser had heroin tablets or that the vanishing Mr Sneidermann had cannabis resin. It is indeed no offence to be in the same building or the same company as people possessing or even using drugs, nor could it reasonably be made an offence. The drugs which Mr Jagger had in his possession must therefore be treated on their own, as a separate issue from the other drugs that other people may have had in their possession at the same time. It may be difficult for lay opinion to make this distinction clearly, but obviously justice cannot be done if one man is to be punished for a purely contingent association with someone else's offence.

We have, therefore, a conviction against Mr Jagger purely on the ground that he possessed four Italian pep pills, quite legally bought but not legally imported without a prescription. Four is not a large number. This is not the quantity which a pusher of drugs would have on him, nor even the quantity one would expect in an addict. In any case Mr Jagger's career is obviously one that does involve great personal strain and exhaustion; his doctor says that he approved the occasional use of these drugs, and it seems likely that similar drugs would have been prescribed if there was a need for them. Millions of similar drugs are prescribed in Britain every year, and for a variety of conditions. One has to ask, therefore, how it is that this technical offence, divorced as it must be from other people's offences, was thought to deserve the penalty of imprisonment. In the courts at large it is most uncommon for imprisonment to be imposed on first offenders where the drugs are not major drugs of addiction and there is no question of drug traffic. The normal penalty is probation, and the purpose of probation is to encourage the offender to develop his career and to avoid the drug risks in the future. It is surprising therefore that

Judge Block should have decided to sentence Mr Jagger to imprisonment, and particularly surprising as Mr Jagger's is about as mild a drug case as can ever have been brought before the Courts.

It would be wrong to speculate on the judge's reasons, which we do not know. It is, however, possible to consider the public reaction. There are many people who take a primitive view of the matter, what one might call a pre-legal view of the matter. They consider that Mr Jagger has 'got what was coming to him'. They resent the anarchic quality of the Rolling Stones' performances, dislike their songs, dislike their influence on teenagers and broadly suspect them of decadence, a word used by Miss Monica Furlong in the *Daily Mail*.

As a sociological concern this may be reasonable enough, and at an emotional level it is very understandable, but it has nothing at all to do with the case. One has to ask a different question: has Mr Jagger received the same treatment as he would have received if he had not been a famous figure, with all the criticism and resentment his celebrity has aroused? If a promising undergraduate had come back from a summer visit to Italy with four pep pills in his pocket would it have been thought right to ruin his career by sending him to prison for three months? Would it also have been thought necessary to display him handcuffed to the public?

There are cases in which a single figure becomes the focus for public concern about some aspect of public morality. The Stephen Ward case, with its dubious evidence and questionable verdict, was one of them, and that verdict killed Stephen Ward. There are elements of the same emotions in the reactions to this case. If we are going to make any case a symbol of the conflict between the sound traditional values of Britain and the new hedonism, then we must be sure that the sound traditional values include those of tolerance and equity. It should be the particular quality of British justice to ensure that Mr Jagger is treated exactly the same as anyone else, no better and no worse. There must remain a suspicion in this case that Mr Jagger received a more severe sentence than would have been thought proper for any purely anonymous young man.

Four weeks later, Jagger's conviction was quashed. If there was a cause-and-effect relationship involving the *Times* editorial, it was carefully concealed from the public gaze. What is certain is that the episode sparked a major public debate whose most notable element was a programme made by a young television producer, John Birt, for the television series *World in Action*, which brought together Jagger, Rees-Mogg and the Bishop of Woolwich, among others, to debate the state of British youth. Jagger received a knighthood in 2003 for services to music, while Birt went on to become the BBC's Director-General and a life peer.

1969

'Think of it! A second Chamber selected by the Whips. A seraglio of eunuchs'

Harold Wilson's Labour government, which came to office in 1964, faced the same problem as previous Labour governments – the inbuilt Conservative majority among hereditary peers in the House of Lords. The arrival of life peers had so far done little to dent this majority, so Wilson convened an all-party group to draft plans for reform. This proposed that hereditary peers should lose the right to vote in the Lords, that enough life peers should be appointed to ensure a small overall majority for the government of the day, that all peers should retire at 75 (with the age later to be lowered to 72), and that peers' powers of delay should be curtailed further.

Peers voted to approve these plans. The House of Commons was a different matter. Two completely different sets of opponents emerged – those, mainly Conservatives, who opposed all reform and wished to uphold the rights of hereditary peers; and those, mainly Labour MPs, who felt that the House of Lords should be abolished altogether. These two groups made common cause, ridiculing the details of the government's bill (which was supported by the Conservative leadership) rather than proclaiming their own very different preferences. This was the speech of the Labour backbencher and future party leader, Michael Foot, in the House of Commons on 3 February 1969.

Michael Foot's speech to Parliament opposing plans to reform the House of Lords

I should like to begin by commenting on a remark of the right hon. Member for Barnet [Reginald Maudling]. He said—and in my opinion this is one of the central features of the whole debate—that great constitutional reforms are better made by agreement between the two Front Benches and the parties. I was somewhat surprised to hear the Leader of the Liberal Party accept that view. I do not think that it would have been shared by Mr.

Gladstone, at any rate in his later years, or by Lord Grey at the height of his fame.

If the right hon. Gentleman looks back at the extremely illuminating history of his great party, he will see that most of the major constitutional innovations for which the Liberal Party was responsible were introduced in the teeth of opposition from the other side of the House, and many of them lasted for a very long time. Major constitutional measures which affect the whole balance of power in the State, the balance of power between different interests in the country, are matters that are resolved only by party Governments who know their own minds and are determined to carry through their leading reforms without conceding to the Oppositions of the day the requirements they may press. That is what a Labour Government should have done in this instance.

I wish, first, to look at the bargain reached between the parties, on which my right hon. Friend the Home Secretary spoke most strongly when he wound up the debate on the White Paper. I do not think that it is an exaggeration to say that the overwhelming majority of opinion in the House of Lords is that the powers are to be retained pretty well as they are, but that the possibility of using them will be greatly enhanced because the place will have been made much more respectable. Theoretically, the powers have been somewhat reduced but, practically, they are to be greatly increased, and such powers will be able to be used in circumstances in which they have been unable to be used during the last 30 years—increasingly so in the last five or 10 years. This is the great constitutional prize to be grabbed. This is what they said there, in another place [the House of Lords].

I recommend right hon. and hon. Members to read the speech by Lord Butler in another place. He could hardly contain himself. I cannot quote him, but I can tell the House the gist of what he said. Lord Butler told his fellow peers, 'Boys and girls, this is marvellous, absolutely marvellous. Look at what we are getting. This is the finest thing we have been offered for many a long year and if you do not seize it you will be even bigger fools than you look to me at the moment.' Lord Butler said all that from the cross-benches, mark you. He went on, 'Do not worry about composition, by the way, or about nomination by the Prime Minister. It is all to be done through the usual channels.'

Think of it! A second Chamber selected by the Whips. A seraglio of eunuchs. That is roughly what Lord Butler said about it. Then he went on to deal in detail with the question of the cross-benchers. We must deal with that again. Not so much has been said about it on this occasion as on previous occasions. But it is a fact that the whole point of this extraordinary constitutional pyramid which we have the wrong way up in the Bill fixes on the question of the cross-benchers and how they are to be selected and how they are to behave.

We could have a national crisis with fierce controversy in the House of Commons. The matter is then referred to the other place. Momentous issues may be at stake. We may have a situation, where, just as in the Suez and Munich crises, parties and, indeed, families are deeply divided. At that stage, everyone is waiting to see what is to be the verdict of the House of Lords.

But the House of Lords may not only settle the issue temporarily. It is no good the Government saying that the House of Lords could settle it only for six months. A matter of a few weeks may be involved. There have been many important legislative Measures which Governments of all kinds have required to get through Parliament within days, even within a single day. Could not such a Measure be settled, in effect, permanently by the cross-benchers in the House of Lords? So, in the midst of a great national crisis, with the country aflame, with everyone having forgotten who these cross-benchers are, what would we hear as the final verdict on such great issues of national policy? We would hear a falsetto chorus from these political castrati. They would be the final arbiters of our destiny in our new constitution.

Nobody can seriously think that these proposals are a proper constitutional device for dealing with the problems which we face. We cannot talk about modernisation when what we are offered is a Heath Robinson House of Lords, a contraption which will fall to pieces in any crisis, which will be laughed out of court on such an occasion and which it would be better for us to laugh out of court now. That would be the best way to deal with it.

Lord Butler said, 'This little Bill, which is to do us'—that is, the Tories—'so much good, and which will set up the Tory Party for the next 30 years or so, is a true lineal descendant of the Life Peerage Bill. I told them then that if only we could get in that thin end of the wedge we would get the rest of the wedge in later'—he did not put it quite in these words. 'Here is the rest of the wedge. Now let us use it as fast as we can to make sure that we establish in this country'—and here, again, I am not using his exact words—'a new kind of second Chamber. We will make it respectable, sedate to the point of stuffy; torpid; quick to prevent any removal of injustice, but longanimous in the toleration of mischief; a perpetual encumbrance across the path of everyone wishing to act boldly; a standing incitement to those who do not wish to act at all.'

I therefore say that we should kill the Bill now if we can; that, if we cannot kill it now, we should kill it in Committee; but that, at any rate, we should prevent the country from being burdened in this modernising age by such an anachronistic and absurd institution as is proposed, not surprisingly, by the collusion between the two Front Benches.

Later that day, the bill received a second reading by a majority of 100. It then went into committee – on this occasion, a committee of the whole House. Although the Conservatives formally supported the bill, they refused to co-operate in limiting debate through the 'guillotine' procedure. Their refusal opened up the prospect of endless argument across the Commons chamber. By mid-April, after eleven days of debate, only five of the bill's twenty clauses had been considered. On 17 April, Wilson announced that the bill would be withdrawn. It took another 30 years before Parliament grappled with the issue again.

1970

'WE INTEND TO MAKE EQUAL PAY FOR EQUAL WORK A REALITY, AND TO TAKE WOMEN WORKERS OUT OF THE SWEATED LABOUR CLASS'

I n 1970, men earned 37 per cent more than women, on average. There was a widespread sense that part of this gulf was caused by women being paid less for doing the same, or broadly similar, work as men. As Employment Secretary at the time, Barbara Castle had the opportunity to do something about it. Politically, she also had good reason to take action that would redeem her reputation with the rest of the Labour Party: despite being associated with the Left of the party, she had come under sustained attack within the party for putting forward plans to reform the trade unions, and had had to retreat on that issue.

On 9 February 1970, Castle introduced the second-reading debate on her Equal Pay Bill, which set out to ban employers from (a) paying women less than men, and (b) offering women a less favourable employment contract for doing 'the same, or "broadly similar"' work as men.

BARBARA CASTLE'S SPEECH ON THE EQUAL PAY BILL

There can be no doubt that this afternoon we are witnessing another historic advance in the struggle against discrimination in our society, this time against discrimination on grounds of sex. While other people have talked – lots of people have talked – we intend to make equal pay for equal work a reality, and, in doing so, to take women workers progressively out of the sweated labour class. We intend to do it, if the House will back us, in ways which will give a lead to other countries whose governments have left us behind in adopting the principles but who are still striving for effective ways of implementing it.

The concept of equal pay for equal work is so self-evidently right and just that it has been part of our national heritage for a very long time. Here, as in other things, it was the trade union movement which gave the lead. Indeed, as far back as 1888, the T.U.C. first endorsed the principle of the same wages for the same work – a very courageous *avant garde* thing to do in those days, long before Queen Victoria's Diamond Jubilee, when women who worked in industry were certainly not considered respectable, even if they were regarded as human beings at all.

Since then the struggle against discrimination against women in rates of pay has had a chequered course. There was that moment during the war when Mrs Cazalet Keir, with strong Labour support, led a successful revolt against the Government on the issue of sex discrimination in teachers' pay and the great man himself, Winston Churchill, had to come down to the House the next day to make the reimposition of sex discrimination a vote of confidence.

Since then, the cause of equal pay has had its partial victories: the non-industrial Civil Service, non-manual local authority workers and teachers all got the first of seven instalments towards equal pay in 1955, and full equality in 1961. But its extension to that far greater number of women in industry for whom the T.U.C. fought so long ago has so far eluded us. The trade union movement has realised that this can be done only by legislation, and previous governments have refused to legislate. Up to now, the extension of equal pay in industry has always foundered on three arguments: how should we define equal pay for equal work? How can we enforce it? And: 'The economic situation is not right.' It is a tremendous credit to this government that they have founded the answer to all three.

The Bill will deal with three different situations. The first situation is where men and women are doing the same or 'broadly similar' work, not only in the same establishment but in different establishments of the same employer where these are covered by common terms and conditions. The second is where they are doing jobs which are different but which have been found to be equivalent under a scheme of job evaluation. The third is where their terms and conditions of employment are laid down in collective agreements, statutory wages orders or employers' pay structures.

This three-pronged approach does all that can be done in legislation, and goes beyond anything in the law of other major countries. It gets away from abstractions like 'equal pay for work of equal value', and brings equal pay out of the debating room and into recognisable situations in factories, offices and shops, and into the black and white of pay agreements.

Clause 1 deals with the first two of the situations I have mentioned. It establishes that where a woman is doing work which is the same or broadly similar to that of men, or work which has been established as being equivalent to that of men by a job evaluation exercise, she qualifies for equal pay, whatever her contract of employment may have said before and whatever any collective agreement may say about her work.

I now come to Clause 3, which deals with the third set of circumstances I have already mentioned. Where, on the operative date, a collective agreement or pay structure specifies a class of work or workers, however defined, to which separate men's and women's rates are attached, the women's rate must be raised to the level of the men's rate.

We also say – and Clause 6 spells this out – that while being entitled to equal treatment in all these respects, a woman shall still retain the right to any favourable treatment accorded by law or through negotiated agreements in connection with childbirth. In other words, we do not consider it preferential treatment for a woman to be given time off to have a baby, or to be paid while she is off – we would do the same for men if they had the courage to have babies.

Clause 8 provides for the Act to come into force on 29th December 1975. This will give the industry over five years to adapt itself to these far-reaching changes. Overall we estimate that equal pay will add about 3½ per cent to the national bill for wages and salaries over five years – something we can certainly assimilate at a time of rising productivity.

Moreover, we believe that by making employers pay economic rates for their women workers we shall be giving a boost to higher productivity. For this is a Bill designed, not only to end injustice, but to stimulate efficiency. As long as women are paid below their economic value, there is no incentive to put their work and their abilities to the best use. Sweated labour is a soporific to management, not a stimulant.

What, then, of evasion? I have no doubt that some employers will try it on. I believe that extensive evasion can be prevented by the extension of job evaluation, properly drawn collective agreements and the 'halo effect'. But, undoubtedly, pockets of discrimination will remain – unless women organise to put a stop to it.

Castle was supported by the shadow employment secretary – Margaret Thatcher. The Equal Pay Act received the royal assent on 29 May 1970. By the time it came into force at the end of 1975, the gap in average pay between men and women had narrowed from 37 per cent to 30 per cent. The Sex Discrimination Act, also passed in 1975, went further and made it illegal for employers to discriminate between men and women in the way they treated staff generally, or when hiring new staff.

1975

'Gone is the principle of accountability to Parliament. The new doctrine is to pass the buck to the people'

Margaret Thatcher succeeded Edward Heath as leader of the Conservative Party on 11 February 1975. Exactly one month later, she delivered her first major speech as party leader to the House of Commons.

Harold Wilson's Labour government had decided to hold a referendum on whether the United Kingdom should remain a member of the European Economic Community (the EEC, more widely known as the Common Market), which it had joined in 1973. It was a major constitutional innovation; a law had to be passed to enable one to take place. No nationwide referendum had ever been held before in Britain, though the idea had been mooted from time to time, and a specific referendum had been held in Northern Ireland in 1973.

On 11 March 1975, a debate was held on the White Paper that preceded the bill for the EEC referendum. Thatcher attacked the government's plans with a forensic speech whose analysis has not dated on the issue of when, if ever, referendums should be held. She stopped short of denouncing referendums in all circumstances, arguing rather that they needed to be considered within a wider context of constitutional reform.

Margaret Thatcher's speech to Parliament in the referendum debate

> **Mrs Thatcher:** The White Paper makes no attempt to discuss the constitutional position once we have had the first referendum, although members of the Government accept that once we have a first referendum things will be different and will never be the same again.
>
> I quote from a letter which appeared in *The Times* of 11th April 1972 from [Roy Jenkins] the Home Secretary:

It may be argued . . . that the EEC referendum would be a once-for-all operation. The device would never be used again. Who can possibly say that? Once the principle of the referendum has been introduced into British politics, it will not rest with any one party to put a convenient limit to its use. And most history shows, as Clem Attlee pointed out with terse force in 1945, that it is a splendid weapon for demagogues and dictators.

Before embarking on a referendum we, as a House, should consider its far-reaching consequences. We should attempt to do so under four heads: parliamentary sovereignty, collective responsibility, representative Parliament, and the consequences for treaty obligations which have already been assumed.

Let me deal first with parliamentary sovereignty. There is no power under which the British constitution can come into rivalry with the legislative sovereignty of Parliament. To subject laws retrospectively to a popular vote suggests a serious breach of this principle.

To use the referendum device at all is to ask the question: to what category of measure should referenda apply? Presumably the answer would be: in cases of constitutional change. But it is hard to define such a change in the British tradition because so much depends on convention and precedent. A referendum may, however, become acceptable if given a proper constitutional foundation—that is to say, if the conditions under which it could be used were defined. But that would mean, like many other democratic countries, going as far as a written constitution or at least part of the way. The implications for parliamentary sovereignty are profound. But if our sense of constitutional rules and conventions is weakening, there may come a time when some such course should be considered.

Secondly, I turn to the principle of collective responsibility. The White Paper makes it clear that the doctrine of collective responsibility will be suspended prior to the poll. But the whole relationship of government with Parliament depends on that principle. No Government can be properly accountable to Parliament unless they acknowledge a collective responsibility with regard to main matters of policy.

The right hon. Gentleman [Edward Short] the Leader of the House described this as the most important issue that has faced the country for many years. What he is saying is that the people must make a decision, Parliament must make a decision, but the Government are incapable of making a decision. On all major matters the essential task of government is decision. That does not mean absence of argument or absence of some differences. It means the capacity to reach a decision after argument and consideration, and sticking to it or resigning.

We now face the new system. If the Government cannot agree, gone is the discipline of resignation, gone is the principle of accountability to Parliament. The new doctrine is to pass the buck to the people. Let the people arbitrate is the view.

What the right hon. Gentleman is doing is to demolish collective responsibility for Labour Party convenience. He has a device so that the Government may stay, even if they are held in no confidence by the people. The people may say 'We object to your main point of policy', but nevertheless they have a device to stay in power, divided though they may be.

The third point I wish to make is the effect of a referendum on representative Government. Our system, which has been copied all over the world, is one of representative Government under which those who have not time to look into every detail of this or that Bill choose people who are honourable and with whose opinions they are in harmony to discuss these matters.

That has been our system of Government for many years, representative Government in which the representatives consider and discuss all the points in detail. In a popular vote, the voter expresses an individual opinion. In a representative institution, the representative would be expected to consider the interests of minorities and see how the separate measure fitted into the whole. I believe that if we have a referendum system, minorities would not receive anything like such a fair deal as they have under the existing system.

The fourth point concerns respect for treaty obligations. The obligations which we assumed by signing and ratifying the treaty were validly, correctly and constitutionally assumed under the full sovereignty and competence of Parliament. The treaty has been in operation for over two years.

THE MINISTER OF STATE FOR FOREIGN AND COMMONWEALTH AFFAIRS (MR. DAVID ENNALS): Without the support of the people.

MRS. THATCHER: Would the right hon. Gentleman wish to put capital punishment to the test of a referendum? Of course he would not, because he is prepared to choose the cases on which he consults the people, according to the convenience of the Government. Perhaps the late Lord Attlee was right when he said that the referendum was a device of dictators and demagogues.

The treaty has been in operation for over two years. I know of no country in the Western World in which a referendum has been used to override a treaty obligation which had been through all its parliamentary stages and had been in operation for two years. Such a step would have a damaging effect on Britain's standing in the world.

It is quite possible to put a democratic case for having referendum provisions. Assuming that we wanted the referendum provisions to apply only to constitutional questions, we should try to define what that means in a British context—an extraordinarily difficult exercise. If we wanted to avoid leaving the decision on whether to have a referendum to the whim of future Governments, we should have to think of some means of limiting its powers.

The White Paper does none of this. It is a practical expedient. It will have far-reaching consequences. The immediate point may be to register a popular view towards staying in the EEC. The longer-term result will be to create a new method of validating laws. What one Minister has used as a tactical advantage on one issue today, others will use for different issues tomorrow. This will lead to a major constitutional change, a change which should only be made if, after full deliberation, it was seriously thought to be a lasting improvement on present practice.

This White Paper has come about because of the Government's concern for internal party interests. It is a licence for Ministers to disagree on central issues but still stay in power. I believe that the right course would be to reject it and to consider the wider constitutional issues properly and at length.

The government got its way. The referendum was held on 5 June. By a two-to-one majority, the public voted for the UK to remain a member of the Common Market. Subsequently, referendums became relatively common in different parts of the UK, generally in connection with proposals for devolution or to establish local, directly elected mayors.

1975

'LET OUR CHILDREN GROW TALL AND SOME TALLER THAN OTHERS'

By the late 1940s, a cross-party consensus had grown that true liberty required greater economic and social equality. Clement Attlee's Labour government built the welfare state on this basis; and for a generation, subsequent Conservative leaders accepted the post-war settlement. Margaret Thatcher challenged that consensus. On 15 September 1975, seven months after becoming leader of the Conservative Party, she delivered a speech in New York which laid the basis for what was to become known as 'Thatcherism': the belief that people and economies – and liberty – flourished most when the State intervened least. Below are excerpts from that speech.*

MARGARET THATCHER'S SPEECH TO THE INSTITUTE OF SOCIO-ECONOMIC STUDIES

A new debate is beginning—or perhaps I should say an old debate is being renewed—about the proper role of government, the Welfare State, and the attitudes on which both rest. The debate centres on what I'll term, for want of a better phrase, the 'progressive consensus'. I should perhaps say here that things that are called progressive are not always progressive in practice—but of course some of them are. And the progressive consensus, I think, is the doctrine that the state should be active on many fronts: in promoting equality, in the provision of social welfare, and in the redistribution of wealth and incomes.

Now, it's not that our people are suddenly reverting to the ideals of *laissez-faire*. Nor are they rejecting the social advances of recent decades. It's rather that they are reviving a constructive interest in the noble ideals

---

* Reproduced with permission from http://www.margaretthatcher.org/, the official website of the Margaret Thatcher Foundation. The full text is available there.

of personal responsibility, because in some respects the concepts of social responsibility have turned sour in practice.

I'll try and concentrate on three broad issues: What are the facts about the distribution of wealth and incomes? Secondly, to what extent is greater equality desired in Britain today? And thirdly, has the economy been strengthened by the promotion of more equality and the extension of the Welfare State?

So let me start with *the facts*. In 1972, incomes after tax in Britain were divided up roughly as follows. At the upper end of the scale, the top one per cent of income earners got four per cent of incomes, or four times the average. If you take the top ten per cent, they had twice the average. And if you take the bottom ten per cent, a bit under half the average. Now, if you look at it, from half the average income at the bottom to four times the average income at the top, is not really a very wide range of incomes. It's not dramatic by any set of rules. Indeed, research has shown that the distribution of incomes in Britain is surprisingly similar to that in Poland—which is a rather shattering conclusion to reach.

Let's turn quickly to have a look at wealth. In 1911, the top one per cent of the population owned 69 per cent of the wealth. By 1938, it had come down to 50 per cent. By 1960, it had come down to 38 per cent. And by 1972, it had come down to 28 per cent and to 16.5 per cent if pension rights are included in wealth holdings. So you have had again an enormous redistribution of wealth over the years.

Now, let me look at the second section: To what extent is more equality desired in Britain today? We've had a massive survey by Political and Economic Planning Group. This is what it showed:

'Our findings show little spontaneous demand for the redistribution of earnings across broad occupational categories. The chief requirement for maintaining general satisfaction with incomes and earnings is steady economic growth.'

Now, can I turn to the third section? A vital one: Is what is called 'socialising' the National Income good for the economy? If it hasn't strengthened the economy, you haven't the means to carry on, let alone improve your welfare. And one of the lessons we are learning in Britain is that you must, first of all, have the creation of wealth before you can put so much attention on to its distribution.

Of course, the public sector has been a large part of the British economy since the early post-war years. The government share of the Gross National Product has steadily got higher and it's been higher in Britain than in most other countries and today the state controls well over half our National

Income. In the later fifties and sixties, the increase in tax and social security payments in effect knocked about one per cent off the growth of private spending each year.

Can you see where the cycle's got us to? Taking too much into public expenditure has meant trying to raise extra taxes. People have rebelled against that. They therefore have demanded extra wages. The companies have suffered, because we've had to have a certain amount of wage control, with price control, with profit control, so that companies have suffered also from extra taxes, also from loss of profits.

What are the lessons then that we've learned from the last thirty years? First, that the pursuit of equality itself is a mirage. What's more desirable and more practicable than the pursuit of equality is the pursuit of equality of opportunity. And opportunity means nothing unless it includes the right to be unequal and the freedom to be different. One of the reasons that we value individuals is not because they're all the same, but because they're all different.

I believe you have a saying in the Middle West: 'Don't cut down the tall poppies. Let them rather grow tall.' I would say, let our children grow tall and some taller than others if they have the ability in them to do so. Because we must build a society in which each citizen can develop his full potential, both for his own benefit and for the community as a whole, a society in which originality, skill, energy and thrift are rewarded, in which we encourage rather than restrict the variety and richness of human nature.

Nothing that I'm saying tonight should in any way be seen as a diminution of our recognised responsibilities to those people who through physical, mental, or social handicap suffer disadvantages. Rather, it is a consciousness that unless we have incentive and opportunity, we shall not have the resources to do as much as we want to do. And having been a Secretary of State for Education, I am the first to understand that.

Second, we must strike a proper balance between the growing demands and powers of the state and the vital role of private enterprise. Private enterprise is by far the best method of harnessing the energy and ambition of the individual to increasing the wealth of the nation, for pioneering new products and technologies, for holding down prices through the mechanism of competition, and for widening the range and choice of goods and services and jobs.

Finally, we must measure the economic and political demands of some of our people against their consequences, and we must have regard to their effect on our political and social framework. In the coming months in Britain, we shall all be thinking particularly of the achievements of the United States in the two hundred years of its existence and of the lessons your country can teach the rest of the world. May I therefore conclude with a modest hope that you will also spare a few minutes to learn from our recent experience? Because it shows how essential it is to escape from the facile arguments, which both our countries have experienced, and to reaffirm before it's too late those true values which both our countries traditionally have shared. Those values have never been more important than they are today.

1976

'WE LIVE IN AN ELECTIVE DICTATORSHIP'

I n October 1976, Lord Hailsham, a former and future Conservative Lord Chancellor, delivered the Dimbleby Lecture – an annual lecture series in honour of the BBC broadcaster Richard Dimbleby, who had died in 1965. In his lecture, Hailsham coined the phrase 'elective dictatorship' to describe Britain's constitution.

In his speech, Hailsham referred to some of the recent disputes that he felt justified his accusation. In the case of Tameside, the local council had resisted the Labour government's direction to introduce comprehensive schooling. When the House of Lords ruled in the council's favour, saying ministers needed fresh legislation to get their way, the government passed a new law imposing comprehensive schools, despite the wishes of local councils. The arguments over Laker's Skytrain turned on the plans of the buccaneering entrepreneur Freddie Laker to introduce a low-budget service to fly between London and New York – a service that threatened the traditional airlines, whose rights to repel new airlines had been protected by national laws and international agreements between Britain and the US. The Skytrain was finally introduced in 1977.

LORD HAILSHAM'S DIMBLEBY LECTURE

The powers of our own Parliament are absolute and unlimited. And in this, we are almost alone. All other free nations impose limitations on their representative assemblies. We impose none on ours. Parliament can take away a man's liberty or his life without a trial, and in past centuries, it has actually done so.

No doubt, in recent times, Parliament has not abused these particular powers. Nonetheless, the point I am making is that, as a result of the changes in its operation and structure, the absence of any legal limitation on the powers of the Parliament has become quite unacceptable. And the questions which I desire to leave for your consideration are, first, whether the time has not come to end or modify this legal theory, and, secondly, whether and how it is possible to do so.

Of course, this doctrine of absolute sovereignty of Parliament has been fully recognised for very many years. Judges may pass judgment on the acts of ministers, as they have recently done in the Tameside dispute, and in the arguments about Laker Skytrain. To this extent, the rule of law applies and prevails here as in other countries. But, once the courts are confronted with an Act of Parliament, all they can do is to ascertain its meaning, if they can, and then apply it as justly and as mercifully as the language of the law permits. So, of the two pillars of our constitution, the rule of law and the sovereignty of parliament, it is the sovereignty of Parliament which is paramount in every case.

The limitations on it are only political and moral. They are found in the consciences of members, in the necessity for periodical elections, and in the so called checks and balances inherent in the composition, structure and practice of Parliament itself.

Only a revolution, bloody or peacefully contrived, can put an end to the situation which I have just described. We live in an elective dictatorship, absolute in theory, if hitherto thought tolerable in practice. How far it is still tolerable is the question I want to raise for discussion.

A good deal of water has flowed under Westminster Bridge since the sovereignty of Parliament was established. And almost every drop has flowed in one direction: an enhancement of the actual use of its powers. To begin with, there has been a continuous enlargement of the scale and range of government itself. Then there has been a change in the relative influence of the different elements in government, so as to place all the effective powers in the hands of one of them, in other words, the checks and balances, which in practice used to prevent abuse, have now disappeared. So both sets of changes have operated in the same direction – to increase the extent to which elective dictatorship is a fact, and not just a lawyer's theory.

How far are the Commons themselves really masters of their own House? Until fairly recently influence was fairly evenly balanced between Government and Opposition, and between front and back benches. Today the centre of gravity has moved decisively towards the Government side of the house, and on that side to the members of the Government itself. The opposition is gradually being reduced to insignificance, and the Government majority, where power resides, is itself becoming a tool in the hands of the Cabinet. Backbenchers, where they show promise, are soon absorbed into the administration, and thus lose their powers of independent action.

The government controls Parliament, and not Parliament the government. Until recently, debate and argument dominated the parliamentary scene. Now, it is the whips and the party caucus. More and more, debate, where it is not actually curtailed, is becoming a ritual dance, sometimes interspersed with catcalls. So the sovereignty of Parliament has increasingly become the sovereignty of the government, which, in addition to its influence in Parliament, controls the party whips, the party machine and the civil service. This means that what has always been an elective dictatorship in theory, but one in which the component parts operate in practice to control one another, has become a machine in which one of those parts has come to exercise a predominant influence over the rest.

At the centre of the web sits the Prime Minister. There he sits with his hand on the lever of dissolution, which he is free to operate at any moment of his choice. In selecting that moment he is able, with the Chancellor of the Exchequer, to manipulate the economy, so as to make it possible for things to appear for a time better than they really are.

1979

'THE INTERFERENCE WITH THE APPLICANTS' FREEDOM OF EXPRESSION WAS NOT JUSTIFIED'

O ne of the most important battles over press freedom took place in the 1970s. Around 10,000 children around the world had been born with deformities in the late 1950s and early '60s because their mothers had taken a sleeping pill, thalidomide, during pregnancy. In Britain, where there were more than 450 thalidomide children, the drug had been sold by Distillers, a company best known for its range of gins and whiskies.

In October 1972, the *Sunday Times* prepared a detailed article on how Distillers had come to sell a drug that proved to have such awful side-effects. The Attorney General issued a writ against the *Sunday Times* to prevent publication. His reason was that a number of parents were still seeking compensation from Distillers, and publication could prejudice future court hearings. In July 1973, the House of Lords ruled that publication would, indeed, constitute contempt – not because the article might influence a jury (the compensation cases were heard by judges sitting alone), but because it might undermine the public's confidence in the administration of justice.

Harold Evans, the editor of the *Sunday Times*, took the case to the European Court of Human Rights in Strasbourg, arguing that the Law Lords had infringed his right to freedom of expression, enshrined in Article 10 (2) of the European Convention on Human Rights. This proved to be a long and expensive process. First, the European Commission of Human Rights had to decide whether the case should go forward to a full hearing of the Court. In May 1977, they did so. For good measure, they added the text of the banned article as an appendix to their ruling, which meant it was available for immediate publication. Finally, in April 1979, the Court delivered its ruling – a narrow 11:9 victory for both the *Sunday Times* and the freedom of the press.

THE RULING OF THE EUROPEAN COURT OF HUMAN RIGHTS ON THE *SUNDAY TIMES* ARTICLE ON THALIDOMIDE

Held, by the plenary Court by 11 votes to 9, that the interference with the applicants' freedom of expression was not justified under Article 10 (2) which permits such restrictions 'as are prescribed by law and are necessary in a democratic society . . . for maintaining the authority and impartiality of the judiciary', the Court deciding that, though prescribed by law and for the purpose of maintaining the authority of the judiciary, the restriction was not justified by a 'pressing social need' and could not therefore be regarded as 'necessary' within the meaning of Article 10 (2). Accordingly, there had been a violation of Article 10.

The reasons why the draft article was regarded as objectionable by the House of Lords all fell within the aim of maintaining the authority of the judiciary, so that the interference with the applicants' freedom of expression had an aim that was legitimate under Article 10 (2).

In the expression 'necessary in a democratic society', the word 'necessary' was not synonymous with 'indispensable', neither had it the flexibility of such expressions as 'inadmissible', 'ordinary', 'useful', 'reasonable' or 'desirable', but it implied the existence of a pressing social need.

Article 10 (2) left to States a margin of appreciation, given both to legislators and to bodies called upon to interpret and apply the laws in force, but that power was not unlimited, the Court having the final ruling on whether a restriction was reconcilable with Article 10.

The Court's supervision was not limited merely to ascertaining whether a State exercised its discretion reasonably, carefully and in good faith.

The scope of the domestic power of appreciation was not identical as regards each of the aims listed in Article 10 (2), so that while State authorities were, for example, in a better position to determine a question as to the 'protection of morals', the same could not be said of the far more objective notion of the 'authority . . . of the judiciary', resulting in a more extensive European supervision and correspondingly less discretionary power of appreciation.

Although contempt of court was peculiar to common law countries and the concluding words of Article 10 (2) might have been designed to cover such a concept, the words provided only that the general aims of the contempt law should be considered legitimate, not every detail of them, so that the test of 'necessity' still fell to be applied in a particular case.

It could not be concluded that the injunction was 'unnecessary' simply because it could or would not have been granted under a different legal system: the Convention did not require absolute uniformity and States remained free to choose the measures which they considered appropriate.

It was necessary to decide whether the 'interference' complained of corresponded to a 'pressing social need', whether it was 'proportionate to the legitimate aim pursued', and whether the reasons given by the national authorities to justify it were 'relevant and sufficient under Article 10 (2)'.

Publication of the article would not have added much to the pressure already on Distillers to settle out of court on better terms.

Since the proposed article was couched in moderate terms and did not present just one side of the evidence, its publication would not have had adverse consequences for the 'authority of the judiciary'.

The Courts could not operate in a vacuum: while they were the forum for settling disputes, this did not mean that there could be no prior discussion of disputes elsewhere, It was incumbent on the mass media to impart information and ideas concerning matters that came before the courts just as in other areas of public interest.

It was not sufficient that the interference belonged to that class of exceptions listed in Article 10 (2), nor that it was imposed because its subject-matter fell within a particular category or was caught by a legal rule formulated in general or absolute terms, but the Court had to be satisfied that it was necessary having regard to the facts and circumstances of the specific case.

The thalidomide disaster was a matter of undisputed public concern and Article 10 guaranteed not only the freedom of the press but also the right of the public to be properly informed.

The families of numerous victims of the tragedy had a vital interest in knowing all the underlying facts, which could be denied them only if it appeared absolutely certain that their diffusion would have presented a threat to the 'authority of the judiciary'.

In view of all the circumstances, the interference did not correspond to a social need sufficiently pressing to outweigh the public interest in freedom of expression; the reasons for the restraint were not therefore sufficient under Article 10 (2); it was not proportionate to the legitimate aim pursued; and it was not necessary in a democratic society for maintaining the authority of the judiciary. Accordingly, Article 10 had been violated.

The *Sunday Times* was unable to celebrate its victory in print: the paper was off the streets at the time because of a long-running dispute with its printers.

However, its campaign for greater compensation for the thalidomide children had long since succeeded in shaming Distillers into paying £20 million to the affected families – ten times its original offer. Distillers' successor company, Diageo, subsequently agreed to make further payments on top of that.

1986

'You see, Bernard, you're the perfect balanced sample'

The television series *Yes Minister* and *Yes, Prime Minister* were originally broadcast between 1980 and 1988. Written by Antony Jay and Jonathan Lynn, they satirised life in Whitehall. Their central characters were Jim Hacker, initially Minister for Administrative Affairs and later prime minister, and Sir Humphrey Appleby, Hacker's Permanent Secretary, and later his Cabinet Secretary. Each episode explored the tensions between Hacker, who had formal power, and Appleby, who manoeuvred to wield real power. Caught between them, with divided loyalties, was Bernard Woolley, Hacker's Principal Private Secretary.

The books that accompanied the series stuck closely to the scripts, but were presented as memoirs published years later, in 2022. In this extract from *Yes, Prime Minister* (actually published in 1986), 'Sir' Bernard Woolley recalls how Appleby proposed undermining Hacker's plan to announce on television his intention to reintroduce national service – an idea that Hacker believed was popular with the public. As well as satirising Whitehall, this scene shows how opinion polls, which ought to enhance the democratic process, can be used to mock it.

ANTONY JAY AND JONATHAN LYNN: *Yes, Prime Minister*

Sir Bernard Woolley recalls:

Humphrey Appleby was not at all pleased that I had failed to have Hacker's speech watered down, in spite of my best efforts. He asked me to drop in on him in the Cabinet Office, to discuss the situation. He was most interested in the party opinion poll, which I had seen as an insuperable obstacle to changing the Prime Minister's mind.

His solution was simple: have another opinion poll, one that would show that the voters were *against* bringing back National Service. I was somewhat *naïf* in those days. I did not understand how the voters could be both for it and against it. Dear old Humphrey showed me how it's done.

The secret is that when the Man In The Street is approached by a nice young attractive lady with a clipboard he is asked a *series* of questions. Naturally the Man In The Street wants to make a good impression and doesn't want to make a fool of himself. So the market researcher asks questions designed to elicit *consistent* answers.

Humphrey demonstrated the system on me. 'Mr Woolley, are you worried about the rise in crime among teenagers?'

'Yes,' I said.

'Do you think there is a lack of discipline and vigorous training in our comprehensive schools?'

'Yes.'

'Do you think young people welcome some structure and leadership in their lives?'

'Yes.'

'Do they respond to a challenge?'

'Yes.'

Might you be in favour of reintroducing National Service?'

'Yes.'

Well, naturally I said yes. One could hardly have said anything else without looking inconsistent. Then what happens is that the opinion poll publishes only the last question and answer.

Of course, the reputable polls didn't conduct themselves like that. But there weren't too many of those. Humphrey suggested that we commission a new survey. Not for the party but for the Ministry of Defence. We did so. He invented the questions there and then.

'Mr Woolley, are you worried about the danger of war?'

'Yes,' I said, quite honestly.

'Are you unhappy about the growth of armaments?'

'Yes.'

'Do you think there's a danger in giving young people guns and teaching them how to kill?'

'Yes.'

'Do you think it is wrong to force people to take up arms against their will?'

'Yes.'

'Would you oppose the reintroduction of National Service?'

I'd said 'yes' even before I'd realised it, d'you see?

Humphrey was crowing with delight. 'You see, Bernard,' he said to me, 'you're the perfect balanced sample.'

1987

'IF WE ACCEPT THE MOTION, WE WOULD BE PLACING THE HOUSE OF COMMONS FOR EVER UNDER THE EFFECTIVE CONTROL OF THE GOVERNMENT'

In 1986, Duncan Campbell, a journalist on the *New Statesman*, made a film for the BBC about a British signals satellite called Zircon that was due to be launched the following year to intercept radio and telephone signals, mainly from the Soviet Union and Eastern Europe. The cost of the project was £500 million – but Parliament and the public had not been told about it.

Once the film was made, nervous BBC executives approached the government and sought its advice. The Ministry of Defence demanded that the programme be shelved in order to protect national security. The BBC complied. The *New Statesman* acted differently and published Campbell's story. A few days later, the Special Branch raided the offices of the *New Statesman* in London and the BBC in Glasgow (Campbell's film had been made for BBC Scotland).

A number of (mainly Labour) MPs were outraged, and planned a viewing of a tape of the programme in a committee room at the House of Commons. The Speaker, Bernard Weatherill, banned it. An emergency debate on this ban was held on 27 January. Because events had moved quickly, Labour MPs had not had time to put down on the order paper an amendment to the government motion which backed the Speaker's decision.

Tony Benn was virtually alone at first in believing that the government could be defeated. He submitted what became known as a 'manuscript amendment' – so-called because he simply wrote it down on a piece of paper – which called for the issue to be referred to the Committee of Privileges. To his credit, and to some surprise, the Speaker accepted Benn's amendment for debate.

TONY BENN'S SPEECH ON THE ZIRCON AFFAIR

I am grateful to you, Mr Speaker, for allowing me to put before the House the manuscript amendment standing in my name that would transfer the matter to the Committee of Privileges. The issue that we are discussing is a fundamental constitutional one of the relationship of the Commons, Members of Parliament and the electors on the one hand; and the Executive and the judiciary on the other.

I do not believe that there is any precedent for the ruling that you gave, Mr Speaker. I have searched carefully through 'Erskine May' and I can find no precedent. I have cited before, and will cite again, the words of Mr Speaker Lenthall. On 4 January 1642 the King came to the Commons to seize the five Members. Mr Speaker Lenthall, described as 'a man of timorous nature', knelt and said:

'May it please your Majesty, I have neither eyes to see nor tongue to speak in this place but as the House is pleased to direct me, whose servant I am here.'

That was the precedent. It could be argued that if it was not in relation to five hon. Members and the King that precedent would not apply. However, we have taken it, ever since, as a statement of your role. Now when a new Speaker is elected he goes to the other place to claim the ancient privileges of the House.

I am sorry to go back to the texts, but people may not always appreciate their importance. In 1688 the 9th article of the Bill of Rights stated:

'That the freedom of speech, and debates or proceedings in Parliament, ought not to be impeached or questioned in any Court or place out of Parliament.'

Hon. Members may ask whether a film shown somewhere else in the Chamber can be described as a proceeding in Parliament. Fortunately, we have a precedent for that as well. In 1938 Duncan Sandys, a Member of the House and also a member of the Territorial Army, received from a colleague in the Territorial Army information that there were defects in the air defence of London. He tabled a question and the person from whom he got the information was charged under the Official Secrets Act 1911. Duncan Sandys came to the House to appeal to the House to protect him by way of privilege and the person who gave him the information. I shall quote from 'Erskine May', page 93, commenting on the Committee that examined the Sandys case:

'Cases may easily be imagined of communication between one Member and another or between a Member and a Minister, so closely relating to some matter pending in, or expected to be brought before the House, that, although they do not take place in the Chamber or committee room, they form part of the business of the House.'

That was one of the most important judgments reached by the House. It entrenched the right of its Members to receive information from someone who is not a Member of the House even when that information is in respect of the security of the country.

I ask the House to ask itself these important questions. First is it right for the Government to engage in major military projects without telling Parliament? The House does not want technical details. However, Parliament must know the general nature of major defence projects, their purpose and their cost. If Parliament does not know that it is abdicating its responsibilities.

The second question is whether it is right that Ministers should be able to go to any court to use the magic words 'national security' as the basis for a court injunction. In a democracy it is for the House and electors to decide what is in the national interest. And when there is a general election, it is the people's judgment as to what is in the national interest that counts. It is not for civil servants, generals, scientists or Ministers to determine what is national security.

The third question that I would like the House to consider is whether it is right that any Speaker – so as not to personalise it – hearing news of an injunction that has been issued should be able, without the explicit and specific authority of the House, to prevent hon. Members from seeking available information that would assist Parliament in its work of holding Governments to account.

The next question is whether we should accept and confirm a limit on our freedom as Members of Parliament that would assist the concealment of any matter by any Government by the use of national security and injunctions. Is it the case that the House could ever allow the courts or a magistrate to send policemen into the Palace, where already a film may not be shown, to discover the source of information of a Member who might be contemplating a parliamentary question?

If we accept the [Government's] motion, we would be placing the House of Commons and Members of Parliament for ever under the effective control of the Government, in that Ministers could bring an injunction, the court could accede to that injunction and – nobody would wish this less than you, Mr Speaker – Mr Speaker would become an agent of the Minister and his injunction and the court that upheld it, to enforce upon Members the denial of the rights for which we were elected. I cannot believe, knowing you Mr Speaker, that it would be your wish to be remembered as a 'counter-Lenthall' whose protection did not extend to hon. Members in this position.

I should like to make a final comment as an old Member of the House. We all take children and visitors round the House. We tell them that we keep Black Rod out. We tell them that the House decides on its own business before it gives attention to the Gracious Speech. We tell them about the five Members. Those are not meaningless rituals. They are reminders of monumental struggles to build democracy against tyranny. In 36 years in the House I cannot recall a debate as important as this and I am grateful to you, Mr Speaker, for allowing my manuscript amendment to be put on the Order Paper tonight along with the motion and the other amendments before us.

By the end of the debate, such was the mood of MPs in all parties that both the Labour and Conservative front benches accepted Benn's amendment. Thus Benn secured a vital principle: that the House should decide for itself what it can and cannot find out, whatever the government or courts may wish. That principle survived, even though the Committee of Privileges subsequently ruled that the film should not be shown at Westminster. It was, however, shown in a building nearby. Years later, Weatherill said that Benn's 'single speech totally swung the House of Commons on that issue. It is my best example of a single speech totally changing the view of other Members.'

As for the BBC, its top management faced blistering criticism from the Left (for agreeing to shelve the programme) and the Right (for allowing it to be made and then failing to keep it under wraps). Two days after the debate, the BBC's Director-General, Alasdair Milne, was summarily sacked. The BBC eventually broadcast Campbell's film in September 1988 – after the Zircon project itself had been cancelled for being too expensive.

1987

'THEY LIVE IN A FREE COUNTRY, BUT THEY DO NOT FEEL FREE'

Of all the attempts to challenge Thatcherism at the height of Margaret Thatcher's powers, Neil Kinnock's speech to the Welsh Labour Party in Llandudno shortly before the 1987 general election is, justly, the best remembered. Not only did its rhetoric soar, it also contained a clear exposition of the case for saying that liberty is enhanced, not diminished, by state provision and greater social equality.

Kinnock had become Labour Party leader in 1983, following Labour's worst post-war defeat at the hands of Thatcher's Conservatives. The most famous line in his speech – 'Why am I the first Kinnock in a thousand generations to be able to get to university?' – did not appear in the text circulated in advance; Kinnock extemporised this passage in order to emphasise the link between collective provision and individual freedom.

NEIL KINNOCK'S SPEECH TO THE WELSH LABOUR PARTY CONFERENCE

Strength is care with compassion – the practical action that is needed to help people lift themselves to their full stature. That's real care – it is not soft or weak. It is tough and strong. But where do we get the strength to provide that care? We co-operate, we collect together, we co-ordinate so that everyone can contribute and everyone can benefit, everyone has responsibilities, everyone has rights. It is called collective strength, collective care. And its whole purpose is individual freedom.

When we speak of collective strength and collective freedom, collectively achieved, we are not fulfilling that nightmare that Mrs Thatcher tries to paint, and all her predecessors have tried to saddle us with. We're not talking about uniformity; we're not talking about regimentation; we're not talking about *conformity* – that's their creed. The uniformity of the dole queue; the regimentation of the unemployed young and their compulsory work schemes. The *conformity* of people who will work in conditions, and take orders, and accept pay *because* of mass unemployment that they would laugh at in a free society with full employment. That kind of freedom for the individual, that kind of liberty can't be secured by most of the people for most of the time if they're just left to themselves, isolated, stranded, with their whole life chances depending on luck!

Why am I the first Kinnock in a thousand generations to be able to get to university? Why is Glenys the first woman in her family in a thousand generations to be able to get to university? Was it because all our predecessors were thick? Did they lack talent, those people who could sing and play and write and recite poetry? Those people who could make wonderful, beautiful things with their hands? Those people who could dream dreams, see visions. Why didn't they get it? Was it because they were weak? Those people who could work eight hours underground and then come up and play football, weak those women who could survive eleven child-bearings? Were they weak? Those people who could stand with their backs and legs straight and face the people who control their lives, the ones who owned their workplaces and tried to own them, tell them 'No, I won't take your orders'. Were they weak? Does anybody really think that they didn't get what we had because they didn't have the talent or the strength or the endurance or the commitment?

Of course not. It was because there was no platform upon which they could stand; no arrangement for their neighbours to subscribe to their welfare; no method by which communities could translate their desires for those individuals into provision for those individuals. And now, Mrs Thatcher, by dint of privatisation, and means test, and deprivation, and division, wants to nudge us back into the situation where everybody can either stand on their own two feet or live on their knees. That's what this election is all about as she parades her vision and values, and we choose to contest them as people with roots in this country, with a future only in this country, with pride in this country. People who know that if we are to have real and sustained individual liberty in this country it requires the collective effort of the whole community.

I think of the youngsters I meet. Three, four, five years out of school. Never had a job. And they say to me, 'Do you think we'll ever work?' They live in a free country, but they do not feel free. I think of the fifty-five-year-old woman I meet who is waiting to go into hospital, her whole existence clouded by pain. She lives in a free country, but she does not feel free. And I think of the old couple who spend months of the winter afraid to turn up the heating, who stay at home because they are afraid to go out after dark, whose lives are turned into a crisis by the need to buy a new pair of shoes. They live in a free country – indeed, they're of the generation that *fought* for a free country – but they do not feel free. How can they – and millions like them – have their individual freedom if there is not collective provision?

Kinnock's speech did little immediate good: one month later, Labour still lost the general election heavily. But while Kinnock survived as party leader for another five years, his words derailed the ambitions of one American politician. In September 1987, Joe Biden was seeking the nomination as the presidential candidate of America's Democrats. In one speech he said:

I started thinking as I was coming over here, why is it that Joe Biden is the first in his family ever to go a university? Why is it that my wife is the first in her family to ever go to college? Is it because our fathers and mothers were not bright? Is it because they didn't work hard? My ancestors who worked in the coal mines of northeast Pennsylvania and would come after 12 hours and play football for four hours? It's because they didn't have a platform on which to stand.

This was not the first time that Biden had adapted Kinnock's hastily scribbled words, but previously he had acknowledged the source. This time he did not. He was accused of plagiarism, and his campaign quickly collapsed. Twenty-one years later, Biden became Barack Obama's running mate and ended up as Vice President. By then, he and Kinnock had become firm friends.

1988

'WE HAVE NOT SUCCESSFULLY ROLLED BACK THE FRONTIERS OF THE STATE IN BRITAIN, ONLY TO SEE THEM REIMPOSED AT A EUROPEAN LEVEL'

Four decades after Churchill proposed that a United States of Europe should emerge from the ashes of the Second World War, Margaret Thatcher proposed a very different vision: a Europe of sovereign nation states choosing to co-operate, rather than pooling their sovereignty within the European Community.

Two years earlier, she had signed Britain up to the single market, which would allow goods, services and people to move freely throughout the Community. Jacques Delors, the President of the European Commission, wished to go further and build a federal Europe which added a single currency and a common defence policy to the single market. Thatcher opposed this, and set out her reasons in these excerpts from her speech to the College of Europe at Bruges, in Belgium, on 20 September 1988.*

MARGARET THATCHER: THE 'BRUGES SPEECH'

Mr Chairman, you have invited me to speak on the subject of Britain and Europe. Perhaps I should congratulate you on your courage. If you believe some of the things said and written about my views on Europe, it must seem rather like inviting Genghis Khan to speak on the virtues of peaceful coexistence!

I want to start by disposing of some myths about my country, Britain, and its relationship with Europe. And to do that I must say something about the identity of Europe itself. Europe is not the creation of the Treaty of Rome. Nor is the European idea the property of any group or institution.

---

*   Reproduced with permission from http://www.margaretthatcher.org/, the official website of the Margaret Thatcher Foundation. The full text is available there.

We British are as much heirs to the legacy of European culture as any other nation. Our links to the rest of Europe, the continent of Europe, have been the dominant factor in our history. For three hundred years we were part of the Roman Empire and our maps still trace the straight lines of the roads the Romans built. Our ancestors – Celts, Saxons and Danes – came from the continent.

Too often the history of Europe is described as a series of interminable wars and quarrels. Yet from our perspective today surely what strikes us most is our common experience. For instance, the story of how Europeans explored and colonised and – yes, without apology – civilised much of the world is an extraordinary tale of talent, skill and courage.

The European Community is one manifestation of that European identity. But it is not the only one. We must never forget that East of the Iron Curtain peoples who once enjoyed a full share of European culture, freedom and identity have been cut off from their roots. We shall always look on Warsaw, Prague and Budapest as great European cities.

The European Community belongs to all its members. It must reflect the traditions and aspirations of all its members. This evening I want to set out some guiding principles for the future which I believe will ensure that Europe does succeed, not just in economic and defence terms but also in the quality of life and the influence of its peoples.

My first guiding principle is this: willing and active cooperation between independent sovereign states is the best way to build a successful European Community. To try to suppress nationhood and concentrate power at the centre of a European conglomerate would be highly damaging and would jeopardise the objectives we seek to achieve.

I am the first to say that on many great issues the countries of Europe should try to speak with a single voice. I want to see us work more closely on the things we can do better together than alone. Europe is stronger when we do so, whether it be in trade, in defence, or in our relations with the rest of the world. But working more closely together does not require power to be centralised in Brussels or decisions to be taken by an appointed bureaucracy. We have not successfully rolled back the frontiers of the state in Britain, only to see them reimposed at a European level, with a European superstate exercising a new dominance from Brussels.

My second guiding principle is this: Community policies must tackle present problems in a practical way, however difficult that may be. If we cannot reform those Community policies which are patently wrong or ineffective and which are rightly causing public disquiet, then we shall not get the public's support for the Community's future development. We must continue to pursue policies which relate supply more closely to market requirements, and which will reduce overproduction and limit costs.

Of course, we must protect the villages and rural areas which are such an important part of our national life – but not by the instrument of agricultural prices. Tackling these problems requires political courage. The Community will only damage itself in the eyes of its own people and the outside world, if that courage is lacking.

My third guiding principle is the need for Community policies which encourage enterprise. If Europe is to flourish and create the jobs of the future, enterprise is the key. The aim of a Europe open to enterprise is the moving force behind the creation of the Single European Market by 1992. By getting rid of barriers, by making it possible for companies to operate on a Europewide scale, we can best compete with the United States, Japan and the other new economic powers emerging in Asia and elsewhere. And that means action to free markets, action to widen choice, action to reduce government intervention.

Our aim should not be more and more detailed regulation from the centre: it should be to deregulate and to remove the constraints on trade. It is the same with the frontiers between our countries. Of course we must make it easier for goods to pass through frontiers. Of course we must make it easier for our people to travel throughout the Community. But it is a matter of plain commonsense that we cannot totally abolish frontier controls if we are also to protect our citizens from crime and stop the movement of drugs, of terrorists, and of illegal immigrants.

My fourth guiding principle is that Europe should not be protectionist. The expansion of the world economy requires us to continue the process of removing barriers to trade and to do so in the multilateral negotiations in the GATT. It would be a betrayal if, while breaking down constraints on trade within Europe, the Community were to erect greater external protection. We must ensure that our approach to world trade is consistent with the liberalisation we preach at home.

We have a responsibility to give a lead on this, a responsibility which is particularly directed towards the less developed countries. They need not only aid; more than anything they need improved trading opportunities if they are to gain the dignity of growing economic strength and independence.

My last guiding principle concerns the most fundamental issue, the European countries' role in defence. Europe must continue to maintain a sure defence through NATO. There can be no question of relaxing our efforts even though it means taking difficult decisions and meeting heavy costs.

Let us never forget that our way of life, our vision, and all that we hope to achieve is secured not by the rightness of our cause but by the strength of our defence. On this we must never falter, never fail.

Let Europe be a family of nations, understanding each other better, appreciating each other more, doing more together but relishing our national identity no less than our common European endeavour.

Let us have a Europe which plays its full part in the wider world, which looks outward not inward, and which preserves that Atlantic Community – that Europe on both sides of the Atlantic – which is our noblest inheritance and our greatest strength.

Thatcher's speech inspired the foundation of the 'Bruges Group' of Eurosceptics. The Group endured, but Thatcher's premiership did not. In October 1990 she returned from a summit of European Community leaders in Rome, having been alone in her opposition to plans for a single European currency. Reporting back to the House of Commons, she gave her reaction to this proposal and to other plans for greater European integration: 'No, no, no.' Two days later, Sir Geoffrey Howe resigned as deputy prime minister, an event that prompted Michael Heseltine to challenge Thatcher for the Conservative leadership. Heseltine succeeded in toppling her, but not in winning the prize for himself. On 27 November, John Major won the vote to become party leader and prime minister.

1993

'WE SHOULD TRUST THE PEOPLE'

I n February 1992, the leaders of the European Community agreed to 'The Treaty of the European Union' – universally known as the Maastricht Treaty, after the Dutch town where it was signed. This paved the way to the single currency; included a 'social chapter', which set out workers' rights; increased the powers of the European Parliament; expanded the Community's role in industrial, transport and educational issues; and changed the name of the Community to the European Union. However, John Major, Britain's prime minister, negotiated opt-outs, which meant that the UK did not have to implement the social chapter or join the single currency.

Britain's Parliament debated the treaty at great length. The fiercest arguments took place within the Conservative Party. The party was re-elected, albeit with a sharply reduced majority, in April 1992, committed to ratifying the treaty. However, a minority of Conservative MPs opposed it. Part of their case was that the treaty should not be ratified without a referendum. This issue came to a head in the debate on 21 April 1993. Two of the most powerful speeches were by Richard Shepherd, a Eurosceptic backbencher, and Douglas Hurd, the Foreign Secretary. Peter Luff and Ian Taylor, who intervened in Shepherd's speech, were pro-European Conservative MPs.

THE MAASTRICHT DEBATE

> **MR. RICHARD SHEPHERD (ALDRIDGE-BROWNHILLS):** Before I became a Member of the House of Commons, it was unthinkable to me that we would be arguing about a transference from democratic government to new arrangements. That is why passion, anger, apprehension and fear are felt by many right hon. and hon. Members and by many other people throughout the country.
>
> Our constitution is founded on the democratic principle, which is government of the people, by the people, for the people, but that is not the system envisaged under the Maastricht treaty. It is, in fact, a system almost of

'arrangements', whereby we transfer decisions over whole areas of life – areas that have been subject to the decisions of the House and have been absolute in that term, subject to such time as we wish to repeal or reform them.

The Bill demonstrates that the British Government are proposing that the British people enter a new political state. It is as simple as that. They give no reasons as to why this is absolutely essential. They indicate that it is in the national interest, but will not give details. The old verity of democratic control – whereby the people, when they voted, could change Governments and thereby change laws – is lost in large measure under the provisions of the Bill.

I feel old fashioned, standing here and trying to propose a new clause called 'Ascertainment of national opinion' – what I would call 'Trust the people.' We cannot doubt that transferring control over economic and monetary policies to an unelected central bank somewhere else means that the institution of government becomes a Council of Ministers, meeting in secret, to pass laws on these matters at the sole suggestion of the centralising bureaucracy – the single institutional framework, as it is called – that permeates the new arrangements. We should use the old tests of democracy – 'How do I change the law?' That is a simple question which we have taken for granted over the years. It is so evident and so obvious – you change your Member of Parliament or convince him by argument. Ultimately, if your Member of Parliament is unsympathetic to your argument, you campaign, argue and reason as part of a democratic debate, which has an outcome in the laws under which you live.

Our rule of law has that as its essential trust: it expects obedience. We in the House all expect obedience to the law, and we can demand it on the basis that there is a proper democratic route by which we can change the law. It is the very basis of our understanding of democracy.

That is at issue here. The debates on the Bill have, if they have done nothing else, demonstrated very clearly the framework of the new constitutional arrangements. I can think of no system of democratic government on earth that would take away the rights of ordinary people, without explanation, and ultimately without regard to their view in the matter.

That is the purpose behind the new clause – to return the question to our own fellow electors. None of us is different from them. We have the privilege to represent them, but the powers that we exercise are their powers. I am now a low Tory – I have had the benefit of high Toryism – but this is a people's democracy. This is our Parliament, which will determine the framework of our lives.

MR. PETER LUFF (WORCESTER): I respect the integrity and sincerity of my hon. Friend's belief that the issue before us is the single most important issue facing the country, and therefore deserves a referendum. However, in my constituency a referendum is already being conducted. There are six questions, not one, on the ballot paper. The first is indeed about Maastricht; another is about the principle of a referendum; another is about a freedom of information Bill. There is also a question about the use of urban rather than rural land for development, and the last two are about live animal transport and hunting with hounds. I have to tell my hon. Friend that the person organising the referendum believes that the last of those six questions is the single most important issue confronting the people of this country, and that is why the referendum is being organised. Does my hon. Friend not accept that he is letting a dangerous genie out of the bottle by proposing a referendum?

MR. SHEPHERD: Clearly my hon. Friend must pursue his own arguments with his own electorate, but I find it deeply disturbing if someone says that the power of the vote is something trivial, and that its passing away is of no consequence. The heart of the matter is that we are trying to take away irrevocably and irreversibly the traditional strengths that our democratic constitution has had.

MR. IAN TAYLOR (ESHER): It increasingly appears that the difference between us is an assessment of how best to look after the interests of our constituents. The effect of the Maastricht treaty is to redefine some of the commitments that we as a country made a considerable time ago, when we accepted that, because sovereignty was not like virginity, which one either has or does not have, but was a multi-layered concept, looking after the interests of our constituents often meant that we as Members of Parliament could have more influence by working together within the Community institutions, rather than by attempting to ignore everything else and saying that only what happened in this place could protect the interests of our constituents.

In my view, Maastricht does not mark a fundamental departure. It marks a continuation of what we set out to do. Indeed, it provides various means of strengthening the process.

MR. SHEPHERD: That is the conveyor-belt argument and I look forward to challenging my hon. Friend in the referendum campaigns around the country. We should trust the people. Let them decide the difference between the two arguments. At the end of the day, that is all I am saying. We are talking about powers that we are moving. They are not my powers or the powers of the House. This House is the symbol of the sovereignty of the people. Those who have the vote and who send us here will be diminished by this measure. Of itself, that is enough to send it back and have a referendum. We should trust the people.

MR. HURD: Tonight's argument is full of echoes from the past. It started many years ago. In 1972, Parliament passed the European Communities Act. Thus, 20 years ago Parliament agreed a system of European lawmaking which we have practised ever since as members of the Community. As I listened to my hon. Friend the Member for Aldridge-Brownhills when, in an eloquent and remarkable speech, he moved the new clause, the echoes were very clear. The arguments, almost the words, were those used by another eloquent and remarkable parliamentary orator, the former Member of Parliament for South Down [Enoch Powell]. The echoes were unmistakable.

If there were ever a case for holding a referendum on Europe, that case was stronger at the time of entry than it has ever been since, yet when the Conservative party in opposition in 1975 had to define its position it came out against a referendum, and it was right to do so. The reasons were spelt out on 11 March of that year by the leader of the party. It was her first major parliamentary speech as Leader of the Opposition. I joined almost all of my party, including many right hon. and hon. Friends here today, and went into the Lobby to vote against the holding of a referendum on our membership of the Community.

As Parliament is sovereign, it is clear that it could decide to hold a referendum, which it could either accept or reject. It could certainly choose, as it has before, to ask for advice from those who sent us here. But I return to the fact that we owe our constituents our judgment, and if we decline to exercise that judgment we are to some extent damaging the authority of Parliament.

I want now to consider the proposal for a referendum on this subject. We have contended throughout the debate that the treaty does not mark a fundamental constitutional shift. When we joined the European Community we joined a body with both an economic and a political dimension. The doctrine of the primacy of Community law that lies at the heart of so many understandable criticisms about the nature of the Community is a doctrine of 1972, not of the treaty of Maastricht.

The use of qualified majority voting is perhaps a test. It was not invented in the treaty of Maastricht. It is in the treaty of Rome. It received its greatest extension in the Single European Act. There was no referendum on that and precious little call for one.

The treaty of Maastricht adds to and, in some helpful ways, redefines and corrects the Single European Act and, I believe, is on the whole less constitutionally innovative than that Act. Of course the treaty provides for the three stages of economic and monetary union. I deal with that point because many hon. Members have stressed it. In respect of the third stage of economic and monetary union, the only stage where compulsion comes into it, the Government have specifically and successfully reserved the decision for the House of Commons.

Ratification of the treaty lies at the heart of our national interest: it is not an optional extra. We have made that point in the House at the cost of some criticism and discomfort. Governments are elected to govern and, in this case, to propose, just as Parliaments in the United Kingdom are elected to decide and, indeed, to dispose.

Let us consider what would happen if the series of new clauses were passed. I shall not dwell on what would have to happen immediately. There would have to be legislation. We would have to spend many hours, days, even weeks, working out the question, the date and how the various organisations would be financed. We would spend many more days not on substance but on procedure. I am not sure that that is what is expected of us.

Of course, all that work would be justified if my hon. Friend the Member for Aldridge-Brownhills were right and we proposed constitutional revolution and destruction. I hope that I have demonstrated that the treaty does not represent that.

The decision for Britain lies where it belongs – in the hands of the British Parliament. We are preparing, in an admittedly untidy, imperfect but I think lively way, for that decision with a thoroughness of parliamentary debate. It would be wrong and foolish to abandon or transfer the work. It would be a shirking of the responsibilities that we were given only a year ago, and it would be a blow to the standing of the House in years to come. We would be saying to our constituents, 'We have examined the matter, but we do not intend to take a decision. We have spent hours, days and weeks examining the issues and now it is over to you. We are going to throw the treaty, with all its diverse controversies and complications, into your laps to make of it what you will.' I agree with the principles set out by Lady Thatcher in 1975. It cannot be right to refuse to do our job, so it cannot be right to accept the new clauses.

◇ ◇ ◇

The government won the vote that night by 299 to 110, with most Labour MPs abstaining. The treaty was finally ratified in August 1993, but not before the Conservative rebels had come close to defeating the treaty; John Major was forced to make the issue a vote of confidence to secure ratification.

When Labour returned to power in 1997, it ended the opt-out on the social chapter, but was more wary about joining the single currency. Gordon Brown, the new Chancellor, effectively vetoed entry, which was backed by Tony Blair, the new prime minister.

As for the argument about the place of referendums in a parliamentary democracy, Labour went further than any previous major party in promising them. In fact, it promised up to six: one each in Scotland and Wales on devolution; one in London on the establishment of a new mayor and assembly; a set in England's regions on the establishment of elected regional assemblies; one on a new voting system for the House of Commons; and one on Europe's single currency, should the government wish Britain to join it.

The first three produced 'yes' majorities. The fourth, on regional assemblies, was abandoned after the first region, the North-East, voted 'no'; and the last two were never held. The government lost interest in electoral reform, and Brown's initial veto on joining the single currency effectively killed that issue. A further referendum was held in Northern Ireland, following the 1998 Good Friday Agreement. And a number of cities, towns and suburbs held referendums to decide whether to elect local mayors.

In 2005, Labour joined the Conservatives in promising a referendum on a new EU constitution, which had been proposed. But referendums in France and Holland both produced 'no' majorities, so the constitution was killed before the UK had the chance to vote. By then, the dam had been breached, for referendums had become a familiar feature of the UK's political landscape.

1995

'The people of Scotland want and deserve democracy'

In the 1970s, the Labour government proposed schemes for devolving power to Scotland and Wales. However, they failed to secure sufficient support at referendums held in March 1979: in Wales because a clear majority voted 'no'; in Scotland because the 'yes' vote, though greater than the 'no' vote, failed to secure the support of 40 per cent of all Scots electors, as Parliament had required.

In 1988, a group of prominent Scots came together to form a constitutional convention to work out a new plan for devolution. The initial committee included all the major political parties in Scotland except for the Conservative Party. However, the Scottish National Party withdrew early in 1989, on the grounds that the Convention did not share the party's view that the goal of the exercise was to achieve eventual independence. The Scottish Constitutional Convention deliberated for the next six years. As well as the Labour, Liberal Democrat and Green Parties, it also included representatives from (among others) the main Scottish Churches, local government, small businesses, trade unions, ethnic minorities and the Scottish Women's Forum. It issued its final report in November 1995.

Report of the Scottish Constitutional Convention

This report is about practical intent. It says: 'Here is what we are going to do,' not 'here is what we would like'. Those who seek inspirational home rule rhetoric are respectfully directed elsewhere, including to the Convention's own previous publications. We have moved on. We regard the argument in principle as compelling. The longing of the people of Scotland for their own Parliament rings clear and true every time opinion is sounded. We believe that the momentum for change is now too great to deny; and that a Scottish Parliament will soon be meeting for the first time in nearly three centuries.

What has been missing has been a practical scheme for bringing the Parliament into existence, and a hard-headed assessment of what it will be able to achieve. That is the gap which this report fills. This report shows that the Parliament can work, and it shows how. In doing so, it answers opponents who have tried to portray a Scottish Parliament as a pipe-dream, a fantasy which the Scots, unlike other peoples around the world, somehow cannot turn into reality.

The Convention has a diverse membership, as diverse as we could make it. Diversity and unanimity are not natural companions. It is the instinct of political parties to disagree with one another, and the instinct of civic groups like the churches, the trade unions and others to be impatient with the preoccupations of politicians. This has meant that a lot of time and effort has been required to arrive at the proposals in this document. But at the end of that process we have an agreed scheme which all the parties involved believe to be the best way forward for Scotland. The way in which that scheme has been hammered out is its strength, not a weakness.

THE CASE FOR CHANGE

The first and greatest reason for creating a Scottish Parliament is that the people of Scotland want and deserve democracy. Their will is powerful and clear. It has been expressed calmly and consistently over a period of decades, and has strengthened rather than diminished with the passing of time. In a responsive and effective democracy, this would be reason enough for change. But present constitutional circumstance denies Scotland responsive and effective democracy. That is the second reason for change.

Scotland approaches a new millennium facing a stark choice. It has a distinguished and distinctive structural heritage, evident in Scotland's legal system, its educational system, its social, cultural and religious traditions. These things are the very fabric of Scottish society, yet Scotland has come to lack democratic control over them. Their conduct is determined by a government for which few Scots voted, operating through a dense tangle of unelected quangos. These bodies now run Scotland's affairs across the board, from Scottish water to Scottish Opera. This is a democratic deficit which runs contrary to Scotland's distinct political identity and system. It is affecting relations with the rest of a United Kingdom in which most Scots wish to remain, and hampering Scotland's ability to make its voice heard in the world, particularly within a fast-developing European Union well attuned to such voices. Redressing the deficit is a matter of fairness and justice, and also of better government. A Scottish Parliament is the means of taking back control without turning our backs on our neighbours; of determining our own strategies; of facing the challenges of a new age in our own way.

A Scottish Parliament will be able to make a real difference to the prosperity of the Scottish people, and to the quality of the life they lead. No modern economy can be viewed in isolation from the others with which it is entwined by ties of trade and ownership – one reason why Scotland needs to remain within the United Kingdom, which is by far its biggest marketplace. But the Scottish economy can be differentiated from those of other parts of the UK, both in its strengths and in its weaknesses. Scotland has a relatively large export trade, for example, but one heavily dependent on a very narrow product base: chiefly computers and whisky. It has a prestigious and successful financial sector, but again skewed towards certain types of services. It has a long-standing difficulty in creating new growth companies and lasting jobs. It has to contend with the communications challenges inherent in a population distributed unevenly across a large land mass. UK economic policy has, hardly surprisingly, failed to address these circumstances closely, systematically or effectively. Scotland's Parliament, equipped with the sort of powers described in the pages that follow, will be able to do much better.

Much the same applies to the field of social welfare – a broad phrase, but the one that best describes the wide range of concerns which have so sharply distinguished the political will of Scotland in recent years. Scotland has consistently declared through the ballot box the wish for an approach to public policy which accords more closely with its collective and community traditions. The frustration which has arisen as that wish is disregarded should be a source of concern to all who hold democracy dear. Scotland's Parliament will provide the means for the will of the people of Scotland, however it may develop, to be acted upon. It will place power in their hands to determine the future course of Scots law and the administration of justice; to decide on the form and the delivery of public services like health, education and housing provision; to boost the development of Scotland's cultural and artistic life. These are matters that touch the lives of us all.

Democracy is a challenge as well as a right and a privilege. It bestows a culture of involvement, and therefore of responsibility. It does not allow blame to be shrugged off on others. The contrast with present public alienation from the processes and structures of government is both compelling and invigorating. There is every reason to expect that the people of Scotland, taking charge of their own destiny, will tackle the issues that confront them more effectively than has Westminster, acting remotely in their stead. There is every reason to believe that Scotland is more than equal to the challenge.

When Labour returned to power in 1997, it adopted the report's proposals for a Scottish Parliament and Executive virtually in their entirety – including the proportional voting system that the Convention recommended. A referendum in September 1997 produced a three-to-one majority for devolution; a second, subsidiary question produced a majority of almost two-to-one for the new Parliament having the power to vary income tax by up to 3p in the pound.

A referendum the following week in Wales for an elected Assembly, which would have some powers, but fewer than the Scottish Parliament, passed much more narrowly. The new Scottish Parliament and Welsh Assembly were elected for the first time in May 1999.

1997

'THE TIME HAS COME TO ENABLE PEOPLE TO ENFORCE THEIR RIGHTS AGAINST THE STATE IN THE BRITISH COURTS'

For almost half a century, since the Council of Europe adopted the European Convention on Human Rights in 1950, Britons had been able to go to court to enforce their rights under the Convention – but not a British court. They had to take their case to the European Court of Human Rights in Strasbourg. As the *Sunday Times*/thalidomide case showed, this was slow, cumbersome and expensive.

One of Labour's commitments in the 1997 general election was to incorporate the rights in the Convention into British law, so that people could enforce their rights in the British courts and no longer have to go to Strasbourg to seek redress. The Home Office published the White Paper 'Rights Brought Home' in October 1997.

WHITE PAPER: 'RIGHTS BROUGHT HOME'

The European Convention is not the only international human rights agreement to which the United Kingdom and other like-minded countries are party, but over the years it has become one of the premier agreements defining standards of behaviour across Europe. It was also for many years unique because of the system which it put in place for people from signatory countries to take complaints to Strasbourg and for those complaints to be judicially determined. These arrangements are by now well tried and tested. The rights and freedoms which are guaranteed under the Convention are ones with which the people of this country are plainly comfortable. They therefore afford an excellent basis for the Human Rights Bill which we are now introducing.

The constitutional arrangements in most continental European countries have meant that their acceptance of the Convention went hand in hand with its incorporation into their domestic law. In this country it was long believed that the rights and freedoms guaranteed by the Convention could be delivered under our common law. In the last two decades, however, there has been a growing awareness that it is not sufficient to rely on the common law and that incorporation is necessary.

The Liberal Democrat Peer, Lord Lester of Herne Hill QC, recently introduced two Bills on incorporation into the House of Lords (in 1994 and 1996). Before that, the then Conservative MP Sir Edward Gardner QC introduced a Private Member's Bill on incorporation into the House of Commons in 1987. At the time of introducing his Bill he commented on the language of the Articles in the Convention, saying: 'It is language which echoes right down the corridors of history. It goes deep into our history and as far back as Magna Carta' (Hansard, 6 February 1987, col.1224). In preparing this White Paper the Government has paid close attention to earlier debates and proposals for incorporation.

The Convention contains Articles which guarantee a number of basic human rights. They deal with the right to life (Article 2); torture or inhuman or degrading treatment or punishment (Article 3); slavery and forced labour (Article 4); liberty and security of person (Article 5); fair trial (Article 6); retrospective criminal laws (Article 7); respect for private and family life, home and correspondence (Article 8); freedom of thought, conscience and religion (Article 9); freedom of expression (Article 10); freedom of peaceful assembly and freedom of association, including the right to join a trade union (Article 11); the right to marry and to found a family (Article 12); and discrimination in the enjoyment of these rights and freedoms (Article 14).

The United Kingdom is also a party to the First Protocol to the Convention, which guarantees the right to the peaceful enjoyment of possessions (Article 1), the right to education (Article 2) and the right to free elections (Article 3).

When the United Kingdom ratified the Convention the view was taken that the rights and freedoms which the Convention guarantees were already, in substance, fully protected in British law. It was not considered necessary to write the Convention itself into British law, or to introduce any new laws in the United Kingdom in order to be sure of being able to comply with the Convention.

However, since its drafting nearly 50 years ago, almost all the States which are party to the European Convention on Human Rights have gradually incorporated it into their domestic law in one way or another.

The effect of non-incorporation on the British people is a very practical one. The rights, originally developed with major help from the United Kingdom Government, are no longer actually seen as British rights. And enforcing them takes too long and costs too much. It takes on average five years to get an action into the European Court of Human Rights once all domestic remedies have been exhausted; and it costs an average of £30,000. Bringing these rights home will mean that the British people will be able to argue for their rights in the British courts – without this inordinate delay and cost. It will also mean that the rights will be brought much more fully into the jurisprudence of the courts throughout the United Kingdom, and their interpretation will thus be far more subtly and powerfully woven into our law. And there will be another distinct benefit. British judges will be enabled to make a distinctively British contribution to the development of the jurisprudence of human rights in Europe.

Moreover, in the Government's view, the approach which the United Kingdom has so far adopted towards the Convention does not sufficiently reflect its importance and has not stood the test of time.

The most obvious proof of this lies in the number of cases in which the European Commission and Court have found that there have been violations of the Convention rights in the United Kingdom. It is plainly unsatisfactory that someone should be the victim of a breach of the Convention standards by the State yet cannot bring any case at all in the British courts, simply because British law does not recognise the right in the same terms as one contained in the Convention.

For individuals, and for those advising them, the road to Strasbourg is long and hard. Even when they get there, the Convention enforcement machinery is subject to long delays. This might be convenient for a government which was half-hearted about the Convention and the right of individuals to apply under it, since it postpones the moment at which changes in domestic law or practice must be made. But it is not in keeping with the importance which this Government attaches to the observance of basic human rights.

We therefore believe that the time has come to enable people to enforce their Convention rights against the State in the British courts, rather than having to incur the delays and expense which are involved in taking a case to the European Human Rights Commission and Court in Strasbourg and which may altogether deter some people from pursuing their rights. If legislation is enacted which is incompatible with the Convention, a ruling by the domestic courts to that effect will be much more direct and immediate than a ruling from the European Court of Human Rights. The

Government of the day, and Parliament, will want to minimise the risk of that happening.

Our aim is a straightforward one. It is to make more directly accessible the rights which the British people already enjoy under the Convention. In other words, to bring those rights home.

The Human Rights Act received royal assent in November 1998. In June 2006, David Cameron, the new leader of the Conservative Party, said a future Conservative government would consider repealing the Act. He told Andrew Marr in a BBC television interview:

We need a new approach. Let's look at getting rid of the Human Rights Act and say instead of that, instead of having an Act that imports a, if you like, foreign convention of rights into British law, why not try and write our own British Bill of rights and responsibilities, clearly and precisely into law, so we can have human rights with common sense.

Cameron's position reflected his party's Euroscepticism and was bolstered by his argument that the European Convention impeded Britain's ability to introduce effective laws to fight terrorism. However, Cameron did not make it clear whether he proposed withdrawing from the Convention or simply devising a new Act that would be consistent with it. Were Britain to remain a signatory to the Convention, Cameron's new Act would still be restricted in what measures could be taken on issues such as terrorism. On the other hand, withdrawal from the Convention would threaten the UK's ability to remain a member of the European Union. (Even though the Convention was drawn up by the Council of Europe rather than the EU, adherence to the Convention is a condition of membership of the EU.)

1998

'OUR TOTAL AND ABSOLUTE COMMITMENT TO EXCLUSIVELY DEMOCRATIC AND PEACEFUL MEANS OF RESOLVING DIFFERENCES ON POLITICAL ISSUES'

On 10 April – Good Friday – 1998, following three centuries of Protestant domination of Northern Ireland, three decades of terrorist violence and three days of intensive negotiations in Belfast, three of the four main political parties in the province agreed to a new system of devolution and power-sharing. The deal had been brokered by the former United States senator, George Mitchell, and Tony Blair, the United Kingdom's new prime minister, who led the final, intense negotiations, which also included Ireland's prime minister, Bertie Ahern. Arriving in Belfast for the final round of talks, Blair said: 'A day like today is not a day for soundbites, really.' He then uttered one of his most memorable soundbites: 'But I feel the hand of history upon our shoulders. I really do.'

The Good Friday Agreement established an Executive and an Assembly for Northern Ireland; they were to be so constructed that every major decision would require cross-community agreement. Of the major parties, only the Democratic Unionist Party declined to sign the agreement.

THE GOOD FRIDAY AGREEMENT

DECLARATION OF SUPPORT

1. We, the participants in the multi-party negotiations, believe that the agreement we have negotiated offers a truly historic opportunity for a new beginning.

2. The tragedies of the past have left a deep and profoundly regrettable legacy of suffering. We must never forget those who have died or been injured, and their families. But we can best honour them through a fresh start, in which we firmly dedicate ourselves to the achievement

of reconciliation, tolerance, and mutual trust, and to the protection and vindication of the human rights of all.

3. We are committed to partnership, equality and mutual respect as the basis of relationships within Northern Ireland, between North and South, and between these islands.

4. We reaffirm our total and absolute commitment to exclusively democratic and peaceful means of resolving differences on political issues, and our opposition to any use or threat of force by others for any political purpose, whether in regard to this agreement or otherwise.

5. We acknowledge the substantial differences between our continuing, and equally legitimate, political aspirations. However, we will endeavour to strive in every practical way towards reconciliation and rapprochement within the framework of democratic and agreed arrangements. We pledge that we will, in good faith, work to ensure the success of each and every one of the arrangements to be established under this agreement. It is accepted that all of the institutional and constitutional arrangements – an Assembly in Northern Ireland, a North/South Ministerial Council, implementation bodies, a British-Irish Council and a British-Irish Intergovernmental Conference and any amendments to British Acts of Parliament and the Constitution of Ireland – are interlocking and interdependent and that in particular the functioning of the Assembly and the North/South Council are so closely inter-related that the success of each depends on that of the other.

6. Accordingly, in a spirit of concord, we strongly commend this agreement to the people, North and South, for their approval.

CONSTITUTIONAL ISSUES

1. The participants endorse the commitment made by the British and Irish Governments that, in a new British-Irish Agreement replacing the Anglo-Irish Agreement, they will:

    i) recognise the legitimacy of whatever choice is freely exercised by a majority of the people of Northern Ireland with regard to its status, whether they prefer to continue to support the Union with Great Britain or a sovereign united Ireland;

    ii) recognise that it is for the people of the island of Ireland alone, by agreement between the two parts respectively and without external impediment, to exercise their right of self-determination on the basis of consent, freely and concurrently given, North and South, to bring about a united Ireland, if that is their wish, accepting that this right must be achieved and exercised with and subject to the agreement and consent of a majority of the people of Northern Ireland;

iii) acknowledge that while a substantial section of the people in Northern Ireland share the legitimate wish of a majority of the people of the island of Ireland for a united Ireland, the present wish of a majority of the people of Northern Ireland, freely exercised and legitimate, is to maintain the Union and, accordingly, that Northern Ireland's status as part of the United Kingdom reflects and relies upon that wish; and that it would be wrong to make any change in the status of Northern Ireland save with the consent of a majority of its people;

iv) affirm that if, in the future, the people of the island of Ireland exercise their right of self-determination on the basis set out in sections (i) and (ii) above to bring about a united Ireland, it will be a binding obligation on both Governments to introduce and support in their respective Parliaments legislation to give effect to that wish;

v) affirm that whatever choice is freely exercised by a majority of the people of Northern Ireland, the power of the sovereign government with jurisdiction there shall be exercised with rigorous impartiality on behalf of all the people in the diversity of their identities and traditions and shall be founded on the principles of full respect for, and equality of, civil, political, social and cultural rights, of freedom from discrimination for all citizens, and of parity of esteem and of just and equal treatment for the identity, ethos, and aspirations of both communities;

vi) recognise the birthright of all the people of Northern Ireland to identify themselves and be accepted as Irish or British, or both, as they may so choose, and accordingly confirm that their right to hold both British and Irish citizenship is accepted by both Governments and would not be affected by any future change in the status of Northern Ireland.

2.   The participants also note that the two Governments have accordingly undertaken in the context of this comprehensive political agreement, to propose and support changes in, respectively, the Constitution of

Ireland and in British legislation relating to the constitutional status of Northern Ireland.

On 22 May, referendums in both Northern Ireland and the Irish Republic approved the agreement. (In the Irish Republic, a referendum was needed to change the country's constitution to withdraw its historic claim to the whole of the island of Ireland.) Elections in June to the new Assembly led to the leaders of the two largest parties becoming First Minister and Deputy First Minister – respectively, David Trimble of the Ulster Unionists and Seamus Mallon of the Social Democratic and Labour Party. In time – far too slowly for many – the main paramilitary organisations, including the Provisional Irish Republican Army, satisfied an international monitoring group that they had put their weapons beyond use.

In the years that followed, Trimble's and Mallon's parties lost support. Friction within the Assembly led to its suspension by the British government and periods of direct rule. But in November 2007, devolution was restored, with Ian Paisley of the Democratic Unionist Party as First Minister and Martin McGuinness of Sinn Fein as his deputy. Despite their history of bitter enmity, they managed not just to coexist but also to form such a close working relationship that they were dubbed 'the Chuckle Brothers'.

1998

'TWO RAINY DAYS OUT OF FIFTEEN WOULD CERTAINLY BE AN ACCEPTABLE RISK FOR PLANNING A PICNIC'

I n the run-up to the 1997 general election, detailed discussions were held between leading Labour and Liberal Democrat politicians to agree a package of constitutional reforms. One of these was that a government commission should propose a new, more proportional way of electing MPs, and that its proposal should be put to a referendum 'within the first term of a new Parliament'.

Lord Jenkins was appointed to chair the commission. A Liberal Democrat, he had previously been a Labour Home Secretary and Chancellor of the Exchequer. He was also a major biographer and arguably the finest writer among top-flight politicians of the twentieth century. The report produced by his commission, published in October 1998, contains traces of Jenkins's distinct and elegant style.

THE 'JENKINS REPORT': THE REPORT OF THE INDEPENDENT COMMISSION ON THE VOTING SYSTEM

The remit we were given by the government in December 1997 was to recommend the best alternative 'system or combination of systems' to the existing commonly-called 'First Past The Post' [FPTP] system of election to the Westminster Parliament. In doing this we were asked to take into account four not entirely compatible 'requirements'. They were (i) broad proportionality; (ii) the need for stable government; (iii) an extension of voter choice; and (iv) the maintenance of a link between MPs and geographical constituencies.

It must be stressed that there is no question of our being asked to impose a new electoral system upon the British public. What we are asked to do is to recommend the best alternative system which will then be put to the British electorate in a referendum.

First the virtues of FPTP. It is the incumbent system. It is familiar to the public, votes are simple to count, and there is no surging popular agitation for change. It usually (though not invariably) leads to a one-party majority government. It thus enables electors, while nominally voting only for a local representative, in fact to choose the party they wish to form a government. It then leaves each member of Parliament with a direct relationship with a particular geographical area, on a basis of at least nominal equality in the sense that they are all elected in the same way. It also enables the electorate sharply and clearly to rid itself of an unwanted government.

These are by no means negligible virtues, partly springing out of and partly providing the reasons why the system has persisted for a long time in Britain (although not, in exactly its present form, as long as is widely thought).

The deficiencies of FPTP are principally the following, many of which derive from a natural tendency of the system to disunite rather than to unite the country. FPTP exaggerates movements of opinion, and when they are strong produces mammoth majorities in the House of Commons. While there is a considerable case for some clear cut results, there are also disadvantages to 'landslide' majorities, which do not in general conduce to the effective working of the House of Commons.

The FPTP system is peculiarly bad at allowing third party support to express itself. The same properties of FPTP tend to make it geographically divisive between the two leading parties. The 1997 election drove the Conservatives out of even minimal representation in Scotland, Wales and the big provincial cities of England. During the 1980s the Labour party was almost equally excluded from the more rapidly growing and prosperous southern half of the country.

The next criticism of FPTP is that it narrows the terrain over which the political battle is fought. The essential contest between the two main parties is fought over about a hundred or at the most 150 swingable constituencies. Outside the chosen arena voters [in 1997] were deprived of (or spared from) the visits of party leaders, saw few canvassers, and were generally treated (by both sides) as either irrevocably damned or sufficiently saved as to qualify for being taken for granted.

Although FPTP is often referred to as a 'majoritarian' system this is an increasing misnomer at the constituency level. To a growing extent it is a 'plurality' rather than a 'majority' system. It is a heavy count against a system which claims the special virtue of each MP being the chosen representative of his or her individual constituency if, in the case of nearly half of them, more of the electors voted against rather than for them.

There is also not merely the regular divergence from a majority but occasionally from a plurality in the country as a whole. In February 1974 the Conservatives had a lead of 0.7%, or 226,000, over Labour, but secured fewer seats. There was also the arguably equally perverse one of 1951, when the Conservatives, although polling 250,000 less votes than Labour, won a small overall majority of 17 seats.

It may be said that, if two elections out of the fifteen since the war have produced perverse results, that is in itself unfortunate, but it nevertheless means that thirteen have given the victory to the party with more votes than any other and that is on average not at all bad. However risks have to be measured by their consequences and not merely by their incidence. Two rainy days out of fifteen would certainly be an acceptable risk for the planning of a picnic, but an air journey which has two chances out of fifteen of ending in a crash would most certainly not be. A false election verdict might be regarded as about halfway between the two categories, which is well short of saying that two distorted results out of fifteen do not matter. Nonetheless, in fairness to FPTP, it should be noted that other electoral systems can also produce occasional irrational results.

The Commission's central recommendation is that the best alternative for Britain to the existing First Past The Post system is a two-vote mixed system. The majority of MPs (80 to 85%) would continue to be elected on an individual constituency basis, with the remainder elected on a corrective top-up basis which would significantly reduce the disproportionality of the geographical divisiveness which are inherent in FPTP. Within this mixed system, the constituency members should be elected by the Alternative Vote.

While few government-commissioned reports have been better written, many have been intellectually more coherent. The commission's proposal was, perhaps inevitably, a compromise – and an incomplete one at that, as no consensus was reached on whether 15 per cent or 20 per cent of MPs should be elected on a 'top-up' basis. When Tony Blair decided to let the report gather dust and to indefinitely postpone a referendum on a new voting system, few expressed much dismay outside the ranks of those Liberal Democrats for whom proportional representation was the transcendent issue facing British politics.

Other recommendations put forward by the original Labour–Lib Dem committee fared better. Its proposals for new laws on devolution, human rights and freedom of information were all carried out.

1999

'No-one shall be a member of the House of Lords by virtue of a hereditary peerage'

Labour's 1997 election manifesto promised to abolish the right of hereditary peers to sit and vote in the House of Lords, as a first stage towards more fundamental reform. In the event, a compromise was reached, which came to light in a farcical manner. On 2 December 1998, William Hague, the Conservative leader, accused Tony Blair of watering down his pledge to remove all hereditary peers from the Lords. Hague was right: the government had agreed to allow 92 hereditary peers to escape the chop. What Hague did not know was that the deal had been agreed by Labour's Leader of the Lords, Baroness Jay, and her Conservative opposite number, Viscount Cranborne. In return for Jay's concession, Cranborne had agreed not to block the rest of the bill.

When Hague learned what had happened, he sacked Cranborne, whereupon the rest of the Conservative front bench in the Lords tendered their resignations as shadow ministers. Over the following days, the Tories tidied up their mess, but Cranborne's career was over. The House of Lords Bill received royal assent on 11 November 1999.

House of Lords Act 1999

An Act to restrict membership of the House of Lords by virtue of a hereditary peerage; to make related provision about disqualifications for voting at elections to, and for membership of, the House of Commons; and for connected purposes.

Be it enacted by the Queen's most Excellent Majesty, by and with the advice and consent of the Lords Spiritual and Temporal, and Commons, in this present Parliament assembled, and by the authority of the same, as follows:—

1   EXCLUSION OF HEREDITARY PEERS

No-one shall be a member of the House of Lords by virtue of a hereditary peerage.

2   EXCEPTION FROM SECTION 1

1. Section 1 shall not apply in relation to anyone excepted from it by or in accordance with Standing Orders of the House.

2. At any one time 90 people shall be excepted from section 1; but anyone excepted as holder of the office of Earl Marshal, or as performing the office of Lord Great Chamberlain, shall not count towards that limit.

3. Once excepted from section 1, a person shall continue to be so throughout his life (until an Act of Parliament provides to the contrary).

4. Standing Orders shall make provision for filling vacancies among the people excepted from section 1; and in any case where—

   a) the vacancy arises on a death occurring after the end of the first Session of the next Parliament after that in which this Act is passed, and

   b) the deceased person was excepted in consequence of an election,

   c) that provision shall require the holding of a by-election.

5. A person may be excepted from section 1 by or in accordance with Standing Orders made in anticipation of the enactment or commencement of this section.

6. Any question whether a person is excepted from section 1 shall be decided by the Clerk of the Parliaments, whose certificate shall be conclusive.

3   REMOVAL OF DISQUALIFICATIONS IN RELATION TO THE HOUSE OF COMMONS

1. The holder of a hereditary peerage shall not be disqualified by virtue of that peerage for—

   a) voting at elections to the House of Commons, or

   b) being, or being elected as, a member of that House.

2. Subsection (1) shall not apply in relation to anyone excepted from section 1 by virtue of section 2.

Viscount Cranborne was not one of the hereditary peers elected by his fellow Conservatives to retain his seat in the Lords. However, he was given a life peerage, along with five other hereditary peers who had served as Leaders of the

House in the past. Cranborne's new incarnation did not last long. In 2001, he took formal 'leave of absence' and so played no further role in the Lords, rather than acceding to new rules on the disclosure of peers' financial interests. He was therefore not in the Lords in 2003 when his father died and he succeeded to a title that had belonged to successive generations of prominent Conservatives: Marquess of Salisbury.

Momentum for further Lords reform – of which the ejection of most hereditary peers was meant to be only the first stage – lasted no longer than Cranborne's career as a life peer. A Royal Commission on Lords reform chaired by Lord Wakeham, a former Conservative Cabinet minister, proposed a mixed chamber of elected and appointed peers. But no consensus could be reached among the main political parties on the details of reform, and the government announced in 2001 that it was abandoning reform for the time being. Spasmodic moves to revive the process in the 2001 and 2005 parliaments fared no better.

2005

'IF WE USE UNDEMOCRATIC MEANS SUCH AS THESE, WE MAY UNINTENTIONALLY WILL NEW AND AWFUL ENDS'

I n 2001, Parliament passed the Anti-terrorism, Crime and Security Act, which allowed foreign people suspected of terrorism to be detained without trial. In December 2004, nine Law Lords, applying the Human Rights Act, voted by eight to one to declare these powers of detention incompatible with the European Convention on Human Rights.

The government responded by introducing a Prevention of Terrorism Bill. This gave the Home Secretary the power to make a 'control order' on named individuals to restrict their liberty without being detained. Control orders could limit such things as an individual's movements, occupation and communication with others; it could also subject the individual to electronic surveillance.

On 23 February 2005, the House of Commons debated the bill. One of the Labour backbenchers who spoke against it was Barbara Follett. Since becoming an MP eight years earlier, she had never rebelled against the government. But on this occasion, as she explained, she had intensely personal reasons for doing so.

BARBARA FOLLETT'S SPEECH TO THE HOUSE OF COMMONS

Like most other Members who have spoken today, I recognise that we have a problem. I recognise, too, like my hon. Friend the Member for Nottingham, North [Graham Allen], that very real attempts have been made by the Home Secretary to solve that problem. I salute him for the work that he has been doing and I value it. I also recognise that, in today's world, control orders are sadly necessary, but I do not see why those control orders have to be initiated and implemented by a single politician. Nor do I see why that politician needs to have only reasonable grounds for suspecting that the individual concerned is, or has been, involved in terrorism-related activity. That seriously worries me.

Those reasonable grounds could be based on intelligence evidence. It is the nature of intelligence gathering that it is unreliable. It is difficult. We have no guarantee that that intelligence will be correct. I know, because I have known the Home Secretary [Charles Clarke] for many years and worked with him for many years, that he is an honourable and fair man. He is acting from the very best of motives and in the public interest, but, with the deepest respect, I think that the end does not justify these means. In fact, I fear that if we use undemocratic means such as these, we may unintentionally will new and awful ends. That is why I will not support the Bill tonight and why I ask my right hon. Friend to think again.

There are better ways of doing this—quite a few have been mentioned in the Chamber tonight. I will not go over them because other hon. Members want to speak, but we should involve a judge from the outset, use the Crown Prosecution Service procedure and have a look at how the Canadians use intercept evidence in court. In other words, look at it again and think again about the kind of example that this sets, as the hon. Member for Gordon said. My right hon. Friend the Member for Southampton, Itchen [John Denham] was right when he said that people can be detained without trial for as long as four years on the continent, but does that mean that we should emulate them? Does that mean that that is something that we should even consider?

I lived for many years in South Africa, during the dark days of apartheid. During that time, Britain's legal system was held up as a beacon of light and hope, as the prison bars of the apartheid state closed around us. In 1961, the South African Government introduced the General Law Amendment Act, which allowed people to be detained for 12 days without trial. By 1963, that had been extended to 90 days. By 1965, it was 180 days. Two years later, it became indefinite. At the same time, the apartheid regime was issuing control orders that restricted the right of some citizens to congregate, to work and, in some cases, to leave the confines of their own homes. Those orders had a devastating effect on the life of the suspect and his or her family. I should know—my first husband was served with one of them in 1971. He lived under it for five years, and it was only thanks to the generosity of the university at which he taught that he did not starve. He could not work, leave his home or travel to Cape Town to see his mother, and he barely saw his children.

I know that this is Britain and not South Africa or Burma, but we must not underestimate the importance of what we are doing today and the message that it sends to countries where we are talking about good governance. The example that we set will stay with us for many years. Removing the hope that we give, as we could tonight, might have a deleterious effect.

ROBERT MARSHALL-ANDREWS: I have been listening to my hon. Friend with considerable admiration and respect. Will she apply her deep knowledge of the matters about which she speaks to clause 1, and especially the provisions in paragraphs (a) to (o) of subsection (3), which set out in detail the restrictions that could be put on people through a non-derogation order? Does she agree that they bear an extraordinary and chilling resemblance to the pass laws in South Africa?

BARBARA FOLLETT: I wish that I did not have to agree with my hon. and learned Friend, but the provisions do bear an extraordinary resemblance to those laws. We must beware of going down that road. Again, I say that this country is not South Africa, but we have an example to set.

My first husband was put under house arrest because the apartheid state believed that he was a threat to its security. He probably was; he was campaigning to give black people the right to vote and join trade unions. Given the structure of the South African state, he probably was threatening it because it believed that only whites could vote and join trade unions. House arrest hampered him, but did not stop him, which was probably why, just before his five-year order was due to expire, he was shot dead in front of our two young daughters in their bedroom. I tried to comfort them in the days that followed by telling them that we were going to go to Britain, where people were not detained without trial or put under house arrest. When one tries to tell a 13-year-old and a nine-year-old that not all parts of the world are as bad as others, one looks for examples, and we in Britain were that example. I am glad that I am here today so that my now 40-year-old and 36-year-old daughters can hear that we are still fighting to uphold that.

I understand that control orders are necessary in some circumstances, which is why, like my right hon. Friend the Member for Holborn and St. Pancras (Mr. Dobson), I supported the Anti-terrorism, Crime and Security Act 2001. However, that Act was a stop-gap measure. It is due to be reviewed in five years and is subject to continual review. The Bill, however, is not a stop-gap measure. It will embed an undemocratic principle in our law. It will remove rights that are guaranteed under the Magna Carta, which says that no free man—I add the word 'woman' to that—shall be arrested or detained except by the lawful judgment of his or her peers. If that was good enough for 1215, surely it is good enough for 2005.

I ask the Home Secretary to think again, please. He should get a judge to implement the orders and consider how to use intelligence evidence in court. He should consider putting a time period on the Bill and review it in five years, rather than committing us to it for ever. Above all, he should take time and care. These principles are the very basis of our democracy and our party. If we destroy them, it destroys us.

Follett abstained in the divisions and other Labour MPs voted against the government; however, the Commons voted overall to support the bill. Following a tussle with the House of Lords, which opposed the bill, it became law on 11 March 2005. This time the courts did not find that the government's powers violated the European Convention on Human Rights. But they did overrule successive Home Secretaries in some specific cases, declaring that they had crossed the line between restriction of liberty (which was allowed) and deprivation of liberty (not allowed). On one occasion, the Law Lords ruled that twelve- and fourteen-hour curfews were acceptable, but eighteen-hour curfews were not.

2007

'LIBERTY IS NOT THE ONLY VALUE WE PRIZE AND NOT THE ONLY PRIORITY FOR GOVERNMENT'

Gordon Brown became prime minister on 27 June 2007. Four months later, he delivered a speech at the University of Westminster on the subject of liberty. He argued that there is a specific British tradition of liberty that needs to be upheld – and also reconciled with other demands on a modern state. He offered a set of principles that should be applied when liberty has to be curtailed.

GORDON BROWN'S SPEECH ON LIBERTY

A passion for liberty has determined the decisive political debates of our history, inspired many of our defining political moments, and those debates, conducted in the crucible of great events, have, in my view, forged over time a distinctly British interpretation of liberty: one that asserts the importance of freedom from prejudice, of rights to privacy, and of limits to the scope of arbitrary state power, but one that also rejects the selfishness of extreme libertarianism and demands that the realm of individual freedom encompasses not just some but all of us.

There is of course always the danger that villains of history become redeemed by the passage of time. There is a human instinct to recast the past as a lost golden age. I do not wish to fall into that trap. Nor should we succumb to an excessively Whig-like interpretation of history that assumes an inevitable stage-by-stage progress. In particular we should neither glorify nor distort what has gone before – and the struggles, both the ups and downs, of empire are not long behind us – to uphold a particular view of where we are now or what we can become. But the single most powerful thread that runs though our history is a succession of chapters in the defence of liberty and toleration.

So I am in no doubt that our freedoms, our openness and tolerance, and our very enterprise and creativity which flow from these qualities – what we value about being British – emerge from this rich and historic tradition.

Yet all too often on the political right, liberty has been reduced to a simplistic libertarianism in which freedom and licence assumed a rough equivalence, and the absence of government from public life seen as essential to maximise liberty. And some politicians of the left have mistakenly seen liberty at odds with equality and were too often prepared to compromise or even ignore the sanctity of freedoms of the individual.

But these simplistic caricatures are unacceptable: we need a more rounded and realistic conception of liberty.

In a world of increasingly rapid change and multiplying challenges – facing for example a terrorist threat or a challenge to our tolerance – democracies must be able to bring people together, mark out common ground, and energise the will and the resources of all.

It is the open society that responds best to new challenges and we are fortunate in being able to do so by drawing on that British story of liberty.

Indeed, the components of our liberty are the building blocks for such a society: our belief in the freedom of speech and expression and conscience and dissent helps create the open society; our determination to subject the state to greater scrutiny and accountability sustains such openness; the reinforcement of civic responsibility and the empowerment of the individual gives our country the underlying strength we need to succeed in the years ahead. I am convinced that both to rebuild our constitution for the modern age and to unify the country to meet and master every challenge, we need to consciously and with determination found the next stage of constitutional development firmly on the story of British liberty.

This will only be possible if we face up to the hard choices that have to be made in government. Precious as it is, liberty is not the only value we prize and not the only priority for government. The test for any government will be how it makes those hard choices, how it strikes the balance. In my view, the key to making these hard choices in a way that is compatible with our traditions of liberty is to, at all times, apply the liberty test, respecting fundamental rights and freedoms, and wherever action is needed by government, it never subjects the citizen to arbitrary treatment, is transparent and proportionate in its measures and at all times also requires proper scrutiny by, and accountability to, Parliament and the people.

By insisting that liberty is and remains at the centre of our constitution, we rightly raise the bar we have to meet when it comes to measures to protect the security of individuals and communities against the terrorist threat.

I believe that trust in our institutions can only be strengthened if our constitutional reforms are explicitly founded on British ideas of liberty – and that it is imperative that in every generation we re-examine areas where the executive has discretion and where to limit that discretion would be in the interests of good government.

Today, Jack Straw is signalling the start of a national consultation on the case for a new British Bill of Rights and Duties – or, as I said in July, for moving towards a written constitution.

This will include a discussion of how we can entrench and enhance our liberties – building upon existing rights and freedoms but not diluting them – but also make more explicit the responsibilities that implicitly accompany rights. The debate about a Bill of Rights and Duties will be of fundamental importance to our liberties and to our constitutional settlement and opens a new chapter in the British story of liberty. So it is right that the discussion should engage those of all parties and none who believe in our democracy and the importance of liberty within it in a constructive dialogue.

At all times in our history we have had to debate how the need for strong and effective government can be combined with the pursuit and preservation of liberty. The challenge for each generation is to conduct an open debate without ever losing sight of the value of our liberties.

Indeed the character of our country will be defined by how we write the next chapter of British liberty – by whether we do so responsibly and in a way that respects and builds on our traditions, and progressively adds to and enlarges rather than reduces the sphere of freedom.

2007

'WHAT, THEN, IS TO BE DONE? THE SHORT ANSWER IS: NOTHING'

I n 2007, the eminent political scientist Anthony King updated Walter Bagehot's *The English Constitution*. King called his book *The British Constitution*. King concluded that the reforms that had taken place since 1997, on top of the reforms of earlier decades, had left Britain with an intellectually incoherent set of constitutional arrangements – but warned that attempts to tidy these up might make matters worse rather than better.

ANTHONY KING: *THE BRITISH CONSTITUTION*

The new British constitution, the small-c constitution actually operating today, is a mess. The word 'mess' is usually understood perjoratively, but in this context it is meant to be understood purely descriptively.

The old constitution possessed a certain monumental grandeur, a certain cruciform, cathedral-like simplicity. Its architecture and ground plan could easily be grasped, at least in their essentials. But that old building now looks as though it has been bombed from above and undermined from below. Parts of the roof have fallen in, at least one of the transepts has collapsed, and workmen have erected an untidy assortment of workshops and sheds inside the few walls still standing. Britain today has neither a brand new church, a post-war Coventry Cathedral, nor a skilful restoration of an old church, like the Frauenkirche, Dresden, but something that looks a little bit like a bombed-out ruin left over from a major war.

The new constitutional structure is certainly more complicated than the old one. The old constitution comprised the prime minister, the cabinet, the civil service and parliament, with the judiciary somewhere in the wings. The new one comprises all those elements plus the European Union, a judiciary far more activist than in the past, a newly established Scottish parliament and executive, a brand new Welsh national assembly and government, many more elections than there once were, the imminent possibility of referendums on important issues, an increasingly assertive House of Lords and a body of government backbenchers that is considerably harder to manage than it used to be.

The most blatant inconsistency – even though it seems hardly ever to be noticed – is that between the organization of the central United Kingdom government and the organization of several of its most important constituent parts. The United Kingdom constitution remains an essentially power-hoarding or power-concentration constitution. The government of the UK governs. Winner takes all. The government of the day is normally a single-party government. First past the post normally determines which of the political parties wins and therefore governs.

But the governments of Scotland and Wales – and, come to that, London and Northern Ireland – are organized on a completely different basis. Their constitutions are power-sharing or power-diffusing constitutions. The government of the day governs, but only through the elected parliament or assembly. Winner does not take all. The government is usually a coalition government. Proportional representation normally ensures that no single party wins. There can be few countries in the world – perhaps there are none – which have within themselves a variety of governing institutions that are based on such fundamentally divergent constitutional conceptions.

That said, there is no going back. The old constitutional structure, however simple, elegant and aesthetically pleasing it may have been in its day, cannot be reconstituted. Europe, the judges, the Scottish and Welsh parliaments and all the rest of it are not going to go away. The world, Britain's constitution and the whole British political system are far more complicated than they used to be, and they are all going to remain so. The past is just that: the past, irretrievable and for that reason largely irrelevant. Nostalgia, as always, is a good companion but a bad guide.

What, then, is to be done? The short answer is: nothing. For the past thirty years, would-be constitutional reformers, notably the constitutional holists, have called, sometimes implicitly, for the summoning of a UK-wide constitutional convention and, usually explicitly, for the adoption of a new, formalized, codified constitution, a Constitution with a capital C. As recently as the autumn of 2006, several ministers of the Crown – including no less than the chancellor of the exchequer and a former solicitor general – aired the idea that Britain should join most of the rest of the world in acquiring a written constitution.

That idea, however, is likely to fall on deaf ears. There is no need for a written constitution. The United Kingdom is not confronted by a major constitutional crisis. There is no popular demand for either a convention or a written constitution. Even if men and women of stature could be attracted, it is not at all clear that attending such a convention would be the most profitable possible use of their time. The United Kingdom faces all kinds of problems, many of them pressing: among them climate change, the domestic economic effects of globalization, old-age pensions and the care of the elderly, the future of the European Union, international terrorism, relations with the worlds (plural) of Islam and the proliferation of nuclear weapons. On the face of it, it would seem eccentric to the point of perversity to redirect the attentions of a significant portion of the country's political class away from the problems such as these towards the problems, such as they are, of Britain's existing constitution.

Finally, but not least, the United Kingdom has already undergone a period of intense and unremitting constitutional change. Good sense would seem to suggest that the time has come to pause, to absorb the changes that have already taken place and to reflect on them. There does not appear on the face of it to be a good case for instituting a Maoist 'permanent revolution' in Britain's constitutional structure. Rather the contrary. Although it is a mess and does look like a ruin, Britain's new constitutional edifice needs propping up, a few major repairs and skilful maintenance. Despite its unfortunate appearance, it does not yet need to be totally rebuilt.

2008

'THE FREEDOM OF THE PRESS IS FAR TOO IMPORTANT TO BE LEFT TO THE SOMEWHAT DESICCATED VALUES OF A SINGLE JUDGE'

Few newspaper editors in Britain have been as successful as Paul Dacre. He made the *Daily Mail* a newspaper that senior politicians variously loved, hated, feared and courted, but seldom ignored. He seldom speaks in public or gives interviews; rather, he lets his paper speak for him. On 9 November 2008, he made an exception. He delivered a speech that condemned the Human Rights Act and the way it had been interpreted by a particular judge, Justice David Eady. In so doing, Dacre implicitly raised a wider question: what should happen when two different rights collide (in this case, the right to privacy and the right to free expression)?

At the heart of Dacre's argument was a legal action in which Max Mosley, the president of the international racing body FIA, had sued the *News of the World* for invading his privacy. The paper had run a story alleging that Mosley had taken part in sadomasochistic sex sessions that had Nazi overtones. Mosley denied the Nazi overtones, said that the sex sessions had been among consenting adults and that his right to enjoy these privately were enshrined in the European Convention on Human Rights. In July 2008, Justice Eady found in Mosley's favour and awarded him damages of £60,000.

Dacre's view was not only that Justice Eady was dangerously wrong but also that the law should not be neutral between 'moral' and 'depraved' sexual behaviour. In this, Dacre was taking a stand against a line of thinking that could be traced back half a century, to the Wolfenden Report of 1957, which argued in relation to homosexuality that 'moral conviction or instinctive feeling, however strong, is not a valid reason for over-riding the individual's privacy'.

PAUL DACRE'S SPEECH TO THE SOCIETY OF EDITORS

The British Press is having a privacy law imposed on it, which – apart from allowing the corrupt and the crooked to sleep easily in their beds – is, I would argue, undermining the ability of mass-circulation newspapers to sell newspapers in an ever more difficult market.

The law is not coming from Parliament – no, that would smack of democracy – but from the arrogant and amoral judgements – words I use very deliberately – of one man. I am referring, of course, to Justice David Eady who has, again and again, under the privacy clause of the Human Rights Act, found against newspapers and their age-old freedom to expose the moral shortcomings of those in high places.

Two cases in particular underline this threat.

Two years ago, Justice Eady ruled that a cuckolded husband couldn't sell his story to the press about another married man – a wealthy sporting celebrity – who had seduced his wife. The judge was worried about the effect of the revelations on the celebrity's wife. Now I agree that any distress caused to innocent parties is regrettable but exactly the same worries could be expressed about the relatives of any individual who transgressed which, if followed to its logical conclusion, would mean that nobody could be condemned for wrongdoing. But the judge – in an unashamed reversal of centuries of moral and social thinking – placed the rights of the adulterer above society's age-old belief that adultery should be condemned.

Recently, of course, the very same Justice Eady effectively ruled that it's perfectly acceptable for the multi-millionaire head of a multibillion-pound sport that is followed by countless young people to pay five women £2,500 to take part in acts of unimaginable sexual depravity with him.

The judge found for Max Mosley because he had not engaged in a 'sick Nazi orgy' as the *News of the World* contested, though some of the participants were dressed in military-style uniform. Mosley was issuing commands in German while one prostitute pretended to pick lice from his hair, a second fellated him and a third caned his backside until blood was drawn.

Now most people would consider such activities to be perverted, depraved, the very abrogation of civilised behaviour of which the law is supposed to be the safeguard. Not Justice Eady. To him such behaviour was merely 'unconventional'. Nor in his mind was there anything wrong in a man of such wealth using his money to exploit women in this way. Would he feel the same way, I wonder, if one of those women had been his wife or daughter?

But what is most worrying about Justice Eady's decision is that he is ruling that – when it comes to morality – the law in Britain is now effectively neutral, which is why I accuse him, in his judgments, of being 'amoral'.

In the sporting celebrity case, he rejected the idea that adultery was a proper cause for public condemnation. Instead, he declared that because family breakdown was now commonplace, there was a strong argument for 'not holding forth about adultery' or, in other words, attaching no greater inherent worth to marriage than to any other lifestyle choice. Thus no moral decision was to be made between marriage and those who would destroy it, between victim and victimiser, between right and wrong.

In the Mosley case, the judge is ruling that there is no public interest in revealing a public figure's involvement in acts of depravity. What the judge loftily calls the 'new rights-based jurisprudence' of the Human Rights Act seems to be ruling out any such thing as public standards of morality and decency, and the right of newspapers to report on digressions from those standards.

But most worrying is that when it comes to suppressing media freedom, the good Justice Eady is seemingly ubiquitous. It was he who was going to preside in Tesco's libel case against the *Guardian*, which was, in the event, recently settled out of court. It was the same Justice Eady who, in Lord Browne versus the *Mail on Sunday*, ruled that BP's shareholders had the right to know that Browne had lied to the court – but did not have the right to know details of his conversations with his partner, despite the paper's case that they had serious public-interest implications.

Again, it was Eady who found in favour of a Canadian folk singer called Loreena McKennitt, who had objected to the publication of a book about her by a former adviser, Niema Ash. Ms McKennitt did not claim that the book was in any way untrue, merely that it had infringed her right to privacy. Never mind Ms Ash's right to freedom of expression.

And it is Eady who, almost unnoticed here, has the distinction of having provoked the US Congress – in what's dubbed the Libel Tourism Bill – to consider making English libel judgments unenforceable in America. This follows the judge's decision to allow a Saudi banker to sue a New York author in the London courts even though she hadn't published her book in Britain. Not for the first time, it seems that our colonial cousins can teach us a thing or two.

But surely the greatest scandal is that while London boasts scores of eminent judges, one man is given a virtual monopoly of all cases against the media enabling him to bring in a privacy law by the back door.

English Common Law is the collective wisdom of many different judges over the ages. The freedom of the press, I would argue, is far too important to be left to the somewhat desiccated values of a single judge who clearly has an animus against the popular press and the right of people to freedom of expression. I personally would rather have never heard of Max Mosley and the squalid purgatory he inhabits. It is the others I care about: the crooks, the liars, the cheats, the rich and the corrupt sheltering behind a law of privacy being created by an unaccountable judge.

If Gordon Brown wanted to force a privacy law, he would have to set out a bill, arguing his case in both Houses of Parliament, withstand public scrutiny and win a series of votes. Now, thanks to the wretched Human Rights Act, one judge with a subjective and highly relativist moral sense can do the same with a stroke of his pen.

BIBLIOGRAPHY

PRINT SOURCES

BOOKS

Amery, L.S., *Thoughts on the Constitution* (Oxford: OUP, 1964)

Ashley, Mike, *Taking Liberties: The Struggle for Britain's Freedoms and Rights* (London: British Library, 2008)

Bagehot, Walter, *The English Constitution*, with introduction by Richard Crossman (London: Fontana, 1963)

Baker, Kenneth, ed., *The Faber Book of Conservatism* (London: Faber and Faber, 1993)

Benn, Tony, ed., *Writings on the Wall* (London: Faber and Faber, 1984)

Blake, Robert, *The Conservative Party from Peel to Thatcher* (London: Fontana, 1985)

Brown, Gordon, and Wright, Tony, eds, *Values, Visions and Voices* (Edinburgh: Mainstream, 1995)

Butler, David, and Butler, Gareth, *Twentieth Century British Political Facts* (London: Macmillan, 2000)

Churchill, Winston, *The Second World War*, 6 vols (London: Cassell, 1948–54)

Winston Churchill's Speeches: Never Give In! ed. Winston S. Churchill (London: Pimlico, 2007)

Cornford, F.M., *Microcosmographia Academica* (London: Bowes & Bowes, 1908)

Craig, F.W.S., *British General Election Manifestos 1900–1974* (London: Macmillan, 1975)

Craig, F.W.S., *British Electoral Facts 1832–1980* (Chichester: Parliamentary Research Services, 1981)

Craig, F.W.S., *Chronology of British Parliamentary By-Elections 1833–1987* (London: Parliamentary Research Services, 1987)

Davies, Norman, *The Isles: A History* (London: Macmillan, 1999)

Elton, G.R., *The Tudor Constitution* (Cambridge: CUP, 1960)

Englefield, Dermot, Seaton, Janet, and White, Isobel, *Facts About the British Prime Ministers* (London: Mansell, 1995)

Foot, Michael, *Aneurin Bevan* (London: Davis-Poynter, 1973)

Frost, David, and Sherrin, Ned, *That Was the Week That Was* (London: W.H. Allen, 1963)

Goodrich, Chauncey, ed., *Select British Eloquence* (New York: Harper & Brothers, 1859)

Grayling, A.C., *Towards the Light* (London: Bloomsbury, 2007)

Hanham, H.J., ed., *The Nineteenth Century Constitution* (Cambridge: CUP, 1969)

Howe, Irving, ed., *Essential Works of Socialism* (New Haven: Yale University Press, 1970)

Kenyon, J.P., ed., *The Stuart Constitution* (Cambridge: CUP, 1986)

King, Anthony, *The British Constitution* (Oxford: OUP, 2007)

Lively, Jack, and Lively, Adam, eds, *Democracy in Britain: A Reader* (Oxford: Blackwell, 1994)

Lynn, Jonathan, and Jay, Antony, *Yes, Prime Minister* (London: BBC, 1986)

MacArthur, Brian, ed., *The Penguin Book of Twentieth Century Speeches* (London: Viking, 1992)

MacArthur, Brian, ed., *The Penguin Book of Historic Speeches* (London: Viking, 1995)

Macfarlane, Alan, *The Origins of English Individualism* (Oxford: Blackwell, 1978)

Machin, Ian, *The Rise of Democracy in Britain 1830–1919* (London: Macmillan, 2001)

Orwell, George, *Coming Up for Air* (London: Secker & Warburg, 1939)

Powell, Enoch, *Great Parliamentary Occasions* (London: Queen Anne Press, 1960)

Rosen, Greg, *Old Labour to New* (London: Politicos, 2005)

Sachs, Albie, and Wilson, Joan, *Sexism and the Law* (London: Martin Robertson, 1978)

Schama, Simon, *A History of Britain*, 3 vols (London: BBC, 2000–02)

Seymour, Charles, *Electoral Reform in England and Wales* (New Haven: Yale University Press, 1915)

Thompson, E.P., *The Making of the English Working Class* (London: Penguin, 1968)

Williams, E.N., ed., *The Eighteenth Century Constitution* (Cambridge: CUP, 1960)

Wilson, Patrick, and Barber, Benjamin, *The Struggle for Democracy* (London: W.H. Allen, 1990)

Young, Hugo, *This Blessed Plot* (London: Macmillan, 1998)

NEWSPAPER REPORTS

The Times (19 January 1865)

The Times (6 June 1945)

The Times (1 July 1967)

PARLIAMENTARY REPORTS

Report of the Committee on Homosexual Offences and Prostitution; HMSO Cmd
  247, 1957

Report of the Independent Commission on the Voting System; HMSO Cmd
  4090–1, 1998

WEB SOURCES

http://avalon.law.yale.edu/subject_menus/medmenu.asp
http://www.bbc.co.uk/radio4/history/voices/
http://www.bibliomania.com/
http://books.google.co.uk
http://www.britannia.com/history/docs/
http://www.british-history.ac.uk/
http://classiclit.about.com/
http://www.constitution.org/
http://courses.essex.ac.uk/gv/
http://ebooks.adelaide.edu.au/meta/titles.html
http://www.fordham.edu/halsall/mod/modsbook20.html
http://www.fullbooks.com/
http://www.gutenberg.org/wiki/Main_Page
http://hansard.millbanksystems.com/
http://www.historyhome.co.uk/
http://www.margaretthatcher.org/speeches/default.asp
http://www.napoleon-series.org/
http://www.nationalarchives.gov.uk/catalogue/default.asp?j=1
http://www.niassembly.gov.uk/io/agreement.htm
http://www.number10.gov.uk/
http://oll.libertyfund.org/
http://www.parliament.uk/publications/index.cfm
http://www.statutelaw.gov.uk/
http://www.thehistorychannel.co.uk/site/encyclopedia/encyclopedia_main_page.
  php
http://www.victorianetexts.com/
http://www.victorianweb.org/history/
http://en.wikisource.org/wiki/Main_Page

Please note that all website details are given by way of copyright attribution and not
by way of endorsement or approval of the contents, over which the publishers have
no control.

INDEX

Aberdeen, Earl of 273, 308, 322
Act of Settlement (1701) 171–4
Act for the Settlement of Ireland
    (1652) 134–7
Act of Union (1707) 175–7
Act of Union (1800) 240–1
Aelfric 37–9
Alfred the Great 34
Alien Act (1705) 176
All Souls College, Oxford 405
Allen, Alderman 139
Allen, Graham 512
Althing 24
The American Crisis 223
Amery, Leo 404–6
Amin, Idi 448
Anarchical Fallacies 234–7
Andrews, Eamonn 437–40
Anglo-Irish Treaty 374–7
Ann and Mary 215–16
Anne, queen 172–5
The Annual Register 251–3
Anonimalle Chronicle 65–6
Anti-Corn Law League 302–3
anti-Semitism 45
Anti-terrorism, Crime and Security
    Act (2001) 512, 514

apartheid 25, 513–14
appeasement 405
Appellate Jurisdiction Act (1876) 325
Appleby, Sir Humphrey 474–5
Apsley House 271
Archbishop of Canterbury 42, 45, 51,
    64, 89, 165, 428, 450
Areopagitica 104–6
Asquith, Herbert 364, 367, 370–2
Assize of Clarendon 42–4
Associated TeleVision 445
Astor, Nancy 373
Athelstan the Glorious 34–36, 45
Attlee, Clement 399, 401–4, 408, 413,
    422, 461, 464
Attorney General 86, 100, 215, 230–1,
    233, 310, 436, 471
Aubrey, Jack 248
Ayr Manuscript 54

Babbage, Charles 30
Bagehot, Walter 25, 332–5, 519
Balfour, Arthur 358
Ball, John 30, 64–5
Ballot Act (1872) 347
Banqueting House 121
Barking 64

Barnstaple 81
Battle of Bannockburn 54
Battle of Brunanburh 34
Battle of Evesham 51
Battle of Falkirk 53
Battle of Hastings 40
Battle of Lewes 50
Battle of Naseby 107
Battle of Stirling Bridge 53
Battle of Waterloo 252, 267, 434
Beaverbrook, Lord 402, 403
Becket, Thomas à 42
Bell, Richard 355
Benedict XIII, pope of Avignon 70, 71
Benn, Tony 32, 434–7, 477–80
Bentham, Jeremy 210, 234–8, 245–50, 326
Bentham, Sir Samuel 326
Berners-Lee, Sir Tim 395
Bevan, Aneurin 389–91, 408–11
Beveridge Report 295–8
Beveridge, William 395
Beyond the Fringe 438
Bible 25, 77, 246, 256
Biden, Joe 483
Bill of Rights 24, 26, 28, 155–9, 163–4, 172, 478, 501, 518
Birt, John 451
Black Death 58
Blackheath 30, 64
Blair, Tony 493, 502, 508, 509
Board of Trade 265
Boleyn, Anne 74
Bonnie Prince Charlie 239
Booker, Christopher 438–41
Bowling, George ('Tubby') 381
Bradshaw, John 117–18, 120–1
Brentwood 64

Brickdale, Matthew 212
Bright, John 25, 302, 336–9
Bristol South-East 434
The British Constitution 27, 519–21
British Medical Association (BMA) 408–11
The Briton 200
Brooke, Henry 438–41
Brougham, Henry 248–51
Brown, Gordon 493, 516–18, 525
Bruce, Henry Austin 344
Bruges Group 487
Brunel, Isambard Kingdom 30
Buckingham, Duke of 94, 96
Burdett, Sir Francis 248–51
Burke, Edmund 211–14, 221–4, 232, 252, 264, 353, 415, 435
Burns, Robert 239–40
Burton-on-Trent 49
Bute, Earl of 200
Butler, Lord 454–5

Camden, Lord 203
Cameron, David 314, 501
Campbell, Duncan 477
Campbell-Bannerman, Sir Henry 191
Canning, George 32, 261–4, 278
Carisbrooke Castle 117
Carnarvon, Lord 345–6
Castle, Barbara 457–9
Castlereagh, Lord 265
Cat and Mouse Act (1913) 367, 369
A Catechism of Parliamentary Reform 245–7
Catesby, Robert 86, 88
Catherine of Aragon 74
Catholic Emancipation 214, 265, 267
Catholic Relief Bill 267
Cavalier Parliament 150

Chamberlain, Joseph 351–3

Chamberlain, Neville 384, 386

Chancellor of the Exchequer 191, 319, 361, 470, 506, 520

Channel Islands 28

Charge of the Light Brigade 322

Charles I, king 94, 96–7, 99–102, 107–8, 111, 116–24, 126, 134, 172, 206, 437

Charles II, king 133, 148–51

Charles VI, king of France 70–1

Charter of the Forest 48

Chartists 296–301, 303, 314, 316

Chichele, Henry 405

Churchill, Winston 364, 384–7, 391, 395, 397–405, 411, 416–19, 422, 434, 458, 484

Chuter Ede, James 415

Civil Partnership Act (2004) 430

Civil War 29–30, 93, 96, 102–3, 107, 123, 126, 134, 148

Clarkson, Thomas 218

Clontarf 310

close borough (*see also* rotten borough) 243, 261–4, 279, 283

Cobbett, William 186, 246, 274, 276–7

Cobden, Richard 302–5, 307–8

Cochrane, Lord 248, 251

Cockburn, Claud 387

Coke, Sir Edward 25, 86–91, 93–4, 120

Collins, Michael 374, 376–7

Combination Acts 233, 285

Coming Up for Air 381–3

Committee of Four 277

Committee of Privileges 434–5, 477–8, 480

Common Market (*see also* European

Economic Community) 422, 460, 463

The Condition of the Working Class in England in 1844 311

Congress of Europe 416–17

Connecticut Women's Suffrage Association 367

Conservative governments 289, 291, 304, 340–1, 353, 428, 431, 437–8, 448, 481, 487–8, 491, 493

Conservative Party 22, 223, 238, 271, 283, 308, 314, 323, 335, 344, 346–7, 349, 350, 354, 358, 361, 364, 373, 384, 386, 401, 405, 408–9, 411–12, 419, 422, 428, 445, 453, 456, 460, 464, 468, 480, 494, 499, 501, 507–11

Considerations on Representative Government 326, 329–31

Constitutions of Clarendon 42

Consultative Committee on Education 380

Convention Parliament 150

Corn Laws 252, 302–8

Cornford, F.M. 359–60

Council of Europe 417–22, 498, 501

Council of State 106, 126–8, 140

Court of High Commission 89

Court of Session 178, 218

Cranborne, Lord 340–3

Cranborne, Viscount (1916–2003) 350

Cranborne, Viscount (1946–) 509–11

Crimean War 322

Criminal Justice Bill 413

Cromwell, Oliver 103, 106–7, 111, 113–17, 123, 126, 128–9, 134, 138–45, 148, 405, 407

Crosby, Brass 185

Curwen, John 243

Curwen's Act 243–4

Dacre, Paul 522–5
Daily Express 403
Daily Mail 451, 522
Daily Worker 387–9, 408
Dance, James 427–8
Darwin, Charles 30–1
Davis, David 314
de Valera, Eamon 374, 376–7
Declaration of Breda 148–50
Declaration of Independence (US) 163, 316
Defoe, Daniel 24, 168–71, 176, 179
Delors, Jacques 484
Democratic Unionist Party 502, 505
Derby 355
Derby, Earl of 305–8, 323–6, 340, 346
Diageo 474
Dickens, Charles 24, 292–5
The Difference Between an Absolute and Limited Monarchy 72–3
Disraeli, Benjamin 297–9, 308, 311–14, 340, 342–3, 349, 392
Distillers 471, 473–4
divine right of kings 91–3, 118, 130, 150, 160
Dooms of King Athelstan 34–6
Douglas-Home, Sir Alec 437
Dublin Castle 241
Dublin St Patrick's 373

Eady, Justice David 522–4
Easte Willes, Sir James 318
Easter Uprising 374
ecclesiastical courts 42, 89
The Economist 332, 428
Eden, Anthony 386, 392–5
Education Act (1944) 380
Edward I, king 50–5, 94
Edward II, king 57

Edward III, king 57
Edward IV, king 91
Egremont, Charles 311–14
El Alamein 397
Eldon, Lord 255
Elizabeth I, queen 81, 83, 86, 88
'The Enfranchisement of Women' 315–17
Engels, Friedrich 311
'England's New Chains' 126–7
The Enlightenment 24, 30, 196
The English Constitution 331, 335, 519
'Epistle to Dr Arbuthnot' 449
Equal Pay Act (1970) 459
Equality Act (2006) 430
Erskine, Thomas 230–3
Essay on the First Principles of Government 208–10
An Essay on Man 203
An Essay on Women 203
'The Essential Nature of the Constitution' 405–7
European Coal and Steel Community 422
European Commission 484
European Commission of Human Rights 471, 500
European Convention on Human Rights (ECHR) 24, 419–22, 471, 498, 499, 501, 512, 515, 522
European Court of Human Rights 419, 471–4, 498, 500
European Economic Community (EEC; see also Common Market) 460
European Union (EU) 26, 422, 488, 495, 501, 519, 521
Evans, Harold 471
Examiner 255

Fawkes, Guy 86, 88–9
Ferrers, Earl 423–5
Fianna Fáil 377
First Lord of the Treasury 187
The First Part of King Henry IV 68
Fleming, Sir Alexander 30
Follett, Barbara 512–15
Foot, Michael 408, 453–6
Forester, C.S. 248
Fortescue, Sir John 29, 72–3
Frankenstein 229
freedom of speech 22, 24–6, 76–7,
    81, 103, 107, 157–8, 160, 164, 200,
    393, 478, 517
friendly societies 362
Friendly Society of Agricultural
    Labourers 285
Frost, David 438–41
Fuller, Nicholas 89, 91
Fuller, Thomas 93
Fulton Report 322
Fyfe, David Maxwell 28, 419

Gallacher, Willie 391
Gay, John 182
George I, king 175, 187
George II, king 187
George III, king 211, 230, 261, 286
George IV, king 267, 271
George V, king 354, 364, 375
Gerard, Sybil 314
Gerard, Walter 314
Gladstone, William 308, 319, 322,
    344, 347–54, 454
Glyn Dŵr, Owain 68–71
Godwin, Mary (*see* Shelley, Mary)
Gollancz, Victor 381
Good Friday Agreement 493, 502–5
Good Parliament 61

Government of Ireland Act (1920)
    374–6
Grampound 261, 263
Grand Remonstrance 97–9
Greenwood, Arthur 395, 405
Grenville, George 200, 202
Grey, Earl 271, 273–74, 277, 283–4,
    289
Grey de Ruthyn, Baron 68, 70
The Guardian (*see also The Manchester
    Guardian*) 21, 254, 524
Gulliver's Travels 179–82
Gunpowder Plot 86, 89

habeas corpus 23–4, 26, 42, 158, 215,
    246
Habeas Corpus Act (1679) 151–4
Hacker, Jim 475–6
Hadow, Sir William Henry 380
The Hague 416–18
Hague, William 569
Hailsham, Lord 437, 468–70
Halifax, Lord 384, 386
Hampden, John 100–1, 206
Hampton Court 99, 111, 116–17
Hansard 186, 248, 297, 499
Hansard, Thomas 186
Hardie, Keir 355–8
Hardy, Thomas 233
Harley, Robert 171, 176
Harrison, John 30
Haselrig, Sir Arthur 100–1
Heath, Edward 438, 445, 460
Henry II, king 25, 42, 45
Henry III, king 48–51
Henry IV, king 68, 70–1
Henry V, king 71
Henry VI, king 72
Henry VIII, king 74

Heseltine, Michael 487
Hill of Tara 309
The History of England 309
Hobbes, Thomas 130–3
Holles, Denzil 100–1
Home Rule 347, 351–4
Hornblower, Horatio 248
House of Commons 32, 96–7, 101–2, 119, 123, 138–9, 174–5, 183, 186, 193–4, 203–7, 243, 261–4, 266–7, 278, 281, 301, 310, 324, 330, 344–50, 365–6, 434–7, 477–80
House of Lords 27, 96, 125, 150, 205, 206, 261–4, 323–5, 344–50, 364–6, 423–5, 434–7, 453–6, 509–11, 520
House of Lords Act (1999) 509–11
Howe, Sir Geoffrey 487
Human Rights Act (1998) 501, 512
Hume, David 25, 192–6
Hunt, Henry 252, 254
Hunt, Leigh 255
Hurd, Douglas 488
Hylton-Foster, Sir Harry 434

Importation Act (1815) 302
Incitement to Mutiny Act (1797) 285
Industrial Revolution 284, 311
Innocent III, pope 45, 48
Innocent VII, pope 70
Instrument of Government 140–4
Ireland 68–70, 99, 101, 134–7, 140–3, 214, 241–2, 265–70, 282, 305–6, 309–10, 319, 331, 351–4, 374–7, 502–5
Ireton, Henry 111–16
Irish Coercion Bill 307
Irish Free State 354, 374–7
Irish Home Rule Bill 351, 354
Irish Parliamentary Party 351

Irish Republican Army (IRA) 374, 505
Isle of Wight 117
Ismay, General 386
Isocrates 103

Jagger, Mick 449–52
James I, king 86, 89, 91–4, 172–3
James II, king 123–4, 151, 155–6, 167–8
James VI, king of Scotland (*see* James I)
Jay, Antony 475–6
Jay, Baroness 509
Jenkins, Lord (*see also* Jenkins, Roy) 506–8
Jenkins, Roy (*see also* Jenkins, Lord) 442–5, 460
John, king 45, 48
John XXII, pope 54, 57
John of Gaunt 61–2, 65

Keynes, John Maynard 30
King, Professor Anthony 27, 519–21
King's Bench 90, 154, 156, 215
King's Speech 200–1
Kinnock, Neil 481–3
Kinross and West Perthshire 437

labour exchanges 395
Labour Party 355, 358, 383, 391, 399, 401, 403, 405, 411, 457, 462, 481, 507
Labour Representation Committee 355, 358
Lagado 179
laissez-faire 199, 464
Laker, Freddie 468–9
Lambeth Palace 65

Langland, William 63
Langton, Stephen 45
Law Lords 350, 471, 512, 515
Leader of the House of Commons 191, 267, 297, 340, 461
Left Book Club 381
Lennox-Boyd, Alan 432, 433
Lenthall, William 100–2, 107, 127, 437, 478–9
Levellers 30, 107–11, 126, 222
Leviathan 130–3
Liberal Democrats 494, 499, 506, 508
Liberal Party 238, 283–4, 289, 291, 308, 331, 335, 344, 346–7, 355, 358, 364, 367, 371, 384–5, 453–4
Liberal Unionists 351, 353, 405
liberalism 74, 238, 400
licensing orders 103, 106, 164–7
life peer 323–5, 350, 423–5, 436, 452–4, 510, 511
Life Peerages Bill 423–5
Lilburne, John 74, 238, 400
Lister, Joseph 30
Liverpool 219, 261–2, 278
Liverpool, Lord 244, 252, 254, 402
Llandudno 481
Lloyd George, David 361–4, 371, 374, 395
Local Government Act (1988) 429
Locke, John 160–3
London Bridge 54
London Corresponding Society 233
London Working Men's Association 296
Lord Chancellor 74, 76–7, 152–4, 215–16, 251, 255, 324, 468
Lord Mayor 185, 435
Louis IX, king of France 72
Louis XVI, king of France 226

Louis, prince of France 48
Loveless, George 285–8
Lovett, William 296, 299
Luff, Peter 488, 490
Luther, Martin 179
Luttrell, Henry 203
Lynn, Jonathan 475–6

Maastricht Treaty 488–93
Macaulay, Thomas 25, 164, 280–2
Macfarlane, Alan 29
McGuinness, Martin 505
Macleod, Iain 433
Macmillan, Harold 433, 437
Madison, James 158–9
Magna Carta 24–5, 45–9, 94–5, 109, 151, 164, 204, 495, 514
Major, John 487–8, 493
Mallon, Seamus 505
Mallorie, Sir Peter 53
'A Man's a Man For A' That' 239–40
Manchester 252, 262, 277, 279, 303, 318, 411
Manchester, Earl of 107
The Manchester Guardian (*see also The Guardian*) 254, 388
Mansfield, Lord 203, 215–17
Mare, Sir Peter de la 61–2
Markievicz, Constance 373
Marney Abbey 311
Mary II, queen 28, 155–6, 160, 172–3, 177
'The Mask of Anarchy' 255–60
Mau Mau rebellion 431, 433, 436
Maxwell, Lily 318
Microcosmographia Academica 359–60
Melbourne, Lord 285, 289, 291
Merthyr Tydfil 365
Mile End 64–6

Mill, John Stuart 317, 326–31, 407
Milne, Alasdair 480
Milton, John 24, 103–6, 145–7
Model Parliament 51
Moll Flanders 168
Monck, General George 148, 150
Montfort, Simon de 24, 49–51
More, Sir Thomas 25, 74–7
Morley, Stephen 314
Morrison, Herbert 387–8, 391, 401
Mosley, Max 522–5
Mowbray Castle 314
Municipal Franchise Act (1869) 318

National Committee for
   Commonwealth Immigrants 442
National Union of Women's Suffrage
   Societies 318
New Model Army 111
New Statesman 477
News Chronicle 381, 404
News of the World 522–3
Newton, Sir Isaac 30
Norman Conquest 34, 37, 443
Northcote, Sir Stafford 319
Northcote–Trevelyan Report 319–22
Nottingham Castle 61, 63

Obama, Barack 26, 223, 483
O'Brian, Patrick 248
O'Connell, Daniel ('The Liberator')
   265–7, 309–10, 436
old-age pension 361
Old Sarum 261, 263, 279
Ombudsman 49
On Liberty 326–9
The Origins of English Individualism 29
Orwell, George 24, 381–3
Overton, Richard 107

Paine, Thomas 26, 223–7, 230–5, 238,
   281
Paisley, Ian 505
Palmerston, Lord 323
Pankhurst, Christabel 367
Pankhurst, Emmeline 24, 367–70
Pankhurst, Sylvia 367
Panorama 448
Parke, Sir James 323, 325
Parliament Act (1911) 364–6, 436
Parliamentary and Municipal
   Elections Bill 345–6
Parnell, Charles Stewart 351
Paxman, Jeremy 21
Peasants' Revolt 30, 60, 63–7
Peel, Sir Robert 267, 283, 289–91,
   304, 307–9
Peelites 308
Pelham, Henry 191
Pennal Letter 70–1
People's Budget 361–4
People's Charter 296–7
Perrers, Alice 61
Peterloo Massacre 252–5, 261, 302
Petition of Right 94–6
Petty, Maximilian 111
Philip IV, king of France 53
The Pickwick Papers 292–5
Picture Post 392
Piers Plowman 63
Pitt the Elder, William 203–5, 264
Pitt the Younger, William 233
*Plan of Parliamentary Reform, in the
   Form of a Catechism* 245–7
Plato 311
Plymouth 299
Plymouth Sutton 373
Pope, Alexander 203, 449
Powell, Enoch 431–3, 445–8, 491

Powell, Mary 103, 106
Priestley, Joseph 208–10, 238
Prince of Wales 68, 124, 187, 230, 233
Prisoners (Temporary Discharge for Ill Health) Act (1913; *see also* Cat and Mouse Act) 367
Private Eye 438
Privy Council 95, 174, 189, 218–20
Protestant Ascendancy 137, 141
Provisional Irish Republican Army 505
Provisions of Oxford 49–50
Pulteney, William 185
Putney Debates 30, 111–16, 134
Pym, John 97, 100–2

Race Relations Acts (1965, 1968, 1976) 442
Radical Whigs 221, 302
Rainsborough, Thomas 111–16
Raleigh, Sir Walter 89
Ramsay, James 195
The Ready and Easy Way to Establish a Free Commonwealth, and the Excellence Thereof, Compared with the Inconveniences and Dangers of Readmitting Kingship in this Nation 145–7
Rees-Mogg, William 449, 451
Reflections on the Revolution in France 221–3
Reform Act (1832) 251, 276, 292, 296–7, 437
Reform Union 336
A Remonstrance of many thousand citizens and other freeborn people of England to their own House of Commons 107–10

Repeal Association 309
The Republic 311
Revolution Society 22
Richard II 61, 63–6, 107
'Rights Brought Home' 498–501
Rights of Man 224–6, 230
The Road to Wigan Pier 381
Robespierre 226
'Robin Hood Society' 185
Robinson Crusoe 168
rotten borough (*see also* close borough) 261, 271, 277, 283
Roundhead 107, 128
Royal Society 179
Rump Parliament 123–5, 138–9, 145, 148, 405
Runnymede 45, 48
Russell, Earl (*see also* Russell, Lord John) 335, 340
Russell, Lord John (*see also* Russell, Earl) 277–80, 288, 297, 299, 305, 308

St Clair, Malcolm 437
Salisbury doctrine 344, 350
Salisbury, Lord 340, 344–7, 350
Sandwich, Earl of 200
Sandys, Duncan 478
Sandys, Samuel 187–9, 191
The Saturday Evening Post 416
Savoy Palace 65
Scholefield, William 336
scot and lot 40–1
Scotland 27, 29–30, 53–7, 68, 70, 134, 140–3, 148, 150, 174, 176–8, 218, 239–40, 283, 429, 493–7, 507, 520
Scottish Constitutional Convention 494–7
Scottish National Party 494
Scottish Parliament 494–7, 519

Scottish Women's Forum 494
Secker & Warburg 381
Second Treatise of Civil Government 160–3
Second World War 28, 350, 381, 392, 399, 416, 484
Secretary for Foreign Tongues 106
Section 28 419, 430
Seditious Meetings Act (1795) 233
'Senate of Magna Lilliputia' 185
Seven Years War 200
Sex Discrimination Act (1975) 459
Shaftesbury, Earl of 151
Shakespeare, William 24, 32, 68, 84–5
Shepherd, Richard 488–91
Shelley, Mary 229
Shelley, Percy Bysshe 24, 229, 255–60
Sidmouth, Viscount 255–6
Silverman, Sydney 413–15
'A Simple Plan of Reform' 332–5
Sinn Fein 373, 505
Six Acts 254, 261
Skytrain 468–9
slave trade 215–20
Slavery Abolition Bill 220
Smith, Adam 30, 196–9
Smithfield 65
social contract 24, 130
social democracy 238
Social Democratic and Labour Party 505
socialism 21, 30, 355–8, 378, 400–1
Society of Editors 522
Sommersett, James 215–17
Sophia, Electress of Hanover 172–5
South Sea Bubble 187
Spanish Civil War 387
Speaker of the House of Commons 61, 74–7, 100–2, 107, 171, 183, 365–6, 425, 434–7, 477–80
Speaker's Conference 371
The Spectator 428
Stanley, Lord (*see* Derby, Earl of)
Stansgate, Viscount 434
Star Chamber 90, 98
Stationers' Company 164–7
Statute of Artificers 78–80
Statute of Labourers 58–60, 64, 78
Steuart, Charles 215–16
Steward of the Chiltern Hundreds 175
Steward of the Manor of Northstead 175
Strauss, George 391
Strode, William 100–1
The Sunday Times 471–4, 498
Swift, Jonathan 24, 179–82, 185
Sybil, or, The Two Nations 311–14

Tameside 468–9
Tamworth Manifesto 289–91
Tawney, R.H. 378–80
Taylor, Ian 488, 490
Taylor, John Edward 254
Taylor Mill, Harriet 315–18, 326
thalidomide 471–4
That Was the Week That Was (*TW3*) 24, 438–41
Thatcher, Margaret 314, 425, 459–67, 481, 484–7
Thatcherism 464, 481
The Theory of Moral Sentiments 196–9
This Is Your Life 438–41
Thomas, George 425
Thomson, George 240
Thoughts on the Cause of the Present Discontents 211–12

The Times 336, 339, 410, 428, 449–52
Tocqueville, Alexis de 311
Tolpuddle Martyrs 285–8
Tories 171, 179, 189, 194, 200, 212,
    252, 261, 267, 283–4, 289, 297,
    307, 309–11, 337–8, 340, 362, 402,
    405, 411, 455, 489, 509
Tower of London 54, 83, 86, 185
Toynbee, Polly 21–2
Trades Union Congress 355
Treasonable and Seditious Practices
    Act (1795) 233
Treaty of Paris 200
trial by jury 24–5, 42, 87, 181, 233, 290
Trimble, David 505
Troilus and Cressida 84
The True-Born Englishman 168–71
Turing, Alan 30
Two Treatises of Government 160
Tyler, Wat 64–6
Tyndale, William 77

Ulster Unionists 505
United Nations 26, 417
University of Westminster 516
utilitarianism 208, 238, 326
Utopia 74–5, 77

Verney, Lord 211–12
Vesey-Fitzgerald, William 265–7
Victims of Whiggery 285–8
Victoria, queen 301, 305, 310, 323,
    350
A Vindication of the Rights of Woman
    227–9
Wakeham, Lord 511
Wales 27, 29, 47, 68–71, 140–1, 170,
    176, 429, 493–4, 497, 507, 520
Wallace, William 53–4

Walpole, Sir Robert 183, 187–91
Walwyn, William 107
Wars of the Roses 29
Wars of Scottish Independence 53
Watt, James 30
The Wealth of Nations 196, 199
Weatherill, Bernard 477, 480
The Week 387–91
Wellington, Duke of 264, 266–73,
    284, 434
Welsh Assembly 497
Wendover 211–12
Wensleydale, Lord (*see* Parke, Sir
    James)
Wentworth, Sir Peter 81–3
Westminster 23–4, 52, 54, 88, 100,
    141, 155, 157, 176, 241–2, 248,
    267, 317, 480, 497, 506
Westminster Hall 117
Westminster Review 315
Whigs 187, 200, 203, 221, 223, 243,
    248, 270–1, 273, 280, 302, 305,
    307–9, 337
Whitelaw, William 425
Wilberforce, William 218–20
Wilkes, John 24–5, 200–7
William I, king 40, 169
William III, king 28, 155, 160, 168,
    172, 177, 194
William IV, king 289
William the Conqueror (*see* William
    I)
William of Orange (*see* William III)
Wilmington, Earl of 191
Wilson, Harold 30, 415, 442, 453,
    456, 460
Wilson, James 332
Winchelsea 248
Windham, William 183–5

Wirrall 34

Wolfenden, Sir John 426

Wolfenden Report 426–9

Wollstonecraft, Mary 227–9

Wolsey, Cardinal Thomas 76–7

Women's Social and Political Union (WSPU) 367

women's suffrage 227–9, 315–18, 331, 367–73

Woolley, Bernard 475–6

Yes Minister 359, 475

Yes, Prime Minister 24, 475–6

Yorke, Sir Philip 215–6

Young Ireland 210

Zircon 477–80